THE PUSHCART PRIZE, XVIII: BEST OF THE SMALL PRESSES

THE PUSHCART PRIZE XVIII

BEST OF THE SMALL PRESSES

Edited by
Bill Henderson
with the
Pushcart Prize
editors.
Poetry Editors:
Richard Jackson,
Susan Mitchell.
Essays Editor:
Anthony Brandt

A Touchstone Book
Published by Simon & Schuster
New York   London
Toronto   Sydney
Tokyo   Singapore

TOUCHSTONE
Rockefeller Center
1230 Avenue of the Americas
New York, New York 10020

First Touchstone Edition 1994
Published by arrangement with Pushcart Press
TOUCHSTONE and colophon are registered trademarks
of Simon & Schuster Inc.
Manufactured in the United States of America

10 9 8 7 6 5 4 3 2 1

Library of Congress Cataloging-in-Publication Data is
available

ISBN: 0-671-73437-7

*Note: Nominations for this series are invited from any
small, independent, literary book press or magazine in
the world. Up to six nominations—tear sheets or copies
selected from work published, or about to be published,
in the calendar year—are accepted by our December 1
deadline each year. Write to Pushcart Press, P.O. Box
380, Wainscott, NY 11975 for more information.*

Acknowledgements

Introduction © 1993 Bill Henderson
Green Grow the Grasses O © 1992 TriQuarterly
Three Protrusions © 1992 Grand Street
In The John Dillinger Museum © 1992 Sycamore Review
Tell Me Everything © 1992 Threepenny Review
Convicta et Combusta © 1992 Conjunctions
Forrest in the Trees © 1992 Ploughshares
Marie © 1992 Paris Review
Days of Heaven © 1992 Ploughshares
A Hunger Artist by Franz Kafka: A Story © 1992 Paris Review
The Parakeet and the Cat © 1992 Conjunctions
The Butcher © 1992 North American Review
Wouldn't a Title Just Make It Worse © 1992 Witness
The Sun, the Rain © 1992 The American Voice
Benjamin Claire, North Dakota Tradesman, Writes to the President of the United States
© 1992 North American Review
The Writer's Model © 1992 Side Show
A Chick From My Dream Life © 1992 Iowa Review
Same Old Big Magic © 1992 Graywolf Press
Somebody © 1992 Kenyon Review
Larabi's Ox © 1992 Milkweed Editions
The Life of the Body © 1992 TriQuarterly
To Write of Repeated Patterns © 1992 Iowa Review
Wallace Stevens © 1992 Threepenny Review
Carla's Story © 1992 ZYZZYVA
Estivation © 1992 Antaeus
Two Cities : On The Iliad © 1992 Kenyon Review
White Hunter © 1992 Threepenny Review © 1993 Alfred Knopf Inc
An Island Notebook © 1992 Georgia Review
Van © 1992 Semiotext (e)
Choosing Your Names © 1992 Raritan: A Quarterly Review
Rough Music © 1992 Provincetown Arts
French Horn © 1992 Iowa Review
Kala: Saturday Night At the Pahala Theatre © 1992 Parnassus: Poetry In Review
The Ladder: Roger Vail's Photo of a Rockface in the Carrara (Italy) Marble Quarries ©
1992 Field
A.M. The Hopeful Monster © 1992 The American Voice
Shelter © 1992 American Poetry Review
Christopher © 1992 New Letters
Somewhere Along the Line © 1992 The Sun
Deaf Poem © 1992 Passages North
"Nearer God, Nearer Realite" © 1992 Indiana Review
Complaint Against the Arsonists© 1992 Virginia Quarterly Review
Monday Her Car Wouldn't Start © 1992 Ploughshares
Guilt Trip © 1992 Antioch Review

In memory of Thomas Lask

INTRODUCTION

IN LAST YEAR'S introduction, I wrote about Pushcart's theory of honest words and I wondered why small press writers bother to revere such words while the media culture around them is hell-bent on profit at any price.

Perhaps, I guessed, because small press writers still care about finding the truths in our funny, lonely, tragic, brave lives on this blue globe lost in space. These writers sense that something important may be going on here, perhaps something sacred. They do not write for money.

These are outlaw ideas in our sad commercial times, where many authors, agents and publishers scream aloud for forgettable bestsellers and major (translation: Minor) motion pictures, as if trash were our highest value.

Over the years, however, the writers who have appeared here and the editors who have worked on this series insist that words are too valuable to be driven by commerce. In this space I would like to thank a few of our editors/readers, with a concentration this year on poetry.

Besides the crackpot idea that words and ideas are important, Pushcart has insisted that the contents of each volume never be picked by a static panel of judges. Each edition sees new Contributing Editors come and go, and new editors sampling what the Contributing Editors contribute.

We have no office staff here at Pushcart's garage in the woods. We are not an institution, or a vast organization or a compromising committee.

I work alone most of the time, aided only by my eleven year old Labrador, Sophie, asleep on the sofa and losing her hearing, and by my five year old Beagle, Opie, who would really rather be tracking rabbits.

The real work is done by the Contributing Editors—160 plus this year—and the changing editors/readers, all of them paid with books or a small fee. We have no meetings and most of us have never met.

Past Poetry Editors include: H. L. Van Brunt, Lynne Spaulding, Naomi Lazard, Herb Leibowitz, Jon Galassi, Siv Cedering, Grace Schulman, Carolyn Forché, Gerald Stern, Stanley Plumly, William Stafford, Philip Levine, David Wojahn, Jorie Graham, David Swickard, Robert Hass, Philip Booth, Jay Meek, Sandra McPherson, Laura Jensen, William Heyen, Elizabeth Spires, Marvin Bell, Carolyn Kizer, Christopher Buckley, and Chase Twichell.

This year Richard Jackson and Susan Mitchell served as Poetry Editors and read the nominations. I have asked them to comment on their experience.

Richard Jackson is the author of three books of poems, most recently *Alive All The Day* (Cleveland State University Press). He is the editor of *The Poetry Miscellany* and *Double Vision: Four Young Slovene Poets* (Aleph Press, Slovenia), plus books of criticism and dozens of articles and reviews. His poems have appeared in two previous *Pushcart Prize* editions and his *New and Selected Poems* is forthcoming from New England University Press. He teaches at the University of Tennessee, Chattanooga and he wears a Braves cap.

Richard Jackson reports:

"To judge by the scant attention poetry seems to get in the press these days, someone attempting to gather a selection of contemporary poems might be tempted to answer, with Persius' 1st century interlocutor, 'Who'll read that sort of thing?' To which, of course, Persius answers with a satire about readers and writers, about who is valued and why, from the effete Greek pastoral imitators to the heart-wrenching poets who take a sort of bubble bath in other people's pain. The point is that this sort of stuff doesn't last, and while it may achieve some considerable audience for a fickle time, it is not the sort of poetry that an enduring, permanent, interested audience returns to. As Persius says: 'Stick to your own judgement,' don't worry about who is neces-

12

sarily fashionable or not. I suppose that's as good a starting point as any for making selections.

"The problem comes when what began as a long list starts to whittle its way down. In my half of the submissions—two large boxes of poems—I found a couple of hundred poems, maybe more, that I thought were outstanding. I suspect that there were an equal number of good poems in Susan Mitchell's batch. Now that is a considerable number of extraordinary poems for any year. The state and health of American poetry is far better than I ever suspected, and the question in Persius' poem—'Who'll read that?'—ought to be answered to the tune of anyone who cares about the health of American culture.

"I know it was a learning experience for me to see exactly this rich storehouse, and it gave me both a better understanding of our poetry, and a sense of pride in what American poetry has accomplished. At their most interesting and compelling, I found, the best poems tend to include or allude to both a personal and public voice, private and political visions, high and popular culture, formal and informal elements, individual and social concerns—that is, a uniquely American sort of blend."

Susan Mitchell is the author of two poetry collections: *The Water Inside The Water* (Wesleyan, 1983, with a new edition planned for 1994) and *Rapture* (HarperCollins, 1992, a National Book Award finalist). She was recently awarded a Guggenheim Fellowship, and a Lannan Foundation Poetry Fellowship, and she is the winner of the Kingsley Tufts Poetry Award. Soon HarperCollins will publish her essay collection.

Susan Mitchell comments:

"What impressed me about reading all these manuscripts was how varied the poems were. There is a great diversity, a wide range of styles. And in my selections for reprint and mention, I have tried to preserve some of that diversity. So you have poems of amazing directness and simplicity of language which have what Keats in one of his letters calls 'the true voice of feeling.' But then you also have poems that are not trying to recreate an experience through language, but to create experience in language, an experience which has no double or equivalent out there in the world. Here I'm thinking of poems like Alice Fulton's 'A.M.: The Hopeful Monster' with its superb opening lines: 'So dawn. A morcellation of the dark, the one / dumb immaculate gives way. / Appetite and breakfast'; and poems like Dennis Schmitz's 'The Ladder: Roger Vail's Photo of a Rockface in the Carrara (Italy) Marble Quarries' where the 'true voice of feeling' is made by all those enjambments—or does it make the enjambments happen, the staccato, syncopated rhythms where the speaker's breath, like the sun in the second line, is 'squeezed dark!'

"For me, poetry begins where ordinary language leaves off—if you can say it in prose, then you don't need to write a poem. Therefore, I'm particularly excited by poems like Deborah Digges' 'Rough Music' which live on the edge between speech and sound, poetry and music, and by poems like Robin Behn's 'French Horn' with its risky leaps and collisions of images, a poem that makes a mad rush for its superb ending. There's a third poem in my selections that has to do with music, Robert Pinsky's 'Ginza Samba,' which like Digges' and Behn's is in love with sounds: 'A monosyllabic European called Sax / Invents a horn, walla whirledly wah, a kind of twisted / Brazen clarinet.'

"All the poems I have chosen I think are in love with risk in one way or another. The honesty of Lois-Ann Yamanaka's narrative, 'Kala: Saturday Night at the Pahala Theatre' is one kind of risk, the made-up dialect of Diane Glancy's 'Christopher' is another kind of risk. Glancy's poem looks at Columbus's discovery of the Indies and America from a fresh viewpoint: *that's* a risk too. And Antler's 'Somewhere Along the Line' risks offending, not because of its language, but because of the utter clarity of its vision."

* * *

A final note: this year, two young readers joined Pushcart as fiction editors: Rick Moody and Lee Smith. Both were in grade school when all this started back in 1976. Next year they will report on their experience in prose reading, as will Tony Brandt, our essays editor.

Our pledge to you, honored reader, is that these introductions will be brief, and not stall your pilgrimage to the annual celebration that follows.

Bill Henderson

THE PEOPLE
WHO HELPED

FOUNDING EDITORS—*Anaïs Nin (1903–1977) Buckminster Fuller (1895–1983), Charles Newman, Daniel Halpern, Gordon Lish, Harry Smith, Hugh Fox, Ishmael Reed, Joyce Carol Oates, Len Fulton, Leonard Randolph, Leslie Fiedler, Nona Balakian (1918–1991), Paul Bowles, Paul Engle (1908–1991), Ralph Ellison, Reynolds Price, Rhoda Schwartz, Richard Morris, Ted Wilentz, Tom Montag, William Phillips, Poetry editor: H. L. Van Brunt.*

EDITORS—*Walter Abish, Ai, Elliott Anderson, John Ashbery, Ed Sanders, Teo Savory, Grace Schulman, Harvey Shapiro, Leslie Silko, Charles Simic, Dave Smith, Elizabeth Spencer, William Stafford, Gerald Stern, David St. John, Bill and Pat Strachan, Ron Sukenick, Anne Tyler, John Updike, Sam Vaughan, David Wagoner, Derek Walcott, Ellen Wilbur, David Wilk, David Wojahn, Jack Gilbert, Louise Glück, David Godine, Jorie Graham, Linda Gregg, Barbara Grossman, Donald Hall, Helen Handley, Michael Harper, Robert Hass, DeWitt Henry, J. R. Humphreys, David Ignatow, John Irving, June Jordan, Edmund Keeley, Karen Kennerly, Galway Kinnell, Carolyn Kizer, Richard Kostelanetz, Maxine Kumin, James Laughlin, Seymour Lawrence, Naomi Lazard, Herb Leibowitz, Denise Levertov, Philip Levine, Stanley Lindberg, Thomas Lux, Mary MacArthur, Jay Meek, Daniel Menaker, Frederick Morgan, Cynthia Ozick, Jayne Anne Phillips, Robert Phillips, George Plimpton, Stanley Plumly, Eugene Redmond, Russell Banks, Joe David Bellamy, Robert Bly, Philip Booth, Robert Boyers, Harold Brodkey, Joseph*

Brodsky, Wesley Brown, Hayden Carruth, Frank Conroy, Paula Deitz, Steve Dixon, Rita Dove, Andre Dubus, M. D. Elevitch, Louise Erdrich, Loris Essary, Ellen Ferber, Carolyn Forché, Stuart Freibert, Jon Galassi, Tess Gallagher, Louis Gallo, George Garrett, Reginald Gibbons, Bill Zavatsky.

CONTRIBUTING EDITORS FOR THIS EDITION—Robert Wrigley, David Lehman, Steve Watkins, Len Roberts, Gary Gildner, Michael Bowden, Campbell McGrath, Lydia Davis, Jane Cooper, Mary Karr, Kathy Callaway, Thomas Kennedy, Michael Collier, Norman Lavers, Christopher Buckley, Gary Young, Timothy Geiger, Susan Moon, David St. John, Dorianne Laux, Carl Dennis, David Jauss, Mark Doty, Linda Bierds, Robert McBrearty, Eliot Weinberger, Vern Rutsala, John Daniel, John Drury, Donald Revell, Tony Hoagland, Carol Muske, Stuart Dybek, Kent Nelson, Marilyn Hacker, Joe Ashby Porter, Carolyn Kizer, Lee Upton, Philip Appleman, Fae Myenne Ng, Paul Zimmer, Pattiann Rogers, David Romtvedt, Mark Jarman, William Matthews, Ted Wilentz, Gordon Weaver, Brenda Hillman, David Wojahn, Josip Novakovich, Ha Jin, Susan Straight, Gordon Lish, Clarence Major, Samuel S. Vaughan, Jean Valentine, Sharon Olds, Judith Ortiz Cofer, Ed Ochester, Greg Pape, Karen Fish, Lloyd Van Brunt, Rita Dove, Lloyd Schwartz, Lynne McFall, Stephen Dunn, Robin Hemley, David Madden, Diane Williams, Laurie Sheck, Ehud Havazelet, C. E. Poverman, Christine Zawadiwsky, Michael Martone, Colette Inez, Jane Flanders, Michael Dennis Browne, George Keithley, Henri Cole, Marvin Bell, Kenneth Gangemi, Jennifer Atkinson, Richard Burgin, Lou Mathews, Robert Phillips, Marianne Boruch, Stanley Lindberg, André Bernard, Rick Bass, Stephen Corey, Gibbons Ruark, Bin Ramke, Kristina McGrath, Barbara Einzig, David St. John, Mary Peterson, Harold Witt, Philip Dacey, Naomi Shihab Nye, Jim Moore, Wesley McNair, Stanley Plumly, Frankie Paino, Pamela Stewart, Liz Inness-Brown, Michael Waters, David Baker, Jack Marshall, Pat Strachan, Maura Stanton, C. K. Williams, Eileen Pollack, Sandra McPherson, Walter Pavlich, John Allman, Pat Gray, Dan Masterson, Ben Groff, Elizabeth Spires, Josephine Jacobsen, James Linville, Lisel Mueller, Wally Lamb, Rosellen Brown, Kelly Cherry, R. A. Sasaki, Maxine Kumin, Dennis Vannatta, Sharman Russell, Melissa Lentricchia, Susan Bergman,

CONTENTS

THE
PUSHCART PRIZE, XVIII:
BEST OF THE
SMALL PRESSES

MARIE

fiction by EDWARD P. JONES

from THE PARIS REVIEW

Every now and again, as if on a whim, the Federal government people would write to Marie Delaveaux Wilson in one of those white, stampless envelopes and tell her to come in to their place so they could take another look at her. They, the Social Security people, wrote to her in a foreign language that she had learned to translate over the years, and for all of the years she had been receiving the letters the same man had been signing them. Once, because she had something important to tell him, Marie called the number the man always put at the top of the letters, but a woman answered Mr. Smith's telephone and told Marie he was in an all-day meeting. Another time she called and a man said Mr. Smith was on vacation. And finally one day a woman answered and told Marie that Mr. Smith was deceased. The woman told her to wait and she would get someone new to talk to her about her case, but Marie thought it bad luck to have telephoned a dead man and she hung up.

Now, years after the woman had told her Mr. Smith was no more, the letters were still being signed by John Smith. Come into our office at Twenty-first and M Streets, Northwest, the letters said in that foreign language. Come in so we can see if you are still blind in one eye. Come in so we can see if you are still old and getting older. Come in so we can see if you still deserve to get Supplemental Security Income payments.

She always obeyed the letters, even if the order now came from a dead man, for she knew people who had been temporarily cut off from SSI for not showing up or even for being late. And once cut off, you had to move heaven and earth to get back on.

So on a not unpleasant day in March, she rose in the morning, even before the day had any sort of character, to give herself plenty of time to bathe, eat, lay out money for the bus, dress, listen to the spirituals on the radio. She was eighty-six years old and had learned that life was all chaos and painful uncertainty and that the only way to get through it was to expect chaos even in the most innocent of moments. Offer a crust of bread to a sick bird and you often draw back a bloody finger.

John Smith's letter had told her to come in at eleven o'clock, his favorite time, and by nine that morning she had had her bath and had eaten. Dressed by 9:30. The walk from Claridge Towers at Twelfth and M down to the bus stop at Fourteenth and K took her about ten minutes, more or less. There was a bus at about 10:30, her schedule told her, but she preferred the one that came a half hour earlier, lest there be trouble with the 10:30 bus. After she dressed, she sat at her dining room table and went over yet again what papers and all else she needed to take. Given the nature of life—particularly the questions asked by the Social Security people—she always took more than they might ask for: her birth certificate, her husband's death certificate, doctors' letters.

One of the last things she put in her pocketbook was a knife that she had, about seven inches long, which she had serrated on both edges with the use of a small saw borrowed from a neighbor. The knife, she was convinced now, had saved her life about two weeks before. Before then she had often been careless about when she took the knife out with her, and she had never taken it out in daylight, but now she never left her apartment without it, even when going down the hall to the trash drop.

She had gone out to buy a simple box of oatmeal, no more, no less. It was about seven in the evening, the streets with enough commuters driving up Thirteenth Street to make her feel safe. Several yards before she reached the store, the young man came from behind her and tried to rip off her coat pocket where he thought she kept her money, for she carried no purse or pocketbook after five o'clock. The money was in the other pocket with the knife, and his hand was caught in the empty pocket long

26

enough for her to reach around with the knife and cut his hand as it came out of her pocket.

He screamed and called her an old bitch. He took a few steps up Thirteenth Street and stood in front of Emerson's Market, examining the hand and shaking off blood. Except for the cars passing up and down Thirteenth Street, they were alone, and she began to pray.

"You cut me," he said, as if he had only been minding his own business when she cut him. "Just look what you done to my hand," he said and looked around as if for some witness to her crime. There was not a great amount of blood, but there was enough for her to see it dripping to the pavement. He seemed to be about twenty, no more than twenty-five, dressed the way they were all dressed nowadays, as if a blind man had matched up their colors. It occurred to her to say that she had seven grandchildren about his age, that telling him this would make him leave her alone. But the more filth he spoke, the more she wanted him only to come toward her again.

"You done crippled me, you old bitch."

"I sure did," she said, without malice, without triumph, but simply the way she would have told him the time of day had he asked and had she known. She gripped the knife tighter, and as she did, she turned her body ever so slightly so that her good eye lined up with him. Her heart was making an awful racket, wanting to be away from him, wanting to be safe at home. I will not be moved, some organ in the neighborhood of the heart told the heart. "And I got plenty more where that come from."

The last words seemed to bring him down some and, still shaking the blood from his hand, he took a step or two back, which disappointed her. I will not be moved, that other organ kept telling her heart. "You just crazy, thas all," he said. "Just a crazy old hag." Then he turned and lumbered up toward Logan Circle, and several times he looked back over his shoulder as if afraid she might be following. A man came out of Emerson's, then a woman with two little boys. She wanted to grab each of them by the arm and tell them she had come close to losing her life. "I saved myself with this here thing," she would have said. She forgot about the oatmeal and took her raging heart back to the apartment. She told herself that she should, but she never washed the fellow's

27

blood off the knife, and over the next few days it dried and then it began to flake off.

Toward ten o'clock that morning Wilamena Mason knocked and let herself in with a key Marie had given her.

"I see you all ready," Wilamena said.

"With the help of the Lord," Marie said. "Want a spot a coffee?"

"No thanks," Wilamena said, and dropped into a chair at the table. "Been drinkin' so much coffee lately, I'm gonna turn into coffee. Was up all night with Calhoun."

"How he doin'?"

Wilamena told her Calhoun was better that morning, his first good morning in over a week. Calhoun Lambeth was Wilamena's boyfriend, a seventy-five-year-old man she had taken up with six or so months before, not long after he moved in. He was the best-dressed old man Marie had ever known, but he had always appeared to be sickly, even while strutting about with his gold-tipped cane. And seeing that she could count his days on the fingers of her hands, Marie had avoided getting to know him. She could not understand why Wilamena, who could have had any man in Claridge Towers or any other senior citizen building for that matter, would take such a man into her bed. "True love," Wilamena had explained. "Avoid heartache," Marie had said, trying to be kind.

They left the apartment. Marie sought help from no one, lest she come to depend on a person too much. But since the encounter with the young man, Wilamena had insisted on escorting her. Marie, to avoid arguments, allowed Wilamena to walk with her from time to time to the bus stop, but no farther.

Nothing fit Marie's theory about life like the weather in Washington. Two days before, the temperature had been in the forties, and yesterday it had dropped to the low twenties, then warmed up a bit with the afternoon, bringing on snow flurries. Today the weather people on the radio had said it would warm enough to wear just a sweater, but Marie was wearing her coat. And tomorrow, the weather people said, it would be in the thirties, with maybe an inch or so of snow.

Appointments near twelve o'clock were always risky, because the Social Security people often took off for lunch long before noon and returned sometime after one. And except for a few employees who seemed to work through their lunch hours, the place shut down. Marie had never been interviewed by someone willing to work through the lunch hour. Today, though the appointment was for eleven, she waited until 1:30 before the woman at the front of the waiting room told her she would have to come back another day, because the woman who handled her case was not in.

"You put my name down when I came in like everything was all right," Marie said after she had been called up to the woman's desk.

"I know," the woman said, "but I thought that Mrs. Brown was in. They told me she was in. I'm sorry." The woman began writing in a logbook that rested between her telephone and a triptych of photographs. She handed Marie a slip and told her again she was sorry.

"Why you have me wait so long if she whatn't here?" She did not want to say too much, appear too upset, for the Social Security people could be unforgiving. And though she was used to waiting three and four hours, she found it especially unfair to wait when there was no one for her at all behind those panels the Social Security people used for offices. "I been here since before eleven."

"I know," the woman behind the desk said. "I know. I saw you there, ma'am, but I really didn't know Mrs. Brown wasn't here." There was a nameplate at the front of the woman's desk and it said Vernelle Wise. The name was surrounded by little hearts, the kind a child might have drawn.

Marie said nothing more and left.

The next appointment was two weeks later, 8:30, a good hour, and the day before a letter signed by John Smith arrived to remind her. She expected to be out at least by twelve. Three minutes before eleven o'clock Marie asked Vernelle Wise if the man, Mr. Green, who was handling her case, was in that day, and each time the woman assured her that he was. At twelve, Marie ate one of the two oranges and three of the five slices of cheese she had brought. At one, she asked again if Mr. Green was indeed in that day and politely reminded Vernelle Wise that she had been waiting since about eight that morning. Vernelle was just as polite and told her the wait would soon be over.

At 1:15, Marie began to watch the clock hands creep around the dial. She had not paid much attention to the people about her, but more and more it seemed that others were being waited on who had arrived long after she had gotten there. After asking about Mr. Green at one, she had taken a seat near the front and, as more time went by, she found herself forced to listen to the conversation that Vernelle was having with the other receptionist next to her.

"I told him . . . I told him . . . I said just get your things and leave," said the other receptionist, who didn't have a nameplate.

"Did he leave?" Vernelle wanted to know.

"Oh, no," the other woman said. "Not at first. But I picked up some of his stuff, that Christian Dior jacket he worships. I picked up my cigarette lighter and that jacket, just like I was gonna do something bad to it, and he started movin' then."

Vernelle began laughing. "I wish I was there to see that." She was filing her fingernails. Now and again she would look at her fingernails to inspect her work, and if it was satisfactory, she would blow on the nails and on the file. "He back?" Vernelle asked.

The other receptionist eyed her. "What you think?" and they both laughed.

Along about two o'clock Marie became hungry again, but she did not want to eat the rest of her food because she did not know how much longer she would be there. There was a soda machine in the corner, but all sodas gave her gas.

"You-know-who gonna call you again?" the other receptionist was asking Vernelle.

"I hope so," Vernelle said. "He pretty fly. Seemed decent too. It kinda put me off when he said he was a car mechanic. I kinda like kept tryin' to take a peek at his fingernails and everything the whole evenin'. See if they was dirty or what."

"Well, that mechanic stuff might be good when you get your car back. My cousin's boyfriend used to do that kinda work and he made good money, girl. I mean real good money."

"Hmmmm," Vernelle said. "Anyway, the kids like him, and you know how peculiar they can be."

30

"Tell me 'bout it. They do the job your mother and father used to do, huh? Only on another level."

"You can say that again," Vernelle said.

Marie went to her and told her how long she had been waiting.

"Listen," Vernelle said, pointing her fingernail file at Marie. "I told you you'll be waited on as soon as possible. This is a busy day. So I think you should just go back to your seat until we call your name." The other receptionist began to giggle.

Marie reached across the desk and slapped Vernelle Wise with all her might. Vernelle dropped the file, which made a cheap, tinny sound when it hit the plastic board her chair was on. But no one heard the file because she had begun to cry right away. She looked at Marie as if, in the moment of her greatest need, Marie had denied her. "Oh, oh," Vernelle Wise said through the tears. "Oh, my dear God. . ."

The other receptionist, in her chair on casters, rolled over to Vernelle and put her arm around her. "Security!" the other receptionist hollered. "We need security here!"

The guard at the front door came quickly around the corner, one hand on his holstered gun and the other pointing accusingly at the people seated in the waiting area. Marie had sat down and was looking at the two women almost sympathetically, as if a stranger had come in, hit Vernelle Wise, and fled.

"She slapped Vernelle!" said the other receptionist.

"Who did it?" the guard said, reaching for the man who was sitting beside Marie. But when the other receptionist said it was the old lady in the blue coat, the guard held back for the longest time, as if to grab her would be like arresting his own grandmother. He stood blinking and he would have gone on blinking had Marie not stood up.

She was too flustered to wait for the bus and so took a cab home. With both chains, she locked herself in the apartment, refusing to answer the door or the telephone the rest of the day and most of the next. But she knew that if her family or friends received no answer at the door or on the telephone, they would think something had happened to her. So the next afternoon, she began answering the phone and spoke with the chain on, telling Wilamena and others that she had a toothache.

For days and days after the incident she ate very little and asked God to forgive her. She was haunted by the way Vernelle's cheek had felt, by what it was like to invade and actually touch the flesh of another person. And when she thought too hard, she imagined that she was slicing through the woman's cheek, the way she had sliced through the young man's hand. But as time went on she began to remember the man's curses and the purplish color of Vernelle's fingernails, and all remorse would momentarily take flight. Finally, one morning nearly two weeks after she slapped the woman, she woke with a phrase she had not used or heard since her children were small: You whatn't raised that way.

It was the next morning that the thin young man in the suit knocked and asked through the door chains if he could speak with her. She thought that he was a Social Security man come to tear up her card and papers and tell her that they would send her no more checks. Even when he pulled out an identification card showing that he was a Howard University student, she did not believe.

In the end, she told him she didn't want to buy anything, not magazines, not candy, not anything.

"No, no," he said. "I just want to talk to you for a bit. About your life and everything. It's for a project for my folklore course. I'm talking to everyone in the building who'll let me. Please . . . I won't be a bother. Just a little bit of your time."

"I don't have anything worth talkin' about," she said. "And I don't keep well these days."

"Oh, ma'am, I'm sorry. But we all got something to say. I promise I won't be a bother."

After fifteen minutes of his pleas, she opened the door to him because of his suit and his tie and his tie clip with a bird in flight, and because his long, dark brown fingers reminded her of delicate twigs. But had he turned out to be death with a gun or a knife or fingers to crush her neck, she would not have been surprised. "My name's George. George Carter. Like the president." He had the kind of voice that old people in her young days would have called womanish. "But I was born right here in D.C. Born, bred and buttered, my mother used to say."

He stayed the rest of the day and she fixed him dinner. It scared her to be able to talk so freely with him, and at first she thought that at long last, as she had always feared, senility had taken hold of her. A few hours after he left, she looked his name up in the telephone book, and when a man who sounded like him answered, she hung up immediately. And the next day she did the same thing. He came back at least twice a week for many weeks and would set his cassette recorder on her coffee table. "He's takin' down my whole life," she told Wilamena, almost the way a woman might speak in awe of a new boyfriend.

One day he played back for the first time some of what she told the recorder:

> . . . My father would be sittin' there readin' the paper. He'd say whenever they put in a new president, "Look like he got the chair for four years." And it got so that's what I saw—this poor man sittin' in that chair for four long years while the rest of the world went on about its business. I don't know if I thought he ever did anything, the president. I just knew that he had to sit in that chair for four years. Maybe I thought that by his sittin' in that chair and doin' nothin' else for four years he made the country what it was and that without him sittin' there the country wouldn't be what it was. Maybe thas what I got from listenin' to father readin' and to my mother askin' him questions 'bout what he was readin'. They was like that, you see. . . .

George stopped the tape and was about to put the other side in when she touched his hand.

"No more, George," she said. "I can't listen to no more. Please . . . please, no more." She had never in her whole life heard her own voice. Nothing had been so stunning in a long, long while, and for a few moments before she found herself, her world turned upside down. There, rising from a machine no bigger than her Bible, was a voice frighteningly familiar and yet unfamiliar, talking about a man whom she knew as well as her husbands and her sons, a man dead and buried sixty years. She reached across to George and he handed her the tape. She turned it over and over, as if the mystery of everything could be discerned if she turned it enough times. She began to cry, and with her other hand she lightly touched the buttons of the machine.

33

Between the time Marie slapped the woman in the Social Security office and the day she heard her voice for the first time, Calhoun Lambeth, Wilamena's boyfriend, had been in and out of the hospital three times. Most evenings when Calhoun's son stayed the night with him, Wilamena would come up to Marie's and spend most of the evening sitting on the couch that was catty-corner to the easy chair facing the big window. She said very little, which was unlike her, a woman with more friends than hairs on her head and who, at sixty-eight, loved a good party. The most attractive woman Marie knew would only curl her legs up under herself and sip whatever Marie put in her hand. She looked out at the city until she took herself to her apartment or went back down to Calhoun's place. In the beginning, after he returned from the hospital the first time, there was the desire in Marie to remind her friend that she wasn't married to Calhoun, that she should just get up and walk away, something Marie had seen her do with other men she had grown tired of.

Late one night, Wilamena called and asked her to come down to the man's apartment, for the man's son had had to work that night and she was there alone with him and she did not want to be alone with him. "Sit with me a spell," Wilamena said. Marie did not protest, even though she had not said more than ten words to the man in all the time she knew him. She threw on her bathrobe, picked up her keys and serrated knife and went down to the second floor.

He was propped up in bed, surprisingly alert, and spoke to Marie with an unforced friendliness. She had seen this in other dying people—a kindness and gentleness came over them that was often embarrassing for those around them. Wilamena sat on the side of the bed. Calhoun asked Marie to sit in a chair beside the bed and then he took her hand and held it for the rest of the night. He talked on throughout the night, not always understandable. Wilamena, exhausted, eventually lay across the foot of the bed. Almost everything the man had to say was about a time when he was young and was married for a year or so to a woman in Nicodemus, Kansas, a town where there were only black people. Whether the woman had died or whether he had left her, Marie could not make out. She only knew that the woman and Nicodemus seemed to have marked him for life.

"You should go to Nicodemus," he said at one point, as if the town was only around the corner. "I stumbled into the place by accident. But you should go on purpose. There ain't much to see, but you should go there and spend some time there.

Toward four o'clock that morning, he stopped talking and moments later he went home to his God. Marie continued holding the dead man's hand and she said the Lord's Prayer over and over until it no longer made sense to her. She did not wake Wilamena. Eventually the sun came through the man's venetian blinds, and she heard the croaking of the pigeons congregating on the window ledge. When she finally placed his hand on his chest, the dead man expelled a burst of air that sounded to Marie like a sigh. It occurred to her that she, a complete stranger, was the last thing he had known in the world and that now that he was no longer in the world. All she knew of him was that Nicodemus place and a lovesick woman slept at the foot of his bed. She thought that she was hungry and thirsty, but the more she looked at the dead man and the sleeping woman, the more she realized that what she felt was a sense of loss.

Two days later, the Social Security people sent her a letter, again signed by John Smith, telling her to come to them one week hence. There was nothing in the letter about the slap, no threat to cut off her SSI payments because of what she had done. Indeed, it was the same sort of letter John Smith usually sent. She called the number at the top of the letter, and the woman who handled her case told her that Mr. White would be expecting her on the day and time stated in the letter. Still, she suspected the Social Security people were planning something for her, something at the very least that would be humiliating. And, right until the day before the appointment, she continued calling to confirm that it was okay to come in. Often, the person she spoke to after the switchboard woman and before the woman handling her case was Vernelle. "Social Security Administration. This is Vernelle Wise. May I help you?" And each time Marie heard the receptionist identify herself she wanted to apologize. "I whatn't raised that way," she wanted to tell the woman.

George Carter came the day she got the letter to present her with a cassette machine and copies of the tapes they had made about her life. It took quite some time for him to teach her how

35

to use the machine, and after he was gone, she was certain it took so long because she really did not want to know how to use it. That evening, after her dinner, she steeled herself and put a tape marked "Parents/Early Childhood" in the machine.

> . . . My mother had this idea that everything could be done in Washington, that a human bein' could take all they troubles to Washington and things would be set right. I think that was all wrapped up with her notion of the gov'ment, the Supreme Court and the president and the like. "Up there," she would say, "things can be made right." "Up there" was her only words for Washington. All them other cities had names, but Washington didn't need a name. It was just called "up there." I was real small and didn't know any better, so somehow I got to thinkin' since things were on the perfect side in Washington, that maybe God lived there. God and his people. . . . When I went back home to visit that first time and told my mother all about my livin' in Washington, she fell into such a cry, like maybe I had managed to make it to heaven without dyin'. Thas how people was back in those days. . . .

The next morning she looked for Vernelle Wise's name in the telephone book. And for several evenings she would call the number and hang up before the phone had rung three times. Finally, on a Sunday, two days before the appointment, she let it ring and what may have been a little boy answered. She could tell he was very young because he said hello in a too loud voice, as if he was not used to talking on the telephone.

"Hello," he said. "Hello, who this? Granddaddy, that you? Hello. Hello. I can see you."

Marie heard Vernelle tell him to put down the telephone, then another child, perhaps a girl somewhat older than the boy, came on the line. "Hello. Hello. Who is this?" she said with authority. The boy began to cry, apparently because he did not want the girl to talk if he couldn't. "Don't touch it," the girl said. "Leave it alone." The boy cried louder and only stopped when Vernelle came to the telephone.

36

"Yes?" Vernelle said. "Yes." Then she went off the line to calm the boy who had begun to cry again. "Loretta," she said, "go get his bottle. . . . Well, look for it. What you got eyes for?"

There seemed to be a second boy, because Vernelle told him to help Loretta look for the bottle. "He always losin' things," Marie heard the second boy say. "You should tie everything to his arms." "Don't tell me what to do," Vernelle said. "Just look for that damn bottle."

"I don't lose noffin'. I don't," the first boy said. "You got snot in your nose."

"Don't say that," Vernelle said before she came back on the line. "I'm sorry," she said to Marie. "Who is this? . . . Don't you dare touch it if you know what's good for you!" she said. "I wanna talk to granddaddy," the first boy said. "Loretta, get me that bottle!"

Marie hung up. She washed her dinner dishes. She called Wilamena because she had not seen her all day, and Wilamena told her that she would be up later. The cassette tapes were on the coffee table beside the machine, and she began picking them up, one by one. She read the labels: Husband No. 1, Working, Husband No. 2, Children, Race Relations, Early D.C. Experiences, Husband No. 3. She had not played another tape since the one about her mother's idea of what Washington was like, but she could still hear the voice, her voice. Without reading its label, she put a tape in the machine.

. . . I never planned to live in Washington, had no idea I would ever even step one foot in this city. This white family my mother worked for, they had a son married and gone to live in Baltimore. He wanted a maid, somebody to take care of his children. So he wrote to his mother and she asked my mother and my mother asked me about goin' to live in Baltimore. Well, I was young. I guess I wanted to see the world, and Baltimore was as good a place to start as anywhere. This man sent me a train ticket and I went off to Baltimore. Hadn't ever been kissed, hadn't ever been anything, but here I was goin' farther from home than my mother and father put together. . . . Well, sir, the train stopped in Washington, and I thought I heard

37

the conductor say we would be stoppin' a bit there, so I got off. I knew I probably wouldn't see no more than that Union Station, but I wanted to be able to say I'd done that, that I step foot in the capital of the United States. I walked down to the end of the platform and looked around, then I peeked into the station. Then I went in. And when I got back, the train and my suitcase was gone. Everything I had in the world on the way to Baltimore . . .

. . . I couldn't calm myself down enough to listen to when the redcap said another train would be leavin' for Baltimore, I was just that upset. I had a buncha addresses of people we knew all the way from home up to Boston, and I used one precious nickel to call a woman I hadn't seen in years, cause I didn't have the white people in Baltimore number. This woman come and got me, took me to her place. I 'member like it was yesterday that we got on this streetcar marked 13TH AND D NE. The more I rode, the more brighter things got. You ain't lived till you been on a streetcar. The further we went on that streetcar—dead down in the middle of the street—the more I knowed I could never go live in Baltimore. I knowed I could never live in a place that didn't have that streetcar and them clackety clack tracks. . . .

She wrapped the tapes in two plastic bags and put them in the dresser drawer that contained all that was valuable to her: birth and death certificates, silver dollars, life insurance policies, pictures of her husbands and the children they had given each other and the grandchildren those children had given her and the great-grands whose names she had trouble remembering. She set the tapes in a back corner of the drawer, away from the things she needed to get her hands on regularly. She knew that however long she lived, she would not ever again listen to them, for in the end, despite all that was on the tapes, she could not stand the sound of her own voice.

Nominated by James Linville

WALLACE STEVENS

by ROBERT HASS

from THE THREEPENNY REVIEW

MY NINETEENTH birthday was also the birthday of one of my college friends. I went to an early class in logic that morning. I think we were reading Aristotle's *Posterior Analytics,* because when I got back to my room a group of my friends was there with several bottles of champagne and I remember that inthe ensuing hilarity there was much speculation about the comic possibilities in the title of that treatise. My friend Tom had been to a class (it was a Catholic men's college, St. Mary's) which somehow involved the Latin names for various illicit sexual positions—*coitus reservatus, coitus interruptus, coitus inter femores,* and so on—and this was also the source of a lot of buffoonery that blent nicely into the subject of posterior analytics, and at some point in the proceedings one of the more advanced of us got out the volume of Wallace Stevens' *Collected Poems* in its handsome soft blue dust jacket and read "The Emperor of Ice Cream." I had never heard the poem before and it seemed to me supremely pleasing. It was March in California, high spring, the hills still green, with grazing cattle in them, plum trees in blossom, the olive trees around the campus whitening whenever a breeze shook them, and at some point a group of us were marching through the field full of mustard flowers and wild radish in the back of the dormitory, banging on pans with spoons and strumming tennis rackets and chanting out the poem, or at least the first stanza of it which I find now is what I still have in memory:

Call the roller of big cigars,
The muscular one, and bid him whip
In kitchen cups concupiscent curds.
Let the wenches dawdle in such dress
As they are used to wear, and let the boys
Bring flowers in last month's newspapers.
Let be be the finale of seem.
The only emperor is the emperor of ice cream.

It is probably significant that I don't have the second stanza by
heart. I don't know if I took in the fact that the poem was a proposition about behavior at a funeral. If I did, it could only have
seemed to me that morning and afternoon immensely droll. I was
a sophomore. I read it as a sophomore poem. The year before in
my freshman year—I make this confession publicly—I had taped
above my desk along with other immortal lines a little poem by
Edna St. Vincent Millay that went something like this:

My candle burns at both its ends.
It will not last the night.
But ah my foes and oh my friends,
It gives a proper light.

I had by the following year understood that it was deeply uncool
to have lines of Millay adorning one's room, and had replaced
them with something appropriately gloomy by Jean-Paul Sartre,
but at that time I took the Stevens line in more or less the same
spirit as Millay's, as permission to have fun, to live in the spirit of
comedy. I see now that they were in fact probably written out of
the same anti-Victorian spirit in the 1920s; they may even have
been written in the same year. And Stevens' poem is more or less
permanently associated for me with that bibulous and raucous
first experience of it. I don't remember for sure what if anything
I knew about Wallace Stevens except that he was a modern poet.
I want to come back to "The Emperor of Ice Cream," but let
me say a word about coming across a couple of other Stevens
poems which complicated my understanding of it. In the fall after
the spring I have been describing, a group of us—eight, I
think—quadruple-dating—were on our way to dinner and a
movie and couldn't decide where we wanted to go or what we

wanted to see, and the driver, in a moment of inspiration, said, "Oh, the hell with it, let's go to Carmel and run on the beach." It was a three-hour drive then from Berkeley to Carmel. We stopped for sandwiches and wine, we had very little money, so there was no question of staying in a motel, which meant sleeping on the beach if we didn't drive back in the middle of the night; people had people to notify if they were going to stay out all night. One woman who had a father whom we all hated—an amazingly unpleasant man who actually made his living by running a lab that tested for venereal disease and who insisted on testing his daughters regularly—was quite worried, which made the rest of us feel appealingly reckless. I don't remember exactly who was there. The driver was a year ahead of me in school, famously smart, a philosophy major who at the end of his senior year read a French novel about Dien Bien Phu and, quoting Nietzsche on the true aristocrat, enlisted in a branch of the service I'd never heard of called Special Forces, where he claimed he would learn to parachute, ski cross-country, and fight barehanded in jungles in places like Annam and Cochin China, which was now called Vietnam. His girlfriend was Philippine, extremely beautiful, the daughter of some kind of politician, we understood, and a French major. It was she who produced the white Vintage paperback volume of Wallace Stevens at some point in the drive and suggested that we take turns reading the stanzas of "Sea Surface Full of Clouds."

I was stunned by the poem. I am still stunned by the poem. After we had read around and gotten over the shock and novelty of the way the adjectives play over and transform the surface of the poem, and had read a few others, and other books were produced and other poems read, the conversation moved on, but I got my hands on Marie's Stevens, and after we had arrived in Carmel and got some more wine and watched the sun set over Carmel Bay in a light rain, I suggested we read the poem again, which we did—to humor me, I think, while the last light smoldered on the horizon. Then we tried to build a fire on the beach, but the rain turned into a lashing Pacific storm and we spent the night quite wet, eight of us crammed into the car in the parking lot, laughing a lot—it was very sexy, as I remember—and making jokes about cars and autoeroticism. I will start to feel like Kinebote, the lunatic annotator of other people's poems with incidents

41

from his own life in Nabokov's *Pale Fire*, if I tell you the story of the lives of each of the people in the car: Marie who returned to the Philippines and who I know had two children and whose spine was badly injured when she was struck by a car, Killpack who did go to Vietnam and then Army Intelligence toward the end of the war and after that seemed to disappear from sight, another friend who was a classics major and later managed a café and wrote poems and died of cancer a couple of years ago. But I will resist, except to say that the poem stays with me in the way that songs you fall in love to stay with you as a kind of figure for that time and those people, and their different lives will always feel to me as if they are playing out in time the way the adjectives of experience play over the adamant nouns in Stevens' poem: rosy chocolate and chophouse chocolate and musky chocolate, perplexed and tense and tranced machine.

And there was the incident of "The Snow Man." It was at a wedding at the end of my sophomore year, of a woman we all liked, large, placid, Irish, a drama major, and the daughter of the man who conducted the last big band in the last seedy, once glamorous dance hall in San Francisco in the 1950s, when dancing to Maury Monohan's orchestra was a city-wide trope for absurdly retro behavior. She was marrying a guy we only grudgingly liked—perhaps we were jealous—but we all showed up for the wedding. And at the reception in one of the rooms of a house that sat over a steep hillside cliff, one of my classmates announced that he was going to kill himself. I came onto this drama late and it's still not clear to me how it began, but when I came into the room, there was a small knot of people standing around one of my friends—his name was Zack and he was an acting student—who was standing by an open window. He looked wild-eyed and he was talking to his friend Tony, with whom I knew he had been in the Navy. They were inseparable friends and they cultivated a certain cool bleakness that was stylish then, so that someone of our group had called them the Laurel and Hardy of tragedy. At that moment it looked to me distinctly as if Tony was goading Zack. They had apparently been talking about "the void," the term for nothingness we all used, and Zack must have spoken of his despair, because Tony was telling him with pure scorn that he didn't feel despair because he didn't feel anything. He was always acting, always a fake, generating histrionics to make himself feel real, feel anything at all. Look, jump, if you want, Tony was saying, Who do you think cares? And you know, he said, you might just have to do it because you've talked yourself into it. It was at that point that Zack said, "I feel it." Hitting his stomach: "I feel it. You know the 'nothing that is not there and the nothing that is'? Well, this is the nothing that fucking is, baby." I thought later that there was something like sexual tension between them, and at that moment I thought that Zack really might jump and that Tony was clearly trying to cut off his avenues of escape, but the truth is I was so besotted with literature at the time that I remember mainly being impressed that someone could quote Wallace Stevens at a moment like that.

As it happened, Zack did not jump. The bride, Agnes, came into the room after Zack had climbed out the window and onto the balcony, and she began talking to him and then suggested we all leave, which we did, and after a while they came downstairs together and danced to her father's orchestra. If I were Nabokov, I could leave them dancing to "Have You Ever Seen a Dream Walking," which I have recently read was one of Wallace Stevens' favorite songs and was the kind of song Agnes' father was apt to play, but I'm not and I have some sense of shame. As for the nothing that is, I was soon enough in graduate school, where the discussion of the poem focused on whether or not it was in favor of a pathetic fallacy, which was another matter; and not long after that I had begun to read around in Buddhism and to see that there were other ways of thinking about the void and that what I loved in the cleanness of the writing of that poem might be connected to those other ways. And sometime in that period I came to see that "the nothing that was," was connected to the way the adjectives in "Sea Surface Full of Clouds" played over the nouns, the way that it seemed the quality of things, the accidents (as someone might say who had been dipped in Aristotle) but not their essence, could be known. And I suppose I must have connected that floating thought to the comedy of "The Emperor of Ice Cream," though I don't exactly remember doing so.

When I was an undergraduate, poetry was much more for me a matter of poems than of poets. But in graduate school I began to acquire some sense of Wallace Stevens. I was never very interested in the Keatsian side of his writing, the wedding cake ba-

43

roque of "The Comedian as the Letter C." What I loved in him was the clarity. I wasn't against the other so much as I just didn't take it in, and I certainly didn't understand the issues implicit in the two sides of his style. I knew a few poems, and almost as soon as I began to acquire an attitude toward Stevens, various things intervened to qualify my first hypnotic attraction to him. A couple of things that can stand for this change are the civil rights movement and my discovery in my senior year of the essays of James Baldwin, and through him the essays of Albert Camus, which began to awaken a different political and moral sense in me. And also the assassination of John Kennedy in 1963 and the ensuing escalation of the war in Vietnam. I was in a lecture course on poetry given by Yvor Winters when I heard the news of Kennedy's assassination; it was the fall of my first year of graduate study. By then I had some idea of who Stevens was and I had read Winters' essay which, though it's clear Winters thought Stevens was a great poet, nevertheless indicts him for a kind of trivial hedonism at the core of his thought. I was disposed to argue with every word Winters spoke, and I thought he was wrong about Stevens, but not entirely wrong. For different reasons from Winters', of course. The country we were growing up into—its racism, the violence it was unleashing in Asia, what seemed in those early years the absolute acquiescence of our elders in that violence—changed the tenor of my thinking about literature, and made Wallace Stevens seem much less attractive as a model.

Arguments about him raged in my group of friends. We knew by then that Stevens had been an executive of the Hartford Insurance Company, that he was making good money during the Depression, and lived well. One of my closest friends among the graduate students was Jiri Wyatt, and he was particularly skeptical of Stevens. Jiri had spent his early childhood hidden with his Jewish parents from the Nazis in the attic of a Slovakian farmhouse. He was much more politically sophisticated than the rest of us, and he was very funny and very bright. I remember specifically arguing with him. I was inclined to take Stevens' side. Jiri had gone to school in Boston. He could be scathing on the subject of what he called Harvard aestheticism, a new category to me, and enraged by the idea of a whole generation of English professors and graduate students fawning over the novels of Virginia Woolf and Henry James and poems of T. S. Eliot as a cover for indulging in their fantasies of belonging to a social class that answered to their aesthetic refinement. "They're cripples," he'd say. "Laughable. I mean, my God, look at this century." At Tressider Union under the oak trees in the spring sun. The war was escalating rapidly. We were all listening to Bob Dylan and the Beatles. "But Stevens' subject," I'd argue, "is epistemology." And Jiri, I think it was Jiri, impatiently: "Oh, come on. At some point epistemology is a bourgeois defense against actually knowing anything."

We did know or had heard that Stevens had written a letter to a friend who was buying tea for him in Ceylon, in which he said that he didn't care what kind of tea he was sent, as long as it couldn't be had in the United States; and I took that story to be, classically, an emblem of our relation to South Asia, and thought that its attitude was connected to what I had learned from Winters and Jiri to think of as Stevens' Harvard aesthete 1910 dandyism—not morally repellent, especially because it was so unconscious and so much of its time, but unsatisfactory, not useful. I also knew (it was widely quoted among us) Stevens' reaction to Mussolini's invasion of Ethiopia: that, if the coons had taken it from the monkeys, the Italians might as well take it from the coons. That too seemed provincial blindness, but less forgivable. I also knew—or sensed, it hadn't quite happened yet—that Stevens was in the process of becoming what I think he was not then thought to be, one of the central modern poets.

It was in this context that I began to replay in my mind the lines from "The Emperor of Ice Cream." The first thing that struck me was its lordliness. Part of our pleasure in chanting it several years before had been its imperiousness. Call the roller of big cigars, no doubt a Cuban or a Puerto Rican, and set him to work in the kitchen, where, in some fantasy out of Henry James or Charles Laughton's *Henry VIII*, "wenches" were employed. In 1963 (my students now don't quite believe this), white men of the older generation in the United States still commonly called the black men who worked in airports handling luggage, "Boy." I listened again to the line that commanded "boys to bring flowers in last month's newspapers." And while I was at it, I noticed that "last month's newspapers" was a figure for history, one I feel the sweetness of now. Who cares about history? Let the boys use it to wrap flowers in when they come courting. But at the time—or

45

was it at that age? I was twenty-two; Stevens was forty-three, twice my age, when he wrote the poem—taking history seriously seemed a central task of poetry.

When I tried myself to write poems about history and politics, I had in mind writing a poem about the California landscape and the United States seizure of California after the Mexican-American War, and about the Dow Chemical plant in the southern part of San Francisco Bay that was manufacturing napalm for the Asian War. And I thought vaguely that I would focus that poem on the person of a woman, the daughter of the first harbormaster of Yerba Buena, as San Francisco was then called. Her fiancé had been murdered by Kit Carson in the skirmishes that occurred when the old Californian families resisted the United States expeditionary force. It was a way of writing about the violence in American history; and when I sat down to the poem—which is published in my first book, *Field Guide*, and is called "Palo Alto: The Marshes"—the first line I wrote was, "She dreamed along the beaches of this coast." It was a couple of days before it occurred to me that I had lifted and transposed the first line of "The Idea of Order at Key West," and when I did, I remembered that the name of the fiancé whom Kit Carson killed was Ramon, and it gave me a place for writing the poem. My consciousness of Stevens' poem fell away as I worked, but its starting point is an instance of how polemical my relation to him felt to me in those years. He felt to me as if he needed to be resisted, as if he were a luxury, like ice cream, that I couldn't indulge.

Years later, though, when I looked at "The Emperor of Ice Cream" again, I felt much more forgiving of the tone of the poem. I said to myself, this isn't Babbitt fantasizing himself a houseful of servants in Hartford, it is Prospero speaking, as I had read, to his daughter, and speaking in the subjunctive at that. But saying it one also had to say that in Shakespeare, and throughout English literature, royalty expressed as power over others is a central figure for the power of imagination. And somewhere in those years it occurred to me that the poem is about death, which I thought made it a more wonderful and darker joke than I had understood. And at some still later stage—I think it must have been after reading Helen Vendler on the use of subjunctive in Stevens, but also after I had had enough experience of failure and disappointment in my own life to get it—I felt the pathos of the wishing in the poem and of the grammar that expresses it, so that by the time I was the age of Stevens when he wrote the poem, the three words "let be be. . ." struck me as a brilliant and sad figure for the fundamental human wish that seems so often impossible for us, and that Stevens had taken for one of his central themes.

And on another occasion—I can remember the shower in which the thought occurred to me, aquamarine tile, the house of a lover—thinking about what I then conceived to be the sadness of the poem, I was wondering about its fundamental gaiety and how it was achieved, and I thought about that delicious phrase that transforms itself from assonance into alliteration, "and bid him whip in kitchen cups concupiscent curds," and lets you know that, at least in language, magic can happen. It struck me suddenly that "bid him whip in kit/chen cups" contained the longest sequence (five in a row) of consecutively assonantal syllables I could think of in a poem. Toweling off, I must have been mumbling the lines to myself. "What are you thinking about," she said. She was wearing a pale, sea-green towel. "I was thinking: Bid him whip in kitchen cups concupiscent curds." "Concupiscent what?" she asked. "Curds," I said, looking her in the eye, trying out an imitation of W. C. Fields, "concupiscent curds."

As I was rereading the poem in the last few weeks, thinking about this essay, I made another discovery. I decided that the crucial thing about it in the end is the rhythm of the first six lines of the second stanza, that stanza I had neglected to take in twenty-five years ago when I was not interested in hearing about death:

> Take from the dresser of deal
> Lacking the three glass knobs, that sheet
> On which she embroidered fantails once
> And spread it so as to cover her face.
> If her horny feet protrude, they come
> To show how cold she is, and dumb.

This is as pitiless as any verse in Stevens, I think. That enjambment at the end of the fifth line and the stutter of a stop in the sixth deliver the last two syllables as baldly as anyone could contrive, and the rhyme—bum, bum—could not be more hollow. It is writing that returns the word "mordant" to its etymological root. And though I still think it is funny, it seems to me now to be, and to be intended to be, point-blank and very dark. And there are other things to notice. I think my disgust with the class-ridden drollery of the first stanza was not altogether misplaced, but it is certainly undercut by that shabby or melancholy or funny, in any case accurate, domestic touch—the glass knobs missing from the deal dresser. And there is a kind of *memento mori* in the peacock tail that had been—"once," he writes, to suggest the pathos of all our efforts at decor—embroidered on the sheet. And there is also something plain-dealing and very like Robert Frost in the diction: "so as to cover"; and if her horny feet protrude, "they come to show. . ." Every detail of the writing is meant to make this death as homely and actual as, what?, not Guatemala certainly. As any death in Emily Dickinson.

The second-to-last line of the poem—"Let the lamp affix its beam"—was for a while the only line in the poem that I thought was pure padding. He needed a rhyme for "cream" and a final flourish, hence a spotlight, hence "beam" and the otherwise meaningless lamp. But once you sense how dark, mordant, sardonic, pitiless a reading this poem can sustain, the lamp becomes an interesting figure for the focus of consciousness. It would seem that the beam is affixed on the stage where the final, now supremely ambiguous refrain is going to occur: "The only emperor. . ." One paraphrase might be: turn your attention to living, seize the day. If it says that, it also says: by all means turn your attention away from those horny toes. A sort of *memento non mori*. Or, to borrow a phrase from Eliot, human-kind cannot bear very much reality. It is also possible to read it to mean the opposite: that one should affix the beam on the horny toes, so that one understands from a clear look at the reality of death that there can be no emperor but ice cream, no real alternative to death but dessert while you can get it. Which is, I suppose, nearer to my first reading of the poem and to what Winters meant by Stevens' hedonism. I think the issue may be undecidable, finally, since both readings are grammatically permissible and both in their way in character. And perhaps the point lies in the poem's seeming poised on the knife edge between these two

48

attitudes. But however one reads these penultimate lines, they carry their darkness into the last line. Which makes for a very different poem from the one those college boys thought they were chanting thirty years ago as they waded through wet hillside grass in the early spring, and brings it nearer to the nothingness spoken of by Zack, whom I see now and then on late night TV playing a psychotic killer or a gaunt, hunted drug dealer in re-runs of *Cagney and Lacey* or *Hill Street Blues*.

It may not be completely accidental that while I was puzzling over the ending of "The Emperor of Ice Cream," a photograph appeared in the newspaper of a pair of stolid Dutch workmen removing a statue of Mikhail Gorbachev (who was briefly and quite literally an emperor) from its stand and carrying it rigidly horizontal, immobilized in a gesture of seigneurial self-assurance, from Madame Tussaud's Wax Museum in Amsterdam. It made me think also that the poem, if it has anything to say about political power, does so by talking about politics and pleasure and death. And it may not be wrong, in its merciless way, about where power usually resides in the world.

I imagine I am not through thinking about this poem, or about "Sunday Morning" or "The Snow Man" or "Thirteen Ways of Looking at a Blackbird" or "The Idea of Order at Key West" or "Of Mere Being" or "The World as Meditation," which are other poems I have been brooding over and arguing with myself about for much of my adult life. But I heard it early and I've lived with it for some time, and I thought that it would serve for one image of the way poems happen in your life when they are lived with, rather than systematically studied. Which I understand is how Stevens, though he was certainly not against the systematic study of anything, thought poetry mainly lived.

Nominated by George Keithley, Philip Levine

IN THE LAND OF THE LOTUS EATERS

by TONY HOAGLAND

from THE GEORGIA REVIEW

What was the name of that bronze-headed god
in charge of the Temple of Distraction?
Around whose shrine the ancient Greeks
would congregate, like flies, for hours
instead of working in their shops and fields?

I remember dying for a drink
about the time my grandmother was ready
to say her final words into someone's ear.
I remember seeing, in the air above her head,
among the tubes and stainless steel,
a vision of a speedboat

with a laughing girl on board—
a red speedboat with the word
ALOHA stenciled on the bow,
ready to take me anywhere. I don't know
I guess I'm the kind of person

who needs to be continually reminded
about love and brevity, about diligence
and loyalty to pain. And maybe my attention
is permanently damaged, never coming back

50

from too much television,
too much silly talk,

the way Ulysses' men turned into swine
from too much recreation in the Lotus Land,
then ran away because they couldn't stand
to see what they'd become.

That's why the newsreels of Cambodia must be divided into
slices by deodorant commercials,
why the lipstick shades to choose between in drugstores
equal the number of remaining whales.
That's why the disintegration of the ozone
is directly proportionate to the number of couples
entering therapy in Kansas City.

It is as if, in another version of *The Odyssey*,
Ulysses' men forgot to tie him to the mast,
and he abandoned ship
to chase the luscious a cappella voices of the sexy siren sisters.
To chase and chase and chase and chase and chase.

And the archers shot their arrows with their eyes closed.
And the workers in the factory denied any knowledge
of what the weapons would be used for.
And the name of the one in charge was forgotten.
And the boat sailed on without a captain.

Nominated by Carl Dennis, Wesley McNair, Robert Wrigley

DAYS OF HEAVEN

fiction by RICK BASS

from PLOUGHSHARES

THEIR PLANS WERE to develop the valley, and my plans were to stop them. I was caretaking this ranch in Montana that the two of them had bought, or were buying. One of them was an alcoholic and the other was a realtor. The alcoholic—the big one—was from New York and did something on the Stock Exchange.

The realtor had narrow, close-together eyes, little pinpoints in his pasty, puffy face, like raisins set in dough. He wore new jeans and a Western shirt with silver buttons and a big metal belt buckle with a horse on it, and he walked in his new cowboy boots in tiny little steps with his toes pointed in. He always walked that way. The realtor—Zim—was from Billings.

The big guy's name was Quentin. He had a big round stomach and small mustache, and looked like a polar bear.

The feeling I got from this big guy was that he was recovering from some kind of breakdown, is why he was out here. And Zim—grinning, loose-necked, giggling pointy-toe-walking-all-the-time, always walking around as if he were an infant who'd just shit his diapers—Zim, the predator, had just the piece of Big Sky Quentin needed. I'll go ahead and say it right now, so that nobody gets the wrong idea: I didn't like Zim.

It was going fast, the Big Sky was, said Zim. All sorts of famous people—celebrities—were vacationing there. Moving there. "Brooke Shields," he said. "Tom Brokaw. Jim Nabors. Rich people, I mean *really* rich people. You could sell them things. Say you owned the little store in this valley—the mercantile—and say

Michael Jackson—well, no, not *him*—say Kirk Douglas lives ten miles down the road. What's he going to do when he's having a party and realizes he doesn't have enough Dom Perignon? Who's he gonna call?

"He'll call your store, if you have such a service. Say the bottle costs $75. You'll sell it to him for $100—you'll *deliver* it, you'll drive that ten miles up the road to take it to him—and he'll be glad to pay that extra money.

"Bing! Bang! Bim, bam!" Zim said, snapping his fingers and then rubbing them together, his mindless raisin eyes set so far back, glittering. His mouth was small and round and pale, like an anus. "You've made twenty-five dollars," he said, and the mouth broke into a grin.

What's twenty-five dollars, to a stockbroker guy? But I saw that Quentin was listening.

I've lived on this ranch for four years now. The guy who used to own this place before Quentin—he was a predator, too. A rough guy from Australia, he had put his life savings into building this mansion, this fortress deep in the woods, looking out over the big meadow.

The previous owner's name was Beauregard. He had built the mansion three stories tall, rising up into the trees like one of Tarzan's haunts. Beauregard had constructed, all over the property, various buildings and structures related to the dismemberment of his quarry: smokehouses with wire screening to keep the other predators out, and butchering houses (long wooden tables, with sinks, and high-intensity interrogating lamps over the long tables, for night work). There were even huge windmill-type hoists all over the property, which would be used to lift the hoof-sprawling animals—moose, bear, elk, their heads and necks limp in death—up into the sky, so that their hides could first be stripped, leaving the meat revealed . . .

It had been Beauregard's life dream to be a hunting guide, and he wanted to take rich people into the woods, so they could come out dragging behind them a deer, or a bear—some wild creature they could kill and then take home with them—and Beauregard made a go of it for three years, before the business went down and the bad spirits set in and he got divorced and had to put the place up for sale to make the alimony payments. The divorce set-

53

tlement would in no way allow either of the parties to live in the mansion—it had to be both or none—and that's where I came in: to caretake the place until it sold. They'd sunk too much money into Beauregard's mansion to just leave it sitting out there in the forest, idle. Beauregard went back to Washington, D.C., where he got a job doing something for the CIA—tracking fugitives was my guess, or maybe even killing them, while his wife went to California with the kids.

Beauregard had been a mercenary for a while. He said the battles were usually fought at dawn and dusk, so sometimes in the middle of the day he'd been able to get away and go hunting. In the mansion, the dark, noble heads of long-ago beasts from all over the world—elephants, and elk, and greater Thomson's gazelles, and giant oryx—lined the walls of all the rooms. There was a giant gleaming sailfish leaping over the headboard of my bed upstairs, and there were woodstoves, and fireplaces, but no electricity. This place is so far into the middle of nowhere. After I took the caretaking position, the ex-wife would send postcards saying how much she enjoyed twenty-four-hour electricity and how she'd get up in the middle of the night—two A.M., four A.M.—and flick on a light switch, just for the hell of it.

I felt like I was taking advantage of Beauregard, moving into his castle while he slaved away in D.C.—but I'm a bit of a killer myself, in some ways, if you get right down to it, and if Beauregard's hard luck was my good luck, well, I tried not to lose any sleep over it.

If anything, I gained sleep over it, especially in the summer. I'd get up kind of late—eight, nine o'clock—and fix a big breakfast, and feed my dogs, and then go out on the porch and sit in the rocking chair, and look out over the valley or read.

Then about noon I'd pack a lunch and go for a walk. I'd take the dogs with me, and a book, and we'd start up the trail behind the house, walking through the centuries-old larch and cedar forest, following the creek up to the big waterfall—heavy, heavy timber. Deer moved quietly through that forest, big deer, and pileated woodpeckers, too, banging away on some of the old dead trees, going at it like cannons. It was shady back in that old forest, and the sun rarely made it down to the ground, stopping instead on all the various levels of leaves. I'd get to the waterfall, and swim—so cold!—with the dogs, and then they'd nap in some ferns while I sat on a rock and read some more.

In mid-afternoon I'd come home—it would be hot then, in the summer—the fields and meadows all around the ranch smelled of wild strawberries, and I'd stop and pick some when I came out of the forest. By that time of day it would be too hot to do anything but take a nap, so that's what I'd do, upstairs, on the bare mattress with no sheets, with the windows all open, no breeze, and a fly buzzing faintly in one of the other rooms, one of the many empty other rooms.

I would sleep in that sun-filled room upstairs, groggy in the heat—sleeping a pure, happy, dreamless sleep—and then when it cooled down enough—around seven or eight in the evening—I'd wake up and take my fly rod over to the other side of the meadow. It didn't get dark until midnight, in the summer. A spring creek wandered along the edge of that far meadow, and I'd catch a brook trout for supper: I'd keep just one. There were too many fish in the little creek, and they were easy to catch, so that after an hour or two I'd get tired of catching them, and I'd take the one I'd decided to keep back to the cabin, and fry him for supper.

Then I would have to decide whether to read some more, or go for another walk, or just sit on the porch with a drink in hand—just one big one—and watch the elk come out into the meadow. Usually I chose that last option—the one about the single big drink—and sometimes, while I was out on the porch, this great gray owl would come flying in from out of the woods. It was always a thrill to see it—that huge, wild, silent creature flying into my front yard.

The great gray owl's a strange creature. It's immense, and so shy that it lives only back in the oldest of the old-growth forests, among giant trees, as if to match its own great size against them. It sits very still for long stretches of time, back in the woods, motionless, watching for prey, until—so say the biologists—*it believes it is invisible*, and a person or a deer can walk right past it—or can even walk right up to it—and so secure is the bird in its invisibility, its psychological cloak of being hidden, that it will not move—even if you're looking straight at it, it's convinced you can't see it, and it won't blink, won't move.

Now *that's* shy.

My job, my only job, was to live in the lodge, and keep intruders out. There had been a "For Sale" sign out front, but I'd taken that down and hidden it in the garage the first day.

After a couple of years, Beauregard, the real killer, did sell the place, and was out of the picture. Pointy-toed Zim got his ten percent, I suppose—ten percent of $350,000, a third of a million for some place with no electricity!—but Quentin, the breaker of stocks, didn't buy it right away. He *said* he was going to buy it, the first day, the first five minutes he saw it—he took me aside and asked if I could stay on, and, like a true predator, I said, Hell yes. I didn't care who owned it, as long as I got to stay there, and as long as the owner lived far away, and wasn't someone who would keep mucking up my life with a lot of visits.

Quentin didn't want to live there, or even visit—he just wanted to *own* it. He wanted to buy the place, but first he wanted to toy with Beauregard for a while, to try and drive the price down five or ten or twenty thousand; he wanted to *flirt* with him, I think.

Myself, I would've been terrified to jack with Beauregard. The man had bullet holes in his arms and legs; he'd been in foreign prisons, and had killed people. A bear had bitten him in the face on one of his hunts, a bear he'd thought was dead.

Quentin and Zim would sometimes come out on "scouting trips," that summer and fall that they were buying the place—Zim's family back in Billings, and Quentin's back in the Big Apple—and they'd show up unannounced, with a bag of stupid groceries—Cheerios, and Pop Tarts, and hot dogs, and a big carton of Marlboro cigarettes—and they'd want to stay for the weekend, to get a better "feel" for the place. I'd have to move my stuff—sleeping bag, and frying pan, and fishing rod—over to the guest house, which was spacious enough. I didn't mind that; I just didn't like the idea of having them in the house.

Once, while Quentin and Zim were walking in the woods behind the house, I looked in one of their dumb little sacks of groceries to see what stupid things they'd brought this time, and a magazine fell out of one of the sacks—a magazine with a picture of naked men on the cover; I mean, dropping penises and all, and the inside of the magazine was worse, with naked little boys, and naked men on motorcycles.

None of the naked men or boys were *doing* anything—they weren't touching each other—but still, the whole magazine, that part of it that I looked at, was nothing but heinies and penises.

Realtors!

I'd see the two boys out on the front porch, the cabin all ablaze with light—those sapsuckers running *my* generator, *my* propane, far into the night, playing *my* Jimmy Buffett records, sitting out on the front porch and singing at the tops of their lungs—and then finally, they'd turn the lights off, shut the generator down, and go to bed.

Except Quentin would stay up a little longer. I'd sit on the porch of the guest house, at the other end of the meadow, my pups asleep at my feet, and I'd see Quentin moving through the house, lighting the gas lanterns, walking from room to room, like a ghost, and then the son of a bitch would start having one of his fits.

He'd break things—my things, and Beauregard's things—though I suppose they were now *his* things, since the deal was in the works: plates, saucers, and lanterns, and windows . . . I'd listen to the crashing of glass, and watch his big polar-bear whirling shape passing from room to room—sometimes he'd have a pistol (they both carried 9mm Blackhawks on their hips, like little cowboys)—and sometimes Quentin would shoot holes in the ceiling, holes in the walls.

I'd tense, there in the dark. . . . This wasn't good for my peace of mind. My days of heaven—I'd gotten used to them, and I wanted to defend them, and protect them, even if they weren't mine in the first place; even if I'd never owned them.

Then I'd see, in that low lamplight, Zim come into the room. Like some old queen, he'd put his arm around Quentin's big shoulders, and lead him away, lead him to bed.

After they left, the house stank of cigarettes, and I wouldn't sleep in the bed for weeks. I'd sleep in one of the many guest rooms. Once I found some mouthwash spray under the bed, and pictured the two of them lying there in bed, spraying it into each other's mouths in the morning, before kissing . . .

I'm talking like a homophobe here. I don't think it's that at all. I think it was just that realtor. He wasn't in it for the love. He was just turning a trick, was all.

57

I felt sorry for Quentin. It was strange how shy he was—how he always tried to cover up his destruction—smearing wood putty into the bullet holes in the ceiling and mopping the food off of the ceiling—this fractured *stockbroker,* doing domestic work—making lame excuses to me the next day about the broken glass—"I was shooting at a bat," he'd say, "a bat came in the window"—and all the while, Zim, in pursuit of that ten percent, would be sitting out on my porch, looking out at my valley—this *Billings* person, from the hot, dry, dusty eastern part of the state—sitting there with his boots propped up on the railing and smoking the cigarettes that would not kill him quick enough.

Once, as the three of us sat there—Quentin asked me some questions about the valley, about how cold it got, in the winter ("Cold," I said, "very, *very* cold")—we saw a coyote and her three pups go trotting, in the middle of the day, across the meadow.

And Zim jumping up, seized a stick of firewood from the front porch (*my* firewood!) and ran, in his dirty-diaper waddle, out into the field after the mother coyote and pups, running like a madman, waving the club. The mother coyote got two of the pups into the trees, picking them up and carrying them by the scruff of their necks, but Zim, Zim got the third one, and stood over it, pounding, in the hot midday sun.

It's an old story, but it was a new one for me—how narrow the boundary is between invisibility and collusion. If you don't stop it, if you don't single-handedly step up and change things, then aren't you just as guilty?

I didn't say anything—not even when Zim came huffing back up the porch, walking like a man who had just gone to get the morning paper. There was blood speckled around the cuffs of his pants, and even then I said nothing. I did not want to lose my job. My love for this valley had me trapped.

We all three sat there on the porch like everything was the same—Zim breathing a bit more heavily, was all—and I thought I would be able to keep my allegiances secret, through my silence. But they knew whose side I was on. It had been *revealed* to them. It was as if they had infrared vision, as if they could see everywhere—and everything.

"Coyotes eat baby deer and livestock," said the raisin-eyed son of a bitch. "Remember," he said, addressing my silence, "it's not your ranch anymore. All you do is live here and keep the pipes from freezing." Zim glanced over at his soulmate. I thought how when Quentin had another crack-up and lost this place, Zim would get the ten percent again, and again and again, each time.

Quentin's face was hard to read; I couldn't tell if he was angry with Zim or not. Everything about Quentin seemed hidden at that moment. How did they do it? How could the sons of bitches be so good at camouflaging themselves when they had to?

I wanted to trick them. I wanted to hide and see them reveal *their* hearts—I wanted to watch them when they did not know I was watching, and see how they really were—not just listening to them shooting the shit about their plans for the valley, but deeper. I wanted to see what was at the *bottom* of their black fucking hearts.

Finally Quentin blinked and turned calmly, still revealing no emotion, and gave his pronouncement.

"If the coyotes eat the little deers, they should go," he said. "Hunters should be the only thing out here getting the little deers."

The woods still felt the same, when I went for my walks after the two old boys departed. Yellow tanagers still flitted through the trees, flashing blazes of gold, and the deer were still tame. Ravens *quorked* as they passed through the dark woods, as if to reassure me that they were still on my side, that I was still with nature, rather than without.

I slept late. I read. I hiked. I fished in the evenings. I saw the most spectacular sights. Northern lights kept me up until four in the morning some nights—coiling in red-and-green spirals across the sky, exploding in iridescent furls and banners. . . . The northern lights never displayed themselves while the killers were there, and for that, I was glad.

In the late mornings and early afternoons, I'd sit by the waterfall and eat my peanut-butter-and-jelly sandwich. I'd see the same magic sights: bull moose, their shovel antlers still in velvet, stepping over fallen, rotting logs; calypso orchids sprouting along the trail, glistening and nodding—but it felt, too, like the woods were a vessel, filling up with something of which they could only hold so much—call it wildness—and when they had absorbed all they could, when they could hold no more, then things would change, and that wildness they could not hold would have to spill out, would have to go somewhere . . .

Zim and Quentin came out only two or three times a year, for two or three days at a time. The rest of the time, heaven was mine—all those days of heaven. You wouldn't think they could hurt anything, coming out so infrequently. But how little of a thing does it take to change—spoil—another thing?

I'll tell you what I think: The cleaner and emptier a place is, the less it can take. It's like some crazy kind of paradox.

After a while Zim came up with the idea of bulldozing the meadow across the way, and building a lake, with sailboats and docks. He hooked Quentin up into a deal with a log-home manufacturer in the southern part of the state, and was going to put shiny new "El Supremo" model log homes all around the lake. He was going to build a small hydro dam on the creek, and bring electricity into the valley with it, which would automatically double real estate values, Zim said. He was going to run cattle in the woods, lots of cattle. And set up a little gold mine operation, over on the north face of Roderick Butte. The two boys had folders and folders of ideas, plans.

They just needed a little investment capital, was all.

In the South, where I had come from, tenants held the power of a barnburning if their landlords got out of hand. Even a poor man or woman can light a match. But not here: a fire in this country wouldn't ever stop.

There seemed like there was nothing—absolutely nothing—I could do. Anything I did short of killing Zim and Quentin would be a token act, a symbol. Before I figured that out, I sacrificed a tree, chopped down a big wind-leaning larch so that it fell on top of the cabin, doing great damage while Zim and Quentin were upstairs. I wanted to show them what a money sink the ranch was, and how dangerous it could be, and I told them how beavers, forest beavers, had chewed down that tree that had missed landing in their bedroom by only a few feet.

I know now that those razor-bastards knew everything; they could *sense* that I'd cut that tree. But for some crazy reason they pretended to go along with my story. Quentin had me spend two days sawing the tree up for firewood, and before he could get the carpenters out to repair the damage, a hard rain blew in and soaked some of my books.

I figured there was nothing I could *do*. Anything I did to harm the land or their property would harm me.

Meanwhile, the valley flowered. Summer came, stretched and yawned, and then it was early fall. Quentin brought his children out, early that second fall—the fall of ownership. Zim didn't make the trip, nor did I spy any of the nekkid magazines. The kids—two teenage girls, and a teenage boy, a younger Quentin— were okay for a day or two (the girls running the generator and watching movies on the VCR the whole day long), but the boy, little Quentin, was going to be trouble, I could tell—the first words out of his mouth when they arrived were "Is it any kind of . . . is there any season for . . . can you *shoot* anything right now? Rabbits? Marmots?"

And sure enough, they made it two days before discovering there were fish—delicate little brook trout, with polka-dotted, flashy, colorful sides, and intelligent little gold-rimmed eyes, spawning on gravel beds in the shallow little creek that ran through the meadow on the other side of the road—and what Quentin's son did, after discovering this fact, was to borrow his dad's shotgun, and he began shooting the fish.

Little Quentin loaded, blasted away, reloaded—it was a pump-action twelve gauge, like the ones used in big-city detective movies, and the motion was like masturbating—jack, jack, *boom*, jack, jack, *boom*—and little Quentin's sisters came running out and rolled up their pants legs and waded out into the stream and began picking up the dead fish, and pieces of fish, and began eating those fish.

Quentin sat up on the porch with his drink in hand, and watched, smiling.

In the first week of November, while out walking—the skies that sweet, dull, purple lead color, and the air frosty, flirting with snow—I heard ravens, and then scented the newly dead smell of a kill, and moved over in that direction.

I saw the ravens' black shapes taking flight up into the trees as I approached; I could see the huge shape of what they'd been feasting on—a body of such immensity that I paused, frightened, even though the huge shape was obviously dead.

It was two bull moose, their antlers locked up from rut-combat—the rut having been over for a month, I knew—and I guessed they'd been locked up for at least that long. One moose was long-ago dead (two weeks?) but the other moose had died so recently (that morning perhaps) that he still had all his hide on him, and wasn't even stiff. The ravens and coyotes had already done a pretty good job on the first moose, stripping what they could while his partner, his enemy, was thrashing and flailing, I could tell; small trees and brush were leveled all around them, and I could see the swath, the direction from which they had come—locked-up, floundering, fighting—to this final resting spot.

I went and borrowed a neighbor's draft horse. The moose that had died that morning wasn't so much heavy as he was just big—he'd lost a lot of weight during the month he'd been tied up with the other moose—and the other one was just a ship of bones, mostly empty air.

Their antlers were locked together as if welded. I tied a big rope around the newly dead moose's rear legs and got the draft horse to drag the cargo out of the woods and down through the forest, to the ranch. It was a couple of miles, and I walked next to the old draft horse, soothing him as he sledded, forty feet behind him, his strange load. Ravens flew behind us, cawing at our theft; some of them filtered down through the trees and landed on top of the newly dead moose's brave, humped back and rode along like that, pecking at the hide, trying to find an opening—but the hide was too thick, they'd have to wait for the coyotes to open it—and so they rode with me like gypsies: myself, and the draft horse, and the ravens, and the dead moose (as if they'd come back to life) moving through the woods like a giant serpent, snaking our way through the trees.

I hid the carcasses at the edge of the woods and then, on the other side of a small clearing, built a blind of branches and leaves where I could hide and watch over the carcasses.

I painted my face camouflage green and brown, and settled into my blind, and waited.

The next day, like buffalo wolves from out of the mist, Quentin and Zim reappeared. I'd hidden my truck a couple of miles away and locked up the cabin so they'd think I was gone.

I wanted to watch without being seen. I wanted to see them in the wild—wanted to see what they were like when humans weren't watching them.

"What the *shit!*" Zim cried as he got out of his big mongo-tire Jeep, the one with the electric winch, electric windows, electric sunroof, electric cattle prod. Ravens were swarming my trap, gorging, and coyotes darted in and out, tearing at that other moose's hide, trying to peel the hide back and reveal the new flesh.

"Shit fire!" Zim cried, running across the yard—hopping the buck-and-rail fence, his flabby ass getting caught astraddle the high bar for a moment. He ran out into the woods, shooing the ravens and coyotes. The ravens all screamed and rose into the sky as if caught in a huge tornado, as if *summoned*. Some of the bolder ones came back down and made passes at Zim's head, but he waved them away, and shouted, "Shit fire!" again, and then, examining the newly dead moose, said, "This meat's still good!"

Zim and Quentin worked by lantern light that night: peeling the hide back with butchering and skinning knives, and hacking at the flesh with hatchets. I stayed in the bushes and watched. The hatchets made whacks when they hit the flesh, and cracking sounds when they hit bone. I could hear the two men laughing. Zim reached over and spread a smear of blood, delicately, on Quentin's cheeks, applying it like makeup, or medicine of some sort, and they paused, catching their breath from their mad chopping, and then they went back to work. They ripped and sawed slabs of meat from the carcass and hooted, cheering each time they pulled a leg off the carcass.

They dragged the meat up to the smokehouse—dragging it through the autumn-dead grass—and cut the head and antlers off last, right before daylight.

I hiked over and got my truck, washed my face in a stream, and drove shakily home.

They waved when they saw me come driving up; they were out on the front porch having breakfast, all clean and fresh-scrubbed.

I went up to the porch, where they were talking among themselves as they always had, talking as normal as pie.

Zim was lecturing to Quentin—waving his arm at the meadow and preaching the catechism of development to him.

63

"You could have a nice hunting camp and send 'em all out into the woods on horses, with a yellow slicker and a gun—boom! They're living the Western Experience. Then in the winter, you could run just a regular guest lodge, like on *Newhart*. Make 'em pay for everything. They want to go cross-country skiing? Rent 'em. They want to race snowmobiles? Rent 'em. Charge 'em for taking a *piss*. Rich people don't mind."

I was just hanging on: shaky. They finished their breakfast and went back inside to plot, or watch VCR movies. I went over to the smokehouse, and peered through the dusty windows. Blood dripped from the gleaming red hindquarters. They'd cut the moose's head off and nailed it, with the antlers, to one of the walls, so that his blue-blind eyes were looking out at his own corpse. There was a baseball cap on his antlers, and a cigar stuck between his big lips.

I went up into the woods.

But I knew I'd come back. I liked living in that cabin, and liked living at the edge of that meadow, and looking out at it.

Later that evening, we were out on the porch again, watching the end of the day come in—the days getting so much shorter—and Quentin and Zim were still pretending to be normal, still pretending that none of the previous night's savagery had happened.

It occurred to me that if they thought I had the power to stop them, they would have put my head in that smokehouse a long time ago. Would have put a baseball cap on my head, stuck a cigar in my mouth.

Quentin, looking especially burned out, had slipped from his chair. He was sitting on the floor with his back to the cabin wall, bottle of rum in hand, looking toward the meadow, where his lake and lots of cabins with lights burning in each of them would someday sit. I was just hanging around to see what was what, to eavesdrop, and to try to slow them down—to talk about those hard winters whenever I got the chance, and to mention how un-friendly the people in the valley were. Which was true, but hard to convince Quentin of, because every time he showed up, they got friendly.

"I'd like that a lot," said Quentin, speaking slowly. Earlier in the day I'd seen a coyote, or possibly a wolf—*sans* pups—trot across the meadow, but I sure hadn't pointed it out to anyone.

Even as we were sitting on the porch, there was the great gray owl—he'd flown in like a plane, ghostly gray, a four-foot wingspan—perched on the falling-down buck-and-rail fence by the road. I hadn't seen the owl in a couple of weeks, and I felt uneasy. It would be nothing for a man like Zim to walk up to that owl with his cowboy pistol, and put a bullet, point blank, into the big bird's ear—the big bird with his eyes set in his face, looking straight at you, the way all predators do.

"I'd like that so much," Quentin said again—meaning Zim's idea of the lodge as a resort, in winter. He was wearing a gold chain around his neck, with a little gold pistol dangling from it. He'd have to get rid of that necklace if he moved out here. It looked like something he might have gotten from a Cracker Jack box, but was, doubtless, real gold.

"It may sound corny," Quentin said, "but if I owned this valley, I'd let people from New York, from California, from wherever come out here for Christmas and New Year's. I'd put a big sixty-foot Christmas tree in the middle of the road, up by the mercantile and the saloon, and string it with lights, and we'd all ride up there in a sleigh, Christmas Eve and New Year's Eve, and we'd sing carols, you know? It would be real small-town and homey," Quentin said. "Maybe corny, but that's what I'd do."

Zim nodded. "There's lonely people who would pay through the nose for something like that," he said.

We sat there and just watched the dusk gliding in over the meadow, cooling things off, blanketing the field's dull warmth of the day and making mist and steam rise from the field.

Quentin and Zim were waiting for money, and Quentin, especially, was still waiting for his nerves to calm: almost a year he'd owned the ranch, a full cycle of seasons, and still he wasn't well.

A little something—peace?—would do him good. I could see that Christmas tree all lit up; I could feel that sense of *community*, of new beginnings.

I wouldn't go to such a festivity; I'd stay back in the woods, like the great gray. But I could see the attraction, could see Quentin's need for peace; how he had to have a place to start anew—though soon enough, too, I knew, he would begin taking ten percent from the newness again.

Around midnight, I knew, he'd take to smashing things—and I couldn't blame him. Quentin was wild, and of course he wanted to come to the woods, too.

65

I didn't know if the woods would have him.

We sat there and watched dusk come sliding in. All I could do was wait. I sat very still, like that owl, and thought about where I could go next, after this place was gone. Maybe, I thought, if I sit very still, they will just go away.

Nominated by Ploughshares, Philip Levine

TELL ME EVERYTHING

fiction by LEONARD MICHAELS

from THE THREEPENNY REVIEW

CLAUDE RUE had a wide face with yellow-green eyes and a long aristocratic nose. The mouth was a line, pointed in the center, lifted slightly at the ends, curving in a faint smile, almost cruelly sensual. He dragged his right foot like a stone, and used a cane, digging it into the floor as he walked. His dark blue suit, cut in the French style, arm holes up near the neck, made him look small in the shoulder, and made his head look too big. I liked nothing about the man that I could see.

"What a face," I whispered to Margaret, "Who would take anything he says seriously?"

She said, "Who wouldn't? Gorgeous. Just gorgeous. And the way he dresses. Such style."

After that, I didn't say much. I hadn't really wanted to go to the lecture in the first place.

Every seat in the auditorium was taken long before Rue appeared on stage. People must have come in from San Francisco, Oakland, Marin, and beyond. There were even sad creatures from the Berkeley streets, some loonies among them, in filthy clothes, open sores on their faces like badges. I supposed few in the audience knew that Claude Rue was a professor of Chinese history who taught at the Sorbonne, but everyone knew he'd written *The Mists of Shanghai*, a thousand-page, best-selling novel.

On stage, Rue looked lonely and baffled. Did all these people actually care to hear his lecture on the loss of classical Chinese?

He glanced about, as if there had been a mistake and he was searching for his replacement, the star of the show, the real Claude Rue. I approved of his modesty, and I might have enjoyed listening to him. But then, as if seized by an irrational impulse, Rue lifted the pages of his lectures for all to witness, and ripped them in half. "I will speak from my heart," he said.

The crowd gasped. I groaned. Margaret leaned toward him, straining, as if to pick up his odor. She squeezed my hand and checked my eyes to see whether I understood her feelings. She needed a reference point, a consciousness aside from her own to slow the rush of her being toward Rue.

"You're terrible," I said.

"Don't spoil my fantasy. Be quiet, O.K.?"

She then flattened her thigh against mine, holding me there while she joined him in her feelings, on stage, fifty feet away. Rue began his speech without pages or notes. The crowd grew still. Many who couldn't find seats stood in the aisles, some with bowed heads, staring at the floor as if they'd been beaten on the shoulders into penitential silence. For me it was also penitential. I work nights. I didn't like wasting a free evening in a crowded lecture hall when I could have been alone with Margaret.

I showed up at her loft an hour before the lecture. She said to her face in the bathroom mirror, "I can hardly wait to see the man. How do I look?"

"Chinese." I put the lid down on the toilet seat, sat on it.

"Answer me. Do I look all right, Herman?"

"You know what the ancient Greeks said about perfume?"

"I'm about to find out."

"To smell sweet is to stink."

"I use very little perfume. There's a reception afterwards, a party. It's in honor of the novel. A thousand pages and I could have kept reading it for another week. I didn't want it to end. I'll tell you the story later."

"Maybe I'll read it, too," I said, trying not to sound the way I felt. "But why must you see what the man looks like? I couldn't care less."

"You won't go with me?" She turned from the mirror, as if, at last, I'd provoked her into full attention.

"I'm not saying I won't."

"What are you saying?"

"Nothing. I asked a question, that's all. It isn't important. Forget it."

"Don't slither. You have another plan for the evening? You'd rather be somewhere else?"

"I have no other plan. I'm asking why should anyone care what an author looks like."

"I'm interested. I have been for months."

"Why?"

"Why not? He made me feel something. His book was an experience. Everybody wants to see him. Besides, my sister met him in Beijing. She knows him. Didn't I read you her letter?"

"I still don't see why. . ."

"Herman, what do you want me to say? I'm interested, I'm curious. I'm going to his lecture. If you don't want to go, don't go."

That is, leave the bathroom. Shut the door. Get out of sight.

Margaret can be too abrupt, too decisive. It's her business style carried into personal life. She buys buildings, has them fixed up, then rents or sells, and buys again. She has supported herself this way since her divorce from Sloan Pierson, professor of linguistics. He told her about Claude Rue's lecture, invited her to the reception afterwards, and put my name on the guest list. Their divorce, compared to some, wasn't bad. No lingering bitterness. They have remained connected—not quite friends— through small courtesies, like the invitation; also, of course, through their daughter, Gracie, ten years old. She lives with Sloan except when Margaret wants her, which is often. Margaret's business won't allow a strict schedule of visits. She has sometimes appeared without notice. "I need her," she says. Gracie scampers to her room, collects school books for the next day, and packs a duffle bag with clothes and woolly animals.

Sloan sighs, shakes his head. "Really, Margaret. Gracie has needs, too. She needs a predictable, daily life." Margaret says, "I'll phone you later. We'll discuss our needs."

She comes out of the house with Gracie. Sloan shouts, "Wait. Gracie's pills."

There's always one more word, one more thing to collect. "Goodbye. Wait." I wait. We all wait. Margaret and Gracie go

69

back inside. I wait just outside. I am uncomfortable inside the house, around Sloan. He's friendly, but I know too much about him. I can't help thinking things, making judgments, and then I feel guilty. He's a fussy type, does everything right. If he'd only fight Margaret, not be so good, so right. Sloan could make trouble about Margaret's unscheduled appearances, even go to court, but he thinks, if Margaret doesn't have her way, Gracie will have no mother. Above all things, Sloan fears chaos. Gracie senses her daddy's fear, shares it. Margaret would die for Gracie, but it's a difficult love, measured by intensities. Would Margaret remember, in such love, about the pills?

Sloan finds the pills, brings them to the foyer, hands them to Margaret. There. He did another right thing. She and Gracie leave the house. We start down the path to the sidewalk. Gracie hands me her books and duffle bag, gives me a kiss, and says, "Hi, Herman German. I have an ear infection. I have to take pills four times a day." She's instructing Margaret, indirectly.

Margaret glares at me to show that she's angry. Her ten-year-old giving her instructions. I pretend not to understand. Gracie is a little version of Margaret, not much like Sloan. Chinese chemistry is dominant. Sloan thinks Gracie is lucky. "That's what I call a face," he says. He thinks he looks like his name—much too white.

I say, "Hi, Gracie Spacey." We get into my Volvo. I drive us away.

Gracie sits in back. Margaret, sitting beside me, stares straight ahead, silent, still pissed, but after awhile she turns, looks at Gracie. Gracie reads her mind, gives her a hug. Margaret feels better, everyone feels better.

While Margaret's houses are being fixed up, she lives in one, part of which becomes her studio where she does her painting. Years ago, at the university, studying with the wonderful painters Joan Brown and Elmer Bischoff, Margaret never discovered a serious commitment in herself. Later, when she married and had Gracie, and her time was limited, seriousness arrived. Then came the divorce, the real estate business, and she had even less time. She paints whenever she can, and she reads fifty or sixty novels a year; also what she calls "philosophy," which is religious literature. Her imagery in paintings comes from mythic, visionary works. From the *Kumulipo*, the Hawaiian cosmological chant, she took visions of land and sea, where creatures of the different realms are mysteriously related. Margaret doesn't own a television set or go to movies. She denies herself common entertainment for the same reason that Rilke refused to be analyzed by Freud. "I don't want my soul diluted," she says.

Sometimes, I sit with her in her loft in Emeryville—in a four-story brick building, her latest purchase—while she paints. "Are you bored?" she asks.

I'm never bored. I like being with her. I like the painting odors, the drag and scratch of brush against canvas. She applies color, I feel it in my eyes. Tingling starts along my forearms, hairs lift and stiffen. We don't talk. Sometimes not a word for hours, yet the time lacks nothing.

I say, "Let's get married."

She says, "We are married."

Another hour goes by.

She asks, "Is that a painting?"

I make a sound to suggest it is.

"Is it good?"

She knows.

When one of her paintings, hanging in a corner of a New York gallery owned by a friend, sold—without a formal show, and without reviews—I became upset. She'll soon be famous, I thought.

"I'll lose you," I said.

She gave me nine paintings, all she had in the loft. "Take this one, this one, this one. . ."

"Why?"

"Take them, take them."

She wanted to prove, maybe, that our friendship is inviolable; she had no ambition to succeed, only to be good. I took the paintings grudgingly, as if I were doing her a favor. In fact, that's how I felt. I was doing her a favor. But I wanted the paintings. They were compensations for her future disappearance from my life. We're best friends, very close. I have no vocation. She owed me the paintings.

I quit graduate school twenty years ago, and began waiting table at Gemma's, a San Francisco restaurant. From year to year, I

71

expected to find other work or to write professionally. My one book, *Local Greens*, which is about salads, was published by a small press in San Francisco. Not a best seller, but it made money. Margaret told me to invest in a condominium and she found one for me, the top floor of a brown shingle house, architect unknown, in the Berkeley hills. I'd been living in Oakland, in a one-room apartment on Harrison Street, near the freeway. I have a sedentary nature. I'd never have moved out. Never really have known, if not for Margaret, that I could have a nicer place, be happier. "I'm happy," I said. "This place is fine." She said my room was squalid. She said the street was noisy and dangerous. She insisted that I talk to a realtor or check the newspapers for another place, exert myself, do something. Suddenly, it seemed, I had two bedrooms, living room, new kitchen, hardwood floors, a deck, a bay view, monthly payments—property.

It didn't seem. I actually lived in a new place, nicer than anything I'd ever known.

My partner, so to speak, lives downstairs. Eighty-year-old Belinda Forster. She gardens once a week by instructing Pilar, a silent Mexican woman who lives with Belinda, where to put the different new plants, where to prune the apple trees. Belinda also lunches with a church group, reviews her will, smokes cigarettes. She told me, if I find her unconscious in the garden, or in the driveway, or wherever, to do nothing to revive her. She looks not very shrunken, not extremely frail. Her eyes are beautifully clear. Her skin is without the soft, puffy surface you often see in old people.

Belinda's husband, a professor of plant pathology, died about fifteen years ago, shortly after his retirement. Belinda talks about his work, their travels in Asia, and his mother. Not a word about herself. She might consider that impolite, or boastful, claiming she too had a life, or a self. She has qualities of reserve, much out of style these days, which I admire greatly, but I become awkward talking to her. I don't quite feel that I say what I mean. Does she intend this effect? Is she protecting herself against the assertions, the assault, of younger energies?

Upstairs, from the deck of my apartment, I see sailboats tilted in the wind. Oil tankers go sliding slowly by Alcatraz Island.

Hovering in the fuchsias, I see hummingbirds. Squirrels fly through the black, light-streaked canopies of Monterey pines. If my temperament were religious, I'd believe there had to be a cause, a divinity in the fantastic theater of clouds above San Francisco Bay.

Rue spoke with urgency, his head and upper body lifting and settling to the rhythm of his sentences. His straight, blond hair, combed straight back, fell toward his eyes. He swept it aside. It fell. He swept it aside, a bravely feminine gesture, vain, distracting. I sighed.

Margaret pinched my elbow. "I want to hear him, not your opinions."

"I only sighed."

"That's an opinion."

I sat quietly. Rue carried on. His subject was the loss to the Chinese people, and to the world, of the classical Chinese language. "I am saying that, after the revolution, the ancients, the great Chinese dead, were torn from their graves. I am saying they have been murdered word by word. And this in the name of nationhood, and a social justice which annihilates language, as well as justice, and anything the world has known as social."

End.

The image of ancient corpses, torn from their graves and murdered, aroused loonies in the audience. They whistled and cried out. Others applauded for a whole minute. Rue had said nothing subversive of America. Even so, Berkeley adored him. Really because of the novel, not the lecture. On the way to the lecture, Margaret talked about the novel, giving me the whole story, not merely the gist, as if to defend it against my negative opinion. She was also apologizing, I think, by talking so much, for having been angry and abrupt earlier. Couldn't just say "I'm sorry." Not Margaret. I drove and said nothing, still slightly injured, but soothed by her voice, giving me the story; giving a good deal, really, more than the story.

She said *The Mists of Shanghai* takes place in nineteenth-century China during the opium wars, when high-quality opium, harvested from British poppy fields in India, was thrust upon the Chinese people. "Isn't that interesting?" she said. "A novel should teach you something. I learned that the production, transportation, and distribution of opium, just as today, was controlled by western military and intelligence agencies, there were black slaves in Macao, and eunuchs were very powerful figures in government."

The central story of the novel, said Margaret, which is told by an evil eunuch named Jujuzi, who is an addict and a dealer, is about two lovers—a woman named Neiping and a man named Goo. First we hear about Neiping's childhood. She is the youngest in a large, very poor family. Her parents sell her to an elegant brothel in Shanghai, where the madam buys little girls, selected for brains and beauty. She tells Neiping that she will be taught to read, and, eventually, she will participate in conversation with patrons. Though only eight years old, Neiping has strong character, learns quickly and becomes psychologically mature. One day a new girl arrives and refuses to talk to anyone. She cries quietly to herself at night. Neiping listens to her crying and she begins to feel sorry for herself. But she refuses to cry. She leaves her bed and crawls into bed with the crying girl who then grows quiet. Neiping hugs her and says, "I am Neiping. What's your name?"

She says, "Dulu."

They talk for hours until they both fall asleep. She and Neiping become dear friends.

It happens that a man named Kang, a longtime patron of the brothel, arrives one evening. He is a Shanghai businessman, dealing in Mexican silver. He also owns an ironworks, and has initiated a lucrative trade in persons, sending laborers to a hellish life in the cane fields of Pacific islands and Cuba. Kang confesses to the madam that he is very unhappy. He can't find anyone to replace his recently deceased wife as his opponent in the ancient game of wei-ch'i. The madam tells Kang not to be unhappy. She has purchased a clever girl who will make a good replacement. Kang can come to the brothel and play wei-ch'i. She brings little Neiping into the room, sits her at a table with Kang, a playing board between them. Kang has a blind eye that looks smokey and gray. He is unashamedly flatulent, and he is garishly tattooed. All in all, rather a monster. Pretty little Neiping is terrified. She nods yes, yes, yes as he tells her the rules of the game, and he

74

explains how one surrounds the opponent's pieces and holds territory on the board. When he asks if she has understood everything, she nods yes again. He says to Neiping, "If you lose, I will eat you the way a snake eats a monkey."

Margaret said, "This is supposed to be a little joke, see? But, since Kang looks sort of like a snake, it's frightening."

Kang takes the black stones and makes the first move. Neiping, in a trance of fear, recalls his explanation of the rules, then places a white stone on the board far from his black stone. They play until Kang becomes sleepy. He goes home. The game resumes the next night and the next. In the end, Kang counts the captured stones, white and black. It appears that Neiping has captured more than he. The madam says, "Let me count them." It also appears Neiping controls more territory than Kang. The madam counts, then looks almost frightened. She twitters apologies, and she coos, begging Kang to forgive Neiping for taking advantage of his kindness, his willingness to let Neiping seem to have done well in the first game. Kang says, "This is how it was with my wife. Sometimes she seemed to win. I will buy this girl."

The madam had been saving Neiping for a courtier, highly placed, close to the emperor, but Kang is a powerful man. She doesn't dare reject the sale. "The potential value of Neiping is immeasurable," she says. Kang says Neiping will cost a great deal before she returns a profit. "The price I am willing to pay is exceptionally good."

The madam says, "In silver?"

Kang says, "Mexican coins."

She bows to Kang, then tells Neiping to say goodbye to the other girls.

Margaret said, "I'll never forget how the madam bows to Kang."

Neiping and Dulu embrace. Dulu cries. Neiping says they will meet again someday. Neiping returns to Kang. He takes her hand. The monster and Neiping walk through the nighttime streets of Shanghai to Kang's house.

For the next seven years, Neiping plays wei-ch'i with Kang. He has her educated by monks, and she is taught to play musical instruments by the evil eunuch, Jujuzi, the one who is telling the story. Kang gives Neiping privileges of a daughter. She learns how he runs his businesses. He discusses problems with her. "If somebody were in my position how might such a person reflect on the matters I have described?" While they talk, Kang asks Neiping to comb his hair. He never touches her. His manner is formal and gentle. He gives everything. Neiping asks for nothing. Kang is a happy monster, but then Neiping falls in love with Goo, the son of a business associate of Kang. Kang discovers this love and he threatens to undo Neiping, sell her back to the brothel, or send her to work in the cane fields at the end of the world. Neiping flees Kang's house that night with Goo. Kang then wanders the streets of Shanghai in a stupor of misery, looking for Neiping.

Years pass. Unable to find a way to live, Goo and Neiping fall in with a guerilla triad. Neiping becomes its leader. Inspired by Neiping, who'd become expert in metals while living with Kang, the triad undertakes to study British war technology. Neiping says they can produce cannons, which could be used against opium merchants. The emperor will be pleased. In fact, he will someday have tons of opium seized and destroyed. But there is no way to approach the emperor until Neiping learns that Dulu, her dear friend in the brothel, is now the emperor's consort. Neiping goes to Dulu.

"The recognition scene," said Margaret, "is heartbreaking. Dulu has become an icy woman who moves slowly beneath layers of silk. But she remembers herself as the little girl who once cried in the arms of Neiping. She and Neiping are now about twenty-three."

Through Dulu's help, Neiping gains the emperor's support. This enrages Jujuzi, the evil eunuch. Opium trade is in his interest, since he is an addict and a dealer. Everything is threatened by Neiping's cannons which are superior to the originals, but the triad's military strategy is betrayed by Jujuzi. Neiping and Goo are captured by British sailors and jailed.

Margaret said, "Guess what happens next. Kang appears. He has vanished for three hundred pages, but he's back in the action."

The British allow Kang to speak to Neiping. He offers to buy her freedom. Neiping says he must also buy Goo's freedom. Kang says she has no right to ask him to buy her lover's freedom. Neiping accepts Kang's offer, and she is freed from jail. She then goes to Dulu and appeals for the emperor's help in freeing Goo. Jujuzi, frustrated by Neiping's escape, demands justice for Goo. The British, who are in debt to Jujuzi, look the other way while he tortures Goo to death.

The emperor, who has heard Neiping's appeal through Dulu, asks to see Neiping. The emperor knows Goo is dead. He was told by Jujuzi. But the emperor is moved by Neiping's beauty and her poignant concern to save the already dead Goo. The emperor tells her that he will save him, but she must forget Goo. Then he says that Neiping, like Dulu, will be his consort. In the final chapter, Neiping is heavy with the emperor's child. She and Dulu wander in the palace gardens. Jujuzi watches the lovely consorts passing amid flowers, and he remembers in slow, microscopic detail the execution of Neiping's lover.

"What a story."

"I left most of it out."

"Is that so?"

"You think it's boring."

"No."

"You do."

"Don't tell me what I think. That's annoying."

"Do you think it's boring?"

"Yes, but how can I know unless I read the book?"

"Well, I liked it a lot. The last chapter is horribly dazzling and so beautiful. Jujuzi watches Neiping and Dulu stroll in the garden, and he remembers Goo in chains, bleeding from the hundred knives Jujuzi stuck in him. To Jujuzi, everything is aesthetic, knives, consorts, even feelings. He has no balls so he collects feelings. You see? Like jewels in a box."

Lights went up in the midst of the applause. Margaret said, "Aren't you glad you came?" Claude Rue bowed. Waves of praise poured onto his head. I applauded, too, a concession to the community. Besides, Margaret loved the lecture. She watched me from the corners of her eyes, suspicious of my enthusiasm. I nodded, as if to say yes, yes. Mainly, I needed to go to the toilet, but I didn't want to do anything that might look like a negative comment on the lecture. I'd go when we arrived at the reception for Rue. This decision was fateful. At the reception, in the Faculty Club, I carried a glass of white wine from the bar to Margaret, then went to the men's room. I stood beside a man who had leaned his cane against the urinal. He patted his straight blond hair with one hand, holding his cock with the other, shaking it. The man was, I suddenly realized, himself, Claude Rue. Surprised into speech, I said I loved his lecture. He said, "You work here?"

Things now seemed to be happening quickly, making thought impossible. I was unable to answer. Exactly what was Rue asking—was I a professor? a men's room attendant? a toilet cruiser? Not waiting for my answer, he said he'd been promised a certain figure for the lecture. A check, made out to him from the regents of the university had been delivered to his hotel room. The check shocked him. He'd almost cancelled the lecture. He was still distressed, unable to contain himself. He'd hurried to the men's room, after the lecture, to look at his check again. The figure was less than promised. I was the first to hear about it. Me. A stranger. He was hysterical, maybe, but I felt very privileged. Money talk is personal, especially in a toilet. "You follow me?" he said.

"Yes. You were promised a certain figure. They gave you a check. It was delivered to your hotel room."

"Precisely. But the figure inscribed on the check is less than promised."

"Somebody made a mistake."

"No mistake. Taxes have been deducted. But I came from Paris with a certain understanding. I was to be paid a certain figure. I have the letter of agreement, and the contract." His green stare, fraught with helpless reproach, held me as he zipped up. He felt that he'd been cheated. He dragged to a sink. His cane, lacquered mahogany, with a black, iron ferrule, clacked the tile floor. He washed his hands. Water raged in the sink.

"It's a mistake, and it can be easily corrected," I said, speaking to his face in the mirror above the sink. "Don't worry, Mr. Rue. You'll get every penny they promised."

"Will you speak to somebody?" he said, taking his cane. "I'm very upset."

"Count on it, Mr. Rue."

"But will you speak to somebody about this matter?"

"Before the evening is over, I'll have their attention."

"But will you speak to a person?"

78

"Definitely."

I could see, standing close to him, that his teeth were heavily stained by cigarette smoke. They looked rotten. I asked if I might introduce him to a friend of mine. Margaret would get a kick out of meeting Claude Rue, I figured, but I mainly wanted her to see his teeth. He seemed thrown off balance, reluctant to meet someone described as a friend. "My time is heavily scheduled," he muttered; but, since he'd just asked me for a favor, he shrugged, shouldering obligation. I led him to Margaret. Rue's green eyes gained brightness. Margaret quickened within, but offered a mere "Hello," no more, not even the wisp of a smile. She didn't say she loved his lecture. Was she overwhelmed, having Claude Rue thrust at her like this? The silence was difficult for me, if not for them. Lacking anything else to say, I started to tell Margaret about Rue's problem with the university check. "It wasn't the promised amount." Rue cut me off:

"Money is offal. Not to be discussed."

His voice was unnaturally high, operatic and crowing at once. He told Margaret, speaking to her eyes—as if I'd ceased to exist—that he would spend the next three days in Berkeley. He was expected at lunches, cocktail parties, and dinner parties. He'd been invited to conduct a seminar, and to address a small gathering at the Asian Art museum.

"But my lecture is over. I have fulfilled my contract. I owe nothing to anybody."

Margaret said, "No point, then, cheapening yourself, is there?"

"I will cancel every engagement."

"How convenient," she said, hesitated, then gambled, adding, "for us."

Her voice was flat and black as an ice slick on asphalt, but I could hear, beneath the surface, a faint trembling. I prayed that she would look at Rue's teeth, which were practically biting her face. She seemed not to notice.

"Do you drive a car?"

She said, "Yes," holding her hand out to the side, toward me, blindly. I slipped the keys to my Volvo into her palm. Tomorrow, I'd ride to her place on my bike and retrieve the car. Margaret wouldn't remember that she'd taken it. She and Rue walked away, but I felt it was I who grew smaller in the gathering distance. Margaret glanced back at me to say goodbye. Rue, staring at Margaret, lost peripheral vision, thus annihilating me. I might have felt insulted, but he'd been seized by hormonal ferocity, and was focused on a woman. I'd have treated him similarly.

Months earlier, I'd heard about Rue from Margaret. She'd heard about him from her sister May who had a PhD in library science from Berkeley, and worked at the university library in Beijing. In a letter to Margaret, May said she'd met Professor Claude Rue, the linguistic historian. He was known in academic circles, but not yet an international celebrity. Rue was in Beijing completing his research for *The Mists of Shanghai*. May said, in her letter, that Rue was a "womanizer." He had bastard children in France and Tahiti. She didn't find him attractive, but other women might. "If you said Claude Rue is charming or has pretty green eyes, I wouldn't disagree, but, as I write to you, I have trouble remembering what he looks like."

Margaret said the word "womanizer" tells more about May than Rue. "She's jealous. She thinks Rue is fucking every woman except her."

"She says she doesn't find him attractive, and she knows what he looks like, what he sounds like, smells like, feels like. May has no respect for personal space. She touches people when she talks to them. She's a shark, with taste sensors in her skin. When May takes your hand, or brushes up against you, she's tasting you. Nobody but sharks and cannibals can do that. She shakes somebody's hand, then tells me, 'Needs salt and a little curry.' "

"All right. Maybe 'womanizer' says something about May, but the word has a meaning. Regardless of May, 'womanizer' means something."

"What?"

"You kidding?"

"Tell me. What does it mean?"

"What do you think? It means a man who sits on the side of the bed at two in the morning, putting on his shoes."

"What do you call women who do that? Don't patronize me, Herman. Don't you tell me what 'womanizer' means."

"Why did you ask?"

"To see if you'd tell me. So patronizing. I know exactly what the word means. 'Womanizer' means my sister May wants Claude Rue to fuck her."

"Get a dictionary. I want to see where it mentions your sister and Claude Rue."

"The dictionary is a cemetery of dead words. All words are dead until somebody uses them. 'Womanizer' is dead. If you use it, it lives, uses you."

"Nonsense."

"People once talked about nymphomaniacs, right? Remember that word? Would you ever use it without feeling it said something embarrassing about you? Get real, Herman. Everyone is constantly on the make—even May. Even you."

"Not me."

"Maybe that's because you're old-fashioned, which is to say narrow-minded. Self-righteous. Incapable of seeing yourself. You disappoint me, Herman. You really do. What about famous men who had bastards? Rousseau, Byron, Shelley, Wordsworth, the Earl of Gloucester, Edward VII."

"I don't care who had bastards. That isn't pertinent. You're trying to make a case for bad behavior."

"Rodin, Hegel, Marx, Castro—they all had bastards. If they are all bad, that's pertinent. My uncle Chan wasn't famous, but he had two families. God knows what else he had. Neither family knew of the other until he died. Then it became pertinent, everyone squabbling over property."

"What's your point, if you have one, which I seriously doubt?"

"And what about Kafka, Camus, Sartre, Picasso, Charlie Chaplin, Charlie Parker, JFK, MLK? What about Chinese emperors and warlords, Arab sheiks, movie actors, thousands of Mormons? Everybody collects women. That's why there are prostitutes, whores, courtesans, consorts, concubines, bimbos, mistresses, wives, flirts, hussies, sluts, etc., etc. How many words are there for man? Not one equivalent for 'cunt,' which can mean a woman. 'Prick' means some kind of jerk. Look at magazine covers, month after month. They're selling clothes and cosmetics? They sell women, stupid. You know you're stupid. Stupid Herman, that's you."

"They're selling happiness, not women."

81

"It's the same thing. Lions, monkeys, horses, goats, people . . . Many, many, many animals collect women animals. When they stop, they become unhappy and they die. Married men live longer than single men. This has long been true. The truth is the truth. What am I talking about? Hug me, please."

"The truth is you're madly in love with Claude Rue."

"I've never met the man. Don't depress me."

"Your sister mentions him in a letter, you imagine she wants him. She wants him, you want him. You're in love, you're jealous."

"You're more jealous."

"You admit it? You never before conceded anything in an argument. I feel like running in the streets, shrieking the news."

"I admit nothing. After reading my sister May's gossipy, puritanical letter, I find that I dislike Claude Rue intensely."

"You never met the man."

"How can that have any bearing on the matter?"

As for the people in the large reception room at the Faculty Club—deans, department heads, assistant professors, students, wives, husbands—gathered to honor Claude Rue—he'd flicked us off like a light. I admired Rue for that, and I wished his plane back to Paris would crash. Behind me, a woman whispered in the exact tone Margaret had used, "I dislike him intensely."

A second woman said, "You know him?"

"Of course not. I've heard things, and this novel is very sexist."

"You read the novel. Good for you."

"I haven't read it. I saw a review in a magazine at my hairdresser's. I have the magazine. I'll look for it tonight when I get home."

"Sexist?" said the first woman. "Odd. I heard he's gay."

"Gay?" said a man. "How interesting. I suppose one can be gay and sexist, but I'd never have guessed he was gay. He looks straight to me. Who told you he's gay? Someone who knows him?"

"Well, not with a capital K, if that's what you mean by 'knows,' but he was told by a friend of Rue's, that he agreed to fly here and give his lecture only because of the Sanfran bath houses. That's what he was told. Gossip in this town spreads quick as genital warts."

"Ho, ho, ho. People are so dreadfully bored. Can you blame them? They have no lives, just careers and Volvos."

"That's good. I intend to use it. Do look for conversational citations in the near future. But who is the Chinese thing? I'll die if I don't find out. She's somebody, isn't she? Ask him."

"Who?"

"Him, him. That man. He was standing with her." Someone plucked my jacket sleeve. I turned. A face desiccated by propriety, leaned close, old eyes, shimmering liquid gray, bulging, rims hanging open with thin crimson labia. It spoke:

"Pardon me, sir. Could you please tell us the name of the Chinese woman who, it now seems, is leaving the reception with Professor Rue?"

"Go fuck yourself."

Margaret said the success of his lecture left Rue giddily deranged, expecting something more palpable from the night. He said, she said, that he couldn't have returned to his hotel room, watched TV, and gone to sleep. " 'Why is it like this for me, do you think?' " he said, she said. " 'It would have no style. You were loved,' " she said, she said, sensing his need to be reminded of the blatant sycophancy of his herdlike audience. " 'Then you appeared,' " he said, she said. " 'You were magnificently cold.' "

Voila! Margaret. She is cold. She is attentive. She is determined to fuck him. He likes her quickness, and her legs. He says that to her. He also likes the way she drives, and her hair—the familiar black Asian kind, but which, because of its dim coppery strain, is rather unusual. He likes her eyes, too. I said: "Margaret, let me. Your gray-tinted glasses give a sensuous glow to your sharply tipped Chinese eyes, which are like precious black glittering pebbles washed by the Yangtze. Also the Yalu."

Margaret said, "Please shut up, dog-eyed white devil. I'm in no mood for jokes."

Her eyes want never to leave Rue's face, she said, but she must concentrate on the road as she drives. The thing is underway for them. I could feel it as she talked, how she was thrilled by the momentum, the invincible rush, the necessity. Resentment built in my sad heart. I thought, 'Margaret is over thirty years old. She has been around the block. But it's never enough. Once more around the block, up the stairs, into the room, and there lies happiness.'

" 'Why shouldn't I have abandoned the party for you?' " he said, she said, imitating his tone, plaintive and arrogant. " 'I wrote a novel.' " He laughs at himself. Margaret laughs, imitating him, an ironic self-deprecatory laugh. The moment seemed to her phony and real at once, said Margaret. He was nervous, as he'd been on stage, unsure of his stardom, unconvinced even by the flood of abject adoration. " 'Would a man write a novel except for love?' " he said, she said, as if he didn't really know. He was sincerely diffident, she said, an amazing quality considering that he'd slept with every woman in the world. But what the hell, he was human. With Margaret, sex will be more meaningful. " 'Except for love?' " she said, she said, gayly, wondering if he slept with her sister. " 'How about your check from the university?' "

" 'You think I'm inconsistent?' " He'd laughed. Spittle shot from his lips and rotten teeth. She saw everything except the trouble, what lay deep in the psychic plasma that rushed between them.

She drove him to her loft, in the warehouse and small factory district of Emeryville, near the bay, where she lived and worked, and bought and sold. Canvases, drawings, clothes—everything was flung about. She apologized.

He said, " 'A great disorder is an order.' ' "

"Did you make that up?"

He kissed her. She kissed him.

" 'Yes,' " he said. Margaret stared at me, begging for pity. He didn't make that up. A bit of an ass, then, but really, who isn't? She expected Rue to get right down to love. He wanted a drink first. He wanted to look at her paintings, wanted to use the bathroom and stayed inside a long time, wanted something to eat, then wanted to read poetry. It was close to midnight. He was reading poems aloud, ravished by beauties of phrasing, shaken by their music. He'd done graduate work at Oxford. Hours passed. Margaret sat on the couch, her legs folded under her. She thought it wasn't going to happen, after all. Ten feet away, he watched her from a low slung, leather chair. The frame was a steel tube bent to form legs, arms, and back-rest. A book of modern poetry lay open in his lap. He was about to read another poem when Margaret said, in the flat black voice. " 'Do you want me to drive you to your hotel?' "

He let the book slide to the floor. Stood up slowly, struggling with leather-wheezing-ass-adhesive chair seat, then came toward her, pulling stone foot. Leaning down to where she sat on the couch, he kissed her. Her hand went up, lightly, slowly, between his legs.

"He wasn't a very great lover," she said.

She had to make him stop, give her time to regather powers of feeling and smoke a joint before trying again. Then, him inside, "working on me," she said, she fingered her clitoris to make herself come. "There would have been no payoff otherwise," she said. "He'd talked too much, maybe. Then he was a tourist looking for sensations in the landscape. He couldn't give. It was like he had a camera. Collecting memories. Savoring the sex, you know what I mean? I could have been in another city." Finally, Margaret said, she screamed, " 'What keeps you from loving me?' " He fell away, damaged.

" 'You didn't enjoy it'?" he said, she said.

She turned on the lamp to roll another joint, and told him to lie still while she studied his cock, which was oddly discolored and twisted left. In the next three days, the sex got better, not great. She'd say, " 'You're losing me.' " He'd moan.

When she left him at the airport, she felt relieved, but, driving back to town, she began to miss him. She thought to phone her psychotherapist, but this wasn't a medical problem. The pain surprised her and it wouldn't quit. She couldn't work, couldn't think. Despite strong reservations—he hadn't been very nice to her—she was in love, had been since she saw him on stage. Yes; definitely love. Now he was gone. She was alone. In the supermarket, she wandered the aisles, unable to remember what she needed. She was disoriented—her books, her plants, her clothes, her hands—nothing seemed really hers. At night, the loneliness was very bad. Sexual. Hurt terribly. She cried herself to sleep.

"Why didn't you phone me?"

"I knew you weren't too sympathetic. I couldn't talk to you. I took Gracie out of school. She'd been here for the last couple of days."

"She likes school."

"That's just what you'd say, isn't it? You know, Herman, you are a kind of person who makes me feel like shit. If Gracie misses a couple of days it is no big deal. She's got a lot of high Q's. I

85

found out she also has head lice. Her father doesn't notice anything. Gracie would have to have convulsions before he'd notice. Too busy advancing himself, writing another ten books that nobody will read, except his pathetic graduate students."

"That isn't fair."

"Yes, it is. It's fair."

"No, it isn't."

"You defending Sloan? Whose friend are you?"

"Talking to you is like cracking nuts with my teeth."

She told me Rue had asked if she knew Chinese. She said she didn't. He proposed to teach her, and said, " 'The emperor forbid foreigners to learn Chinese, except imperfectly, only for purposes of trade. Did you know that?' "

" 'No. Let's begin.' "

Minutes into the lesson, he said, " 'You're pretending not to know Chinese. I am a serious person. Deceive your American lovers. Not me.' "

She said, "Nobody ever talked to me like that. He was furious."

"Didn't you tell him to go to hell?"

"I felt sorry for him."

She told him that she really didn't know a word of Chinese. Her family had lived in America for over a hundred years. She was raised in Sacramento. Her parents spoke only English. All her friends had been white. Her father was a partner in a construction firm. His associates were white. When the Asian population of the Bay Area greatly increased, she saw herself, for the first time, as distinctly Chinese. She thought of joining Chinese cultural organizations, but was too busy. She sent money.

" 'You don't know who you are,' " said Rue.

" 'But that's who I am. What do you mean?' "

" 'Where are my cigarettes?' "

"Arrogant bastard. Did you?"

"What I did is irrelevant. He felt ridiculed. He thought I was being contemptuous. I was in love. I could have learned anything. Chinese is only a language. It didn't occur to me to act stupid."

"What you did is relevant. Did you get his cigarettes?"

"He has a bald spot in the middle of his head."

"Is there anything really interesting about Rue?"

"There's a small blue tattoo on his right shoulder. I liked it. Black moles are scattered on his back like buckshot. The tattoo is an ideograph. I saw him minutely, you know what I mean? I was on the verge of hatred, really in love. But you wouldn't understand. I won't tell you anymore."

"Answer my question."

She didn't.

"You felt sorry for him. I feel sorry for you. Is it over now?"

"Did it begin? I don't really know. Anyhow, so what?"

"Don't you want to tell me? I want to know. Tell me everything."

"I must keep a little for myself. Do you mind? It's my life. I want to keep my feelings. You can be slightly insensitive, Herman."

"I never dumped YOU at a party in front of the whole town. You want to keep your feelings? Good. If you talk, you'll remember feelings you don't know you had. It's the way to keep them."

"No, it isn't. They go out of you. Then they're not even feelings anymore. They're chit-chat commodities. Some asshole like Claude will stick them in a novel."

"Why don't you just fly to Paris? Live with him."

"He's married. I liked him for not saying that he doesn't get along with his wife, or they're separated. I asked if he had an open marriage."

"What did he say?"

"He said, 'Of course not.' "

Margaret spoke more ill than good of Rue. Nevertheless, she was in love. Felt it every minute, she said, and wanted to phone him, but his wife might answer. He'd promised to write a letter, telling her where they would meet. There were going to be publication parties for his book in Rome and Madrid. He said that his letter would contain airline tickets and notification about her hotel.

"Then you pack a bag? You run out the door?"

"And up into the sky. To Rome. To Madrid."

"Just like that? What about your work? What about Gracie?"

"Just like that."

I bought a copy of *The Mists of Shanghai*, and began reading with primitive, fiendish curiosity. Who the hell was Claude Rue? The morning passed, then the afternoon. I quit reading at twilight, when I had to leave for work. I'd reached the point where Dulu comes to the brothel. It was an old-fashioned novel, something like Dickens, lots of characters and sentimental situations, but carefully written to seem mindless, and so clear that you hardly feel you're reading. Jujuzi's voice gives a weird edge to the story. Neiping suffers terribly, he says, but she imagines life in the brothel is not real, and that someday she will go home and her mother will be happy to see her. Just as I began to think Rue was a nitwit, Jujuzi reflects on Neiping's pain. He says she will never go home, and a child's pain is more terrible than an adult's, but it is the nourishment of sublime dreaming. When Dulu arrives, Neiping wishes the new girl would stop crying. It makes Neiping sad. She can't sleep. She stands beside the new girl, staring down through the dark, listening to her sob, wanting to smack her, make her be quiet. But then Neiping slides under the blanket and hugs the new girl. They tell each other their names. They talk. Dulu begins slowly to turn. She hugs Neiping. The little bodies lie in each other's arms, face to face. They talk until they fall asleep.

Did Claude Rue imagine himself as Neiping? Considering Rue's limp, he'd known pain. But maybe pain made him cold, like Jujuzi, master of sentimental feelings, master of cruelty. Was Claude Rue like Jujuzi?

A week passed. Margaret called, told me to come to her loft. She sounded low. I didn't ask why. When I arrived, she gave me a brutal greeting. "How come you and me never happened?"

"What do you mean?"

"How come we never fucked?"

She had a torn-looking smile.

"We're best friends, aren't we?"

I sat on the couch. She followed, plopped beside me. We sat beside each other, beside ourselves. Dumb. She leaned against me, put her head on my shoulder. I loved her so much it hurt my teeth. Light went down in the tall, steel-mullioned, factory windows. The air of the loft grew chilly.

"Why did you phone?" I asked.

"I needed you to be here."

"Do you want to talk?"

"No."

88

The perfume of her dark hair came to me. I saw dents on the side of her nose, left by her eyeglasses. They made her eyes look naked, vulnerable. She'd removed her glasses to see less clearly. Twisted the ends of her hair. Chewed her lip. I stood up, unable to continue doing nothing, crossed to a lamp, then didn't turn it on. Electric light was violent. Besides, it wasn't very dark in the loft, and the shadows were pleasant. I looked back. Her eyes had followed me. She asked what I'd like to drink.

"What do you have?"

"Black tea?"

"All right."

She put on her glasses and walked to the kitchen area. The cup and saucer rattled as she set them on the low table. I took her hands. "Sit," I said. "Talk."

She sat, but said nothing.

"Do you want to go out somewhere? Take a walk, maybe."

"We were together for three days," she said.

"Did he write to you?"

"We were together for hours and hours. There was so much feeling. Then I get this letter."

"What does he say? Rome? Barcelona?"

"He says I stole his watch. He says I behaved like a whore, going through his pockets when he was asleep."

"Literally, he says that?"

"Read it yourself."

"It's in French." I handed it back to her.

"An heirloom, he says. His most precious material possession, he says. He understands my motive, and finds it contemptible. He wants his watch back. He'll pay. How much am I asking?"

"You have his heirloom?"

"I never saw it."

"Let's look."

"Please, Herman, don't be tedious. There is no watch."

With the chaos of art materials scattered on the vast floor, and on table tops, dressers, chairs, and couch, it took twenty minutes before she found Claude Rue's watch jammed between a bedpost and the wall.

I laughed. She didn't laugh. I wished I could redeem the moment. Her fist closed around the watch, then opened slowly. She said, "Why did he write that letter?"

89

"Send him the watch and forget it."

"He'll believe he was right about me."

"Who cares what he believes?"

"He hurt me."

"Oh, just send him the watch."

"He hurt me, really hurt me. Three days of feeling, then that letter."

"Send it to him," I said.

But there was a set look in Margaret's eyes. She seemed to hear nothing.

Nominated by Sam Halpert

NOTE I LEFT FOR GERALD STERN IN AN OFFICE I BORROWED, AND HE WOULD NEXT, AT A SUMMER WRITERS' CONFERENCE

by WILLIAM MATTHEWS

from NEW ENGLAND REVIEW

Welcome, good heart. I hope you like—I did—
the bust of Schiller, the reproduction
of Casper David Friedrich's painting
of Coleridge, with his walking stick, gazing
over the peaks of German thought (the Grand
Teutons?), and the many Goethe pin-ups.
The life of the mind is celebrated here,

so why's the place so sad? I hate the way
academic life can function as a sort
of methadone program for the depressed,
keeping the inmates steadily fatigued

91

and just morose enough that a day's full
measure of glum work gets done. Inquilines
like us will have to put in our two weeks' worth

before the studied gloom begins to leak
forth from the files, the books, the postcards sent
back by colleagues from their Fullbright venues,
Tubingen, Dubrovnik, Rome, and Oslo.
Of course our own offices wait for us
and fall is coming on. To teach, Freud warned,
is one of three impossible jobs

(the others are to govern and to cure),
but to teach what you know—laughter, ignorance,
curiosity and the erotic thrall
of work as a restraint against despair—
is as close to freedom as anyone pays
wages for. The classroom's fine. Meetings are not,
those slow afternoons of the living dead,

and to watch academics isolate
some colleague they don't like is to look on
while an oilslick engulfs and coats a gull.
You can witness like torture in most jobs,
though not the drenched-in-sanctimony prose
by which it is excused. The louder they quote
Dr. Johnson, the faster I count the spoons.

Well, the grunts always kvetch about the food
and the scant morals of their officers.
Who'd want to skip that part? In the office,
though, alone with the books, postcards, busts
and sentimental clutter, we feel rage
dim and joy recede. These dusty keepsakes
block from view the very love they're meant to be

an emblem of, the love whose name is books.
It's as if we'd been kidnapped by the space
people and whisked around the galaxies,
whirred past wonders that would render Shakespeare

mute and make poor stolid Goethe whimper
like a beagle. The stellar dust, debris
agleam in the black light, the fell silence,

the arrogant and gratuitous scale of it
all, the speed of attack and decay each
blurred, incised impression made, the sure greed
we'd feel to describe it, and how we'd fail
that greed. . . . And then we're back, alone
not with the past but with how fast the past
eludes us, though surely, friend, we were there.

Nominated by Philip Levine, Arthur Smith, David Wojahn

LARABI'S OX

fiction by TONY ARDIZZONE

from LARABI'S OX (MILKWEED EDITIONS) and
PRAIRIE SCHOONER

IN A DITCH alongside the highway between Casablanca and Rabat lies Larabi's ox. Even in death the blue-black beast appears huge. Its open eye stares unfocused at the sky, streaked tangerine from the sun setting over the Atlantic. The ox's left foreleg, snowy white from hoof to knee, lies curled nearly to the swell of its stomach. The dying light lends its sallow horn a yellow cast. By the time Larabi finds his beast, the eye will be entirely milked over and covered with flies buzzing with greedy madness. Already the flies have settled on the blood clotted around the nostrils, lips, the black tongue bulging from the mouth. Other flies cling to the coarse hairs on the muzzle and the thinner lashes surrounding the eye, waiting their chance to bite something choice. Three egrets, white plumes unruffled in the still air, pick at a gash in the animal's side where its sweet blood has congealed, where a jagged spike of rib has torn through the skin. Beneath the skin the organs have bloated from the day's heat.

The ox has been struck by a shuttle bus from the Casablanca airport, then been prodded into the ditch by the bus's angry driver and by a dreamy boy pushing a red wheelbarrow loaded with two aluminum cannisters of milk. It is mid-morning on the highway to Rabat. The driver stands on the hot stretch of road in front of his idling bus, a curse on his lips, his foot eager to kick the stupid snorting animal his bus has just struck. The driver is dark, built as thickly as the steamer trunks stowed in the bus's cargo drawers. Despite the bus's air conditioning he has sweated

94

through his shirt. Dark loops of sweat droop from his armpits. A rounded triangle of sweat stains the center of his chest. His pants cling to his thighs. He smokes so continuously that his first and second fingers are stained gold from nicotine. He has never had a driving accident. He believes in *maktub*, that what is written is sure to pass. Afraid to veer off the road and risk a flat or, worse, a broken axle, he drives down the road's center, with as much horn as wheel. The road belongs to the strong, he believes. The ox failed to understand this.

The stupid beast. It gasps on the road before him, sitting on its folded legs. Why, when other animals run from the bus, did this one stroll into its path? The driver cares nothing for the animal's pain. His sole concern is the worry that if the bus is damaged he may lose his job. For a moment he turns from the ox and a wide-eyed country boy, who hurries from behind a red wheelbarrow, and studies the front of the bus.

At least the headlight is intact, he thinks. The bumper and front panel are dented, spotted with blood. He glances back at the ox, fearing if he is not careful it will rear up and charge him. His hands try to jerk the bumper straight. Once he slit a sheep's throat for the feast celebrating the birth of his first son, and when he turned for a moment the animal stood and charged him. The dented bumper does not budge. After the birth of his second son he held the sheep to the ground. He jerks at the stubborn bumper. He straddled the animal and held the neck fast while the dumb thing's life spilled between his legs into the earth. He stares at the stupid ox, then steps into the bus and returns with a rag with which he begins wiping away the blood and the many dark hairs smearing the bumper and front panel and headlight.

He'll lose his job. The thought is too terrible to consider. His job is a big step up from what he used to do, which was drive a city bus. No, he was not in the wrong. The right of way belongs to the strong. He's no fellah from the countryside. He has opinions on many issues, his time spent behind the wheel being ample. Also he has observed much from the high seat of his bus. Force is what makes life work. No matter the situation, the world belongs to the strong.

He remembers when he was young, after they buried his mother and burned her things so the disease would not spread, her brother came and took him to Casablanca. All he knew was life of the fellahin. The brother told him to stop acting like a donkey, to dry his tears, learn to open his eyes, use his brain. The brother taught him how to lead tourists into shops owned by their friends, who would later share with him a percentage of whatever was bought. When he was older the brother taught him to steer and to shift the grinding gears of a friend's truck, and with luck and connections got him a job as a city bus driver. In the cool morning when the sun broke the darkness of the horizon, spreading over Casablanca's tan walls like a racing fire, and there were seats and room for everyone, the young driver saw that his countrymen could behave as decently as Europeans sipping mint tea. But in the thick heat of the afternoon when three buses wouldn't be enough—well, you risked your life sometimes trying to get aboard, to ride with the others, standing. Of course the weak ones were left behind at the curb, pushed aside, occasionally knocked down in the rush. With no room for them, he'd have no choice but to shut the door. Once, a woman with his mother's face was nearly trampled by a crowd thronging onto his bus. He watched her fall, remembers still her dark eyes and the curve of her raised arm as the mob swirled around her.

He sees his image in the headlight as he folds the rag he used to clean the front of the bus. In the headlight he is fat and upside-down. The bumper and front panel look as they always look, he thinks. They must. A dent here, one there. And if someone were to point them out, why, the dents were always there, weren't they? No one needs to know the bus struck anything.

Then he hears the boy with his wheelbarrow sighing. The boy is filthy, wide-eyed, so thin his hips hardly hold up his ragged pants. He wears a man's T-shirt torn at the neck. The driver takes out a cigarette, then spits with disgust. He was just like him before he was rescued by his mother's brother.

"Oh, oh, oh," the boy says, his dirty hands fluttering in front of his face. He leans over the fallen beast, which thrashes its legs on the ground. The driver would like to slap some sense into the boy, at least to shut him up. He steps toward the boy, raising his hand. The beast lets loose a great quantity of shit. The ox must have been saving it for just this moment, the driver thinks. He lowers his hand. The shit lies repulsively in a mound, shimmering wetly. The stench is very high.

96

The driver considers for a moment the farmer who owned the animal. He might demand to be paid. Well, screw him. The stupid ox came out of nowhere, charged the bus. If blame is to be laid at someone's step, blame the fence the ox broke through or the sleepy shepherd boy who should have been watching it. The driver lights the cigarette, inhales deeply. There was no opportunity to stop without risking harm to the passengers. Of course, if accused, he can blame the passengers. He nods, looking back at the bus. The passengers are pushed against the windshield, gawking out like sheep at a fence. One, a fat American in a fedora and safari shirt, is taking photographs.

The driver waves for him to stop. "This damn American thinks it's amusing," he shouts into the bus's doorway. He speaks in Arabic to the group of Moroccans standing by the window.

"This is our life," one of the Moroccans answers, vigorously nodding, "the reality we live with each day, and he makes of it souvenirs."

The American smiles at the driver, then snaps his picture.

Screw him, the driver thinks as he walks back to the ox. Already he has decided his bus hasn't struck a thing. The dents were there when he drove the bus from its station. He grabs the animal's horns, lifts its head, trying to pull it from the road. The ox was already on the highway. The muscles in the dark neck twist against his grip. The black tongue lolls in the mouth. The country kid will have to help him.

The driver rolls what has happened around in his mind. He wants to put the events straight. He was driving along until he stopped the bus for a few moments to move an animal blocking the road. Obviously something hit it, then sped off. A car, a truck, a motorbike, perhaps another ox. Who can say how the beast was hurt? Who else but he knows what took place?

Not too bad a way to go, the American in the safari shirt reflects. He nods at his thought, then looks again at the beast through his camera. Quick, out of the blue, mouth full of tasty grass. Maybe dreaming about a cool drink of water, green pastures, a juicy heifer. You step out onto a road and then honk, honk, BAM! Welcome to the twentieth century. Probably broke the poor thing's ribs, punctured a lung, a few of the vital organs.

The American lowers his camera and pouts. He looks somewhat like an egg and knows it, feels sometimes like a big

97

Humpty-Dumpty as he plods about. His face is very pink and since the chemotherapy fairly hairless, and he is quite fat, particularly now that he no longer cares what or how much he eats. Funny how they call them vital organs, he thinks, as if there's anything inside you that isn't. Well, there's the appendix. But who knows for sure? Life offers no reliability. You think your cells are inside your skin where they belong, minding their own business, behaving and carrying out their various God-given functions, and then you find out that a whole bunch have been traveling about your body acting like promiscuous sluts. Multiplying and dividing in places where there should be no arithmetic. He pushes his abdomen with the flat of his meaty hand and feels nothing but the hand's pressure. No pain. Funny how when it all goes haywire you don't even feel pain. As sure as his name is Henry Goodson, he'd bet the animal on the road feels pain.

"He hit an immense black ox," he announces loudly, turning away from the windshield toward the Westerners, then the Moroccans, on the bus.

No one responds. Henry wishes someone would respond. Because whenever he remembers how his body turned Benedict Arnold on him, he aches to be touched, or at least acknowledged. He fears his loneliness is so strong sometimes it can be smelled. His eyes scan the others with visible urgency. Oh, see me and smile. No one does.

Pressed around him are several Moroccans, staring indifferently out the window or gesturing and talking with one another in Arabic. Others relax in their seats. A pretty American traveling by herself smokes a cigarette and fidgets, chewing her fingernails, pulling at the ends of her red hair, which is shoulder length, unwashed, breathtakingly lovely. What a shame beauty like hers is wasted on boys in their twenties, he thinks. When he was a boy in his twenties he had the sensitivity of a toad. He remembers what a bumbler he'd been in bed. Like a bottle rocket. No sooner did he get all the way up than he popped. He shakes his head, feeling pity for the girl and all young women in general. Then he feels himself beginning to harden.

Oh Body, he thinks, how at times you amaze me. He covers the front of his pants with one hand and blushes, not having felt desire as strong as this in longer than he can remember. The young woman peers out her window, puffing dribs of smoke out the side of her mouth.

What a shame she smokes. What a shame she doesn't wash her hair. Hair that beautiful should be shampooed, gently dried, brushed, then held back from her face with fine combs. In a louder voice aimed at her he repeats, "Our driver has killed an ox."

Instead of looking up, the young woman ignores him, eyes and fingers busy with her cigarette and the ends of her hair.

Then he notices the older woman, reading in her seat. The drabness of her turtleneck and men's hiking boots and trousers makes him wonder if she's from England. Few American women dress that way, he considers, at least the ones he's had the fortune to know.

Is she in her forties? Fifties? Her complexion is quite fair. Her nose, forehead, and the backs of her hands and her wrists are lightly brushed with freckles. Irish? Scotch? He imagines sitting next to her. What would he say? Surely she'll put down her book before they arrive in Rabat.

Then he sees the other American—or is he Spanish?—the one in the brown tie, gold-rimmed sunglasses. Corduroy jacket neatly folded next to him on the seat. Looking about like a cornered rat. No, he's from the States. You can tell by the button-down collar. Though the air inside the bus is still quite cool, the man is visibly sweating. Too tense a guy to go up to, sit down with, say how-de-do.

He turns and looks out the window as the Moroccans around him at first give him room, then press in against him like a wave. They lean freely on him, touch his back, push against his legs, his arms, in their attempts to see out the windshield. Henry doesn't mind the contact, no, not in the slightest. It has been many years since he's been touched. He thinks perhaps that's why he has come to Morocco.

For a moment he closes his eyes and concentrates on the men around him. He feels their shoulders and hands rock against him, smells the sweet mix of their sweat and hair lotion and tobacco and some unidentifiable spice, listens to the lovely tumbling cadence of their speech. He turns, steals a glance at the young woman. She chews the ends of her hair, her tender face now buried in a guidebook. What a waste, he thinks. If only he could help her to be not wasted. He tips back his hat and gazes again out the windshield.

The boy with the heavy wheelbarrow is glad he was not hit. Surely if he had been, his father would beat him. He is taking two cannisters of goat milk several kilometers down the road to his uncle. Then his uncle will sell the milk or take it where it will be made into cheese. The boy does not know what arrangement his father and uncle have made. All he knows is that he must not tip the wheelbarrow.

He has tipped many wheelbarrows in his short life. He has the welts to show for it. If he is as useless as his father and uncle tell him he is, he is sure to tip many more. Pushing a wheelbarrow is simple enough, difficult perhaps only over rock or in deep mud. But pushing a wheelbarrow usually leads him to dreaming. As his uncle and father have told him, daydreaming distracts him and leads to mistakes. Dreamy boys tip wheelbarrows. He must not allow the wheelbarrow to tip.

Earlier, as the boy moved down the road, he daydreamed he was a horseman, like the ones he saw last summer in the magnificent fantasia held during the festival of Sidi Moussa el Doukkali, a saint buried outside Salé, where his father's family lives. Traveling to the festival had been the most exciting event of the boy's life. Sidi Moussa had lived on wild onions and the salty air and could appear and disappear whenever and wherever he wished, leaping through any distance, no matter how great. He had given bread to the poor. Each year he had made a hajj to Mecca. He was the village's favorite saint.

The boy was imagining that he was a saint, a great horseman who lived on couscous and lamb and *bulfaf*—pieces of sheep liver rolled in luscious layers of fat—and who could fly through the air with his horse, and who rode in every fantasia in Morocco. In a fantasia the country's best horsemen, dressed in turbans and their finest robes, gathered at the far end of a field, forming a line, their steeds meticulously combed and decorated in red tassels and brilliant saddle blankets. At the field's other end waits the eager crowd. A hush falls. Then the horsemen charge, bright white capes flowing, raising and then twirling their long rifles above their heads. The horses break into a gallop loud as thunder. The men scream, *"Allaho-akbar! Allaho-akbar!*

Allaho-akbar!" Allah is the most great! The earth trembles. The crowd falls back and screams. At the very last instant, when the crowd is certain it will be cut down by the horsemen like wheat beneath a sickle, the riders rein in and fire their rifles simultaneously into the air, and then the great horses rear and the riders stand victorious in their stirrups, again twirling their rifles above their heads. Then they retreat.

The boy imagines the red wheelbarrow is an elegant tasseled bay and he is starting the charge, crying, *"Allaho-akbar! Allaho-akbar!"* He pushes the wheelbarrow down the road with what for him is reckless speed. Then he hears the terrible honking bus. He raises his eyes to the sound. From his angle the bus appears to be charging a black ox standing alongside a slight ditch. How exciting, the boy thinks. A fantasia. Surely at the last moment the bus will brake. The ox takes a step onto the roadway. The boy readies his mouth with the sound of rifles. "Pa-tchoo! tchoo! tchoo!" the boy says. The bus speeds nearer, and the beast— Larabi's ox, the boy realizes—continues on its way, seeming to chew its tongue, the boy notices, gazing first vacantly at him and then casually in the direction of the honking. For a moment the boy has the giddy desire that the bus might actually hit the ox. No. Yes, yes, it would be something to see. Then horribly, as all of time collapses to a single moment, the bus does exactly as he wishes, glancing into the ox's side, causing the great animal to skid drunkenly up the road until its useless legs bend and then crumple and it tumbles down onto its side, neck arched, its horned head raised to the sky as it lows as if saying, "Oh, I am in such trouble and pain!" There is much dust then and honking as the bus slides through the dust to a stop above the fallen animal.

For several moments the beast twitches and snorts, sides heaving like a punctured bellows. The driver rushes down from the bus, flares his nostrils, spits. The boy hears the man's dark curse and lowers his eyes. At that moment the animal begins emptying its bowels. The feces is soft, dark as pitch, and smells of fear and metal. Or is the metal just the taste on his tongue? The boy tries to taste his tongue, but it has turned to sand. He tries to swallow but cannot. He fears that by desiring the accident he has caused it.

The stench of the feces is so strong his eyes are tearing. He takes a deep breath and smells fear. Through the smell of fear he

101

looks up, back at the ox. Blood bubbles like a spring from the wound where the bone protrudes. The bone is torn, tipped with pink. The boy steps over the mound of feces and puts out his hand to touch the bone. Perhaps he can push it back in place.

The driver tries to pull the beast to its feet. The ox seems to snore, as if asleep. The driver gives it a kick. The boy cannot comprehend why a man would kick an animal he is trying to save, though the boy knows that men often kick for no good reason the things around them. His two cannisters of milk reflect the morning sun with a glare that is dizzying and blinding. In the same blinding light the dying ox's side flutters wetly.

"Wake up," the driver shouts. Again he kicks the ox, which lies now on its side. "Hey, donkey boy! Help me with this damn thing."

"As you like," the boy answers with a heavy heart. He knows if he had not imagined the tragedy nothing would have happened.

Together they try to encourage the ox into the ditch beside the road, with the driver grabbing the beast's horns, and the boy tugging the animal's right foreleg. The ox doesn't budge, shaking its head free of the driver's grasp and kicking the boy's hands, all the while lowing plaintively. Blood pools on the road beneath it. At the end of each of its labored breaths there is a gurgling, soft as a stream. The ox's hind legs scissor the air, and the driver and the boy stand back. The ox tries to right itself. It tucks in its forelegs, kicks its legs. Then, as if understanding the man's intent, it rolls and works itself to its knees. The driver holds its horns, trying to twist the head toward the ditch. The ox follows its head, crawling on its knees through its blood and feces toward the man, who steps backward as he pulls its horns. Then the beast collapses alongside the road.

The morning sun blazes brightly in the corner of the bus's windshield. The passengers stare down from behind the tinted glass. The boy watches the driver pick up from the road a blood-stained rag and then fold it into smaller and smaller squares and then place the smallest square into his back pocket. Why does he want to keep the blood? the boy wonders. Tears fill his eyes. Oh, fantasia! Instead of a festival and celebration there is tragedy.

He returns slowly to the wheelbarrow. Without thinking, his hands fall to the wooden handles, which he lifts with a soft grunt. The boy knows he doesn't push his load so much as try to keep up with it. The weight of the load presses down on the wheel, which turns beneath the weight, covering the ground between where the barrow is and where it wants to go. His father told him it is the same with life. You run between the handles, trying your best to guide the wheel's direction and to prevent the load from tipping. The bus roars now like a horrible monster. The boy is careful to push his load around the slash of feces. The bus's gears engage with a clank. Then the bus starts up the roadway, moving

For a moment the three—boy, driver, ox—are in a line perpendicular to the road. The bus is in the center between the boy and the beast, which has stopped lowing and is nearly numb, feeling only a growing heaviness of breath and the familiar, teasing sting of the flies. The driver gives the bus gas, thinking no one else knows what has happened. The chugging sound of the bus's engine soothes him. No matter what, he will not give up the comfort of his seat. The American in the safari shirt and fedora waves at the boy with the wheelbarrow as he passes below. The boy does not notice the wave. His eyes dumbly watch the road and the two cannisters in front of him as he trudges in the opposite direction. But then he looks up and sees behind the window the lovely face of the woman with red hair. Her face is turned fully toward the window. Her beauty surprises him. The boy thinks her large, heavy-lidded eyes look sad. He stares at her openly, smitten by the ripe fullness of her lips, as the bus pulls even with him. The young woman looks beyond him and the rocky field west of the road toward a blue sliver of the ocean, which she has just noticed, and which pleases her, brings a smile to her lips. She knew the road from the airport to Rabat ran parallel to the coast, though she did not expect the ocean to be this close.

The boy's heart catches when he sees her smile. He imagines she smiles at him because he is so handsome, so strong, so brave as to drive an ox into a ditch. The idea is too delicious for him to endure. His wheelbarrow strikes a sudden stone and all at once tips, one cannister shifting from the left side to the right with a bang, causing the cannister's top to pop off and some of the milk inside to splash out. The milk splashes onto the side of the road, which drinks it greedily, and into the belly of the wheelbarrow.

The images of the woman's smile, the dizzy tipping, and the splashing milk tumble in the boy's mind as the roaring bus speeds past.

From a distance the boy's uncle watches the bus move past his nephew and the wheelbarrow. The uncle stands sideways on the inside slope of a slight ridge between the road and the pounding sea. In a moment the boy will notice him, he thinks.

He has just peed, not without effort and pain, straining with all his might to push out the last lazy drops that seem always to wish to remain. He is pleased that this morning he's been successful. He is sure the heavy drops contain grit from the food he has eaten in the past day. That's why it's so difficult to cleanse the body of them. Like the sediment you see settled on the bottom of a jug of clear water, so it is with a man's tubes, he believes. If a person is not careful, the grit builds up like silt at the bottom of a slowly moving stream. The grit clings to itself, forming peculiarly shaped pebbles. He has seen several such pebbles, picked up from the ground by men just his age after they'd painfully urinated. He knew a few men whose tubes became so choked with grit they died. There are far better ways to die than to die of clogged tubes, he thinks.

He shakes a stubborn drop from the mouth of his penis, then pushes his penis back inside the pantaloons he wears beneath his djellaba, which is wool, tan with sienna brown stripes. His dark eyes are set deeply in his skull. He has wrapped his shaved head in a white turban. Twice a month for a full day he fasts, and on the second day to break his fast he drinks bottled mineral water from Sidi Harazem, near Fez, to flush the grit from his bowels. During the thirty days of Ramadan, the ninth month, when Muslims forego all food, drink and sexual relations from sunrise to sunset, his body purifies itself further, becoming a flame of thirst and desire.

At first the flame flares brightly. The edge of desire is keen. The body cries out in need, like a pampered child. But then after several days the needs stop crying out. The flame of physical desire flickers, dies back to an ember, and the person becomes self-contained, like a plant, the uncle thinks, which takes in nothing, surviving on itself. Then appetite becomes more suggestion than demand. The body becomes servant to the soul. The mind is then content, and the soul is better able to submit to the will of

Allah. Fasting is a pillar of Islam, which means submission or self-surrender, a voluntary act whereby a person places his or her destiny in the hands of God and submits to God's rule as revealed through the commands given to the Prophet.

In the pocket of his *choukkara*, his fingers touch his beads. The voice beneath his breath falls into prayer. *"La ilaha ill'Allah, Mohammed rasul'Allah."* There is no god but Allah, and Mohammed is His Prophet. He runs the beads through his fingers as the prayer spills from his lips. The prayers have not yet become part of his body, companion to each breath, heartbeat. His hand still needs to feel the beads. But sometimes once he has started to finger the beads he is able to pray through to their knot without a distracting thought.

He watches his nephew stop to balance the cannisters in his wheelbarrow. Dawdler, inventor of excuses, dreamer and creator of unbelievable tales, the boy will need much discipline before he grows older, the uncle thinks. The man frowns, more from habit than displeasure. He deeply loves his nephew and would forgive him any sin. The boy is like the body, he thinks, full of need and desire. He is to the boy as the mind is to the body.

He notices far behind the boy an egret circle and then settle near a mound alongside the road. He does not know the dark shape is Larabi's dying ox. From where he stands it resembles a pile of freshly dug earth. He thinks no more of it, envying his brother, even though envy is a useless feeling and his brother is miserably poor. His poor brother lives in a shack made of scrap wood and tin with his wife, seven children, and skinny goats.

The sea rages against the rocky coast. The man turns into his shadow, fingers his prayer beads, reflects. *"La ilaha ill'Allah."* The waves pound the rocky shore, shatter into droplets. *"Mohammed rasul'Allah."* The water recedes, and the shore resists, though with repetition and time the sea will reduce even the hardest rock into sand. *"La ilaha ill'Allah."* With time and repetition the body learns complete submission. *"Mohammed rasul'Allah."* The rock and the sea act in accord with Allah's will.

The uncle looks off into the distance, to the south outside Casablanca, where there stands a refinery's flaming smokestack. This morning the sky over the refinery is especially gray, unclean. The man can remember when there was no flaming dirt in the sky. In time, he considers, even the refinery will be reduced. The candle will flicker, die. The towering cylinder of bricks will tumble. All of man's works will be reduced during the last hour, when the sun will be shrouded and the stars will no longer give light, when the mountains will vanish and the seas will boil over, and all people will be coupled with their deeds. Then the scrolls will be unfolded, and all will come to know what they have prepared for themselves. And the earth will be rocked in her last convulsion. The man returns his gaze to the furious whitecaps biting their way into the shore.

He knows his nephew nears, recognizes him, is thinking of a fantastic tale to explain why he is so late. Though the uncle is pleased to see his nephew, he clears his face.

Breathless, shouting with a high voice as he makes his approach, the boy tells him in a single tumbling sentence the story of the ox, the fantasia, the honking bus. As he begins to describe how the beautiful woman with hair the color of sunrise looked down and smiled with admiration at his bravery, the uncle chides him for the wasted milk puddled in the belly of the wheelbarrow. The uncle believes the entire tale is a fantasy and is tempted to lecture the boy on the dangers of such idleness, but then he thinks better of it and holds his nephew to his chest and in greeting kisses both his cheeks, and the boy tells him no more of his story.

The boy tells no more of Larabi, the simple fellah, who, untold, will set out on foot in search of his stray beast as the tangerine sun streaks the sky and dips into the pounding blue Atlantic. No one will watch Larabi walk into the dying light, shielding his eyes with one hand, his other hand grasping the staff he uses to drive his herds. He will walk into the sun, to the sea. The birds in the air will lead him to it. At first Larabi's mind will deny what he sees, will tell him the animal is only resting, or asleep, or at worst has slipped, injured its snow-white left foreleg. Then when his eyes protest that the beast in the ditch is dead, he will think that it only resembles his lively animal. Surely this dead, bloated beast is another man's misfortune, Larabi will think.

Then he will fall to his knees in mourning and in recognition of God's will, and his fingers will scratch sad furrows into the darkened earth.

Nominated by Milkweed Editions

CARLA'S STORY

by PETER COYOTE

from ZYZZYVA

I MET CARLA IN 1968 when she was 17, a big, voluptuous teen-ager with a throaty laugh and a baby. I was 27, the de facto head-man of the Free Family commune in Olema. I lost track of her around 1971 when our truck caravan broke up in Boulder. My father had just died and I went East to help my mother. Others scattered to their own needs and purposes, Carla with them.

I ran into her once by chance in San Rafael around 1975. We went back to her room to share a bag of dope and catch up. After that, I lost track of her for 16 years until she called me one day, out of the blue. We met and talked for hours, breathless with the good fortune of having found one another again. This is largely her story, but it is also mine.

It was autumn. I had moved my lady, Sam, and our daughter, Ariel, out of the overcrowded Olema ranch house into a small, abandoned outbuilding, a cattle shed we had tarpapered against the winter, insulating the windows with plastic and the rough wood floors with old carpets. I had installed a wood-burning stove and built a loft for sleeping. It was quite lovely lying in bed at night, listening to the dull comforting murmur of the winter rains on the slate roof.

According to Carla, I was away at Black Bear Ranch, another Free Family site deep in the Trinity-Siskiyou wilderness, when she and her gangly, boisterous boyfriend, Jeff, arrived. Jeff had already been living at Olema and had been introduced to Carla through a mutual friend from one of Carla's foster families when the two had traveled south for some r&r. Carla gleaned from others that I was a "significant" person and that she would need my okay to stay. I suppose I was the nominal headman by virtue of having been the first to colonize the place and supplying the overarching vision of Olema's dovetail with the rest of the Free Family. It was commonly agreed by all who lived there that Olema was "free turf"; one could do and be whatever one chose to be there.

Carla remembers that I made her feel at home when I returned and that my lady, Sam, appeared to her as omnicompetent and everything she might ever want to be. Sam was ten years older than Carla, a tall blonde from Shreveport whose family had once trained her for beauty pageants. She was beautiful and imposing with witchy powers. Emmett Grogan used to call her "the swamp bitch." Like most of us, she was picking her way through the rubble of her own psyche; to Carla, she appeared as a goddess, fully formed and worthy of emulation.

Sam taught her to tan the deer hides we retrieved in numbers from the Pt. Reyes garbage dump during hunting season; to make an oatmeal-thick mash from wood ashes and water to slip the hair; to pickle the skins in a sulfuric acid bath or rub them with brains, and break them to softness over a fence post or the back of an ax jammed into a stump. Though the ultimate utility of such skills might have been marginal, they contributed to a sense of independence from the larger culture and supported our intentions to be in continuity with indigenous people who had lived where we were living, centuries earlier. Such skills also enabled us to create tradegoods and currency from found objects, personal skills, and time. One could create wealth by re-defining it in a game that was not stacked against you.

Carla's deficiencies as an immature mother were absorbed by Phyllis and other members of the community who would grab her baby, Malachi, and take him off with them on their errands and whims for hours at a time. Carla was stupefied and relieved at this display of group concern and generosity, not surprisingly, considering her own memories of home. Her parents were both teachers. Her mother was also a fairly talented painter of portraits, the type that grace middle-class homes, implying status and discretionary income. Her stepfather was discovered with pornographic photos of some of the girls in his class. Carla remembers him as a "sick son of a bitch." One day when Carla was 14, he ripped off her blouse and pinned her to the living room floor. Her mother walked in, regarded them for an instant, then continued to her own room, slamming the door without a word. That was when Carla began running away.

Before long Carla was stitched to the rest of us seamlessly. She participated in creating our group mythology and she inspired others, once serving as the inspiration for one of Lew Welch's best throwaway lines. Lew was a famous Beat poet, a tall, freckled, sad-eyed Irishman whose characteristic expression was childish wonder and delight. He lived sporadically and stormily with a thick, powerful Slavic woman named Magda. When she tired of his drunken escapades, he would move out of their Marin City pad and in with us. He loved jazz and Magda's two children and was proud of tutoring their musical abilities. He introduced me to Magda's oldest, Huey, when he was ten years old. Lew beamed with delight as the child scatted the tricky jazz riffs Lew had taught him. He might well have been proud: Lew's Huey grew up to be his own Huey Lewis and the News.

I was pleased to have Lew at the ranch, because I felt his presence conferred on us a legitimate descent from the Beats. I was also extremely proud that Lew had dedicated a poem to me, "Olema Satori."

On the day he honored Carla, Lew was sitting on the floor of the Olema living room cradling a jug of Cribari red in his lap. He was deep in his cups. The room was pulsing with music and dense with marijuana smoke. Carla was lost in sinuous dancing, naked from the waist up. Lew watched her with undisguised lust. He turned to me, grinning crookedly, raised one finger, and said, very slowly and very clearly, "The . . . worst . . . Persian . . . voluptuary . . . could . . . not . . . imagine . . . our . . . most . . . ordinary . . . day." Having managed this, he pitched over, unconscious.

There was no clue in Lew's joy that day, that not long afterwards he would leave his wallet and a note in Gary Snyder's kitchen and walk into the Sierra foothills with his rifle, to commit

109

suicide. If he had hidden his private griefs in his life, he remained consistent in death. To this day, his body has never been found.

About this time, Rick "Doc" Holiday, a small, delicate junkie with black hair, a con-man's politesse, and a soft, smokey voice, showed up with a tall, androgynously beautiful girl who might have been Mick Jagger's sister. This was Daney. Junk-sick as she was when she arrived, she radiated sexual energy and Carla took to her immediately.

Basically, Doc abandoned her with us to clean up. Daney did her best, and before long she was baking bread, laughing, throwing sparks off her cat's-eyes, and radiating a feral energy that made it apparent that she would not linger very long in the land of brown rice and black beans. Both girls were ready for a break from the poverty of ranch life when Carla came and asked me for some money to get high.

The reason she asked me was because, that day, I was in charge of the Free Bank, a Digger institution: everyone put their money, food stamps, and personal wealth into a kitty, to be divided up at group meetings according to consensual priorities. What was left after the kids, trucks, and groceries had been covered, could be taken out on an as-needed basis, and simply recorded in the Free Bankbook.

I tried to talk Carla out of doing drugs, but she and Daney were already gassed up and idling at half-throttle. They left together, Carla in her work boots, floor-length skirt, and flannel shirt, baby on her hip, and Daney, looking fabulous and "reeking of sex," as Carla remembers. Daney did not have any money for herself, and Carla overlooked her assertion that she would "get some" when they arrived in Sausalito.

The two girls and the baby hitchhiked to the Trident Restaurant, a favorite hangout for drug dealers and wannabes. Daney was in her element there, gliding into the room like a shark, leaving Carla at the bar while she went "to score some money."

"I couldn't figure out how," Carla said incredulously. "Even when I saw her crawling out from under a tablecloth, some slickster handing her some bread, I *still* didn't get it!"

The girls left with an archetypical dope dealer in tight leathers, roaring through town in his BMW-with-sound-system-to-blow-out-windows. In his bachelor pad in the Sausalito hills, Carla filled the sunken tub while Daney went into the bedroom and fucked the guy into unconsciousness. After putting him to sleep, she joined Carla for a luxurious soak while they waited for their heroin to be delivered. While lounging in the suds, Daney confessed her occupation to Carla, who, far from being shocked, was impressed.

"Hey, it didn't sound half bad to me at *all*! Great pads, good cars, easy money, and all the dope you want, being *delivered*! I couldn't believe it." She lay back in the luxurious hot water, playing with the baby in the shimmering, scented bubble bath, and put that idea on hold for use at a later date.

In April 1970 we were evicted from Olema. A new cowboy had leased the pastures and didn't want to share them with 30 hippies. We left peacefully, cleaning the house and grounds, down to the last cigarette butt and bottle cap, paying every outstanding bill in town. The citizens of Pt. Reyes and the new lessee understood and appreciated the gesture. While we were definitely freaks to them, they liked us. We had been honest in our business dealings and had certainly supplied ample entertainment and gossip. Tom Quinn, the new lessee's brother, was a local commercial artist. He made an elegant wooden sign with a coyote footprint painted on it. Under the footprint he wrote ". . . and company have gone." As we drove out for the last time, I wrote the word "on" after the "gone." Six months later I returned and took the sign itself. I still have it.

The Free Family was preparing a caravan at that time. Our idea was to travel to far-flung locales and use our neutrality as newcomers to create meetings, détentes, and political alliances among people who should, but did not, know one another. Things were to commence with a trip to southern Colorado for a peyote meeting with members of the Red Rockers and the Triple-A communes in the Huerfano Valley.

I loved the act of preparing my truck for such trips. Each task I accomplished inventoried a useful skill I had developed since leaving college with a degree in English literature. I had discovered a passion for the deductive, problem-solving capacities required to live without the money to hire professionals to solve life's inevitable dilemmas. My engine had been lovingly re-built

111

on my kitchen table; each bolt torqued to specifications and locked against vibrations with Loc-Tite. I had balanced the flywheel and clutch pressure-plate together and it idled like a whisper. Metal strapping from the bed of an abandoned truck had been arched over the sideboards of mine and covered with canvas, so that my '49 Chevy deuce-and-a-half-flat-bed resembled a Conestoga wagon. In honor of the scars and lacerations I incurred during its construction, I named it Dr. Knucklefunky.

Nineteen adults and eleven children trundled nine homemade house-trucks over the Sierras and on through the sage and scrub of Nevada. Outside Provo, Utah we camped in a broad flat meadow overlooking a reservoir. It was idyllic: groves of aspens offered pleasant shelter from the wind, the grass was thick and long, the weather balmy. Everyone was having a great time. Everyone but Simon. Simon had joined us from Black Bear. He was tall and skinny with red pimples all over his body, so painful that he took to walking around naked. He also had a huge boil on his tongue that made speech almost impossible. I smashed up some Oregon grape root to make a blood-purifying tonic for him; it seemed to help, but he decided he needed vitamin C and went to town to steal some oranges. He was brought back by an apologetic sheriff. He had tried to be nice to us, he complained, had not hassled us during our stay, but now we had embarrassed him. Simon kept blubbering protestations which were unintelligible due to the boil festering in his mouth. We told him to shut up and apologized to the sheriff, promising to keep Simon confined to camp.

One day, as Simon was wandering around naked, a car nosed along the trail and around a clump of aspen. Simon was either too stupefied from poisoned blood or too arrogantly proud to pay attention and cover himself. The driver floored his car and raced away. As we discovered later, the angry man was the owner of the property and his wife had been sitting next to him.

That night, at around 11, the sheriff, apologetic again, woke us up: the Range Riders were coming to arrest us.

We thanked him for the warning and broke camp by headlights. Only a little trampled grass showed we had been resting there almost a week. We drove down the road a while and pulled in at a diner-bar joined at the hip to a small gas station. A

Saturday-night cowboy frolic was in full swing. While we filled our thermoses and gave the kids hot chocolate, the men parlayed and tried to decide where we would camp. From time to time a cowboy would wander out from the bar, survey us drunkenly, then disappear back into the whining maelstrom of the dance. I was beginning to get nervous.

We got everyone loaded into the trucks and were lined up ready to go, when I noticed that Peter Berg and his truck, The Albigensian Ambulance Service, were not among us. I began searching for him. Cowboys clutching pool cues were beginning to cluster in the doorways, and you could see that serious trouble was brewing.

I spotted Berg's truck at the gas station and ran over. He was nowhere to be seen, so I pounded on the rest-room door. It was flung open and I was greeted by a sight that I was certain would be my next-to-last on earth. Peter was back-lit in the doorway. He was wearing his brown leather trench coat. He was still bald from where he had been shaved by the Nevada police. His eyes behind his rimless glasses were crazed by stimulants, and in his hand was a large and bloody butcher knife. Behind him, half in and half out of the blood-stained sink, was what I took to be a flayed human baby!

All I could imagine was one of the cowboys peering over my shoulder. I knew, with paralyzing insight, that we would all be lynched, strung up among the winking bar lights, as a warning to others, the way the locals in that area killed coyotes and casually hung them from fences along the highway.

It was a jack rabbit that Peter was skinning. He had run it over on the way out and had not wanted to waste a possible addition to a stew. I regained enough voice to convey my urgency to him, and we gathered up the remains and fled, leaving the blood-stained washroom for the locals to ponder.

After four months on the road, Carla was "ready for a hot bath and some dope." She and Jeff traded their Chevy for a little red MGB and piled themselves, Malachi, and all their gear into it and drove straight back to Church Street in San Francisco, where they moved in with Little Paula and the Cockettes.

Little Paula was a short, effervescent brunette I had met during my time at the S.F. Mime Troupe. She was one of those girls

113

who substitutes aggressive personality for physical beauty. She wore thick-lensed glasses that made her eyes appear large and manic, independent of the rest of her face. Since leaving the Mime Troupe, Little Paula had become a skilled criminal, working hot credit cards and using extraordinary amounts of drugs. She also owned a gargantuan tomcat who had been trained to crap in the toilet, a feat that kept the house odor-free and was also guaranteed to stun brain-numbed stragglers who stumbled into the bathroom to confront the cat spread-eagling over the toilet bowl. This was the atmosphere that Carla had been seeking, and it was not long before she had a jones going.

Paula's roommates, the Cockettes, were a drag-queen review that favored Shirley Temple crinolines and tutus, unshaved legs and beards. One of their spectaculars featured Hibiscus reprising Jeanette MacDonald numbers while being pushed on a large, flowered swing. They loved to shock straight people by going shopping while sucking popcicles that were shaped like penises.

Like most everyone else in the counter-culture, the Cockettes were anti-war activists, and they invented a unique brand of draft resistance. They would pull their van up to the Oakland Army depot and offer free blow-jobs to young men about to take their physicals. Afterwards, they would offer Polaroid pictures of the event as hard evidence of homosexuality to be presented to the draft officials!

Jeff began to hang around with the Hell's Angels. I don't know whether he was an active prospect for admission or just waiting around hoping to be asked. He was doing B&E's (breaking and entering) and fencing stuff to get by, when Carla became pregnant. They moved out to the suburbs of San Anselmo, where they sold dope for a sweet guy named Kelly, who controlled all the Mexican salt-and-pepper heroin in Marin. He was a stand-up guy; no matter how many times he was ripped off, he took it as the dues that came with the territory. His counts were always fair. He would extend credit. He never ground up the nuggets of brown heroin into the material that it was cut with, so it was easy to pick out the active lumps and throw away the lactose. Everyone liked him.

Kelly's old lady, Carol, however, was hated and feared. A sultry, flashy girl with thick blonde hair, she rode roughshod over

114

Kelly's undying affection. Junkies who got into arguments with her would get cut off. She was famous for leaving people dope-sick and waiting while she shopped for clothes. She didn't like men very much. Her mother had been a hooker, and she had eight brothers and sisters, each by a different father.

One day, while Carla and Jeff were selling for Kelly, the DEA raided their house in one of those B-movie *blitzkriegs* where furniture is upended, and all the spices are dumped in a huge pile in the middle of the rug. Baby Malachi sat in the middle of the floor with his crayons, coloring diligently, while the house was being dismembered around him. Carla was screaming "would you like me to *open* it for you?" but the cops were oblivious to her ironies. They smashed down doors and shredded pillows, having much too much fun to slow down.

One cop, Jerry, a handsome Kirk Douglas look-alike with shoulder-length hair, was obviously embarrassed by the whole procedure. He just sat in a chair covering his face with his hands, repeating over and over, "Guys, you can *see* they're not scared of us. There's obviously nothing here." Carla noted and appreciated his mannerliness and demeanor; coincidentally, he figured prominently in her life a few years later.

The raid helped Carla decide that a future of imprisonment was becoming increasingly probable. Because she could not even consider "the possibility of life without dope," she entered the methadone program in San Rafael, and moved in with Nichole, an occasional girlfriend of mine, who had joined us, much to Sam's displeasure, on The Caravan. Some years later Nichole lived with me, after coming to Pennsylvania at Sam's invitation, and soon displaced her as my lady. Nichole was and still is a great singer. She was dating Stephen Stills at this time. This would have impressed Carla inordinately, if Nichole had not also taken a shine to Jeff. Sexual generosity, as well as great personal charm, were two of Nichole's endearing qualities, however, so no one ever stayed angry with her for long.

Things went fairly well for a while. Willow was born in that house, with Baby Malachi in attendance, holding his little red wagon prepared with a pillow and blanket to take his baby sister for a ride. "Malachi was the adult in our relationship," Carla used to say. "He adored his sister. Told me when she was hungry, when she needed her diapers changed. He took her everywhere, God bless him, because I could barely take myself anywhere, let alone take care of them." Malachi was three.

With a larger family now, Carla moved to San Rafael. Jeff was hard at work building trucks with fake compartments for Kelly's drug runs to Mexico. Jeff's fascination with the Angels had continued and he had attached himself to Moose, a gregarious rogue with a quick temper and a steel-trap mind. Moose was everyone's uncle. He had to come to Olema often in his huge white Cadillac. His Harley-Davidson was painted white too, with a large red cross on the gas tank. I always assumed this was because Moose never traveled without medicines for aid and comfort, particularly high-quality methedrine. He enjoyed "kidnapping" me, as he called it, taking me away for runs of days at a time. On one occasion we left so rapidly that he had to stop at Angel Larry's to commandeer a pair of boots for me, solid black Chippewas I still wear.

Moose's real name was Lorenzo and he intimated a connection with the Mafia. He had, according to his own mythology, been imprisoned for life-without-possibility-of-parole at 19 for killing three guys with a screwdriver after they'd made the mistake of jumping him outside a waterfront bar. He *was* awesome when provoked to violence and I considered this story as possibly true. Once, as we were leaving on one of our runs, he asked to look at my scarf. When I took it off and gave it to him, he returned it without looking at it. "If I can get *that* from you, I can get everything you own." He was full of little epiphanies like that.

Jeff thought he could slide by the Angels' prohibition about needles, and with anyone but Moose he might have, but when Moose discovered needle tracks on Jeff's arm, he beat him so badly he broke a baseball bat over his body.

Carla and Jeff were best buddies at this time, but living separately. Jeff claimed that he was being paid by the Angels, but whether or not his status had formally been elevated to "prospect" was unclear. He was making many trips north to Oregon, and would appear on Friday nights to eat, sleep with Carla, play with his kids, and leave her some rent money.

One day, Moose suggested that Jeff prospect in San Rafael in Marin County instead of Oakland, said that it would be closer to

116

home and less of a strain on him. He was put under the charge of a guy named Red, who ran a gas station there.

Soon afterwards, Jeff came to Carla's truly horrified. He couldn't sit still, couldn't concentrate, couldn't focus his attention. He spoke agitatedly, with big gestures, gulping for air. He kept alluding to something, but all he could actually say was "I'm freaked, Carla. Really, I'm freaked."

She could only determine that Jeff had been wheel-man on an errand with Red and had seen something that had scared him beyond measure. He told her that he was going to talk to Red in the morning and that he'd get back to her. He didn't.

The next day Carla's temporary roommate pulled a robbery that went sour and had to leave town, leaving Carla without one-third of her rent. By the second Friday, without Jeff's contribution, she was down to two-thirds and nervous, so she went to the garage to see Red. When she asked about Jeff, Red looked at her blankly and said, "Jeff who?" She knew then he was dead. She called Moose, her only ally in the Angels and he gave her a song and dance about Jeff just being gone for a few days.

"I knew this was bullshit," she said, "and I freaked." She went to the police and tried to convince them that her husband had been murdered, "but all they saw was some hysterical biker's broad and laughed me off."

They must have laughed all the way to Red's as well, because the next day an unlit Molotov cocktail crashed through Carla's front window with a note attached to it about not going back to the police.

Carla left the kids asleep in the house to slip around the corner to the market. When she returned, all her furniture was piled up in the yard with the kids sitting on it, her clothes in a big puddle at their feet. Despite that fact that her rent had always been regular and there had never been any trouble, the landlord's only response to her entreaties was, "You're outta here."

Carla took what she could and left. Despite the help of friends who took her in and gave her dope—without a phone she could not service her regular customers and buy her own—she slept on the streets, in Goodwill boxes, for weeks. Finally, two of her friends, Mitchell Brothers porn stars who had "done a geographic" from some trouble, took pity on Carla, and offered to take care of the kids, until Carla could get her scene back together.

Carla was grateful, but unfortunately one of the friends, the one Carla knew best, got hurt in an accident shortly afterwards, so *she* gave the kids to the *other* girl, Barbara, who promptly moved them to faraway Coos Bay.

Relieved of the children for the moment, Carla was scuffling determinedly now, trying to grubstake a house and a means of supporting her drug habit. Hitchhiking over the Wolf Grade one day, a fat cat in a big Mercedes picked her up and offered her $50 for a blow-job. Carla was stunned.

"Fifty fucking dollars," she thought, "now that's something I can do." So she did, and not only loved the money, but the rush. She liked the rush so much that in later years, even after she and her friends had established a solid house and a substantial client list, she confesses that they would sometimes sneak off into the city and "work guys in cars, for the adrenaline."

She rented a sweet little house in San Rafael, and between selling dope and turning tricks, paid for a cozy nursery with fresh paint and sweet pictures. She stuffed it with toys, books and pictures, clean bedding, and clothes, and prepared to get her kids back.

When she got to Coos Bay and finally located Barbara, she was horrified. They were living in a filthy tepee. Her children had runny noses and chapped lips, and were covered with mud. Barbara had fallen in love with them and was not about to give them back. She had alerted the town to the threat of Carla's arrival and everywhere Carla went she was tailed by hostile people who had been told God-knows-what about her relationship with the kids—maybe the truth.

Carla finally struck a deal with Barbara to let Carla have her own kids for 30 days. If the children didn't want to live with her after that, Barbara could have them back. Carla returned home with Malachi and Willow.

Two days later Barbara appeared at their San Rafael doorstep and moved in.

Carla knew that she had to hide her habit and her business dealings from Barbara. To meet her various customers and keep the money rolling in, Carla was forced to make a dozen trips to the store, pleading absentmindedness. She would lock herself into the bathroom and take half her normal dose of heroin so that she would not nod out and drop a burning cigarette into her lap.

Finally, the wear and tear of inventing excuses and juggling schedules got to be too much, so Carla demanded that Barbara leave and come back at the end of the agreed-upon 30 days. Barbara asked to be allowed to take the kids to visit her own foster mother first. She said she would return with them that night.

It was not until the next morning that Barbara ended Carla's all-night vigil with the news that she had given both children to the police and told them about Carla's prostitution and drug business. Carla became hysterical. Instead of simply going to the police to report that her children had been taken by a crazy babysitter, she made the understandable, but stupid, mistake of going to see a lawyer.

Marvin the Con, as I'll call him, had a penchant for young hookers, and in lieu of money (although Carla estimates that she gave him about twenty grand in cash over the years), he was happy to fuck Carla himself and pimp her to his friends. He gave her a lot of lawyerly advice, which, "if I'd of followed, I'd probably have my kids back today," Carla confesses fairly enough, "but he's still a scumbag."

He sent Carla to a social worker named Jane, a kindly, understanding-looking woman that Carla fell in love with and "just trusted! I told her *everything*," she says. "I came clean: the drugs, the tricks, the selling, everything." Jane went to a judge to have both children made wards of the court.

She met and moved in with Clint, Kelly's muscular delivery man. The next two years became a blur of moves between every cheap hotel, motel, and rooming house in Marin, until November 11, 1975, when Carla picked up the *Examiner* and saw the front-page photo of a large, algae-covered 50-gallon drum, dripping wet and wrapped in chains, which had just been dredged up from beneath the Richmond Bridge. The caption identified it as her husband's coffin. The police had caught Jeff's "friend," Boneyard, on that bridge with a car-trunk full of cocaine. In searching around for something to deal for his freedom Boneyard turned over some *people*—and Jeff's final resting place.

The next night one of Carla's customers told her that the Angels were looking for her. Carla figured that if her *customers* knew the Angels wanted her, it would not be long before she crossed paths with the boys themselves. So for the next month,

119

she and Clint slept in a different place every night. It was nerve-wracking never knowing when she kept an appointment, whether or not she might find an Angel there waiting for her. Clint and Carla drifted that way for months, skimming the nether world of Marin like fallen leaves before the wind.

Malachi and Willow were by this time in a foster home in San Anselmo. They were thriving with a wholesome, nurturing couple who had a yard, rabbits, swings. Carla's appearances there were becoming more and more traumatic. On her final visit, Malachi had clung to her leg screaming and begging, "Take me with you, take me with you, Mommy."

Carla recognized that her life was a shambles; she believed, with good reason, that she could possibly be dead very soon. Reluctantly, she signed adoption papers, delivering her children to these good people. "I cried for five straight days," she remembers. Clint and Kelly held her, rocked her, fed her, kept her stoned, and never left her alone for five minutes.

Meanwhile, Kelly was on his way to jail. Even the brilliant Terry Hallinan, friend of civil liberties, radical causes, and underdogs, a man who had often helped the Diggers without charge, could not help Kelly this time. Kelly didn't help much, either. At his trial when the IRS compounded the charges against him by over-valuing the street-price of his dope and demanding $45 in unpaid taxes for each $20 bag of dope he'd allegedly sold, Kelly became irate, jumped out of his chair, and yelled, "If you can get that kinda fucking money for it, I'll sell it to *you!*"

Kelly owed Carla and Clint about 80 grand for bail and lawyers they had extended him during the course of his troubles. As recompense, he introduced them to his primary connection in Mexico, so they could take over his business. All he asked—begged for, actually—was that they "take care of Carol." This was a lot to ask because, as I've mentioned earlier, *everyone* hated Carol. Clint and Carla agreed, nonetheless, so Kelly could go off to prison without worrying.

The night before he went to jail, Kelly rented a big sailboat and catered a haute-cuisine candle-lit dinner with fine tableware and sparkling crystal. He bought matching handmade white doeskin outfits for himself and Carol, and some fabulous jewelry for her. He had prepared a magnificent romantic farewell, but Carol never showed up. Kelly spent his last night of freedom lying on the bed of the boat weeping. At dawn, he delivered himself to San Quentin.

After Kelly left, Carol finally appeared. Carla, infuriated at her cruelty, beat her bloody. In tears, Carol recounted *her* side of the story—the details of life with a man rendered impotent by junk. Carla was certainly sympathetic to the idea of sex as a basic need, and Carol's tale mollified her and Clint just enough to assure her that they would deliver her maintenance-level quantities of dope. She would have to cover her own rent. Even this was difficult for Carol, because she had grown lazy and dull after years of Kelly's largesse. Carla gave her the phone numbers of some tricks and told her to go to work and see if she liked it.

Not surprisingly, Carol turned out to be a phenomenal hustler. "She got more outta those guys than I could," Carla reports. Carol moved in with a girl named Pam and they started doing "doubles." Then Clint got very hot with the police and had to disappear, so Carla moved in with Carol and Pam. They let a snazzy house on Sunset in Mill Valley, with a lovely view of trees and an easy walk to the park.

Life was good. They had plenty of customers and lots of calls for doubles and triples. A cab would come every morning, with orange juice and donuts, to take them to the methadone program. All their neighbors liked them, in spite of guessing what they were up to, because they were sweet girls with sunny dispositions.

In the curious way that opposites often attract, Carla and Carol fell in love. Carla explains, "I mean we were bathing together, sleeping together, fucking together, getting high together, what do you expect? Besides, Carol was great with me, helping me through bad depressions about my kids and really looking after me. Bein' real sweet."

Clint was incensed about this, but Carla was adamant: if he wanted her he would have to take Carol as well. Clint did move in, but things didn't work out. One day when Carla returned with the groceries, she found Clint and Carol loading weapons on either side of the living room. This was too much and Carla walked out.

She relented a few days later, picked up Clint, and the two of them moved in together and started a "whole new deal." Carla got a job in a pizza spot in Tiburon, and they both broke their rigs. Alcohol was still allowed—and methadone—and she still turned an occasional trick for fun-money, but compared to their past, they were almost civilians.

But Clint began killing a fifth of vodka before noon. By evening he'd be blind drunk and dangerous. He was a big, strong guy and gave Carla several serious beatings he would blot out of his mind by the next morning. Carla would present herself at breakfast, black-eyed and puffy: "This is you, Clint." Clint would insist that he would never treat her that way; he refused to believe that her condition had anything to do with his behavior.

One day the cops picked her up hitchhiking. They "suggested" she come to the station for a talk. It is a measure of the loyalty that Carla inspires in people that when her favorite trick saw her enter the police car, he risked following her to the police station, demanding to know the charges against her and what her bail would be. The cops assured Carla (and the trick) that she was not under arrest. They told her that they wanted Clint. They had a warrant for his arrest, for a hand-to-hand sale of two ounces of heroin to an undercover cop. They had him cold. Terry Hallinan couldn't help him because of a conflict with Kelly's case; this made Clint crazy as a cutworm. That night, Carla heard him careening down the hallway toward their flat. She decided she'd been beaten enough for one life and hid behind the door. When he stomped into their apartment, calling for her drunkenly, she flattened him with a lamp and fled to her sister's.

Despite their disagreements, Carla didn't want Clint to face his bit in prison without the prospect of conjugal visits, so she married him. The day after their wedding Clint's trial began. The star witness for the prosecution was the undercover cop that had bought the dope directly from Clint. Carla recognized him as Jerry, the polite, Kirk Douglas look-alike from the destructive DEA raid on her house. She still liked him. "He was just doing his job," she said. "He caught Clint fair and square, nothing personal."

On the witness stand, Jerry kept alluding to his notes. Clint's lawyer rose and told the court that he had petitioned Jerry countless times for these notes and had never received them. Jerry confessed sheepishly that he had recently moved and that during the move the bottom drawer of his file cabinet had become hopelessly jumbled . . . he had used papers from that bottom drawer to start the first fire in his new house. Clint's lawyer looked at Clint, then at Carla. The prosecutor looked at Jerry. Everyone looked at the judge, who looked at everyone else before he shrugged helplessly and said, "Case dismissed!"

Carla and Clint figured that God had favored them and that perhaps they owed him the commitment of turning over a new leaf. Both got jobs and kicked heroin (again) by using a lot of pot (and methadone) and by going to bars and drinking themselves into a stupor, "because we thought that's what straight people did!" It all took its toll, however, and finally they split up for good.

Carla met a guy at the methadone clinic: slim, feminine-looking, waist-length black hair, a stab-your-mother street hustler, named Gino. He had approached her very aggressively at first and she hadn't liked him, but then for several weeks he had been courteous and polite. One day she left the clinic with Gino, and they went to a hotel and "fucked for two weeks." After a sexless life of several years with Clint, Carla thought that the God of flesh had finally answered her prayers.

Gino's stated occupation was rock'n'roll drummer, but actually he was a con artist. He wasn't above sticking a gun in your ribs, but what he really liked were stings. He was a master at the pigeon drop, the world's oldest switcheroo hustle, but he prided himself on inventing this con: he and a friend would meet sailors coming into port and offer them "girls, any kind you can imagine." He would put together a party of six to eight guys, while his buddy went around the corner to steal a car. On the way to the hotel, he primed the sailors with lurid descriptions of the particular appetites of each girl in his "trap line." They would arrive at a hotel and Gino would park "for a second" in a no-parking zone. He and his buddy would collect the girls' fees, towel deposits, bribes for the madame and the police—and sometimes extra for particular costumes or fetishes he swore excited the girls. Then he and his buddy would enter the hotel and exit through a rear door. The pièce de résistance for Gino was that he had also stolen their liberty by leaving the sailors in a stolen car!

Gino also sold fake drugs. He would let oregano sit in a cookie tin for a couple of weeks until it had lost its scent and then mix it with henna and egg yolks. He would scalp tickets to rock concerts, then sell the dope inside. He also robbed gay drug-dealers, using his feminine looks and guile to get in the door. He called that one "playing the sugar," because it was so sweet. Once, Carla remembers, "he stole a fag dealer's dog and held it for ransom."

One night Carla's friend Steve appeared at her door bloodied and shaken, having been stabbed by two black girls while trying to cop dope in Marin City. When one of these girls showed up at Carla's methadone program the next morning, Carla jumped her and pounded the living hell out of her. This was a serious violation of program rules, and not even Paula McCoy, our old friend and the most elegant hostess in the hip scene, on the program herself *and* Carla's counselor, could save her from a suspension for 30 days.

With the insouciance of the young and naive, Carla told everyone to fuck themselves; that she was going to *quit* methadone rather than to have to put up with their bullshit, and quit she did. It is a testament to Carla's will that she stayed clean and virtually sleepless for *three months,* while Gino was still taking his maintenance doses. When she finally broke and walked into the clinic, she weighed 90 pounds and was shaking like a leaf. Dr. Charlie took one look at her, waived the obligatory two-week waiting period, and gave her an immediate dose.

A little later, the same hard-luck, stabbed-in-Marin-City Steve showed up bloody and ragged *again!* He had propositioned the wife of a guy named Danny in front of Danny's friend Worm. To save his own honor, Danny had smashed Steve in the face with a glass ashtray. Gino retaliated for his friend and kicked Danny's ass publicly in front of a bar on Fourth Street in San Rafael the next day. Unfortunately for Gino, Danny was an unhinged—actually hinge-less—Vietnam vet. After his beating, he returned to Carla's house with a baseball bat and a focused intention to murder Gino. Carla fled out the back door and warned Gino at work. Consequently, Gino was prepared when he encountered Danny later that afternoon and preemptively stabbed him in the chest. Danny lost a lung, but, to his credit, never turned Gino over.

After the stabbing, Gino was too hot to stay in San Rafael, so he fled to New York, leaving Carla a Greyhound bus ticket.

She arranged the transfer of her detox clinic (and enough metha-done to travel with), and joined with Gino at his mother's in Connecticut.

Gino straightened up and got a job at a warehouse. Carla got a job tending bar at a Howard Johnson's. She walked five miles there and back every day, so they could save toward a place of their own. One night God smiled on her again. She found a wal-let with $1200 in it, stripped of I.D., in one of her booths at HoJo's. She stashed it in the back and, two weeks later, when no one had claimed it, used the money to bankroll an apartment for her and Gino.

They began a couple of years of holding down several jobs, scrimping to make ends meet, struggling to fend off boredom and despair; a normal working existence. Then, homey normalcy be-gan to pall, and Carla announced her decision to return to California.

Gino did not want to lose her. His dad had worked for a big company, and his mom, moved by Gino's late-blooming domestic-ity, forged his credit record and denied his arrests on the com-pany's application . . . so Gino was hired to work for a West Coast branch. He applied all his street smarts and inventiveness to his new work, and today is thriving as one of the company's top service reps. . . .

Back in California, Carla became fixated on the possibility that if there *were* an earthquake, the seismic jitterbugging might cre-ate a condition where they would be cut off from their metha-done. The doctors at the program pooh-poohed this fear and assured her that all they had to do was turn up at *any* hospital and demand their dose. Carla's knowledge of the world predicted a different scenario. "I could just see it," she says, "turning up at the trauma ward among the bodies, the wrecked-up and the fucked-up, two junkies looking for a fix. Imagine how long we'd have waited in the back of *that* bus?"

She and Gino decided that it would be prudent to kick meth-adone in anticipation of "the big one." They tossed a coin, and Gino won (or lost) the toss and quit first. He began slacking off by a couple of milligrams every couple of weeks until he felt nor-mal at that dosage. He'd "keep the edge off" a while and then

125

diminish it another couple milligrams. He began jogging and getting really fit. Carla maintained them both by selling half her doses and the rest of his, and working.

When her turn came, Carla stayed true to her word and cleaned up, although it took her two full years. She then entered a period of intense isolation. Her mother was dying, and she introduced Carla to *The Aquarian Gospel*. Carla began reading anything spiritual she could find, even Jehovah's Witness pamphlets she found on buses. She had no idea how she would be able to live without dope and felt these books might help. One "adjustment problem" was that Carla's newly awakened body remembered sex. She was now constantly aroused, but all of Gino's surplus energy appeared to be dedicated to regaining his physical fitness through exercise. Soon they cashed it in as a couple.

Carla got a job with Marin Towing, a company that hauled away disabled and illegally parked vehicles with snazzy yellow-and-chrome towtrucks. She felt comfortable there, because the business reminded her of prostitution, especially the litany of services and prices: $25 to unlock; $50 for a straight tow; $75 with dollies.

"It was legal stealing," she laughs. "The cops back it up, even set the rates. A shop owner sets out a little sign that says if you park here your vehicle gets towed. The sign cites some numbers in the public law books, and the towtruck boys are in business, working on straight commission."

She and the boys used to sit on the hills over Sausalito scanning the parking lots with binoculars, looking for illegally parked cars. "Hell, we busted Kenny Rogers' car, and Todd Rundgren's," Carla recalls. "Todd was so impressed that we towed his car correctly that he hired the towtruck driver as his driver. We worked 17 hours a day and I didn't have *time* to be junk-sick." Besides the excitement of the work, an added perk was being surrounded with vigorous young drivers: "I fucked everything in sight." she remembers dreamily.

She stayed with Marin Towing for three years, until she was virtually running the office, augmenting her pay checks by towing race cars on weekends. Finally, the owner couldn't afford to pay her what she needed, and, with regrets and great memories, she was forced to leave her first real oasis in many years.

She applied for a job as a cashier at one of America's great brokerage houses. She loved it. Stockbrokers drank like fish and partied hard. They were as unabashedly materialistic as hookers, played all the angles, and according to Carla, worked their customers "just like Johns." Friday through Sunday, she held her demons at bay by drinking herself into oblivion.

One Friday night, her boss gave her his credit card and told her to reward the girls in the office for a tough week by taking them out to party. Carla piled them into her lovingly restored Pontiac Firebird and took them out for the night, firmly resolved to have just one glass of wine and then go home.

"But I can't have just one," Carla says reflectively. By the time the boss joined them, she was so out of control that he took her car keys and put her in a cab. Carla did not want to wake up in Richmond, 30 minutes away, without her car so she ordered the driver back. She used a hidden key to start her car and head for home.

She doesn't remember much about the trip except smashing into a Volvo as she headed the wrong way down a one-way street. When she finally recovered perception and memory, she was in the middle of the Chevron oil-refinery complex, having crashed through a set of heavy gates, and wrapping the car around herself like extravagant steel clothing.

The firemen took three hours to extract her from the wreckage. Another hour later, at the police station, her blood alcohol measured, .23, over twice the legal limit.

Carla called her boss from jail at about four in the morning and told him to leave her there because she needed a vacation. . . .

After all those years and escapades, she was in jail for abusing a legal drug.

It was two years ago that Carla joined AA. She's found her children and is working hard to repair what can be salvaged of their tattered relationship. She is still stunning. Her shoulder-length hair is punk-short in front. Her adolescent baby fat has been burned away, exposing chiseled cheekbones and a slender, aquiline nose. The only trace of her old life I can detect, besides her street-smarts, is the excessive polished way she says "Good evening," when she answers the phone. I inquired about that, suspecting that she might still be using the phone for business. She looked at me for a minute. Her dark eyes were as bright and undiminished at 39 as they were at 17. She took a drag of her cigarette. She smiled. "I always thought it would be low-rent to turn tricks after thirty, Coyote, so I stopped."

Nominated by Dorianne Laux

CONVICTA ET COMBUSTA

fiction by JOANNA SCOTT

from CONJUNCTIONS

THE FIRST THING I DO in the morning every morning is recite the Lord's Prayer. I haven't made a mistake in seventeen years. Then I put on my gray linen skirt and lavender blouse with buttons and machine lace, the same clothes every day, rain or shine. In winter I feed Zerobabel, my Indian myna bird, and then open a book and wait for warm weather. In summer after I feed Zerobabel I leave my room and lock the door behind me. I don't always have a plan in mind. If I spend my time wandering inconspicuously that's good enough. It's not as easy as you might think, even on Coney Island in the middle of summer. When you're nearly as old as Tammany Hall, people look twice. Especially children. They stop dead in their tracks and stare until their mothers slap their faces. For this they grow up despising women like me, as though we were to blame. But wait until they're old and just as poor, an eyesore, a symbol of all that's wrong with America. Maybe you'll be fortunate and never experience old age, but if you plan to take your time you'd better start practicing the Lord's Prayer now, that's all I can say.

Because if you can't recite the Lord's Prayer without making a mistake you will be condemned and burned alive at the stake. I'm inclined toward superstition, I admit it. All those books I've read. You know if you spend just two hours a day reading, in fifty years it adds up to an awful eight years and four months of precious time. I don't believe in witches. But I am scared nearly to death of being accused. You never can tell what a passionate be-

129

liever will do, maybe kiss you on the lips, maybe shoot you in the head. Or maybe scream, *Witch!* I am scared nearly to death of being burned alive. Not that I believe in witches. But how can I tell what other people will believe?

Take my own father, for example, a cook at Tilyou's Surf House. One day he persuaded himself that he was a fish, and before the month was out he had drowned off Coney Island Point trying to prove it. And then there's the history to consider, Pope Innocent's bull of 1488 calling upon Europe to rescue the Church of Christ from witches and launching the slaughter that continues to this day: of women, it was said, who transformed themselves into cats and danced on the back of black goats, women who roasted babies over a slow fire and with the fat that trickled down anointed the hair and beard of Satan, women who vomited needles, women who caused famines and plagues. And not only women. In Salem, Massachusetts in 1692 nineteen witches were condemned and burned including a five-year-old child and a dog. Pope Innocent, what do you think about that? A five-year-old child and a dog.

Four hundred and twenty-three years after the celebrated bull an old woman can't be too careful. You never know who is going to accuse you of bewitching his little girl, his wife, even the horse he's gunning for at Gravesend double or nothing. You never know who is a witch-finder and who an ordinary cop on the beat. *Countrymen: Hang her! Beat her! Kill her!* Maybe they don't use the same words anymore, nor do they put you in a room, tie you to a chair, and wait for your familiar to appear in the form of a fly or a mosquito. Sometimes they don't say anything at all when they gather around you, they just poke you and snatch your purse. I know from experience. I don't carry a purse on me anymore, I don't carry anything at all except a dime for a malted milkshake from Nathan's, which I drink as I walk out to the end of the Iron Pier and back again. But here I am getting ahead of myself, I was telling you what I do in the morning and I don't buy my milkshake until two in the afternoon.

What I do in the summer season after I leave Julius's where I have lived for seventeen years is this: I walk along the boardwalk looking around like it's all a novelty to me and I am one visitor among thousands, no one special. There is so much to see: the El Dorado triple-decked carousel, Babar's Bathing Pavilion, the

130

Stratton Hotel, the Elephant. If you have never seen the Elephant, with its four-foot-high glass eyes and legs sixty feet in circumference, you've missed one of Coney's feature attractions. There's a room in the trunk eleven feet high, eleven feet in diameter. "See you at the Elephant" is what men say, never women, you figure out why.

Then there's the Brighton Beach Hotel, where Mama worked after she was widowed, champagne on draft at twenty-five cents a glass. And at the end of the boardwalk is the Manhattan Beach Hotel, the finest of them all because it is far away from the roughs and their doxies, the pickpockets, the confidence men, the till-tappers and moll-buzzers and rowdies. If I had the means and if it were open year-round I would move to the Manhattan Beach Hotel. But means I lack so I stay where I am, Julius's Boarding House, and spend warm-weather days walking through crowds, mingling, making myself as thin as air, like the souls of stillborn children.

It used to be I'd go to Steeplechase when I grew tired of looking at the hotels on one side, the ocean on the other. But it was at Steeplechase I had my purse snatched, one dollar twenty-nine cents. Lucky for me I kept the rest of my savings in a hole in the wall behind my bureau, otherwise I would have been reduced to beggary and the witch-finders would have had an easy job. I was watching the metal horses slide toward the finish line, their riders whooping, the crowd whooping back, when I felt a tug and I looked down and saw the straps of my purse hanging from my arm like seaweed. The little boy squeezing through the crowd looked up at me, grinned as though we were in league together, and disappeared. I turned to watch the end of the race, then I walked home to Julius's.

What good would it have done to report what happened? I learned long ago from Mama to keep my mouth shut. But later that night I couldn't help thinking about that boy, and I wondered was he put up to the caper, was there some pineapple waiting for the loot, was he happy-go-lucky because he'd done a good day's work and wouldn't be beaten? He was dark-skinned, black-haired, maybe one of the Romany gypsies advertised on billboards in front of Luna. I thought so much about him that I stopped frequenting Steeplechase and went to Luna instead, at

131

first to look for the gypsy boy and then to admire the elephant Topsy. I never saw that boy again, which was all right with me. What would I have said if I found him? What would he have done?

So for the next few summers I went to see the elephant. I'd say to Zerobabel, no one else, "I'm off to see the elephant." I've already explained: men are supposed to say this, not ladies. But Zerobabel is only a bird and it was our little joke. "I'm off to see the elephant," I'd say to him, and one day he said it back to me. "I'm off to see the elephant." He still says it, stupid bird, not out of spite, he doesn't mean any harm. He grows used to my company off-season and tries to impress me so I won't leave him alone in the hot weather. He doesn't know that I stopped going to see the elephant last year. I stopped going to Luna altogether, and here's why:

Topsy couldn't waltz or smoke a pipe or eat her meals from a table like Little Hip and some of the other elephants. She couldn't do much at all but trumpet mightily—for this she was a star attraction. An extravaganza wasn't complete until Topsy raised her trunk and blew. And whenever Topsy was in the arena, I stood behind the chain-link fence with everyone else who couldn't afford a bleacher seat.

I was there the first time Topsy went berserk, thinking to myself how safe I felt in such a captivated group of chumps, especially now that I no longer carried a purse. I was thinking I couldn't be more invisible than this, one crooked body in gray and lavender among hundreds. But an old woman should never feel safe, no one should feel safe as long as people can be persuaded to do evil. Who persuaded the workman standing ringside to throw a lit cigarette into Topsy's open mouth as she was trumpeting I don't know. But that's what he did, and Topsy stopped trumpeting and started screaming. There's no way to describe an elephant's scream—no sound is comparable. The next thing I knew the man with the shovel was dangling like a wet shirt from one of Topsy's tusks.

But Topsy was the star of Luna's animal act, and who would sacrifice a legitimate operation because of an unpleasant accident? So after a suitable period of time had passed—two weeks—Topsy was trumpeting again. And I was back at the fence, standing in the push that had swelled because of Topsy's infamy. Man-killers are always great attractions.

Topsy wasn't going to let the summer pass, though, without tasting blood again. She waited for another, milder provocation— one of the assistant trainers lashed a whip into her eye, and Topsy killed a second man. Since this was during rehearsal only the crew on hand were witnesses. Thompson and Dundy, Luna's owners, tried to keep the story out of the papers, and failing that they decided to retire Topsy. It was the middle of August. Though Thompson and Dundy didn't say so, we all knew Topsy would be back in the arena next June.

We. Don't think I use the word casually. *We* was what I wanted to be—I was a child of Coney Island and for years had no life separate from the life of crowds. Then I grew old, and age deprives a lady of her place in the midst. But with Topsy at the center of attention and everyone a comer, I was once more *we* that summer, as anonymous as I'd been when I was young, a speck of color in the background. And the following winter, during those long, solitary hours in my room at Julius's, no one but Zerobabel for company, I tried to sleep and dream the crowd around me. "I'm off to see the elephant," Zerobabel would croak to help me along, and I'd be back at the chain-link fence, blending in beautifully.

And when I was back again the next summer for Topsy's first performance, which never took place because Topsy decided to smash a foolish janitor who threw a peanut in her mouth. Smashed him flat as a flounder, so the rumor went, and as far as I'm concerned there's nothing truer than a rumor, nothing more expressive.

So on the first Saturday of the summer season a notice was posted outside the arena announcing that the elephant Topsy had become irretrievably vicious and was to be publicly executed the Saturday next, at noon, admission ten cents. Now being as I was an admirer of Topsy's you might think I would have chosen to miss the final scene. But I did more than attend the public execution, I even paid the admission and sacrificed my malted milkshake. Don't think I ordinarily go in for such things. On the contrary. I attended the execution because I had a prophetic feeling—call it an intuition, it sounds less supernatural—that Topsy would survive.

133

I climbed to the top of the bleachers and found a seat. The woman in front of me wore feathers in her hat that blocked my view, white, frosty feathers, like the print of cold on my window in winter. I had to stand to see Topsy as she lumbered into the arena. Her trainer walked with his head bent, making it perfectly clear that he wanted no part of this but was a slave to his bosses, just as Topsy was a slave to him. The master showmen themselves, Thompson and Dundy, arrived wearing velvet top hats and tails, the dust smoking around their ankles as they strolled toward the center of the ring, poisoned carrots in their gloved fists.

At first I felt as though I'd lost my way, like one of the wild Coney rabbits you sometimes see hopping in circles along the boardwalk. Unlike the rest of the audience, I had no appetite for public executions. But when Topsy stubbornly kept her mouth closed, refusing Thompson's carrots, and the crowd began to cheer, I felt fine, in harmony, you might say, with the general mood. We were on Topsy's side. We wanted the elephant to live. After three quarters of an hour had passed and Thompson and Dundy had failed to nudge, thrust, or stuff the carrots into Topsy's mouth, they announced that the show was over and that they would try again the following Saturday.

We filed out of the ring, only a few among us grumbling that they had spent ten cents to see an execution and since there hadn't been any execution they wanted their money back. The rest of us were thoroughly pleased and ready to spend another dime to witness the indomitable Topsy outwit those blockheads again. The sweetest music in the world was Topsy's trumpeting as her proud trainer led her back to her pen.

All through the week the elephant ring was closed while workmen built a huge scaffold. Word spread that Topsy was to be hanged. I could have told those men to save their breath. On Saturday I spent another dime and watched as Thompson and Dundy and various assistant trainers tried to pull and push the elephant up the steep plank to the platform. Topsy wouldn't budge without her trainer, though, and he, following the animal's example, refused to collaborate. Thompson finally announced that if they couldn't lead the killer elephant to death, they would bring death to the elephant. Thompson is an insane lush, everybody knows the truth, and I heard the madness in his voice. I knew he meant to carry out the execution—from that moment on Topsy was doomed.

Still I paid my dime for the third week, don't ask why, I knew there was no hope left. We gathered around Topsy's cage and watched silently as workers wrapped her legs in chains. In the right leg of the Elephant Hotel there is a tobacco shop, in the left leg there is a jungle diorama. Wrap chains around the Elephant Hotel and pull the switch, see what happens. What happened to Topsy that day when they pulled the switch and sent 25,000 volts through her was smoke poured out of her ears and mouth, out of her joints, through her hide, her eyes melted like candy into syrup, and she stood as still as the Elephant Hotel itself for five, maybe ten seconds and then collapsed forward and flipped onto her side.

Five, maybe ten seconds. To the elephant it must have lasted ten thousand years.

I never went back to Luna. I wandered along the boardwalk and sat on benches and watched the seagulls and bathers. People noticed me, some of the guilty idlers began to leave handouts on the bench beside me—half a sandwich, a penny, a bottle of pop. Once they recognize you it's the beginning of the end. So I was grateful for nightfall when people didn't have the time or take the time to notice. You see, at heart I'm a society girl, I like people, if only I trusted them. And always after dark my eyes would wander to the three-hundred-and-seventy-five-foot-high tower rising from the middle of Dreamland.

Dreamland was Coney Island's third amusement park, the newest, boasting twice as many turnabouts as Luna's, twice as many tunnels-of-love and shoot-the-chutes, and a Lilliputian village with three hundred midget inhabitants. I had never been to Dreamland and never planned to go. It was lit by one million incandescent light bulbs. The white tower at its center glowed as though it were on fire, a burning stake. If such a thing as I have described could happen at Luna, what could happen at Dreamland?

What could happen? Who was it who wrote, "Curiosity is the master passion?" I couldn't wait the rest of my life wondering, I had to take a few chances, especially now that I had so little to lose. On the first day of the season I woke up with a premonition

135

that this summer would be full of discoveries. Since I knew what I'd find at Steeplechase and Luna, the only place left for discoveries was Dreamland.

The dime tucked into the top of my stocking was the last of my mama's legacy. Whatever you might say about my mama, as a mother she was blameless. She always cooked my dinner or else brought me a hogie from the hotel kitchen, she warned off my roving lechers, and she bequeathed an inheritance that she thought would keep me to the end of my days. How could she have foreseen that I would live so long? In the weeks since I've spent that dime I've made ends meet one way or another. If worse comes to worse I'll sell Zerobabel—I'll take him over to the lobby of the Elephant and auction him off. In such a place the price I get for him will far exceed his value. I may not have much of a sense of money but I know about men and their humors. All those years spent watching and listening. Maybe I should write a book.

But I was telling you about the first eventful day of the summer. With Dreamland as my destination, I locked Zerobabel in my room and went out to bide time. The park was nothing until night, its whitewashed lath and staff as comfortless as asphalt. Only after darkness had fallen and one million bulbs were lit did the park deserve its name.

My first milkshake of the summer tasted just like the last milkshake from the summer before, chalky, rich with malt. The sky looked like last summer's sky. The crowds looked like the same old crowds. This has always been reassuring: despite the innovations, you'll find the same kinds of people in the same giddy mood year after year. I wanted to be in the mood of the crowd like I'd been when Topsy had made fools of her executioners. But by midafternoon I'd spent my mama's last dime and I was feeling sour. Maybe even then, in the back of my mind, I was thinking about betraying Zerobabel.

Darkness came at last and improved my spirits. I stood up and strolled along with the rest of humanity then turned toward the entrance of Dreamland, where a giant plaster Adam straddled the threshold. As soon as I was inside I understood why I'd stayed away from Dreamland. However magnificent its skyline was at night, inside it was Luna's inferior—it may have had more rides and booths, but it lacked the population. The boulevard beside the lagoon was too spacious, the crowds too sparse. The barkers couldn't collect a push for their shows, the pickpockets couldn't hustle, the mitt-joints were empty and the fortune-tellers sat on stools outside the tents, cooling themselves with fans made of playing cards.

If anyone had asked me for advice I would have said to cut the scale by half. But the man behind Dreamland, the Senator he was called, had long since decided immensity would be the draw. If he wasn't going to listen to me he might have taken a lesson from his own park. What do you think was the main attraction? Not Madame Morelli and her seven leopards. Not the Alpine train or the flotilla of gondolas. Dreamland's most popular show was the Incubator Babies, where the main players all weighed less than three pounds and slept in glass boxes. The hospitals didn't want the Incubator Babies, no more than a church wants freaks among its congregation. Which was why the Senator got them cheap.

Dreamland had been designed to be better, brighter, more excessive than Luna and Steeplechase, but it failed to draw the numbers that would have made the excess profitable. It had been open for three years when I first entered that day through Adam's portal. It would be quick in dying. I knew it was dying just as sure as I'd known Mama was dying way back when. She'd do her face every day and head off to work, but the eyebrows were crooked, the lipstick smeared, like she'd made herself up with her left hand. Toward the end I cooked her scrambled eggs, but feeding her was like trying to reach the gong on the high-striker. Each day I hit the teeter-board, each day the rubber ball fell further from the mark until I couldn't make it rise at all.

Despite one million incandescent bulbs, by 1911 Dreamland was on its last breath. From the outside it was still a spectacle, but up close it was pitiful. Like Mama. Like my daddy the fish. Like anyone near the end, I guess. And when you're an object of pity you can be sure you're an object of contempt as well. So if you're not going to hide in the crawl space beneath the boardwalk and go quietly, privately, like a blind old cat, expect to die a fiery death in the manner of Topsy.

Outside the building with the Incubator Babies the Wild Man from Borneo announced the feeding schedule. Without a nickel for admission I had to be satisfied looking at the flash on the

137

walls, the valentines and photographs of babies as small as the palm of a large man's hand. In the animal arena Captain Bonavita whipped his twenty-seven lions into order. I heard their roaring, like the sound of waves crashing against the pilings of the Iron Pier. In front of the gates of the Lilliputian Village a midget invited people to enter and threatened them with retribution when they walked by.

There was no sign that the Senator had plans of closing Dreamland's doors and giving up. Instead, he was still trying to revamp the enterprise and that night a crew striped the white tower fire-engine red. But just as no shark will find a cure for old age any day soon, no senator will make a dying amusement park inviting. I could have told them what was going to happen, but I would have made myself an easy target—a prophet is always the first to be accused. So I minded my own business and thought about the lesson to be learned from Dreamland.

What I couldn't have told them was when and how, and here's where the story gets fantastic. You'll think I'm lying when I tell you I had nothing to do with the fire that broke out in Dreamland in the middle of that first night. I don't blame you. I think I'm lying. My vision of what would happen nearly coincided with the event, maybe even caused it.

I left Dreamland shortly before midnight, thinking about the smoke that one day would pour through the Creation entrance and seep through the white walls. Shortly after midnight the fire began. This is my testimony. I no longer believe in my innocence because I no longer know what innocence is.

I'd seen West Brighton burn in 1899. I'd seen the Bowery go up in smoke in 1903. I'd even paid admission to the burning ruins of Steeplechase after the fire of 1907. So why I slept through this fire, the fire of fires, the fire that might very well have been my own perfidious work, I don't know. They say that the fire began in Hell Gate, where a crew was caulking a water spillway. A lightbulb popped in the heat, someone kicked over a tub of hot pitch, and in a few seconds Hell Gate was in flames. They say that the fire spread first to the building housing the Incubator Babies but that all the babies were saved. They say that over eighty animals perished and that the Shetland ponies were spared because their heroic keeper stayed with them and fought the flames single-handedly. The burning tower collapsed at 3:00

a.m., and the cascade of sparks poured like water from a faucet. I slept through most of the night and woke up only when I heard the distant popping sound of gunfire.

By the time I arrived at Dreamland the fire had almost burned itself out and the only animal to escape from the arena—a Nubian lion called Black Prince—was already dead. He had been cornered at the top of the Rocky Road to Dublin railway. They fired twenty-four bullets into his head, and when he still kept twitching they split open his skull with an ax. I learned all this from bystanders gathered around the lion's carcass that had been dragged out to the sidewalk in front of Adam.

While I stood there a man called for a pair of pliers—I recognized him as a local carny who worked the roller coaster over at Luna. A few minutes later pliers were produced. I watched the carny take the pliers first in his left hand, then in his right, and open them slowly as though testing their resistance. I heard what I thought were sirens. Only later did I realize that the sirens had long since stopped and that these were the last shrieks of the animals burning to death in the park. I watched the carny pry open Black Prince's bloody lips. He secured the pliers around a tooth and jerked it out by the root. I almost expected the lion to leap up. The carny pulled another tooth. If I hadn't known any better I might have thought the Nubian's teeth were being extracted for sanitary purposes. But I am a child of Coney Island and understand this mean world of cons and pitches and shills— anything that comes free becomes a souvenir and sooner or later will cost a pretty penny. The carny didn't quit until all of the lion's teeth were in his pocket. And when the crowd dispersed, I did too.

What goes through the mind when the flames have wrapped around the body? That's what no one will ever figure. Still, I can't help but think about much of anything else these days. It doesn't look like the Senator is going to rebuild Dreamland or even open up the ruins to the public. Which everyone agrees is a shame. Though Dreamland was only a poor imitation, something essential has been lost.

I still go out for a daily perambulation and a milkshake, if I'm lucky enough to find a dime. Then I come home and sit in my gray skirt and lavender blouse waiting for the word to spread like Dreamland's conflagration. I'll be accused—rightly or wrongly, it doesn't make much difference because the end is the same. What goes through the mind, I keep wondering. Any mind. Maybe I will sell Zerobabel tomorrow and with the money purchase one of Black Prince's teeth. With the few hairs left on my head I'll make a necklace and I'll be wearing the tooth when they come for me.

They will come, I have little doubt, just as they came for the others. And when I hear the doorknob turn I will start reciting the Lord's Prayer. Maybe I will wait until they are in the room to be sure they hear every word. I will recite the Lord's Prayer without making a mistake. And then, to spite them, I will say it backwards.

Nominated by Conjunctions

140

ROUGH MUSIC

by DEBORAH DIGGES

from PROVINCETOWN ARTS

This is how it's done.
The villagers surround the house,
beat pots and pans, beat shovels to drain spouts,
crowbars to shutters, rakes
raining rake tines on corrugated washtubs, or wire
whips, or pitchforks, or horseshoes.
At first they keep their distance
as if to wake you like blackbirds, though the birds
have long since fled, flown deep into the field.
And for a while you lie still, you stand it,
even smile up at your crimes
accompanying, each one, the sunrise stuttering across the ceiling
like the sounds within the sounds,
like lightning inside thrum-tink, woman-in-wood-shoes-fall-
down-wooden-stairs, like wrong-wrong inside rung-rung,
brick-smacking-brick housing ice-breaking-ice-
breaking glass . . .
I mention this since this is what my dreams
are lately, rough music,
as if all the boys to women I have been, the muses, ghost-
girls and the shadows of the ancestors
circled my bed in their cheap accoutrements
and banged my silver spoons on iron skillets, moor
rock on moor rock, thrust yardsticks into the fans.
Though I wake and dress and try
to go about my day,

room to room to room they follow me.
By evening, believe me, I'd give back everything,
throw open my closets, pull out my drawers spilling my hoard
of dance cards, full for the afterlife,
but my ears are bleeding.
I'm trapped in the bell tower during wind,
or I'm the wind itself against the furious, unmetered,
anarchical applause of leaves late autumns
in the topmost branches.
Now the orchestra throws down at once its instruments.
The doors in the house of God tear off their hinges—
I'm the child's fist drumming its mother's back,
rock that hits the skull that silences the martyr,
or I'm the martyr's tongue cut out, fire inside fire,
clapper back to ore, ore into the mountain.
I'm gone, glad, empty, good
riddance, some shoulder to the sea, the likeness
of a wing, or the horizon, merely, that weird mirage, stone-
skipping moon, the night filled up with crows.
I clap my hands.
They scatter, scatter, fistful after
fistful of sand on watër, desert for desert, far from here.

Nominated by Stanley Plumly

ESTIVATION

by SUSAN BERGMAN

from ANTAEUS

It is you   who   I wish   to share my body with   she said.
—Cat Stevens

In my dictionary under *"estivation"* are listed twenty types of prefloration, each with a compelling name and small inky diagram. These are the variety of ways a plant infolds within the bud, and the way the plant will show itself, at the time of its blossoming. There are pinwheels and concentric rings, Ionic pods and nests of opposed scales. I wonder if the list is exhaustive or if, like the elements of the periodic table, the patterns of the hidden life of plants are still being discovered. Each sign is an allegory of waiting. Each form, the form of an ongoing preparation.

Think of enacting each of the patterns with your fingers; you need both hands, the enveloping, the curling like the several ways a fetus lies cocooned and tucked within the womb, almost ready. I am thinking of the patterns as the many designs of first love, first kiss, first sex, and the many other flabbergasting beginnings I (unremittingly try) keep trying TRY to repeat, again. If a young girl's father pays her even a minute's notice, lifts her one time onto his shoulders so she can almost reach the fruit on the gnarled tree, he is that first love. He becomes the template along which the constructs of desire trace and are retraced. Hence the word *patern-al*. His is the proportion of God. Hers these intricate foldings and unfoldings according to the pattern: involute, revolute, induplicate, valvate, equitant, circinate, twisted, quincunx, cochlear, curvative. There are more.

In the photograph he is my groom. We are smiling at my mother, though my face is covered with a white net. I am six; he

143

has a flat blond crew cut. I have long blond braids and a cocked smile. My nose, which has too wide a bridge for me to have been a beautiful child, flares slightly at the tip. I was pretending he was a distant cousin, having heard from the girl across the street of the blood-relation matrimonial taboos. Our children's heads would be so large they would not fit on a pillow. They would be unmarriageable. Her father would not play along. He was married to her mother. She would have to find her own true love. But my father, until he grew so ill we had to lift him from his bed, posed for my wedding pictures a ringmaster, or a thoughtful gardener. The gardener does not design the patterns but he cultivates them. The ringmaster does not tame the tigers that pace their ornate gold-barred wagons.

Now I am eleven as the sun sifts through the trees in glimpses. Light has a shadow-self, has a presence in water as dusty beads strewn around us, displaced. It is the evening of my baptism. In the shallow end of the neighbor's pool my borrowed raincoat clings like the shroud I mean it to be: to die in the span of one held breath. Sown in weakness, raised in power. That first year of baby-sitting for the salesman's children I could not help slipping his magazines into my notebook to look at them. To lift slightly off my haunches, my hands locked behind my head, to twist to see them watching my back arch, my mouth shaped like the women's on the glossy pages into O's, now licking our fingers, now barely touching the tip of my tongue to my top teeth. The men must want us to stroke ourselves. I do. I am the bride of Christ. Sown in dishonor, raised in glory. Lying back in the preacher's arms, dusk's late warmth releases unevenly in air. I let him press me under, his trousers' full legs washing up at his ankles, his jacket tails a wake. *In the name of the Father,* I hear, and then inside the Spirit-of-Jesus cold I close my eyes. We are virgins, our chastity a consummation. The waters are enchanted; everyone is watching. His hands are covering my mouth and nose. It is not mine to dispute; he can feel my body rising with the water's muscle against gravity, he must know, or toward it.

My mother and her best friend wrapped me in a warm towel. I had been quizzed on doctrine and recited the Scripture from memory. There was a lot of me to put to rest and a lot of Christ to rise in me. I identified with Jesus, three days in the tomb and then, because of His perfection, resurrected. I identified with the Church, His spotless Bride. I wanted to make a public ceremony out of my faith so that others could help me not forget. Sitting on the roof, where I read in the hot smell of shingles and out of range of my mother's calls to help, I had discovered in the book of Revelation the story of the wedding feast. Some would marry, some would be guests. Some were not invited at all. I didn't want to take that chance.

In the salesman's bedroom closet, though, I risked it all. Behind his perfect rows of suits and the angled shelves of polished shoes he had built a bookcase with rows and rows of paperback smut. I would prop his children in front of the television, or wait until they went to bed—he stayed out late—and then, over the course of six weeks or so, I read all the way through *Naked Came the Stranger*. She would just show up and in ten minutes an impotent man was cured. There were all sorts of bursts and sighs and a general wetness wherever the Stranger went. She did not discriminate. She knew their names or didn't, or forgot her underwear, or almost made him drive the car into the ditch. I'm making up what I can't remember. It's been all these years. Somewhere I read once that the book had been a sort of party game that a group of writers devised. Each chapter was a different writer's fantasy, which was a disappointment, probably because as I read I had pictured one man writing who had mastered the depiction of such vile beauty as this, and instead there was a confederacy, who could know how extensive, of men and women in the thrall of secrecy and the many faces of the stranger.

Inside me there were these two chronic susceptibilities of body and spirit. By thirteen my interior landscape was overrun with their mutual contagion. We had moved from the country, where I had been raised among the Amish people, quilting, canning, watching the butchery of pigs and freedoms and eating what I saw. The boy I loved I loved purely for his love of the maps and places he would never see. By a kerosene light he traced the rivers for me, transposing dry ground into connective estuaries or canals with a small stick he had whittled to a point. What he did not take into account were the headstrong currents of his imaginary waters. North or south he could navigate the interiors of continents, equatorial or polar, even the deserts, but for him there was no culminating Ocean. We were Baptist. We could float away, someday. And now we were in the city with all our legalisms incongruous but intact. We were not allowed to swim with people of the opposite sex. If we were women we wore head coverings, no jewelry or makeup, and skirts to the middle of our knees. We had broken ties with one small congregation and joined together with five families to form another. We did not dance. TOTAL DEPRAVITY. We did not celebrate the holidays, except Thanksgiving, because we were not pagan UNCONDITIONAL ELECTION nor did we follow rituals of pagan institution. Nor drink, nor smoke LIMITED ATONEMENT nor frequent theaters, nor stand for a child's deviations. IRRESISTIBLE GRACE. At school I kept to myself as much as possible, waiting for the weekends, when I wouldn't have to answer for my anachronisms. I could baby-sit. Maybe there would be a pot-luck supper PERSEVERANCE OF THE SAINTS and Charlie-O would come.

The Osbornes were our church's poor whose care the five families that met together several times a week for worship or meals or teaching took turns shouldering. They lived in Cleveland city proper, down behind the art museum. There was the mother and her six children whose father was presumed no good for having left them indigent. It was their dogs that my father disliked feeding with the slim allowance he afforded them. The dogs, the children joked, were always pregnant at the same time as their mother. The children smelled of animals as they piled into our station wagon on the Sunday mornings when it was our turn to pick them up. He disliked the dogs, and Charlie, the only son, whose high black boots, and guitar strapped over one shoulder, whose manly stature at eighteen exerted a pressure that the inside of my heart's walls could not sustain. Charlie would not sing the hymns, but he held the book for me and stroked the back of my hand, weaving his fingers between mine while I sang out the alto line. He didn't come more than a few times. His sister was sick with lupus and I saw him at the hospital once. As though he didn't remember me, he turned around when I pushed open the door to his sister's room and then turned back without saying anything to look out the window onto the parking lot. There was one flower in a beaded white vase. Her wrists looked inflated, the blue veins of her hands stretched taught beneath the translucent skin. She slept sitting up and leaning over a little in her bed.

The year of my father's first grave illness I turned sixteen. We had moved back to the country, to a different town. I drove on Sunday evenings to a new church that met in a Jewish synagogue and where the people were caught up in love. They did not shake hands but embraced one another at the door. The group had not yet settled into organizational hierarchies or personal scandal. My brother and sisters began to ask me if they could come along, and gradually, even our parents grew overburdened with the old rules. As a family we began to celebrate holidays for the first time ever. My father had given up hearing-aid sales for interior design. He had met someone and signed up for classes. It had been too difficult to convince the deaf of their need to hear.

"They're paranoid that everyone is talking about them," he would say, shaking his head, "but they're too vain to put the tiniest battery in their ears." He wanted to adapt his perfect eye for color, or his perfectly pitched ear to a profession more suitable to his skills. So we moved to the town where his first design client had a weekend home. He was gone a lot for training. He had to check on progress at the drapery workrooms downtown where he manned the design studio for his new partners. Along the way he had met a man who gave him dozens of brightly colored striped and patterned shirts. Every week he would come home with more: short sleeves, red animal-patterned lace, a purple-and-white-striped silk that I begged him for.

"Why does he give you all these shirts?" my mother would ask him, giddy with that much generosity. "This beautiful pale blue linen!" though she didn't care as much for the loud prints.

"He doesn't wear them anymore," my father told her. For most of that year my father lived in his bathrobe once the hepatitis took control of his body. It was the bad lobster he had eaten. Yes, that was it.

"Shouldn't we tell the restaurant?" I asked. "Wouldn't their insurance help us?"

"I should look into that," he said, but knowing he had eaten no lobster, he never did. It was all right, the doctor told my parents, to have sex. My mother kept a towel folded on the kitchen counter with his bottles of medication and a spoon and cup she sterilized with boiling water after feeding him.

"Do you want me to go on reading?" she asked quietly, thinking he might have fallen asleep. His breathing was almost imper-

147

ceptible. Even the automatic body functions taxed his weakness. His eyelids fluttered open, the skin the same stained yellow as the yellow of his eyes.

"Please," he whispered, and she read on. There were days he could walk in the yard, but mostly he lay sunk into the corner of the sofa in the living room, a sheet draped over the blue-and-white-flowered upholstery and over him. The sofa was pushed against the long wall with no windows; the light exhausted him. The younger children lived the best they could in a hush.

For my birthday, though, he insisted that my mother get him dressed. In a restaurant with sixteen classmates he pretended were my friends, he had arranged sixteen roses with a ten-dollar bill tied to each stem. I think the boy I went with to the prom was most impressed. The boy was silly, I knew, even then, and the roses seemed too lavish a display for the occasion, the money flaunted on the roses' wired heads. The effort would initiate a deepening collapse that drove my mother nearly to despair. She could not get him to drink the broth from his spoon. He would not improve. There was no income. He must have borrowed the money, so I gave it back.

By then there was someone else whom I imagined had given me the roses. I would sit in the third row of his Shakespeare class so that the other girls could not see me watch him—the place where his olive-skinned arm met the loose cloth of his T-shirt sleeve, the fade of his jeans, his long black hair like the lover's in the Song of Songs. He had participated in the Kent State riots, and smoked pot with the seniors in his van. He was the sole faculty member who sided with the students on the issue of a smoking lounge, and rallied for free paint for the cafeteria walls. His was a rebel's courage. We were both left-handed. He carried his tall lean body like a cause, forward and sure, but with enough relaxed slowness that he had the appearance of already having won. In front of the whole class he would dance with our imaginations' spoils. Near the end of the period he would turn to me, after waiting all those minutes. Maybe it would be a question he had written on the board that only I could answer, or a paper he would hand back with comments in the margin like "droll" or "just so." His family was not American—Arabic, I thought I heard him tell someone, or Jewish. But I don't remember asking him. His past didn't involve me. What he believed about Her-

148

man Hesse, or Andrew Marvell, or Carson McCullers did. And what he believed about what I thought but had never said aloud before, what kind of an artist I was, how did I know? The dialogue was taken up in the pages of my assignments I turned in for grades, the thought-papers that registered more of me than of the books assigned, and that he seemed to treasure.

"Whatever you may think, it's beyond a crush," I wrote in my journal. "He loves *me,* too. It is how we will resist our love that will save us." The journal was his idea. I addressed my thoughts to an unspecified "you." In it I tried to record the accelerating rivalry of desires, the one day pressing my mouth onto the page and writing over the marks of lips and breath, the next tearing the page into repentant shreds. I was a temple of the Holy Spirit. I would win his soul to Christ. He would initiate me into His eternity I dreamed of and woke to the whole year I was sixteen. A quick breakfast, the bus a blur. He would arrive earlier than I could so we didn't have to wait.

In my journals—as in my life—there was the problem of what to call him. I knew his given name, of course, but having called him, along with all the other students, by his surname the year before, the name was how I thought of him. Which felt absurd. Didn't he call me Susan? So I didn't call him anything most of the time or I called him Mister, as in you'd better watch it, Mister, or, I love you, Mister. On the page he sometimes shows up by initial, or I have someone else refer to him. What he called discretion became my layered dishonesties. A show for them, a show for us. How we avoided speaking of his infidelity was to feature in our trysts the problems of Time and Age. He was twenty-seven. I had another year of high school. We had fifteen minutes to be alone.

There are entries about student government and about art. I had drawn a series of self-portraits with multiple images on a single page. My face is looking both straight ahead and to the side, and I write about this. The central running theme is "the other sex," the incidence of encounter heightening the pitch of the diction until an entry either expires in a prayer of thanks, or is signed—as though the page itself were masculine—"Love, Susan." There is an insistence in the writing, when attraction flares, on what I refer to throughout as "the platonic." Platonic meant that both the male and the female could "resist the physical" and interact by mutual agreement in mental and spiritual harmony. My spirit was willing but my flesh was not. She is confused in front of herself. She turns away. On one page the grandiloquence of righteousness, on the next the flat bathos of a sixteen-year-old girl's moondreams.

The way it started was that I had fallen off my bicycle and crushed my mouth against the curb. One lip split open and the other was swollen. I held the back of my hand up to my mouth when I opened the English-office door. The department chairman (my after-school tutor in the formal elements of poetry, the tests of rhythm, shape, meter, caesura) rose to leave when I arrived, mumbling his excuses of preparation, glancing back and meeting, I think, both of our eyes for an instant before he closed the door behind him.

My hand with the bitten fingernails in front of my face; the hand he took and kissed in mock gallantry, not noticing yet, and then pulling me into him gently he looked from my mouth with the dried blood along the corner to my eyes. It was not that this was the best tenderness of its kind—I had no measure to compare—but that it was the first. "Don't look at me," I said, turning my face away, and staying right up next to him. This was as far as I had envisioned. But he had my head in his hands and was touching faintly around the bruise and the cut lower lip with his tongue, like a dog, I thought, confusedly, the thought tossed up out of my awkwardness and longing. The severe tenderness soothed my mouth, though I couldn't let it.

The body, flowering, is greedy, and secretive, its pleasures hoard the mind, hoard guilt as though there were no help for its fecund devouring. The way the spirit grows is steady too once it begins, though its evolution is more difficult to recognize. You cannot make it happen by a volitional strike, suddenly. The visible bursts. The unseen foliates. The arrangement with the bud must begin of its own accord to loosen.

I had a friend who walked with me along a spiritual path for a while. When Matthew came back from Princeton for the summer we drove his Jeep with the top off to go look for shoes for him. He had a size-fourteen foot so narrow that nothing fit. Matthew was holy already, and the smell of him so strong I think the lake

150

we swam in changed its fragrance when he dove in. He smelled like an African market, and eucalyptus, and tansy, and gasoline. Whatever else I had been was over. We spent the summer between our houses and at his family's lodge. We took our separate blankets out into the field at midnight and lay there until we could pick out the constellation we'd elected from the planisphere. It is because of those nights I can find the wide-mouthed W that is Cassiopeia and Orion's studded belt—the summer stars that year after year in honor of the equinoxes return to their places right on time. Between us there was the impossibility of spoiling the ideal form of friendship; as if we were a model, not quite actual, we didn't dare to touch. Though my father refused to believe it. Part of the energy he needed to recover trickled from him in allusions to the effect that I was lying to myself. Fueled by the surfeit of his own sexual dread, he did not believe me either.

But now I had nothing to hide. Matthew had apprenticed himself to a Greek Orthodox priest and was teaching the lives of the eastern saints to me. His family was perplexed. All five of the handsome brothers had their talents and capacities, but none like his. It was not until the shortening days of that summer that he took his orthodox name and left us all. We were encumbrances he had loved well but whom he now believed could not partake in his ultimate spiritual quest. He came to the front door and knocked instead of the usual walk right in. I slid down the stairway railing from my bedroom when I saw his Jeep pull into the drive, all packed for where? His greeting was stiff, his head sitting back too far on his neck so that as he looked from my gold-hoop earrings to my Danskin leotard I wore under a long print skirt I felt what seemed like condemnation. I had no shoes on and so stood exposed.

From someone else's monologue he intoned, "It is heaven I need to follow." I could see he had rehearsed, "I've come to see you last, to say goodbye," though he was not pretending.

"You haven't told me anything about this!" I was startled. We hadn't been together for a week, maybe eight days, but "Where do you think you're going, Mister?" He was nothing like Mister, but I called him that as he stood by the door and wouldn't grab on when I reached for his hands. He was going to California, to the monastery where he would complete his Greek studies and

151

prepare himself to help the church fathers with translation. "Is she beautiful?" I tried to joke, then stiffened myself at the awesomeness of the high call I knew he would not betray. He had just a few minutes more to talk about his plans. I offered my regard for his dedication, feebly.

"There can be no help from you," he said. "You are not part of the plan." I didn't deserve to be, I knew, which made me cry a little.

"I'm going to miss you like crazy, then." Tomorrow, I thought, he'll call, but no. Matthew belonged to the Platonic ranks of the five regular geometric solids. His mineral to my vegetable, we could not corrupt each other, being as we were from separate orders. That was how we had preserved the ether between us, and perhaps why he still will not answer my letters.

It was near closing time at the end of the summer, after Matthew had already gone away, that I saw the familiar van pull into the garden center where I worked. The flowering plants in the front rooms had all been watered, the metal picks attached to the artificial flowers Mrs. Hisset would arrange in imitation of the Tela-Flora photograph. She saw him coming in the front door and quickly smeared on the coral-colored lipstick she reapplied in front of the tiny office mirror for her best customers. He told her he was going to need a little time to look around, for a gift, not seeing me at first. Then as Mrs. Hisset answered the phone he ducked out the front door, pulling me after him into the fading summer evening.

"We're going for a ride," he said, sliding back the door of his van. He had driven me places before. Inside was like the inside of a genie's lair, with carpets and the blended aromas of patchouli and untamed smokes. All this time I hadn't thought of school, or him, and now his friend, my history teacher—the one with the acne scars and the sense of the world as a grand sports metaphor—was sitting in the front passenger's seat.

"Mr. Mendiola," I said, surprised.

"Make it Mike," he nodded, blearily. He too had been corrupted, I understood, his pot-face blurring into a flatter and flatter smile with the new sensation of his high. I breathed in and out the heavy spice of the closed space, not wanting to see my whole set of saints, and my devotion, spinning into orbit right

152

then. Why were we stopping on a country road not far from my house? Mister opened the back door again and I hopped out. It was time for me to be home for dinner. I hadn't said goodbye to anyone at work.

"Why is *he* here?" I asked, tossing my head in the direction of the front window. In my mind our secret was completely hidden from view. I would get passes out of chemistry lab if I finished early because that was his free period. Or we would stagger our escapes into the woods behind the school if the coast was clear. He would wrap the deep red-velvet curtains backstage in the school auditorium around us until we were just another prop. But to my mind our attraction and its acts had been invisible. There was no place for it in the world and so for the world it did not exist. He had covered with a friendliness, a light touch, or a considerate length of after-school contact with several other students we both knew. I sneaked into the band-practice rooms when no one was watching and would wait for him there, playing Gershwin and Judy Collins on the piano, or practicing my scales. "Do you know what I want you to do?" he would ask me when I was far enough under the spell of his mesmerism to comply. Or was it my malign charms? Ours was an unspoken complicity and he was breaking open the secret without having offered the choice to me.

"What, are you afraid Mike's going to tell your mother?" he asked. There was derision in his voice. A car threw up dust and gravel behind it on the road. Out there in the coming dark the rows of corn, the crickets turning on, with his friend pretending to keep busy in the front seat, I couldn't think of anything to say. He wasn't my teacher anymore. He must have fought with his wife. He didn't even have the pretense of a desk or books or lesson plan. Whenever I walked down the hallways I had been superior, somehow, I was his favorite, but after a summer apart I envied my friend who had a boyfriend her own age she might marry. My body wouldn't come on. I leaned on him with my back and shoulders against his chest, not wanting to feel his erection.

"Do you ever get jealous?" I asked to mute the silence.

"Of what!" He was pulling my blouse tail out of my shorts.

"Of who else I will love?" I tucked my shirt back in.

153

"No, I don't." He was sure without having to think about his answer. His only rival for my heart was God, who seemed so pale and helpless next to this vivid man.

I turned around into him, my arms bent in front of me like a soft shield, and leaned my face into his shoulder. He wrapped me up in him until he felt me release my future, my history, my father's illness, and what would be my mother's horror to see me in my teacher's arms. I could feel his cheek stroking my face up toward his. They were almost black eyes.

"I'm moving out west," he whispered, like a part of my own body speaking. It was already August. We had three weeks.

My father moved slowly, like a stiff-legged heron about to take flight as his body gained strength and then relapsed. When he grew strong enough to eat at the table, we burned his snagged blue bathrobe. We could not wash the sickness out of it or look at it limp on the back of the bathroom door for one more day. The summer was ending with promise. A halting resuscitation in our household stirred us all to plans. It would be my last year at home. My father would be well again.

Maybe I would still adore my teacher—I keeping wanting to say *she* would adore *her* teacher. Still I dream about him. He comes back. When he sees me he hesitates for a moment, making sure nobody is watching us, then he motions for me to follow him into a room with no windows, and once we are inside, no doors. I was drunk on his fondling, but more so on his gifts of books and ideas. I am trying to cultivate that early passion without sneaking off to a father surrogate. Let me try again.

The way it started was after school one day he was sitting on top of a teacher's desk in an empty classroom and we were talking about Howard Roark and Dominique from Ayn Rand's *Fountainhead*. Roark was an architect who could, for principle's sake, explode the very building he had designed. Dominique could slash her neck and arms until she fell unconscious to disguise her love for a man. I was sitting in front of him and stood up suddenly, overcome with the characters' pure sufficiency. In one passage she is lying on a wide bed upstairs, the whole plot conspiring to have Roark open the door and want her. But he leaves before they make love, I think before they even touch, and the whole book quivers with the strength of his self-denial.

Or I quivered, and standing up I took the two or three steps ahead to him and straddled his one knee so that my thighs surrounded and rode his thigh. I just did it, astonishing myself, and him. He had to grab me around my waist or I would have lost my balance. Beyond that he didn't respond by touching me. Only by trying to look in farther to what I must be thinking. I looked back hard.

"Lady"—he left a long pause hanging—"do you know what you're doing?" he asked.

It was not my parents' rules, or the schools, or the Bible's I was transgressing so much as my own developing spirit. I wanted to take in all experience that could teach me without destroying the light. But when I touched him, at the same moment that my body pulsed on, the light inside me flickered. The whole thing was there together. I would have to divide it into parts and put the one outside and the other over there. The parts would be wrapped in separate colored papers. I would open them up when I was ready. The mind begins to legislate. The body craves its equal time. The spirit rises to sing and is placed far away, under something that will muffle it. And the clamor of conflicting passions sounds outlying passions like a gong. I stepped back and ran from the room.

The way it started—however far back I can go along the avenue of a glance (she knows he is watching her and she is watching him), beyond the compelling drive, back to nurture, and a lack of nurture, into the genetic codes of addiction and great need—the way it started, the prescient start, like a first principle, encodes in its embryo its end.

I had just finished my period. I was dry. He was moving to Colorado so I went to see him for the last time at his apartment. I had been there before on his enormous waterbed, but I would leave my clothes on as we touched, lightly, more like wrestling. Once I wore my favorite caramel-colored lambswool sweater with the tiny moth hole at the neck. What he liked best was the feel of me in my father's purple-and-white-striped silk shirt without a bra. When I got there this time he didn't want me to go into his apartment so I stood outside in the hallway waiting for him to

155

finish whatever it was he had to do and then lock the door. He was all packed to move, or his wife might come home, but he had a key for an empty apartment down the hall with a few pieces of inexpensive furniture, including, in a single back bedroom, one twin bed without any sheets.

Usually we had music. There were the remains of the last tenant's plants on the windowsills, dead from the heat and neglect. August's trill of heat. The walls were thick with an overpainting, this incarnation they were what would have normally been a forgettable mustard gold. I must have been wearing a skirt. I had brought my journal to let him read the last few pages. They were poems about him now that he was going away and about me. I would let the light burn beyond the wind of our desire now. They were a girl's poems troubled with the drifts of sex and faith and words. When he finished reading them he read a few lines out loud to me, with great deliberation, as though they had been written by an ancient bard. Wallace Stevens says:

> We do not say ourselves like that in poems.
> We say ourselves in syllables that rise
> From the floor, rising in speech we do not speak.

As he read them I sat on the arm of the sofa with my feet in his lap, his arm draped over my knees.

"These are by far your best," he told me. "You are right there in the words, and the words are transparent."

To desire virtue, I pretended not to notice, is its own form of seduction. I admitted the magnetisms of a game of chess, how the opening moves lock you and your opponent into moats of dependency. I knew the maddening itch being ignored worked up, but not that purity is a dare.

His fingers followed along the front of my thighs and hooked under the elastic of my panties. I had resolved not to and chose my oldest cotton pair. He helped me stand up on the couch and step out of them. They fell there like a useless skin shedding that he picked up to smell. At the same time he reached for me I let my legs swing around his hips so he could carry me to the other room. We were going to, without music, at the callow end of the interminable summer of my abandonment.

156

He took his penis out of his pants and rubbed against me, on my belly, high up between my legs; I tried to help him, on the dry folds of my labia. This was going all wrong. There was no time to unwrap the right elements so that even one of them could be included, could begin its justifications to the other parts. Yet this sense of being an accomplice. I couldn't help it. He pushed in and I felt his zipper cut into my skin as he rocked two or three times and as abruptly pulled out. As if he had been thrown from me he reared back and fell against the wall.

"There was no way I was going to let that happen." He moans, shaking. I finish buckling his belt for him. I draw him back down to the bed and make him lie down on his back so I can lie along the whole length of him. There is a song I am humming before I think of what the words are and when I think of the words I stop. It is I who am no good at ending. The torn. That was it, wasn't it? Was that it? I smooth his hair away from where it has stuck to the sweat on his neck and he shudders. I have to drive home fast and get into the shower.

The blasting heat a farewell, the shock of walking past people on the way to my car who will forget this day's significance. The green lights a farewell. Go on, go on. The woman placing a pale envelope into the mailbox—if her sorrow is deep it is as my sorrow. The white lines of the road, interrupted, but going on, and beyond the place where I turn off onto the gravel roads that will take me to my road, the white lines continuing.

Nominated by Joyce Carol Oates

QUESTIONS FOR ECCLESIASTES

by MARK JARMAN

from NEW ENGLAND REVIEW

What if on a foggy night in a beachtown, a night when the
   Pacific leans close like the face of a wet cliff, a preacher were
   called to the house of a suicide, a house of strangers, where a
   child had discharged a rifle through the roof of her mouth and
   the top of her skull?

What if he went to the house where the parents, stunned into
   plaster statues, sat behind their coffee table and what if he
   assured them that the sun would rise and go down, the wind
   blow south, then turn north, whirling constantly, rivers—even
   the concrete flume of the great Los Angeles—run into the
   sea, and fourteen-year-old girls would manage to spirit
   themselves out of life, nothing was new under the sun?

What if he said the eye is not satisfied with seeing, nor the ear
   filled with hearing? Would he want to view the bedroom
   vandalized by self-murder or hear the quiet before the
   tremendous shout of the gun or the people inside the house,
   shouting or screaming, crying and pounding to get into the
   room, kicking through the hollow core door and making a new
   sound and becoming a new silence—the silence he entered
   with his comfort?

What if as comfort he said to the survivors I praise the dead which are dead already more than the living, and better is he than both dead and living who is not yet alive? What if he folded his hands together and ate his own flesh in prayer? For he did pray with them. He asked them, the mother and father, if they wished to pray to do so in any way they felt comfortable, and the father knelt at the coffee table and the mother turned to squeeze her eyes into a corner of the couch, and they prayed by first listening to his prayer, then clawing at his measured cadences with tears (the man cried) and curses (the woman swore). What if, then, the preacher said be not rash with thy mouth and let not thine heart be hasty to utter anything before God: for God is in heaven?

What if the parents collected themselves, then, and asked him to follow them to their daughter's room, and stood at the shattered door, the darkness of the room beyond, and the father reached in to put his hand on the light switch and asked if the comforter, the preacher they were meeting for the first time in their lives, would like to see the aftermath, and instead of recoiling and apologizing, he said that the dead know not anything for the memory of them is forgotten? And while standing in the hallway, he noticed the shag carpet underfoot, like the fur of a cartoon animal, the sort that requires combing with a plastic rake, leading into the bedroom, where it would have to be taken up, skinned off the concrete slab of the floor, and still he said for their love and hatred and envy are now perished, neither have the dead any more portion forever in anything that is done under the sun?

What if as an act of mercy so acute it pierced the preacher's skull and traveled the length of his spine, the man did not make him regard the memory of his daughter as it must have filled her room, but guided the wise man, the comforter, to the front door, with his wife with her arms crossed before her in that gesture we use to show a stranger to the door, acting out a rite of closure, compelled to be social, as we try to extricate ourselves by breaking off the extensions of our bodies, as raccoons gnaw their legs from traps, turning aside

our gaze, letting only the numb tissue of valedictory speech
ease us apart, and the preacher said live joyfully the days of
the life of thy vanity, for that is thy portion in this life?

They all seem worse than heartless, don't they, these crass and
irrelevant platitudes, albeit stoical and final, oracular, stony,
and comfortless? But they were at the center of that night,
even if they were unspoken.

And what if one with only a casual connection to the tragedy
remembers a man, younger than I am today, going out after
dinner and returning, then sitting in the living room, drinking
a cup of tea, slowly finding the strength to say he had visited
these grieving strangers and spent some time with them?

Still that night exists for people I do not know in ways I do not
know, though I have tried to imagine them. I remember my
father going out and my father coming back. The fog, like the
underskin of a broken wave, made a low ceiling that the street
lights pierced and illuminated. And God who shall bring every
work into judgment, with every secret thing, whether it be
good or whether it be evil, who could have shared what He
knew with people who needed urgently to hear it, God kept
a secret.

Nominated by Christopher Buckley, Edward Hirsch, Dorianne Laux, Philip Levine

A.M.: THE HOPEFUL MONSTER

by ALICE FULTON

from THE AMERICAN VOICE

For John H. Holland

So dawn. A morcellation of the dark, the one
dumb immaculate gives way.
Appetite and breakfast.
        The light is enlarged
to show detail. It strokes the earth
with no boring or fumbling, with just
        enough. So dawn. Like charity it spreads
itself thin, "envieth not, vaunteth not,
beareth all things. . . ."
It circulates
but has no currency;
        it scraps the dark
for fluctuation and rough justice,
puts a lean on the fields,
glittering like insect flesh.
        A vastation, it braces
every thistle, scrub, and burr. Each minnow, morsel,
swimming in its limber glue, each cell
        strung with elation. The dirt dances in yields.
Look at it that way and give
wonder. The light is enlarged to show detail.
        It bareth all things, it maketh all things

161

naked, a slater, stripping
the flesh from the hide.
It circulates, but has no currency.
     It takes shape from what blocks it,
the obstacles, like criticism, a kind of birth
control. So scathe
the one who made the pus and suffering
of the stray. He has twenty-six toes
and twenty-six claws to break the spines of mice.
Fleas suck his blood
     and that's how he will die. Nice nature,
nice. Kitten is a pretty thing,
bred to pet. "Cute" is a baby
human concept. Toddler in utopia,
     undergulfed by nothing all
the night, give wonder. And give fear.
Everything that knows it lives
is shivering. Everything
that lives predicts.
     Terror is just
the confidence of prophecy:
what from the gut
the nerve emerges—
     step by step and sweat by sweat.

Nominated by Mark Jarman

A CHICK FROM MY DREAM LIFE

fiction by KAREN E. BENDER

from THE IOWA REVIEW

I LOVED HELPING my sister Betsy hide her bad hand in the morning. By eight, she'd be standing on the side of the bathtub, looking at her body in the bathroom mirror. "Okay," she'd say. She would fling out her bad hand: "Make it fashionable." I'd flip through my tube tops, finding one the same color as her swimsuit. Betsy examined her tan lines or put on Sea Coral lipstick because she thought that was right for the beach. She ignored me when I pulled her bad hand—the one with no fingers—toward me and put a tube over it. She liked tube tops because they hid her hand completely but made her look like she was carrying something bright. "Maybe tape it shut," I said. "Or paper clip it. And bunch it at your wrist. There." Betsy would hold the tube top up and examine it. "Cool," she said. I smiled, the expert. I wanted the tube top to look natural. I wanted to slip the tube top over her and see a good hand push through.

My parents were the ones who started helping Betsy hide her bad hand. After my mother hemmed the bottom of Betsy's coats, she would sew the extra material to one sleeve. Betsy always had sleeves that were too long for her; I thought all her coats looked like they were coming alive and taking over her body. My mother took forever with those sleeves. I hated watching her with Betsy. Because of her hand, Betsy possessed my parents in a way that I didn't. Sometimes when I played with Betsy, I pulled my coat

163

sleeves down over my hands; but the sight of me with gigantic sleeves always seemed to annoy my mother. "You don't want to look like a waif," she said, and rolled my coat sleeves all the way to the elbow.

Helping Betsy with her hand was the only thing I could do right that summer. Betsy was only eleven, a year younger than me, but had become pretty. The sun went into her skin and she held it easy, her hair, knees, glowing. Everyone knew her walk at our junior high school, a slow, watery step, her hair lifting and slapping her shoulders. Betsy understood something that I didn't, and as her older sister it was my job to stop this.

That was the summer when my father moved from his bed to the couch every morning and when my mother tried to figure out what was wrong with him. My father was tired. He woke up at night, cold, when it was warm outside. He had a little cough. All over the house I could hear him; he always sounded as though he was about to spit. Part of the day, my father lay on the couch in the den. Wrapped in a blanket, he watched the news reports. Before he felt tired, I used to sit with him on that couch and watch Sherylline Rivers talk disasters: 3,000 evacuated after chemical spill. Tornado ravages Kansas. My father would say two things to me: "Listen Sally," or "This is sick." "Listen Sally" included countries being invaded and teenagers who were more successful than I was. "This is sick" included everything else. I wanted to sit on that couch until my father organized the world for me.

Now he didn't want us in the den, so we sat where the carpet turned from rust to brown and watched him. It was Betsy's idea to toss balls of paper with messages at our sleeping father. She wanted to see how far she could throw a ball of paper if it were placed on her bad hand. She said if the messages hit him, maybe he would feel better. We scribbled notes we thought might work: The Greatest Father in the Universe!, Smile!, Hugs and Kisses!, We Luv You! I crumpled up Smile! and put it carefully on her bad hand.

She reached her arm back and served Smile!, full force, into the den. The ball bonked our father on the forehead.

He opened his eyes. We waited for him to thank us.

I knew our father was different when he woke up after our message hit him. He didn't thank us, which he could have done;

he didn't instruct us about the world, something he would usually do. He threw back the blanket and sat up.

"Enough, girls," he said. "Out."

Hearing our father talk that way sent Betsy all the way across the yard. She put her towel as far from the den as she could. She said she was going to make a project of thoroughly reading all of her *Seventeens*.

I couldn't decide where to sit. I didn't know what we had done. Sometimes I sat with her across the yard. Sometimes I sat on the edge of the den, like an anchor.

Our mother began to walk through the house. She walked hard through each room, as though into a wind. She was different, too. She wasn't in her face when she looked at us; she was with our father.

When my mother yelled at my father to go see a doctor, I ran to Betsy, who was involved in her *Seventeens*.

"What do we do!" I yelled at her.

She turned the page on a quiz on kissable lip gloss. "How should I know?" she asked.

I started to walk away until we heard our mother's voice rise again, louder than I had ever heard it.

Betsy jumped up. She began to run, arms flapping, I ran, too. She turned on the sprinklers. "Doe," she sang. "A deer. A female deer. Ray, a drop of golden sun. . ."

"Me, a name, I call myself. . ." We ran. We ran over the water, we ran as though we had practiced. I followed her around the yard, over the magazines, cover girls all wavy under the water.

We ran as far from the house as we could. We sang so loud their voices blurred. The house shimmered through the water. It almost looked beautiful.

Before my father got sick, he took us driving. He wanted to take us somewhere we had never seen. Sometimes he reached over the seat to us; his arm waved in front of our faces, and Betsy and I would decide what to put in his hand. "Guess what this is," we'd say, giving him anything—a shoe, a comic book.

I hated the game the moment Betsy put her bad hand into his. My father would rub her bad hand gently, as though he was trying to erase something, and then his fingers would close completely over her. "It's . . . a banana," my father would say. "A

165

croissant." Betsy would fall into the seat, giggling. "Wrong," she'd say. "It's a boomerang tip." Sometimes I would also put my hand in my father's. He would lightly lace his fingers into mine. "This is—um," he would say, thinking. I waited for him to tell me something special I could be.

I had to be good at something. I was the older sister. That's what I could do. My favorite older sister job with Betsy was when I was in charge of her bad hand. Before we played, she put her hand into my lap. I had so many ideas. We pushed it into Play-Doh to see the dents it made. We molded chocolate chip cookie dough around it to make a cookie that was full of air.

When Betsy was six, we were sitting in the yard and I was holding her bad hand, wondering what would happen if we put on a sprinkler, when she took it away and put it in her lap.

"Why is it different on me?"

"What? What's different?"

"Tell me."

I told her what our father had told me: You're the same as me, you just can't take piano lessons.

She began to bang her bad hand on the grass.

"Give me a thumb," she said to me.

"What?" I asked.

"Come on," she said. She put her bad hand into my lap.

I had no idea what to do.

I took her into our bedroom and we looked through our closet. Mr. Potato Head, Clue, nothing seemed right. Our 52-color marker set.

"Sit," I said. I held her bad hand in mine and I began to draw. Bumps of aqua, olive green, burgundy. I wanted to find the color combination that would make her fingers sprout.

When I was finished, Betsy had five colorful fingers drawn on her bad hand. We had a good day. I carried her around the yard, we sang. I lifted her up, she giggled, her bad hand raised like a beautiful flower.

When she woke up the next morning, the colors had run. Her hand looked like it had been beaten up. "What did you do!" I shrieked. I was afraid I had deformed Betsy in a new, horrible way; now she would also be purple. But as soon as we had cleaned her off, Betsy turned around and put it in my lap.

"Do it again," she said to me.

166

Betsy's bad hand wasn't exactly a hand. Her arm just ended in a point, like the tail end of whipped cream. I thought it looked like Betsy's arm just didn't want to stop when it entered the world. I thought her arm sensed something wonderful in the world and was shooting right out to meet it. Like Betsy. She seemed always to have some new way to leave me behind her. A few days after we had been sitting by the gate, she stood up and said, "I'm going to the beach."

That was an older sister's idea. She went ahead and stole it. Betsy headed out the next day. I couldn't believe it. I sat in the backyard and waited; I was afraid of the world. I opened the gate and started walking, walked until I hit the busy street. At the intersection, I stopped, feeling the car wind on my arms. I stood there, hoping, lifted my arms. But I was grounded without Betsy. There was nothing to do but turn around and go home.

The next day, I let her pull me with her. We took the blue bus to Santa Monica. We dropped off the bus and looked. The sand rolled, sparkling, to the flat silver of the Pacific Ocean. Betsy pushed out toward the water so fast I thought she'd belly-down the air, skid toward the sparkling blue.

I was slower. The fear started from nothing sometimes. I felt it rise through my body. Betsy looked fine, flapping out the towel; all I could think of was our father pulling at me, trying to bring me back home. "The ocean's polluted, Sherylline Rivers said," I told her.

"It is not," said Betsy.

I started unfolding the bus schedule. Betsy chewed her hair, watching me. "Wait," she said.

She grabbed my arm and started walking. She led me past a few lifeguard stations and up a hill. From the top of the hill, I saw a group of boys standing and pissing into a ditch.

"How incredibly gross," I said.

The boys were standing in a zigzag row along the ditch, which was shallow but dark with something I didn't want to think about. We were far enough away to lose the smell, but we could see the thin yellow lines go down into the ditch. We put our towels on the top of the hill and watched the boys walk up to the ditch. They unzipped themselves quickly and stood, hips forward, all aiming for the same place.

167

Betsy pointed at her discovery. "The one on the right could be named John," she said. "Beside him might be Gus and across could be Harvey." I was impressed; that was more information than I knew about any boy.

"Lay down," said Betsy, and we did; she said we could hold them on the lengths of our arms. She said if we could get all the boys in our arms, they would be ours. We lay face down, fingertips touching, but we couldn't quite do it; there were a couple of boys that kept getting away from us.

I breathed slow, my chest pressing into the sand. I decided that I needed these boys to turn all at once and call: Sally. I imagined their voices filling me until I rose above them all. But the boys just stood, holding themselves, looking into the air. "John's cute. Ted's a grosso, I don't know about Ed," said Betsy. Her good hand was in mine, hot and sticky. I could feel the air in my palm as she pushed toward them, let go.

We made it to the hill by ten every day; we could spend forever watching the boys. They came by twos or threes to the ditch and left quickly; after a few days we knew them all. "There's the cute guy we saw yesterday, the one who thinks he's James Dean," Betsy might say. "Okay. He's . . . I think he's . . . okay. He's going. He's going. God, what did he drink this morning?"

That was the fun part.

"Grape Kool-Aid," I said. "A gallon."

"Minutemaid, instant," said Betsy.

James Dean yanked his shorts shut. He was replaced by Fonz Wanna-be.

"Lemonade," I said. We watched, open-mouthed, as he went and went and went.

The hill was the one place in the world where I began to feel good. We sat for hours, waiting to see who would walk up next. Betsy and I made up things the boys would say if they liked us.

"You are a total foxy babe," said Betsy.

"You are one hunk o'woman," I tried.

"You are a chick from my dream life," she said.

Betsy and I rolled close to each other. For a second we owned the boys, all of them.

We looked at each other. Our faces were so close I could feel her breath.

"How do they not bump noses," I said.

She leaned over and quickly kissed me on the lips.

"Ow," I said, though it didn't hurt.

She kissed me again. She didn't bump my nose that time either.

"Ow," I said, again.

Betsy rolled away. I loved her.

"Ow," she said.

Up on the hill, Betsy and I never talked about our father. We did that only on the long block between our house and the busstop; then, we discussed our theories about what was wrong with him.

One day I told her I thought he wasn't doing anything because he was part of a contest. "Like how much TV you can watch," I said. "He's going to win a trip to Hawaii for four."

"No," said Betsy. "But maybe he's getting ready to go on a game show."

"He's going to win the *car*," I shrieked.

We hugged each other and jumped up and down. We were proud of our father. But the idea seemed strange when we got closer to the house. Our father was not going to Hawaii.

I moved close to Betsy. "There's a bug on your shoulder!" I shrieked.

"There is not," she said.

"Yes!" I shrieked. I swatted an invisible bug off her back and left my hand there. She didn't move.

We also had different theories about what would make our father feel better. That day I decided it was French braids. Betsy pulled her *Seventeen* from her tote bag and we sat on the curb, braiding each other's hair. We marched up to the house, arm in arm, giggling. We looked nice. He was going to love us. I began to knock, but Betsy grabbed me, hard.

"He's not going to like them," said Betsy.

"Yes, he will," I said.

"No," she squeaked. "He's not going to know who we are."

I don't know why I believed her, but it seemed better than believing myself. We destroyed our French braids, quickly and viciously. We stood by the front door, quietly. Betsy put her hand on my back.

"There's a bug on you," she said.

169

When Betsy was eight, I tried to suck her fingers out. We sat, backs pressed against old games of Clue and Candyland in our bedroom closet, legs tucked so our knees hit our chins. First I kissed her bad hand. I was delicate as a suitor; a circle of kisses around her wrist. "Eat it," she said. Her bad hand was spongy and a little salty. My mouth rode it as though it were corn on the cob. I thought of fingers. I bent down and tried to wish them out of her, making us, finally, the same.

"What?" she asked, excited.

I wiped her on the carpet and inspected; nothing.

"What?" asked Betsy. She was three years from becoming pretty. She put her bad hand in my lap.

"Please," she said to me.

It happened by the snack stand. Betsy was plucking straws out of the container while I held our drinks. A row of boys leaned against a wall that said in loopy, black writing, NO FAT CHICKS.

Betsy was struggling with the straw container. One of the boys, a cute one, walked right to her. He slapped a hand on the metal container. A few straws rumbled down. He plucked them out, very gently; then he held them out to Betsy as though they were a bouquet.

Betsy looked at the straws and, slowly, at the boy. He was just standing there, being a boy, but that was too much for me. I stared down at the sand. Betsy took the straw from him. And then she ran to me.

"What!"

"He said his name was Barry and he hung out at Station 5," she said.

"Oh my God," I said.

We ran across the sand, the ice in our drinks jingling.

"What does that mean?"

"He likes you," I said.

She shrieked. "Do you think he's cute?"

"No."

"Are you sure?"

"Yes."

"Oh," she said. She stabbed her straw into her drink top. The boy was still there, watching. It took too long for him to disappear.

Betsy and I both crawled into my bed at night. She liked to run her bad hand along my arms. Starting at my wrist, she slid it up to my elbow; then she stopped and slid back down again. We wrapped our legs around each other, Betsy smoothing me over and over, and often fell asleep like that, my mouth wet against her hair.

Sometimes, when we held each other, she would try to figure things out. "Daddy chopped them off when I was born," she whispered. "He came into the hospital and chopped them off with a knife." Or, "Mommy shoved them back in when I was a baby. Probably when I was crying too hard." Her imaginary good hand was destroyed by can openers or car washes; it was savaged by parents or music teachers; but it was never ruined by me. I waited for her to say it—"You, Sally, slammed it in a car door—" but, instead, she just looked at me, waiting for my answer. "That is totally whacked," was what I usually told her. "Really?" she asked me. "You think so, Sally?" Some nights she leaned so hard against my body I thought she might empty into me.

After Betsy had been picked at the snack stand, I decided there had to be a change in our boy-watching. "The one who could be Jake looks too much like Donny Osmond." I said. "The one who could be Todd has weird lips." Now all I could see were the mistakes in the boys. Pat's tubby stomach. Bob's spindly legs.

Betsy seemed loosened from her body, able to fly out and away whenever the chance came. "The one who might be Fred is a total hunkola," she said. "The one who could be John has cool hair."

I told her she was blind. Or just sick. I was the older sister. I knew these things. She shrugged. Since the day of the boy by the snack stand, she was spending a lot of time looking in mirrors; I think she was wondering why she had been picked.

The day she went down we were debating the one who could be Earl. "The most disgusting thing on the planet," I said. "I mean, if I were born looking like that I wouldn't ever leave the house. . ."

"Oh, come on. He's not *that* bad," she said.

"Not *that* bad," I said. "Are you crazy? Are you in love with him?"

Betsy stood up.

171

"Bye," she said.

She turned and sailed down to the ditch. I leaned over the edge of the hill, as though I could reel her back, but she was already there, she was already walking. The boys saw her and a few comments came, like the first zippy pieces of popcorn that explode inside a pan:

"Hey."

"You have a name?"

"Nice day, sweetie?"

"Wanna come hold it for me?"

"Bitch," I said, quietly, into the sand. She stopped. I hoped she'd run then, make a break for the parking lot, but she didn't; she was brave. She zeroed in on one boy who had finished and was standing away from the others. He was thin-armed, freckled, pressing a boogie board close to his chest. Betsy walked right over and stood beside him. She kept the tube top wrapped tight around her bad hand. You couldn't see her bad hand, couldn't see that there was anything different about her. She was just a really pretty girl who was trying to make this boy like her. The boy kept his eyes on the sand and she kept talking. Then she leaned forward and touched his arm with her bad hand.

I thought he'd know it in a second, feel the bump through her tube top and run. I thought that would teach her, and all those boys would come running to me. But she had him. My sister made him like her. The boy toed the sand, practically smiling. And even though he wasn't a very cute boy, even though he was probably named something like Earl, I had never wanted so much to be like her.

I flopped onto my back and closed my eyes so she wouldn't know that I had been watching. When I opened them, she was there.

"You know what," she said.

"What."

"I think he liked it."

"What? Speak English."

And she held up her bad hand.

"That?"

Betsy smiled.

"I think he did," she said.

172

That night, when our father fell asleep in front of the TV, we slipped in, low, flat, to sit beside him. Once we made it, once we were finally beside our father, I wasn't sure what I was supposed to do. Betsy sat, staring into the bright white of the TV; then she unwrapped her tube top and took out her bad hand. Her bad hand glowed in the light of the TV set. I thought it looked as though it entered the world more purely, simply, than a complete hand would. Betsy pulled my father's feet on her lap; then she began to rub her bad hand back and forth along them. "Idiot," I hissed. "What are you doing? What are you *do*-ing?" I thought, this was it. She was going to be Queen of the Hill; now she would cure our father in some sick mutant way.

"Fine. Fine," I hissed. "Wake him up. Just kill him, while you're at it." But nothing happened. Betsy stopped. "Bitch," she whispered, "I'm not doing anything." Neither of us moved from our father. We looked at him for a long time.

As soon as we got to the hill the next day, she announced, "I'm going to kiss a boy an hour and I'm going to tell them my name is Sally."

She ran down the hill; I followed. She put me against a truck. I started to go back to my towel but I stopped; I had to see what she was going to do with my name. Betsy steered clear of the boy she had picked the last time and found one I thought was cute. Clutching the boy with her good hand, she led him over to the truck. She stopped about ten feet from me, turned him so he couldn't see me. All I could see of the boy was his pinkish back. She stepped close to him, fiddling her good hand in his hair. I stood against the truck, pretending to look at the seagulls circling. Then Betsy, my sister, reached up and kissed him.

I could almost feel it inside me when she did that, I could almost taste that boy. But I wasn't kissing him. It wasn't me. I was just there, in the shadows, trapped against a truck.

I wanted to say things. Tramp. Slut o' the Universe. Crazed Maniac of the World. Major Bitch. Of course, I didn't. There was nothing to do but stand quietly and watch my sister pull love out of someone else.

I left the beach early and headed for Sav-On. It was where our family went when we needed to fix things. I went down the Cosmetics aisle and thought of my mother. I thought hard about her, trying to make her stop yelling. I went down Toilet Seats and thought of Betsy. I tried to keep her from taking over the world. I went down Lawn Chairs and I thought of my father. I tried to make him well.

I found it by Gardening. A small bottle filled with bright blue fluid: Fern Encourager. In small print: Bring your thirsty ferns to life.

I think I had to take Fern Encourager because nothing else had worked.

I did something I had never done before: I put Fern Encourager in my pocket and went for the door. I walked out past the girls ringing the cash machines, stepping right into the parking lot. I didn't stop walking for five blocks. In front of me the sidewalk rose up, shining.

I showed it to her in the bathroom that night.

She rolled up her bikini top, flashing her brown nipples, her tiny breasts. Then she ducked, knocking the bottle out of my hand.

"Are you insane," she said to me.

I watched her move into the mirror as though she were in love with it.

"I can make you sprout fingers," I said.

"Sally, you're such a geek," she said.

I swallowed. I stood so hard on the floor I hoped it would tilt, spill Betsy, my family somewhere.

"I can," I told her.

I went outside and sat with my father.

"Do you have cancer?"

He shook his head. "No," he said.

I felt something, full as a balloon, shrink inside of me. "Do you have heart failure?"

"No," he said.

"Well then, what?" I said.

He held out his arms. I stood inside them. They did not surround me the way I wanted.

"I get tired after I read the newspaper," he said. "I get tired after I walk one block." His voice swelled. "I get chills almost every night, and still no one says there's anything wrong with me." He rolled over. "Forget it, Sally. Go play with your sister."

I didn't know what to think. I wasn't a contest. It wasn't a fatal disease. It wasn't that he just liked to lay around. My father had just stopped.

My father closed his eyes. He looked like he could just sink into the lawn chair and disappear. It wouldn't take long for me to follow. I wouldn't even have to try. I tried to tell one of the boys at the beach to come get me. The one who could be Craig, pushing open the gate and walking right to me, leaning over, knowing how to kiss.

That was the first time in ages that I sat right beside my father.

That night, I woke up, blinking into the dark. I moved down the long hallway to the kitchen. I stood in the doorway and scanned the utensils. The can opener wasn't sharp enough. I didn't know how to put together the Cuisinart. So I took the biggest steak knife, silver and heavy. And I put it against my left hand.

That knife was stubborn. I held it hard, stood there breathing; I thought of all the love I would possibly get. But the knife wouldn't go down. It wouldn't move.

I lifted the knife off my skin. I put it in the very last trash can in the garage. I dumped garbage over it—old TV dinners, soda bottles, banana peels—until I was sure no one would know it was there. In bed, my hands went slowly all over my body: my body, still ridiculously complete.

When I woke up, I told Betsy I wasn't going with her to the hill anymore.

"It's boring," I said.

She was stepping into that day's swimsuit; she stopped.

"How?"

"It just is," I said.

Betsy slapped her arms at her sides. "Fine," she said. "Be that way." She whirled around. "What color do I wear?"

"I don't care."

"Pink," she said. "I totally need pink." She began to hurl shirts and towels. "Fonz Wanna-be looks like a fish when he kisses," she said. "It's really gross. You have to see."

"No," I said.

175

She zoomed out of the bedroom. I listened. She was running. She was also throwing: magazines, big pillows, chairs.

"Sally," she yelled.

She was in the kitchen.

"You stole my pink one," she said.

"I wouldn't want it," I said.

"Bitch," she said. "You know you do."

She grabbed a spatula lying on a counter. "You know you do," she yelled, and went for me with the spatula. I leaped on Betsy. She whacked the spatula everywhere: into my chest, under my armpit, between my legs. I hit her all over; I didn't want to miss a spot.

She shoved me off and ran to the den. I couldn't believe it; she ran inside.

"Daddy!" Betsy yelled.

She began to jump all over the den. I did, too. We bounced up and off chairs, the card table. I pretended our father wasn't sleeping. He wasn't even there.

Our father opened his eyes. "Girls, out," he said.

Betsy hopped, gently, on top of the TV set. Under her feet, a contestant touched a new Buick. Betsy was the tallest thing in the room.

Again, she had picked the center of the universe. She had found the best place to be. I wriggled toward Betsy, getting ready to push her off.

Our father was faster. He lifted her off the TV. Betsy started kicking. He was holding her, in the air, kicking. It was the first father thing I saw him do the whole summer. It was the first thing he did that made him look strong.

He gently set Betsy on the floor. I loved him then, instantly, ridiculously. Now he would talk to us again; now he would tell us what to do.

But our father didn't say anything to us. He didn't even smile. He stepped away from us as though he thought we were ugly.

I let out a big breath. I wondered how our father felt, watching me and Betsy leave for the beach every day. I imagined how mad he must be, being tired when it was so beautiful outside.

Our father was alone in the den again and I had no idea how to save him.

Our father turned away from us. Betsy shot out of the room. I followed. When we made it to the bathroom, she began to cry.

She leaned into me, her whole face salty. I wanted to help her stop. I frantically scanned the bathroom. Blowdryers, lip gloss, a loofah sponge. The bottle of Fern Encourager was beside my toothbrush. I grabbed it and held it out to her.

"Oh, please," she said.

I poured out some blue on a paper towel and touched her bad hand with it. I knew the Fern Encourager wouldn't work. I knew she didn't think it would, either. But it was all I could think of then, in the bathroom.

"Idiot," she said, softly.

I kept pouring the bottle of Fern Encourager. I poured so the blue dripped off her onto the floor. Betsy squatted and rubbed her bad hand in the blue that was pooling around her feet.

I bet she thought I was stupid. I know I did. But it was just us then in the bathroom. Finally Betsy held her bad hand to me. And she shrugged.

"Do it," she said.

We didn't take the bus this time; we ran the whole way. Betsy dashed up the hill first, sand flying from her feet like white sparks. When we got to the top, we turned to the sun and I lifted her arm.

She twisted away from me, embarrassed, but I held her arm there, hard. "Higher," I said. "On your toes."

The boys at the ditch turned toward us, but they were too far away, I think, to see anything but that she had kissed some of them by the parking lot.

"Hey," a couple of them began to call. "Hey."

Betsy was frozen in her salute, and the boys began running, slowly toward us. I stood behind her and held her arm so it was closer to the sun.

"Try," I said. "Push."

Betsy closed her eyes. It seemed like she was trying to fling her whole self into that hand. I wrapped my arms around her skinny waist and lifted her, kicking, to the sky.

"Push."

The boys coming up the hill saw me holding Betsy and started slowing down. I squeezed my sister, tighter, tighter. I waited for

177

something beautiful to come out of her; I waited for anything at all. Then Betsy started to cough and we fell, separate, on the sand.

Betsy was still. I took her hand out of the sand. She kept her face down as I shook the sand off. She must have known there was no difference. And, of course, there wasn't. Because when her hand was out, I could see that it was the same. It was still my sister's bad hand.

The boys began to rush the hill. And they began calling her by the name she had given them. Sally. Sally.

When she heard they were still coming, Betsy sat up, yanked her bad hand back.

"Oh, great," she said. "Give me something."

"What?"

"Don't be stupid. Your shirt."

She snapped up my shirt with her good hand and then I was on the top of that hill in my bikini top, the wind touching my shoulders. Betsy wrapped my shirt around her bad hand in about a half a second, whip-fast after years of practice. The boys were coming for us. They were coming. Betsy pulled me. "Let's go," she said. She took my hand with her good one. Her good hand fit into mine perfectly. It had never fit so well.

"Come on," she said. And we walked off the beach, all the boys calling Sally, Sally, the whole beach ringing with my name.

Nominated by The Iowa Review

GREEN GROW THE GRASSES O

fiction by D. R. MACDONALD

from TRIQUARTERLY

A SUSPICION HAD come down that Kenneth Munro was using dope in the house he rented above the road. "Harboring drugs" was the way Millie Patterson put it.

"I don't think he's that kind," Fiona Cameron said, in whose parlor Mr. Munro was being discussed. She had seen him coming and going, a thirtyish man with dark gray hair nearly to his shoulders. It was the only extravagant thing about him, how the wind would gust it across his eyes. He had left St. Aubin as a tot and returned suddenly now for reasons unclear.

"Drinking's one thing," Millie said. "But *this*."

"This what?" Fiona said. She was curious about him too, but in a different way. And Kenneth Munro, after all, was not just any outsider. His family was long gone but still remembered.

After some coaxing, Lloyd David, Millie's son, described how Munro's kitchen had been full of the smell the day he'd dropped by to cut the high wild grass out front. "There's no other smell like it," he said.

This expertise got him a hot glance from his mother. Millie missed no opportunity to point up the evils of drugs.

"But Millie," Fiona said, "a smell in his kitchen is hardly criminal."

"Fiona dear, you have no idea." Millie, a nurse for twenty-six years, recalled with horror a young man the Mounties brought

179

into the emergency ward last winter: "In that weather, crawling down the highway in his undershorts, barking like a dog." Lloyd David chuckled, then caught himself. "He was that cold," Millie went on, "he was blue." She paused. "Marijuana." But the word came out of her mouth erotically rounded somehow, lush and foreign.

"But we hardly know Kenneth Munro," Fiona said. She knew he often stood shirtless on his little front porch late in the morning, stretching his limbs. He'd just got up, it was plain to see. He was brown from the sun, though he'd brought the brown with him. Fiona could not imagine him crawling along a highway or barking either. What she could imagine she was not likely to admit. She was from the Isle of Harris in the Outer Hebrides but had lived in Cape Breton all her married life, nearly twenty years. Her eyes were an unusual pale green, peppered with colors you couldn't pin down, and they looked merry even when she was not. No, Millie would not easily let go of this matter. Kenneth Munro. And drugs. They had come to Cape Breton like everywhere else, and of course people saw on TV what drugs out there in the world could do. Marijuana? Just a hair's breadth from heroin, in Millie's eyes, whereas alcohol was as familiar as the weather. Hadn't there been a nasty murder over in Sydney where two kids on drugs stabbed an old man for his money? That shook everyone, murder being rare among Cape Bretoners, despite a reputation for lesser violence. Fiona glanced out the front window; she hadn't seen Munro all day. His bedroom window was flung high and the curtains, green as June grass, whipped in the wind.

"He's got a telescope in the backyard," Lloyd David said.

"What's he up to?" Millie said.

"Well, that's the point." Fiona took a sip of tea. It was cool. "We can't say."

"He seems like a nice fella." Harald, Fiona's husband, had come in from haying and stood stout and perspiring in his overalls. "Fiona's right," he said from the doorway. "Yesterday he was asking me about the bobolinks."

"About the *what*?"

"Birds, Ma. Tweet, tweet?"

She glared at her son; she hated his Oakland Raiders T-shirt with the insolent pirate face on the front.

"Well," Fiona said. "He's just over the road. We'll have to find out about him. Harald, won't we?"

At a table by the west window of the Sealladh Na Mara Restaurant Kenneth Munro took in the postcard view. Whatever he saw he measured against the descriptions his father had given him years ago. He could see a portion of Goose Cove and the mountain behind it whose profile darkened the water this time of the afternoon, calming the bay. Terns squabbled on a sandy bar. The waitress, whom he fancied and who, he felt, was ready for a move, came up behind him, her slender figure reflected in the glass. In her unflattering uniform—a bland aqua, the hem too long—she seemed all the more pretty. She'd worn her fine brown hair unfashionably long down her back when he had seen her walking along the road, but now it was clasped in a bun.

"Ginny, suppose I was to take you to dinner some night soon? In Sydney?"

"Oh, I don't know. You're older than I am, by more than a bit." Ginny had graduated from McGill this summer and was back home, pondering her future. She loved the country she'd grown up in but knew she would work in a big city before long.

"I can't deny it," Munro said. "I'm up in years. I expect your parents wouldn't approve."

"No, No, they wouldn't much. And they've always known just about everything I've done around here." She looked over at two elderly women picking daintily at their lobster salads. "There's no need they should keep on knowing."

"I'll get you home early," he said. "Early as you like."

"I suppose we could. I'm thinking we might." She went off to another table and stood with her back to him. Munro drank from his water glass, running the ice around his tongue, and smiled comfortably at the immobile brilliance of the bay, its surface inked in shadow.

That was the kind of light he imagined in his special afternoon, an ambience like that.

They ate in a steakhouse too open and noisy, but after a bottle of wine they talked freely in raised voices, discovering that they might be distantly related through a great-grandmother, and that brought them a few inches closer. Munro told her about his carpentry work in San Francisco, cabinetmaking and remodeling, and how he liked working for gays because they paid him well and were particular. Ginny told him about Montreal and how she always tried to speak French there because she got to know the people. She asked him why he was living alone over there in St. Aubin with hay and woods all around him.

"Only for a while," Munro said. He took a photograph out of his coat and laid it on the white tablecloth, moving his face closer to hers. "That man there is my father, Ginny. The women I don't know."

"I'd say they like him, eh?"

"Something more than that going on. Look at his face."

"Is he your age there, your dad?"

"About."

"I like your gray hair. It's a bit long. His looks black."

"And very proud of it he was. Vain, even."

"He's dead?"

"He is." Munro tapped the photo. "But not here. Here, he is very much alive." He touched her hand. "Would you come with me to a field like that? Would you be one of those women, for an afternoon?"

Ginny laughed. He looked so serious in the smoldering light of the candle jar. But the people in the photograph, the man and the two women, seemed happy, and she felt quite good herself after three glasses of wine.

"You mean like a picnic?" she said.

On the way back to Rooster Hill Munro pulled off the highway near South Gut so they could take in the bay. Along the mountain ridge the lost sun threw long red embers. In the evening water below them, still as a pond, lay the blackened timbers of an old wharf.

"My father had a picture of that," Munro said. "From back in the twenties when he was a kid. There was a schooner tied up to it. Looked like another century. Here, you want a hit of this?"

He proffered what she thought was a cigarette. She stared at it.

"Am I shocking you?" Munro said.

"I've run across it, and I don't shock easy as all that."

He was afraid he had blown it with her, but he was in a hurry, and for him puffs of grass were part of almost any pleasure.

"You *are* a woman," he said.

"At home here, I am still a girl."

"Well, then." He made to stub out the joint but she grabbed his wrist and took it from him, drawing a long hit.

"God help us if the Mounties come by," she said through the smoke. "And you with relatives here."

"Never met any. One afternoon of my own is all I want. With the sun out, and a warm wind coming up from the field. And women like those in the photo, at their ease. That's what I came for—to take that back with me."

"I don't want to be a woman in a picture."

"Ah, Ginny, you'll be more than that."

They kissed in the car as it idled by her mailbox, once quickly like friends, then again with a long deep taste of something further. After Ginny got out, she kissed the window on the passenger side. The fierce twilight made her reckless. Through the rosy smudge on the glass, Munro watched her walk up the hill to her house, twirling her bag.

Fiona parted the parlor curtains: Kenneth Munro's car was turning slowly up his driveway, its broad taillights reminding her, in the foggy dark, of a spaceship. Wee men would be coming out of it, heading for the scattered houses of St. Aubin. *Feasgar math,* she'd say, I've been waiting. *Fuirich beagan.* Certain feelings had no shape in English, and sometimes she whispered them to herself. Harald was not a speaker above the odd phrase, but Gaelic came to her now and then like old voices. *Air á ghainmhich.* The sands of Harris, the long shell-sand beaches that even on a dour day opened up white like a stroke of sun, still warm to your bare feet after the wind went cold and the clouds glowered over the gusting sea. Those strange and lovely summers, so distant now—brief, with emotions as wild as the weather, days whose light stretched long into evening and you went to bed in a blue dusk.

"Harald," she said, "is it time for a call on Mr. Munro?" But Harald, pink from haying, had dozed off in his chair. A rerun of *Love Boat* undulated across the television, the signals bouncing

183

badly off the mountain tonight. Fiona loathed the program. When she turned off the set Harald woke. He kissed her on the cheek, then wandered upstairs seeking his bed.

So why not go up to Munro's? Yet when she thought of him opening the door, her breath caught. Of course she could phone him first, but that was not the same thing, was it?

Fiona had shared a life with Harald for a long time, here in the country. She'd left Harris for a small farm in Nova Scotia because she loved the man who asked her away, the seaman she'd met in Stornoway where she worked in a woolen shop. Love. *An gaol.* Yes, she had no reservations about that word, and all it carried, never had. She loved his company, even when he was dull (and wasn't she the dull one too sometimes, shut into herself, beaten down by a mood?). The two of them together had always seemed enough, and although they liked other people, they never longed for them. Small delights could suffice, if you were close in that way you couldn't explain to anyone else: it was the robin who nested every summer in the lilac bush at the front door, huddled in the delicate branches as they came and went, always aware of her, pleased that she didn't flee, and the families of deer they watched from the big window at the foot of their bed, grazing elegantly one moment and exploding into motion the next, and every day the Great Bras D'Eau, the different suns on its surface, the water shaded and etched by tides, stilled by winter, the crush of drift ice, and the long mountain in autumn, swept with the brilliance of leaves. And just the day-by-day work of living seemed to have a reason that lay in their being together, but they could never have said what it was. A meal, a task, a domestic calamity—who could say what made them glad for having it? They talked about some things, but left most unsaid. She loved . . . what? Harald's presence? Was that the word, *làthair*? In some way that no one else could embrace? It was like a bit of music that was always there, behind everything, often too faint to be noticed, but there, and sometimes powerful. He knew her, and he loved her, without question. She had not yearned for any different thing between them.

Yet something shocked her out of sleep now and then, her heart galloping hard until the dream yielded to the bedroom, to the familiar window, and she knew again where she was. An impossible longing came on as she lay there in the dark, whether there was a bright moon out, or snow raging or flickering down, or a deep rain drumming on her nerves as she waited for thunder. Harald would mutter on in his own dreams. She wondered if they were anything like her own. He never said. And why anyway? They were his, he needed them. But in some dreams, she made another man care about her: his attentions were utterly new and like that first keen love when everything is on the tips of your fingers. Each time, in whatever dream place, the feeling was the same: rich in sensation, strange, like none she knew in her waking life, and there were no words for it in Gaelic or English either.

Munro's front light burned in the fog, a gathering coolness on her skin. In Harris as a girl, mists had sometimes frightened her because of the tales she'd heard and because sights would suddenly appear in her path, ambiguous shapes in a gray sea, and as she approached Munro's house, she thought maybe that was why he looked out his window a moment before disappearing from it fast. She rapped on his door. What had she seemed like to him? A specter? *Tannasg?* He was slow to answer. She stamped her feet lightly though the wind was not cold.

"Did I scare you?" she said, pleased to have that edge.

"I don 't get many callers, not at night. Mrs. Cameron is it?"

He looked tense but he ushered her inside, smiling. There was an odd smoke in the air and she blushed.

"Am I interrupting you? Harald's asleep. Tired to the bone." Was she rattling on?

"Something to drink?" he said. "Rum and ginger ale maybe?"

"Well I think I will. A wee one. Thank you."

Munro pryed an ice tray from his snowy freezer, scattering frost on the floor. He jabbered on about bobolinks in the hayfield. Wouldn't the tractor mow through their nests, the females drab but the males decked out in cream cravats? Were the fledglings gone, was that it? He held ice cubes in his hands.

"Oh, yes," she said. "They've flown by now."

He poured rum into a glass. The ice crackled.

"I've seen your husband cutting hay," he said. His face was pleasantly creased, as if he'd spent time outdoors, but comfortably, skiing or swimming perhaps. His long hair looked recently trimmed.

"He sells it. Three thousand bales." She smiled. At the tips of her cheekbones she felt spots of red. Like rouge, but hot. "I used to help him."

Munro handed her the drink, then peered out the window. "I'm glad it was you coming out of that fog," he said. "Jumped out of my skin."

"Nothing to harm you here."

"I know. Sometimes I'm sensitive to surprises." He sat down at the wooden table he used for a desk. "This little house is fine for me. The roof leaks a bit, in the kitchen."

"A family of seven lived here once. Less than fine." She had taken a good swallow and could feel the rum in her blood. She was startled to see her white knees crossed at the hem of her skirt since she'd intended to wear slacks. "I'll send Lloyd David over. He'll patch your roof."

"Lloyd David's mother showed up here this morning," Munro said as if it had just come back to him. "She asked me if I knew about the Knox Church and would I like to attend." He laughed. "She was really looking me over. I said no thanks, and she said it was only what she expected. What do I make of that?"

"Millie is just concerned about your soul, Mr. Munro. Some people here feel a kind of responsibility toward you, and they don't know what you're like."

"Because I was born here?"

"Your father grew up here, your grandpa too. He's buried over in the churchyard." She nodded toward the small white church that on a clear night could be seen from the kitchen. "That's part of why Millie came to your door."

"And you?"

"It wasn't for church, Mr. Munro. I'm not a deep kneeler myself."

"Folks don't usually care about my soul, especially strangers."

"You've got kin around here, if you want to know them."

"Really, I don't." He bent a gooseneck lamp low to the table. "That is, I have something I want to live, or relive, while I'm here. It doesn't involve cousins. Just myself, and two others."

She set the glass down on the carpet, most of it gone. The rum made her bold.

"Has it anything to do with what I smell in the air? Mind you, I'm only asking."

He went still and looked at her. There was a touch of smile in his voice. "Asking's plenty, at this point."

"I'm not snooping."

"And I'm not dangerous. Every Presbyterian is safe."

"It doesn't matter, believe me. Not in my book."

"Would you come here to the table? I'll try to show you what I'm after, something I missed a long time ago."

A photograph was arranged under the table lamp like a document. "I never saw my family except in snapshots," Munro said. "My father would lay them out and tap a face or a house or a field somewhere, places I'd never seen. Bits of a puzzle, to me. People posing in kitchen chairs out back, gray shingles behind them, in Cape Breton. St. Aubin, other places. You know what I mean . . . a guy standing by a horse with his hand on its nose, and my father would say, 'Now that's cousin Murdock John Rory, and he's nearly a hundred.' And my mother would chime in, 'And isn't that Donald's Heather when she was small, with the dog Uncle Freddie left behind?' She knew all the pictures by heart. But not this one. I found it in the lining of his suitcase, after he died. No, my mother never saw this. She would have said, even though she isn't in it."

His father, shirtless, lies on his back in an unmown field. Closed in delight, his eyes are directed toward the camera through a veil of summer grass into which he seems to be settling. His smile is one of selfconscious bliss, unfeigned. A plump woman with dark hair hugs him, her cheek pressed to his bare chest as if she is listening to his heart, while a second woman, younger, her light blond hair pulled tightly back, sits in a sidesaddle way beside his head, her hand playing in his hair. Her smile, pursed with mischief, would warm any man near it. Fiona can see that. Her shorts have cuffs and her tucked-back legs are pale but pretty. It is like the photos Fiona grew up with, in its black-and-white tones of the past. Behind the father and his two women, neglected fields recede toward gray water. Shy spruce trees stand singly in the far reaches of meadow, awash in wild blond grass. Visible at the edge of the picture is a boarded window. The old house lists like a grounded ship.

"The farm was long abandoned by this time," Munro said. "Granny was dead. The land is going back to woods, slowly, and my dad didn't care. He'd had to stay home into his thirties, being the youngest. Had to see to his mother. But you see, he was cut off, for years, there in the country. No electricity. No plumbing. Nothing to tune into. A caretaker, a nurse. And Granny was hard to live with sometimes. So when he was free of all that, he took off west. He only came back here once, and this is it, I know it. On a whim he's come out to the old place, with two women. There's something he has to taste, one more time, and it's all in the air of that afternoon."

"And who *took* the picture?" Fiona said.

Munro looked the question off, his eyes still on the photograph. "I'm trying to *see* this, you understand, to get inside it. An afternoon like this one, just once. No camera has to record, only me. And the two women."

"And what happens when that day dies down and you all have to go home?"

"I'll still have the day. And I can enter it whenever I wish." He showed her a stubby joint from his shirt pocket. "This helps me. Does that make any sense?"

"Portions of it." Fiona could see right into that old house: the lamps were dry and the cold air was damp with absence. She could smell the mildewed cushions and clothes and bedding, on the beds or in the drawers. And that man in the grass, he would never be back. The women touching him were neither his wife nor his wife-to-be. What was he like? What kind of man had he been?

"But why do you need help from that?" she said, pointing to the roach in the palm of his hand. "I'm sure I sound naive."

"It helps me see things I've missed. And it makes me high." He smiled. "Are you going to evict me?"

"You're not noisy. Your rent's paid. And it's only you up here, isn't it?"

"You do understand what I'm after here? A kind of re-enactment?"

"And where will you do all this?"

"At my grandmother's old place, of course. Nobody's there. Are they?"

"No." Fiona looked to the window that faced the strait and the mountain. "But I have to tell you that your grandmother's property is gone for a gravel pit. There's little of it now but a bare cliff. I'm sorry."

188

Kenneth Munro spread the tripod legs and focused his telescope on the bare brown scar across the water: dust blew about it like smoke, and yes, it was mostly cliff now, gravel mounded for hauling at the base of it. He could just make out the monotonous grind of a stone crusher. A dump truck rumbled off with a heaped load and disappeared into the dense green mountainside.

When Harald's tractor started up the hill from the road, Munro hailed him and waited in the row he was mowing. Harald stopped and got down, leaving the engine running.

"I wanted to ask you," Munro said, offering Harald the photo and nodding toward the mountain. "How could they do *that* to *this*? How is it legal?"

Harald doffed his cap and wiped his startlingly white scalp with a red bandana. He studied the picture. "It was fallow, you know, your grandma's place, a long while. Nothing coming out, nothing going in. Just deer and hunters. So, goes for taxes. Goes for what money might be made of it."

"Gravel?"

"Gravel. God, they took ton after ton out. All under the highway now."

"Where I live you could fight that."

"Fight what? We had nice farms all over here once. The place was full of people. Lots of trees now, as you see it, everywhere." Harald patted the hood of his tractor as if it were flesh. "You liking it up here, in the house?"

They both looked at the house. Lloyd David was kneeling on the roof wielding a thick black brush. He waved.

"It's fine. Look." Munro brandished the photo. "Is there a meadow like this anywhere over there, on the other side?"

"Look east a bit. That patch. I used to cut hay for the old widow but she's gone. It's clear yet, I think. Funny how trees don't come back into certain places, just don't. Further up lies a stone house, what's left of it. We didn't build with stone. Plowed up too damn much, I guess."

"Is it grassy there?"

"Old hay and whatever." Harald yanked a stalk from the ground. "There's no single grass called hay. It's a mixture, varies from place to place. Over at the stone house, I can't recall." He blew on the timothy in his hand. "See that powder? Pollen."

"Flower tops," Munro said. "Them I know about."

189

He glanced back at the roof. Lloyd David flashed him an ambiguous peace sign and then put his forked fingers to his lips. Munro ignored him.

"Look through your scope there and you'll see the spot I'm talking about." Harald climbed up on the tractor seat. "Or is that just for stars?"

"There's a comet due pretty soon. Next Friday, I think. Come up and have a look."

"Can't stay awake for a comet, Mr. Munro. That time of night I'm sawing heavy wood." He looked toward his house where Fiona had come out. "Now, Fiona, she'd love to. You show her the stars." Harald released the brake lever and fell instantly into the rhythm of mowing. The man would keep it up until dark, and if the weather shifted, he had other things to do. Had he noticed how lovely his wife looked?

Down by her lilac bush, Fiona was taking in the morning, her face up to the sun, or so it seemed, a mist of lavender still left in the branches behind her. When she saw him, she crossed the road and came slowly up the field, the wind in her clothes, billowing her pale green skirt. She stopped short of him and shaded her eyes. The sun warmed her honey-colored hair.

"There's a stone house over there I'd like to go to," Munro said.

"I heard it's dangerous." She was a bit out of breath and her cheeks had reddened. "It's falling in."

"I suppose there's some danger, sure," he said. He looked down at her white house and the green shutters. The barn, the big doors of its threshing floor thrown wide, was painted and trimmed the same, neatly. All of a piece. "Why did my father hate his own farm so much he let it be ground up into nothing? The fields have been hauled away in trucks."

"He wasn't happy there," Fiona said.

"He was at times. At times."

The sound of the tractor was fading out beyond the rise.

"I guess you've been to the stone house," Munro said.

"I never have. I know it's there."

"Do you like comets?"

"How couldn't I?"

At the big rock behind his house he helped her up to the telescope, his hands shaping her waist. Fiona looked into the eye-

190

piece where the stone house was supposed to be. He watched her looking, her hands on her bare prim knees. Something in the tension of the skin there made him want to touch her.

"It fair puts you right there, doesn't it?" she said. She tapped the barrel of the scope. "That could find mischief far and wide." She looked down at him. "Why the stone house?"

"My afternoon lies over there. Would you come along? We'll have a look."

Harald was returning over the hill. Lloyd David had hauled his ladder down and stood smoking a cigarette. He grinned at Munro as if they both shared some secret.

"But," Fiona said, "how would I fit into an afternoon like that?"

"Just fine." He gave her his hand and she hopped down off the rock. A strap of her blouse slipped down and Munro plucked it quickly back in place. "You see," he said, "I know the mood of that day. My father could go away again any moment he wanted to. His mother wasn't in the house anymore, cranky, dying." Munro looked at the tall, almost platinum grass beside his house, beautiful as a woman's hair. He'd told Lloyd David not to cut it, to leave it as it was. "My father had the smells of summer in that grass, that air. The women felt it too. So could we, I think."

A breeze rushed through the old maples along the hayfield, a warm sound in the leaves. The ripe hay shimmered. Crows roamed the stubble like portly deacons. Down on the road a red Lada crept past, Millie hugging the wheel.

"When?" Fiona said.

Since there was an old path, she let Munro and his excitement lead the way through the foothill woods until they stepped out into a meadow, clear except for a sprinkling of wild apple, gnarled and stunted by browsing deer.

"Up there!" Munro said. In the upper boundary of the meadow sat the ruins of the house, its stones the color of damp sand. It seemed to be merging with the ground. All these years and Fiona had never seen it: strange to look upon the open gut of it, all tumbledown, mossed, grassed in, tufted with wildflowers. But then she had had no cause to come here before. Harald came haying but how would he have known she'd take an odd pleasure in beholding a stone house half broken back to where it came from? Munro pulled her away to a pair of apple trees so old they knelt, their trunks extending out like thick branches, and he sat her down in the tall, fine grass.

"My father's trees were straighter," he said. He was flushed and proprietary, as if all he saw were his. "These are hardly breathing. Leaves, but not a fruit on them."

"Och, they needed pruning and propping in their later years, and who was here to do it?" Harald tended their own small orchard, and Fiona loved the apple blossoms in June, the white perfume of a new summer. Rain scattered the petals like snow.

"This can be the place," Munro said. "I know it, I feel it."

"It is a place already. People worked here, lived here."

"I'll borrow it for a day. That's all right, isn't it?"

"If there's ghosts, I doubt they'd mind."

Munro was lighting a joint as if it were no more than a cigarette, his eyes absorbed in the flame.

"They might well mind that, though," Fiona said.

"You mean they never got high, these people. Can't believe it."

"I didn't say that. But I wouldn't think you'd need that stuff up here," she said.

"My father had a bottle up here." Munro hissed more smoke from the joint and blew it out with a long sigh. "Background music, Fiona. Here, try a little. We'll see things the same way."

"Thanks, no. I'm seeing fine."

He was on his feet and striding toward the ruined house. That smoke changed him, she could see that clear enough: he took a little turn of his own and left her a step behind. What was it like? She had to wonder. She liked his eyes, but they were too light sometimes, like water in a swimming pool, and she could imagine him leaning against a palm tree. But that was unfair. His long hair suited him somehow, carefully trimmed, and the rough clothes too, the denim shirts and jeans that made no distinction between leisure and work.

She followed him up the hill, drawn more to the house itself than to Munro's investigation. She knew stone houses, growing up in Harris they were all she knew. But here she had never seen one like this, rude as an old hearth. Two of the walls, thick with stacked stones of many sizes, were nearly intact, their outer surfaces sealed in a layer of rough mortar (some crude version of harling?), but the inner ones exposed like a tall fence of field-stones, weathered and stained from rains and the earth they'd been pulled from (but chosen with the patient eye and hand of a stone setter), smaller ones (pebbles even) wedged between larger, all to complete this solid unwavering puzzle, this wall. At the corners, broken or joined, the stones had been dressed to fit flat. The lintels of the low, cramped windows were long, chiseled blocks. Never fancy, this house, but Highland skill and labor had formed it. The roof had long ago pitched itself into the living space, atumble with split timbers, gray as driftwood, and with broken stone. Among them grass and hardy flowers sprouted from sod clumps. Rubble from the collapsed sections had spilled into the fruitcellar, a cell-like pit lined with stones dressed into neat blocks like the lintels. But all was collapse now, a giving in. It must have been dark indeed, but she could attest there was nothing like two feet of stone between you and the world, a kind of safety, coming as she did from an island of wind. Wind cowered her mother's flowers, but howl as it might, the house did not budge. Only neglect could bring it down—an open roof, and no one caring.

"Look!" Munro was running his hands over an outer wall where lichen blossomed like bits of ochre. "Feel the *mass*. It's not like a wooden house going down at all, is it. See that?" Faint marks in the mortar. "Bird tracks."

She touched the wall. Odd what things stones had in them. St. Clements. On Harris, the church in Rodel so old it was worshipped rather than worshipped in. When she and her friend Morag visited there, awed by its stone mysteries inside and out, it was two sculptures that forced their glances as they wandered the wild grass of the grounds, the tombs and graves: high above a door in the east wall were two lewd sandstone effigies, a woman squatting to display her unmistakable cunt (as plain as that) still swollen after four hundred years of blurring wind and water, and balancing her out was a male also embedded in the wall stones, gripping rigidly his huge implement as if he had hold of life itself. What was this lurid couple doing high up the wall of a church, papist though it had been, burial place of MacLeod chiefs? The devil put them there, if you ask me, Morag had said, and Fiona only laughed, knowing better.

"But what bird walks on walls?" Fiona said.

"There are birds you don't know about, my dear Fiona."

His eyes had taken on that abstracted, detached look she noticed the other night. The stones felt cool, like cave rock. She shivered. Munro brought his face close and when she didn't move, he kissed her mouth, her chin.

"They must've been lovely cozy in that house," he whispered.

"How lovely we'll never know," she said.

"We might, we might." He smiled and moved away into the foliage that hugged the ruins. She listened to him pushing through the branches. "They must've had a garden or something here," he called back, his voice muffled in the trees, a different voice than he'd come up the hill with. She wished she had said no, had let him come alone, even that she had come herself alone, for she liked this place, liked the day, the feel of it. She hadn't kissed him, he had kissed her. She liked his mouth and that warm moment before the kiss, his eyes soft and blind, taken up with what was coming, a look she had not seen in so long she wasn't quite sure it was there. Kenneth was younger, a desirable man, a mystery of sorts—and yet not. How could she say what she was after in him? It was something beyond him, something maybe impossible, even unwise, to reach for. She caught again that smoke: a whiff of burnt grass.

Munro called out to her, "Yes there has been a garden!" He was shaking the branches of a tall shrub. "See? Lilac!" At the tips of its bony, dead-gray stalks were dry but visible blossoms, and yes, it was in leaf. Lost in the slender fir trees they found a spindly rose bush too tall to be wild, and further away a single apple tree, hoary but filled with tiny green fruit. "They had flowers here," Munro said, "no doubt about it." Then they nearly stumbled over a low stone wall, disguised by grass, much of it, and what they could make out here and there showed it as an enclosure within which the wild trees had checked their growth, the birches almost thinly decorous, the spruce lightly branched and airy. "How strange," Fiona said. A walled garden behind a small farmhouse like this, in this country, walled not to keep anything out but just to define a place, to contain pleasure. No vegetables in this space, their potatoes and turnips would have ripened elsewhere. How strong the scent of flowers must have been in the midsummer air when the people of the house came walking here, the same people who hauled and chiseled and hoisted those great

194

stones ten feet up for windows and walls. It would have been peaceful, for the men as well as the women, with the fields cleared, the wind off the water. She sat down on a mossy patch of wall and imagined the garden without the invading trees. Daisies bloomed at her feet. What other flowers of their own had they put in the ground? Was it the women of this stone house who planted them? She wanted to think it had been a man, the kind of man who, after grappling with stones in those hard days, would have, with a splayed finger, poked tiny seeds into the dirt of a flower garden.

Munro had knelt behind her and was parting, as he might a curtain, the back of her hair. He kissed her nape, and that was all she felt, just that sensation, unexpected, its surprise moving warm like wine into her face. She closed her eyes and turned her mouth to his. They slid down into the grass outside the wall. His fingers smelled of balsam, and very faintly of the lilac that had brushed him. Yes, the garden, and a coppery evening sun, the wind down, the flowers tense, waiting for the night, birds merging into trees and leaves. She felt the warm sun on her legs, and then his fingers, almost cold so that she tensed and gave into him at the same moment, and it seemed they were sinking gently into the grass, she whispering to him but not words, his mouth hot through the cloth of her blouse as his breath moved down her waist. Then he stopped, his muscles hardening and he sat up out of her arms: "Someone's coming." Her own breath stopped, then she pulled her skirt down and smoothed it over her knees. Who was the someone coming? She didn't move. To flee would look more foolish than lying in the grass, a man on his knees next to you. In her daze she nearly laughed: oh Millie, turning her tongue on them both, fiercely, first at this suspect man who had surely tricked Fiona into the trees, and then at Fiona who would have to be some kind of a thing herself to lie down in the weeds with him in the middle of a working day. Lord, the racket in the teacups, sipping her name, and his, and Harald's. Fiona sat up but stirred no further, nor did Munro while feet tramped nearer and took the forms of Lloyd David and a pal, a taller boy Fiona didn't know, their voices preceding them, earnest but unintelligible in the noise of the leaves and snapping branches as they ducked and staggered through the trees. Lloyd David was holding in his fingers a cigarette butt like a captured bug and the boys paused long enough to share its smoke, taking it gravely to their lips in turn. They were not looking for anyone, were headed elsewhere, heads down, intent, guileless, the woods just something to be got through. They passed within a few yards of Munro and Fiona, stumbling on, oblivious, their bluejeans fading out into the thicker trees.

"He had a bottle in his back pocket, that squirt," Munro said. "God, I thought he was working with Harald."

"He was, this morning. He comes and goes."

Fiona brushed off her skirt and redid two buttons of her blouse, her fingers cool and clumsy. Over on a wall of the stone house a tree shadow swayed like a flame. She stood up: something had both happened and not happened. Munro lay back in the grass, his shirt open. There was a silver medallion in the thick hair of his chest.

"What was it my father used to say?" he said. " 'Hot as Scotch love'?"

She saw in his closed eyes, in their fluttering lids, something of the father in the photo: something that had to be satisfied, but never would be.

"You're looking pleased with yourself," she said. "Does it not bother you a wee bit?"

"Does what?" He got to his feet and climbed on the stones so he could see down the hillside.

"I'm married," Fiona said. "You do know the man. You have met him."

"I like Harald. He's a worker, he is. But what have we done, you and me?"

"Half what we would do, I suppose. Isn't that part of your 'afternoon'?"

"We don't have to make love . . . . if you'd rather not."

"You're an arrogant man, you are. You know I like you, and like the feel of you. But there's an ache I'll carry home with me. I don't think you know anything about that. Do you feel it at all?"

"Feel what?"

"Guilt, they call it around here."

"Over *this*?"

"Somebody could be hurt over this."

"Nobody knows, nobody will. Lloyd David and his buddy were stoned blind." He jumped off the wall and put his face close to

196

hers. "You have beautiful eyes, extraordinary eyes. And listen: I'll be gone in a month, less."

Munro went off down the hill to pick a spot for the next visit. The wind had turned and the weather with it, chilly out of the east, the sun gone behind the rolling gray clouds. Fiona hung back. She picked up a chip of stone. How cold and damp this house must have been at times, here where the winters were so much colder than in Harris, deep frosts and blizzards. The night Harald brought her to St. Aubin it was winter and deeply cold, colder yet to her, a stranger. Harald soon put a fire in the old coal stove and she ran outside yelling into the snow, snow so cold it had bits of blue in it, and she stood there, panicked: a fire like that in a wooden house, wood from sills to rooftree? All she could think of were flames, creeping, then roaring up the walls. She soon enough felt the freezing air, Harald at the back door calling to her, laughing. Wood and paper, she'd thought, that's all this house is. But he came out into the windy snow and put himself around her like a cape. He said you're warmer now, aren't you? Aye, she said, let's go inside.

Munro beckoned to her from a heap of fieldstones in the meadow. "We'll have a picnic down here! Look at the soft grass!" He brushed his hand through it. Fiona wandered down, the chip in her fist.

"In the photograph," she said, "weren't they lying under an apple tree?"

"We're not slaves to the photo. It's the spirit we're after, Fiona. Besides, I've got to have a hand in it. I'm scripting this play. The original afternoon was as easy as living. Anyone can live. The hard part is ours."

A sweep of wind up the hillside brought a few hard, cold drops of rain.

"There were *two* women, in that picture," Fiona said.

"I have the other one," he said. "She's perfect."

Ginny was at the roadside, waiting against a tree. In a full red skirt and white blouse, there was a touch of peasant about her that he liked, the way she hailed him as she shouldered her bag: he might've been driving a bus. Beside him on the seat she was all talk and faint perfume, happy to be released from the restaurant, the duties of food. "Do I smell like a kitchen?" she said, brushing her rich brown hair. He said no, that she smelled like something he had never tasted but had always wanted to.

"You've been smoking, haven't you?" she said.

Munro smiled. He described the stone-house meadow as he drove, how perfect it was, the very place.

"And what happened to your dad's then?"

"Dug up and dispersed. There might be some of it under us right now."

"Gravel?"

"Gravel."

"Kenneth, I'm not sure who I'm supposed to be in this," she said. "The women in the picture were older than I am."

"But not prettier. I consider it a bonus. And you don't have to *be* anyone but yourself. The day will do the rest."

"But I'd like to visit the spot first."

Munro touched a fold of her skirt. "Of course. We'll go up there today."

Ginny said nothing more until they had turned onto the main highway at South Gut, passing the big motel that looked up the bay. Its restaurant's windows were cluttered with tourists and they reminded her somehow of busy chickens, feeding away, packed into that one place and cocking their heads now and then at the country around them.

"I should've worn jeans," she said, "if we're going in grass."

Munro accelerated up the mountain highway, praying the weather would hold.

Perfect? What did he mean?

Maybe he had said it only to get a rise out of her.

Fiona had not seen Munro up at his house since yesterday. To-night the comet was due. Was he there and she'd missed his car? She picked up the phone. No. A foolish schoolgirl, wanting to hear his voice, thick with sleep even this late in the morning. What did other women do when a certain man set them wondering? Dream it out?

She set about dusting the parlor, but suddenly she flung the feather duster to the floor. What a silly object, and how silly she felt bustling around with it. Was there really another woman in this? Did he mean beauty? Youth? Someone more inclined to be the way he wanted? When they had parted that day, Fiona said yes, maybe she would meet him again at the stone house when the weather was to his liking, and it would be another step, her life into his. But a kind of acting, for a day, part of a day. And what would she say afterward, to herself, to him? Something would be altered for good. She liked being in his arms, no lie there. He was a different man and she could not get the details of him out of her mind, those she knew and those she might. Two days since they talked and she missed him, even the complication the sight of him brought.

But this other woman? Where? Fiona could not conjure her up. Why did he insist on this fantasy when common sense would tell him that his father was not out sporting with two women that afternoon, that surely there had been another man behind the lens of that camera? He couldn't wish him away, though perhaps he could smoke him away.

Kenneth had told her what the comet might look like, but her anticipation was not celestial. They would be up there alone. She would know before long whether she would go with him down below the stone house and be arranged in the grass according to an old photo, where Kenneth would be hoping to find what he was after, old moments he knew little about.

From the kitchen window she could see Harald starting in on the lower and last field, the felled hay a wake of darker green following him toward the shore. She knew the look he would be wearing: absorbed, contented, a slight smile as he rocked along in the sun, calm as a boatman. By the time he was done for the day it would be near dark, and later she would spot him in the hayloft, the bare light bulb throwing shadows around him.

Did Kenneth mean the *two* of them, to have herself and that nameless woman, both . . . ?

Fiona went out to her flower bed and weeded furiously, panting with amazement, trying to will images out of her mind before they dizzied her daft. My lover? *Mo gràdh?*

After lunch she walked up to the mailbox. Millie pulled up slowly in her car and spoke out the window.

"They caught a bunch of smugglers last night," she said, out of breath as if she'd been running instead of driving. "Along the north shore. Drugs, bales of it."

Fiona sorted through letters. "Anyone we know, Millie?"

"They were Americans, wouldn't you know! The ones behind it. And mainlanders."

Fiona could feel what was coming. Her cheeks were already hot and she ripped open an ad for weedkiller instead of looking at Millie.

"Well, anyway," Millie said. She revved the engine a little. "What about that Munro fellow over there? What did you find?"

Fiona nearly said I found your son in the woods and he wasn't hunting rabbits. "He'll be going home soon, Millie, so don't concern yourself."

She took her anger into the house, anger with herself, with everything. Not the day to have run into Millie Patterson. She banged around upstairs, cleaning their bedroom that did not need it. This was a big house but why did it seem so small, so cramped? Soon she was standing at the picture window: its view was clean and wide and took in miles up and down the strait. The water lay out blue and sheer on a slack tide. Without meaning to, she was staring at that part of the mountain where she had been with him. She could see the patch of field, and some flicker of movement there, deer, or dogs. She reached for Harald's field glasses, the powerful ones he spotted ships with. She moved the circle of vision up and down until she found them. Kenneth, for sure. And a girl with him. Kenneth was jogging ahead, towing her along by the hand. They'd soon be breathless at that clip. But she was young. And he young enough yet to take a hill on a beautiful afternoon. She watched them tumble into the grass and lie there like children, their arms flung open to the sky. Was he handing her something, like a flower? It was not a flower. Fiona was aware of her own eyes against the glasses, of the weight of them in her hands, and she set them back on the sill. Munro and the girl were up and running now, flecks of color on the green hill, but she didn't care to look at them any closer again. They'd be heading for the stone house, for the lovely ruins of the garden. You're making a mistake, she wanted to tell this girl, you don't know that man at all. But how stupid: Fiona did not know him either, and the girl was free to be foolish if she wished. And what did that girl, so much younger than herself, see in Kenneth Munro? What made her take his hand and disappear into the trees of that mountain? When they parted, what would she take away? Humbled that she had no answers, Fiona stepped back into the shadow of the room, a vague ache in her chest. Along the shoreline, Harald's tractor was passing against the strait, rocking like a boat over the uneven ground, while, unknown to him, Lloyd David danced a distance behind, spinning in circles, flinging cut hay into the air like flowers.

"Are you coming up to Kenneth Munro's? The comet is on." Fiona stood over Harald in his easy chair. "It's a right clear evening for it." She half wanted him to say yes because that might make things easier but he said no, and her heart shifted. "I'm whacked out, dear. Anyway, what's come of your investigation up there? Was the man inhaling terrible fumes or what was he doing?"

"There's nothing there Millie need fash herself about, or anyone else either," she said with more heat than she'd intended.

Harald smiled. "I just wondered where the comets might be coming from."

"That's more than I can say. Where do they usually?"

"Oh, I guess there's all kinds," Harald said, getting up.

Fiona glanced through the curtains. "That comet, it won't come around again for sixty years," she said.

Harald kissed her as he passed. "Then we'll both miss the next one. Eh?"

She skirted the house where he'd left the lamp on, briefly annoyed that he would carelessly burn a light all day while he was off with the girl who was perfect. It illuminated the table by the front window where he did his reading and snacking, and smoking too, no doubt. Out back on the big rock the telescope waited, a spindly silhouette in the deep blue of the night. He had aimed it where he figured the comet would appear, not in the direction of the stone house but somewhere over the westerly woods. The smell of the mown grass lifted with the wind. Frogs in the spring pond chirped like sleepy birds but they were well awake. In the humid nights of the last week she had heard them shrill at the fitful corners of her sleep. The telescope trembled on its thin legs and she steadied it, startled by the cold metal. He wasn't coming.

She tried the back door and of course it was open. Hadn't she herself told him you needn't lock up here like you would in San

Francisco? She moved slowly through the darkened kitchen and its spicy smell she didn't recognize, into the lighted living room where his things lay about as he'd left them, trench coat tossed across the sofa (it smelled of the rain he'd worn it in), a few empties of Old Scotia Ale on the table, reeking of stale malt, a dinner plate holding two bits of butt-ends (how could he have smoked them to nubs like that? She flicked her tongue over her lips). She thumbed through his bird book, noted the kinds he'd checked off in the index. Had he really seen a Tennessee Warbler? She had never heard of one, but then he saw things here that she did not, perhaps could not, without smoking those leaves. There was visible dust on the bureau and she ran her finger through it, tempted to write him a mischievous message but realizing she had passed that stage with him. She hefted the walking stick he had whittled from a driftwood branch. Stacked neatly were letters in a woman's hand but she did not disturb them. A magnifying glass, a book about stargazing, a jar of peanuts uncapped. Harald would distrust this sort of leisure. What Harald was not using he put away in sheds or chests or closets. He would never surround himself with things as idle as these. There were no leavings of his pleasure for others to peruse. But Kenneth's were all over this house. And there was the photograph.

Stretched out in the grass, stripped to the waist of his baggy trousers, the father looks somehow naked. The women's bare legs are sexy in a way now lost, Fiona thinks. A bottle of liquor is propped against the apple tree. The tree needs pruning badly. All those years he had been under his mother's stern and jealous eye, but today no one watches him from the house. And the land, now his, is turning wild. He is free to drink inside the house or out, to play in the unruly grass of his own fields, to ignore the decaying roof, the spoor of hunters (surely that's their work—the splintered door, the riddled pail), the stealthy trees new in the distance. He's free, as dusk comes down, to steal back toward his old bedroom where wind sighs through shot-out windows, his shoes crunching over glass, a finger to his lips, mocking his mother's prohibitions. Drink, drink, drink, he wants to shout in the dark hallway, the woman behind him hugging his back, giggling with a fear she hardly understands, there in that summer twilight that smells of damp and age. He cups his ear. He pretends, for a laugh, that his mother lies listening down the hall. And of course she does, even now; years after her death she is still in this house, and even on the slashed stuffing of his old mattress, in a desolate smell of winter and wet cotton where he makes the kind of noises he never dared, like love in a storm, he feels her hard rain on his back. And this his son will never know, will never see.

Fiona turned out the light.

On the rock, she put her eye to the telescope, holding down her skirt. Kenneth said it would have no fizzing tail, it wasn't that kind of comet. Far from flashing across the sky, its motion seemed little more than a waver, like a star, just brighter, more restless and low in the sky. Wasn't just the word charged with speed and color? Was it something like that he got from his smoke, from that brittle smell? The comet flared, south of west. She let her skirt go, the gusts took it away from her legs and whipped it about. If she turned the telescope toward the stone house, she wouldn't see anything now but the cold, yawning walls, heavy as dreams.

When she got into bed, she lay looking out the big window at the end of the room. Harald stirred beside her. "Did you see it?" he said. Fiona could tell from his voice that he'd been sleeping.

"The tail was magnificent. Fiery. The way you'd think it would be."

"Streaked across the sky, did it?"

"No," she said. "No, it took longer than that."

Harald touched her face, then turned back into sleep.

She remembered waking one cold, cold February morning, unaware that Harald had wakened too. From their pillows they could see that the water of the Great Bras D'Eau had vanished, become a long white field. The men had not laid down a bushline yet but someone was crossing the new ice anyway, a woman, making her way slowly over the rough snow of the surface, her trail as fragile as a bird's. Her danger seemed to enter the room, and they watched her, she and Harald, saying nothing about her, this dark, tiny figure. They never saw where she came ashore, and they never found out what woman she was, coming so early, and finding her own way across.

Nominated by John Daniel, Ehud Havazelet, Norman Lavers, TriQuarterly.

TO WRITE OF
REPEATED PATTERNS

by ALBERT GOLDBARTH

from THE IOWA REVIEW

THEY SAY HE'S 16. They say in the dead of the night—they really *do* say this, "the dead of the night"—he sneaks to the attic, planned or unplanned nobody yet knows, he lifts his daddy's "squirrel gun" from its case, then sneaks back down with it, carefully opens the door to the room in which they're sleeping, and blasts them out of this life, one shot to the temple each, in quick succession. The neighbors are interviewed, ". . . shocked" ". . . a *wonderful* boy" ". . . he *loved* his parents." Then the camera brings him into its painfully clear-edged imagery. He's seated behind a desk at headquarters, confused by himself, by everything and everyone. He doesn't look over 12, a limp rag doll of a child, being questioned for parricide.

Skyler and I are at Sarah's and Eric's. "Change the channel!" What we'd wanted was mild diversion floating in over our afternoon beers. There's TV snow and lightningbolts; then, a couple of numbers up or down the dial, the news is into its loonier wrap-up phase: "There was three of them, three feet high. They were green." A trucker spotted them trotting down a playground-slideish gangplank "from a silver ship. It looked like, you know. . ." ". . . A shark's fin fitted with lateral wings," the one other observer, a priest, chimes in. A *priest*? "They peered around, returned to the ship, and took off. That's all. I think they were trying to bring us a *message*."

Tonight, while Skyler's asnooze, I'm up with a book. It says, in the voice of classical lamentation, "A man looks on his own son as his enemy. The heart is aggressive, blood is everywhere, no office functions properly. The rich wake poor, the poor wake rich, the land whirls around like a potter's wheel." Verily. The television yeasayeth this with every snoopy camcorder shot of a Presidential rally or a weekend convention of skateboard and dirtbike enthusiasts. Some group of PTA sex education fanatics, costumed á la birds and bees. Some show of support for a local pastor in jail on charges of fondling a 10-year-old girl. The remains of an airliner: yes, a three member suicide squadron smuggled a plastic gun on board in six unrecognizable segments. "Everywhere men are killed wrongfully."

This text, however, is from the Egyptian Old Kingdom—2500 B.C. Some nights—this isn't the first time I've consulted it after overmuch media brouhaha—its cannily contempo applicability leaves me shaking my head in a bleary wonder, blinking my eyes not so much at a world gone mad (which would, at least, be an adventure) but a world that's always been, and is continually, mad.

I may as well also admit that Skyler and I have squabbled. I'm downstairs reading inside an invisible bubble of self-righteousness. She's upstairs in bed, and emanating waves of anger out of her body, regular convection currents the instruments would pick up as scarlets and indigos. We'll make up soon— tomorrow, most likely. We'll add our latest display of this commonest syndrome to its history. We've done it before, the billions before us have done it before, the tiffing couples on pleasure barges beached along the Nile have had their ritual version of skirmish-and-smooch, and some nights when I finally tamp myself under the sheets beside her, I see we're two strokes of an all-over pattern repeated—past where sight thins out—across the fabric of being human, or being alive at all.

*

If I'm going to write of repeated patterns, let me mention the relatively well-known mid-12th century report of William of Newburgh, about "an unheard-of prodigy, which took place during the reign of King Stephen." Incredible though its details are, he

205

"was so overwhelmed by the weight of so many and such competent witnesses" that he feels, finally, "no regret at having recorded an event so miraculous."

By a village of East Anglia, at harvest time, two children
emerged from "some very ancient cavities" near the fields, where
the reapers found them wandering in a daze—"a boy and a girl,
completely green in their persons, and clad in garments of a
strange colour, and unknown materials."

They couldn't speak English; for months they ate only raw
beans from the pod, "until they learned the use of bread. At
length, by degrees, they changed their original colour, through
the natural effect of our food, and became like ourselves."
(*reader, let a bell go off*)

Then they told a story of having been whisked here from "the
land of St. Martin" where the sun doesn't rise, and all is perpetual twilight, but the countryfolk are Christian. They were tending their father's flocks when they both "heard a great sound . . .
we became on a sudden entranced, and found ourselves among
you in the fields."

The boy died not long after. His sister "continued in good
health" and "was married at Lynne, and was living a few years
since."

This isn't the earliest sighting of green otherpeople by any
means, but something in its narrative and phrasing gives it the
first truly modern *cachet*. It's tempting to think of it as the
patriarch-story (siblingarch-story, really) from which an anecdotal
family of wünderkind and aliens descend, yet it's more properly
just one very fine retelling in a line of tellings immeasurably
long.

Eight hundred years away from William of Newburgh, I pick
up one of those supermarket tabloids devoted to cheap astonishment. June 12, 1990: MOM ON VEGGIE DIET GIVES BIRTH
TO GREEN BABY. " 'Even the whites of his eyes are pale green,'
notes stunned Dr. Dominic Valenso." He's the cover story, staring
out at me cute and gooing. He's printed in no inconclusive hint of
light lime, but a deep and even St.-Paddy's-Day-green inked
freely from a tube that's labeled *Shamrock*. " 'It'll take some
time, but with a well-balanced diet the baby should lose the
green color eventually,' Dr. Valenso promises." (*reader, does this*

ring a bell?) Meanwhile, "teary-eyed mom Consuela Alvarez" wrings her lovely cocoa-colored caucasian hands.

*

I've zeroed it down to that handful of seconds of TV sputter while Sarah was switching channels. Before that, everything was copacetic. Right after, Skyler started with those only-Albert-can-recognize-them petulant glances that—well, but she'd have another version. I brought up subject x or y; I cranked on into my supercilious mode, with that look I beam out by tilting my head down and glaring *over* the rims of my glasses . . .

The truth is, neither one of us has a clue as to why we've suddenly lowered the interpersonal temperature of our house to that of a meat-locker. There's no issue being battled. Ideas of right and wrong aren't at stake. We only know we brought a sliver of coolness home from Sarah's and Eric's, and managed to fan the thing—a snideness here, a willful misinterpretation there—into a berg.

This "isn't like us." We're normally sweet in our love, and sane. In a truce of a few talky minutes' duration before bed, Skyler says, "I think we've been taken over by outerspace beings. I can feel it. They're growing some gunk in our heads. Seeds." She's really *into* it now. "If our heads were sliced open they'd look like cantaloupes: all those alien seeds in the center."

So that's when it happened, I'm theorizing: the TV fizz was an interdimensional portal, through which the little green creatures from Planet Unimaginable grabbed hold of our unwary minds. That way, the two of us aren't at fault. That way, external agency as large as science fiction bears the blame.

And I mean it, too, if by the formulation "little green creatures" I get to mean our reptilian selves, that were there in the primal underdrift of our brains before our brains were even undifferentiated plasm laboring toward shape—our gilled and serpent-tailed lizard selves, our circulating of cold blood through the rockbottom saurian folds.

*

What I'd like to do now is remind you of some 14th-century narrative goings-on. The scene is Christmastide at Camelot, and at

207

the Round Table *with all the meat and the mirth that men could devise* are Arthur, *the comeliest king,* and his courtly followers, *the most noble knights known under Christ, and the loveliest ladies that lived on earth ever.* All is ceremonially festive. Their initial course is served, to the accompaniment of trumpets, drums and *noble pipes,* and all of the world seems good and in order to these good, orderly personages, but—*scarce were the sweet strains still in the hall* when *there hurtles in at the hall-door an unknown rider.* Larry D. Benson says, "the action is suddenly suspended, and over ninety lines are devoted to a carefully detailed portrait."

Put simply, the man is *oureal enker grene,* entirely green. His lavish beard is green. His *raiment noble* is green; the ermine mantle, the hood, the hose, the spurs, the belt and its bosses, the saddle—*all his vestiture verily (is) verdant green* and he rides *a green horse great and thick.* A tang of wildness radiates like green aurora borealis, emerald, celadon, flickering poplar. Something hugely out of the ordinary is glowering over the roast.

There hurtles in at the hall-door. . . .   In the still of this civilized gathering, it must be as if an interdimensional portal—*zzzt!*—has opened wide.

*

By its own Middle English audience, the aspect of the Green Knight in *Sir Gawain and the Green Knight*—or the facets of his aspect—would have been easily read. A literary figure himself, he incorporates stock folk art figures that trail back, by ballad and creaking tavern sign, to some preliterate origin lost in green fog.

The "green man" is a "wild man"—Benson says "in folk ritual they are interchangeable." Here, at the court of Arthur, the clues are clanked onstage: the intruder is rude in speech and in action, he brandishes an axe, his look is savage and it culminates in that formidable beard, as *big as a bush on his breast,* the poet says, referring us to the color again. And Benson: "In medieval art the wild man often wears both hair and leaves." He is stern, perhaps hostile, and "the enemy of the knight and the opponent of the values represented by the romance courts."

At the same time, the figure in green is Youth (I was a fresh-man, green at the game myself, when I first encountered the poem) and, not surprisingly, Nature in benign guise. In *The Parlement of the Thre Ages*, Youth is *gerede alle in grene*. "One finds the same green-clad figure throughout fourteenth-century literature"—vital, sweet to look upon, laughing musically into the breeze—and, by uncomplicated association, the figure comes to be symbolic of love, of springtime foliage, finally of Life itself. In the 14th-century work *Le Songe vert*, the narrator contemplates suicide, swoons, but then is revived by Venus and her attendants, and clothed by them *entire de vert*. In *Death and Life*, the latter figure is *comlye clad in kirtle and mantle of goodliest greene that euer groome ware*.

If you subscribe to a full year of a supermarket tabloid, it's those same opposing twins you'll meet in alternate issues, repeat-edly: the evil aliens bent on enslavement, nabbing up late-night drivers from behind the wheel, strapping them onto the tables of weirdly-wired Martian-scientific surgery; and the aliens of light, of peace (I think of the dove descending with the green sprig in its beak), they bring advice, and hope, they bear the shoots of other, older worlds, by which a new green Eden will blossom for us in our soil and in our hearts.

*

We can follow these figures through time along unbroken vines, the figures themselves now tuber-like, below our daily notice, and now bunched up in splashy clumps.

It seems unquestionable that the wild man, the representor of everything feral lurking inside green shadow (or: in am/bush), is a presence of unfathomably ancient creation. Cain, the farmer and fratricide, is his ancestor. So is Enkidu the beast-man, foe at first and then the blood-brother of King Gilgamesh: we see him on cylinder-seals battling lions no more lushly maned than he is, and often this battle is formulaically rendered to look more like the ballroom whorl of happy partners. How far back does he go, this figure? How far back do our psyches extend?

As a character with a number of type associations, the wild man "survived among the peasantry of continental Europe well into the nineteenth century" (Benson), and a study titled *Homo Sapiens Ferus* (1988) reports "A girl of nine or ten years entered the village of Songy at dusk. Her feet were naked, her body was covered with rags and skins of animals. She wore a piece of bottle-gourd on her head. She carried a club in her hand, and when someone in the village set a dog at her she gave it such a heavy blow on the head that the animal fell over dead at her feet." The threatening pod people lurching amok in s-f movies are cousins to her, the scaly and often antenna'ed creatures that stalk the streets of our fairest cities, the green blob/slime that carries whole groups of supporting actors and extras out of party scenes in its oozy amoeboid grip.

Likewise, the life-bestowing vegetable god precedes the Green Knight by millennia, but the two are in alliance, leafy link by link. Tammuz, consort of Ishtar and annual bringer of renewal to the Babylonian fields. Osiris, who fertilized Egypt by using his own dismembered body for seeds, who therefore tends to reviving the dead amidst the Sacred Lotus Fields of Eternity. Their largesse, over time, becomes the wealth that's redistributed by a green-outfitted Robin Hood, quartered in his arboreal hold—or Tarzan of the Apes, in whom the law of fang and claw becomes transmuted to the vehicle of our rescue: out of the heavens, out of the thickly bough-canopied heavens, on his magic liana, he'll arc low, lofting us up from our direst moment.

The same green-chapleted face that peers down from the corbeled arch of a 13th-century chapel smiles winningly when pushing canned peas and green beans in The Valley of the Jolly (HO-HO-HO) Green Giant (who would later, with the growing kiddie audience in mind, be awarded the youthful sidekick Sprout). It isn't much of a secret that Jung washes clean for us, out of the murk of the ages: "Green is the color of the Holy Ghost, of life, procreation and resurrection."

Frazer, in *The Golden Bough*, details numerous "leaf-clad May Day mummers"—the Leaf King, the Grass King, Jack-in-the Green. . . . Ronald Johnson quotes Lewis Spence: "I have seen him at South Queensferry . . . where he is known as the 'Burry Man,' a boy on whose clothes large numbers of burrs or seedcases have been so closely sewn that he presents the appearance of a moving mass of vegetation."

In Kenneth Koch's kookily feisty poem "Fresh Air," the stifled spirit of 1950s American poetry—all too hangdog and dyspeptic—

is saved from its enemies in the halls of publishing houses and universities, by a breath of sexual fervor, intuitive consciousness, and unchained craziness, blowing in over the green of the ocean: "O green, beneath which all of them shall drown!"

*

Nobody knows what to think. No, make that: *everybody* knows what to think. It simply isn't the same thought.

In the days that follow his being booked on murder charges, Vonnie Coleman, 16, is become a *cause célèbre*, and certain do-good groups are organized in his defense. He's young, his face has a ruggedly puppydog power that attracts, and encourages kindness. There are rumors that the father was in debt to local hoods, and Vonnie became the easy fall guy. His various versions of that night conflict. His so-called confession was hammered together, after all, from the splinters of trauma. Anyway, if he *did* pull the trigger, the rumors say that his parents abused him and photographed it. What about the legal rights of underage suspects? Much media flap.

It doesn't help, however, that his fingerprints are coating the gun. Killing one's parents in sleep takes on a grisliness unnatural even in houses long accommodated to TV reportage of running blood. If the average result of the average roving reporter is to be believed, our average Joe-and-Jane-in-the-street would like to see Vonnie Coleman brought to trial as an adult, and have him sentenced to being eaten alive by rats, an inch or two a day, until only the flesh of his head is with us, begging mercy, and then the rats start at his mouth.

But for my friends and myself, the tragedy and its grievous components are part of a picture so large, we can't look at Vonnie Coleman except through a historyscope or mythologyscope— and, caught in this focus, he takes his place in a sad continuum sized to the cosmos we live in. He dips sharply out of our consciousness for a couple of hours, then sneakily stitches back in. A day is made of its zillion-and-umpteen stitches, joyous, tormenting, whatever; in the immediate moment, any one of them, half-a-brainwave long, can knock our breath into orbit and drop us to our knees. They're like the stones comprising those

211

"Nazca lines" in Peru—you need to see them from an airplane's height, and *then* there's a chameleon or monkey or star, a meaningful pattern.

At PANDORA'S BOX! EXOTIC DANCERS! I buy a lady called Angel a drink when her set is over. Onstage, she threw sexual heat like an opened furnace. Now, she nearly cowers inside the minimal spandex bands of some chartreuse excuse-of-a-costume. She says, "His face is so innocent. *I* know he didn't do it! And if he did, then we should give him money, you know, government money, and let him start a new life in a different country, don't you think?" I think we should have five minutes of the innocently flirtatious discussion I'd guessed her overpriced drink would buy. But she's heard all the stories, including mine. I know: there are only so many stories.

Later, on my way out, a guy says, "Start by chopping off the sonofabitch's trigger finger. Then his gun hand. Then the arm. I'd like to make my own kid watch that, so he'd learn."

Outside—a patron's left his car lights on, who knows how long? It reminds me, somehow, of Vonnie's face as the cameras always deliver it: his eyes wide open, the rest of him blank, and beams of useless energy I can't understand are burning out into the void.

We've seen this face before: this isn't our first broadcasted pathos. This is Vonnie's face, is Vonnie Coleman's specific face, who could be you or me but for genetic dice in Chance's hands. Yet we can see that this face is cut from a template: the face has preceded the boy, the face will remain when he's only a thimble of elements spilled out, recombining.

*

Confusion can be useful.

For instance: the casserole of opposite meanings attached to the Green Knight, Benson finds an intentional "ambiguity (that is) part of the Green Knight's essential character." Merry, then scowling; intruder and, later, host; unappeasable fiend but, in a snap, indulgent friend—"the poet," says Benson, "capitalizes on this ambiguity . . . taking care that his audience remains unsure of whether the green implies good or evil until the very end of the romance."

212

And what these seemingly conflicting meanings have, at bottom, in common is the Green Knight's utter otherness. As Benson claims, "he comes from another world altogether." Saviour or nemesis; citizen of our own psychological shadows or sudden visitor from some "actual" but undiscovered kingdom; nature in all of its howling fury or nature in all of its mysterious verdant nurturing . . . the green is an economy for stating all of these and more, at once—because, no matter the immediate nuance, above all else the Green Knight "always represents a mode of life completely opposed to that represented by (Gawain)."

You betcha. That humongoid presence equestrienned there in the light of the sconces, his skin the color of spinach leaves. Whatever we are, he's else.

In Henry Reed's lyrical novel *The Green Child*, published in 1935, the title character is in many ways a different creature wholly from that figure hulking enormously into Camelot 800 years before: a slim defenseless girl, a foundling, she grows up into a slim defenseless woman, with "the same ageless innocent features" informing her countenance now, as in her childhood. Wraithlike. Fey.

Distinctions notwithstanding, though, her lineage is the green warrior's. Her "skin was not white, but a faint green shade, the colour of a duck's egg. It was, moreover, an unusually transparent tegument, and through its pallor the branches spread, not blue and scarlet, but vivid green. . . ." And what this betokens, obviously, is someone from an Earth that's not *our* Earth—from "a mode of life completely opposed," as Benson puts it. Reed: "The psychology of the Green Child was a different matter; in a sense, it did not exist."

I say: in a sense it's always existed, parallel to our own, and it will clatter through the castle's staunch portcullis when we least expect.

*

Green can't be more "other" than as elvin-green, the leafy and briery hiding-places of troll and of gnome, often their skin color too (think quick of the witch in *The Wizard of Oz*); when the Green Knight first bursts into Arthur's stronghold, *phantom and faerie the folk there deemed* that startling being.

213

We're talking pointed ears and impossible laws of physics, we're talking magic rings and chariots drawn by caparisoned mice. In a way, then, the alliance of "green otherness" with fairy lore is its consummate expression.

Or: its consummate expression at a given moment. We live in another moment. This is why Michell and Rickard say: "The little people who, by unanimous report, played an intrusive part in daily life up to the Middle Ages, had long been dwindling from their accustomed haunts when suddenly they reappeared, airborne and technologized and up to all their same old tricks. We refer of course to the 'UFO people.' We take this connection seriously. For modern accounts of fairies and the like we must turn to such books as *Flying Saucer Occupants* and *The Unidentified*, where a common phenomenal source for both the fairy and the UFO legend is emphasized."

It's not much more than a matter of adding "atomic propulsion" or "hyper-drive" or "star thrust" into the fairies' forges. Ronald Johnson, describing one more variant of the traditional May Day "green man" figure: "In former times he was also marched in the London Lord Mayor Day's Parade enclosed in a wooden framework on which leaves were clustered and from which came explosions of fireworks." (Picture it landing.) "Chimney sweeps paraded beneath the same pyramidal frameworks on May Day until the nineteenth century. One imagines them coming like small boxwood topiary, crackling and sparkling through the streets."

(Imagine the "sparkling" stopping, the engine turned off. Imagine them removing their helmets. They venture from the craft. They're saying—what are they saying?—can you make it out?—"Take me to your. . ."—then garble.)

And *their* world, what it's like?—we'll never know. We only have *our* language for it, and that's by definition insufficient. I can give you Dorothy's first view of The Emerald City, however: "The window panes were of green glass; even the sky above the City had a green tint, and the rays of the sun were green. There were many people, men, women and children, walking about, and these were all dressed in green clothes and had greenish skins. At one place a man was selling green lemonade, and when the children bought it Dorothy could see that they paid for it with green pennies."

Here, *she's* the alien. She's come in her frightening flying machine (a standard Kansas farmhouse). " 'What do you wish here in the Emerald City?' 'We came here to see the Great Oz,' said Dorothy." She wants to meet their leader.

*

Reed's *The Green Child* takes its inspiration from a version of the same folk tale William of Newburgh reports—the brother and sister stumbling dazed from the pits, their eating of the beans, the girl's eventual adventures among humankind (in Reed's chosen version, she marries a knight "and was rather loose and wanton in her conduct"). From this green seed his novel flourishes, the children now found wandering in the year 1830, the girl become a water nymph—a naiad—instead of a forest figure: at story's end, she and its human hero sink together "hand in hand . . . below the surface of the pool," those watery recesses being as "other" a realm as the warrens below a fairy knoll.

I first read William of Newburgh's account in John Carey's smart anthology *Eyewitness to History*: 700 pages of first-hand reportage that go from plague in ancient Athens, to the fleeing of President Marcos from the Philippines in 1982. In his introduction, Carey makes the savvy, persuasive case that we can "view reportage as the natural successor to religion."

He reminds us of the constant all-pervadingness of "the media" in our lives; then: "if we ask what took the place of reportage in the ages before it was made available to its millions of consumers, the likeliest answer seems to be religion. Not, of course, that we should assume pre-communication-age man was deeply religious, in the main. There is plenty of evidence to suggest he was not. But religion was the permanent backdrop to his existence"—and, as reportage currently "supplies modern man with a constant and reassuring sense of events going on beyond his immediate horizon" and with "a release from his trivial routines, and a habitual daily illusion of communication with a reality greater than himself," it's easy to see (among many other revealed connections) our tabloidbabble servicing us the way the wonderworking tales of charlatan relic-peddlers must have, once.

If we admit the fairy denizens—the green-girdled, pipestootling, impishly tricks-playing Pucks and Pans of the whispered tales—are truly the residua of ancient gods, diminished but refusing to be hooked totally off the psychic stage . . . then we can see our saucermen, yes and Consuela Alvarez's celery-dermis boy-child, as the permutations of raw needs and faint glimmerings of understandings that cycle with steadfast fixity through the surface burble-and-flux of human history.

Skyler and I have "made up"—tonight there's the ritual smooching. All of the details some aspiring short-story-writer might observe and scribble into an entry book—the gooey pet names, the shared reserve of reference-cues that trigger giggling, the hundred niknak specifics through the room—are ours, are ours alone, and we've toiled long in their compilation. But who would deny the case that our love, as much as our sorrows, reenacts the patterns we're part of, inevitably, from cloverleafs and infinity-signs of submolecular needlepoint, to red-shift, supergalaxy, Big Bang universe swoosh? A flush. A fondle.

Jung relates our deities with our bug-eyed extraterrestrials: "In the threatening situation of the world today, when people are beginning to see that everything is at stake, the projection-creating fantasy soars beyond the realm of earthly organizations and powers into the heavens, into interstellar space, where the rulers of human fate, the gods, once had their abode in the planets."

Reed, with one apt metaphor, connects his water nixie—she of the aqueous depths—with skyscape: at the last, when she returns to her pool after thirty years passed among humans, "her face was transfigured," the narrator tells us, "radiant as an angel's."

*

But Tasha Coleman, 15, doesn't want to hear that the pain in her heart is part of a graphable, overgoverning schema of repetitions. She really does say it that way, "There's a pain," and she points with a wickedly polished but raggedly chewed-at nail, "in my heart." Her face in the TV screen is so very hurt it's barely composed into faceness, and it seems to shimmer in front of us, is more like the reflection of a face, in trembled water.

She had spent the night at a girlfriend's home. She woke up on a different Earth, Earth-X, a world where her parents are dead and her older brother ("I love him still" and she makes another

216

heart-tap) is supposedly their murderer. I don't imagine sleep will ever be the same for her again. Or being awake, for that matter. Do they let her walk through the house? What does she think, approaching that bedroom door? "Think" may not be the word for it; what she *feels*, though, she's said—a pain in her heart. I believe it's a "real" physical excruciation she's talking about, is something like a fish hook stitched beneath the cardiac skin.

And she won't stand your hi-falutin' b.s. or mine about the general shape of pain, and its many guises including the Greek myths blah blah blah. She's had it up to here and we can just go fuck ourselves. The only thing she has in the world right now is that pain, in the back-and-forth threads of nucleic jelly in every cell of Tasha Coleman: that pain. There's no assuagement, but at least she has the knowledge that her pain is monumentally singular, never before such agony and never again, and she doesn't want one syllable that will deprive her of this, so take your chart of literary motifs, shove hard, and waddle on home with your butt clamped tight around it.

Later on, I suspect, she'll turn to one of those larger shapes for comforting. An example: in 1945, when *Amazing Stories* published a "factual" article by Richard Shaver, an exposé of the civilization that lives inside our (hollow) Earth, the number of letters from readers leaped from 40 a month to 2,500 and stayed that way for the next four years while the Shaver reports continued. In the Earth live "Deros," evil creatures whose "tech machines" shoot rays that cause our wars and traffic accidents, our cancer and our sexual dysfunction. When "a hobo is arrested while attempting to wreck a train because a 'voice' directed the action"?—*Deros at work!* Like Satan's minions, they relieve us— they relieve a Vonnie Coleman—of a pure responsibility.

Or maybe Tasha will join up with the saucer-spotting priest, awaiting The Grand Arrival, the day salvation will simply be handed over to us, no questions asked, and those who want can leave this vale of suffering in the rounded titanium belly of the Mother Ship. In this cosmology, Jesus Christ is the greatest extraterrestrial of all.

She'll see it—that Organizational Shapes, recurrent matrices, cannot be escaped. They form a unity on macrolevels as surely as

217

we're the momentary cohering of subatomic particles, dot and wave, that dance their stately pavanes in the least of our gestures.

She'll see it—but not now. Now, she walks at night through the house she was born in, whimpering at its familiarity, stopping a moment to feel her own self beat like an ocean in storm at her own self's borders, and clutching—actually pantomiming clutching—her pain to her breast.

I'm going to stretch next to Skyler tonight and love her with all of the luck we've been given (so far) and I suggest you set down this page and do that with somebody too.

Who *is* it we see when we look in the mirror, that rounds the weary corners of our own eyes, furtively, gone in an instant? *Wild man, mild man, monster, saint.*

*

This began with the Egyptian Old Kingdom, 2500 B.C., and it can end there well enough. I have a textbook of "religious art through the centuries," and it starts with the wingèd *ka*—a form of soul—as it flutters over a Pharaoh inside the tomb. It looks like a fledgling hawk, though with the head of a human: the face is concerned.

Many pages later, there's a sample of Marc Chagall's *Message Biblique*. Perhaps you know it: the world, the sky, are done from a palette of pinks, an urgent damask, a more rougey pastel, the range of rose and pouting shell-lip, pink, all pink. And through these heavens glides a single angel bearing a candelabrum. All of the suffering she's seen becomes the accentlines of her eyes and mouth, with a tenderness. Her face is deeply green: against such pink, she's like green fire.

Is it a prayer? I don't know; it's annealing.

Nominated by David Baker, Stephen Corey, Stephen Dunn, Kent Nelson

THE FIRST SIX SEALS

by DAVID WOJAHN

from POETRY NORTHWEST

THE FIRST SIX SEALS

*"I saw a scroll. It had writing on both sides and was
sealed with seven seals. . ."*

—Revelation 5:1

SEAL I.
THE THREE CHRISTS OF YPSILANTI

All three Christs in a locked room for a year—sharing meals.
A daily "business meeting," conducted, of course,
To *Robert's Rules of Order.* Each session commences
With a different song: *"Blue Moon," "Yankee Doodle."*
Never hymns, for they spark untherapeutic
Theological debates, which leave each Christ
Exhausted. Tonight they talk back to a TV set
Bolted to the wall. Joseph screams Leon's "a her-e-tic"
Who'll burn for watching *Sea Hunt, Milton Berle.*
Leon Almighty, Clyde Christus Est, Joseph Hallowed-
Be-Thy Name. Pre-Thorazine and manic, their godhead
Is degenerative. The experiment will fail.
For what could shame them into human form? Joseph bewails
Another lost Yahtzee game. Leon, scowling, changes channels.

SEAL II.
THE PROPHECY

"Then Mrs. Clark received the final message,
Spoken to us from her trance: prepare for the saucer

219

To land at midnight by the patio. December
In Wisconsin, it had snowed all day. She urged
Us to stay calm, to remove all metal objects
From our pockets and clothes, for in the spacecraft's heat
They'd scorch our skin. We threw down earrings, belts
And coins, sliced the zippers from our pants
And skirts. We gathered in a circle in the yard
And waited for The Mother Ship's approach
On this final day of the world. Someone spoke
Of *this* snow as the world's last. Mrs. Clark
Led us all in *Amazing Grace*. Then the silence settled in,
The snow swirling up. We huddled that way 'til dawn."

SEAL III.
SEMIOTICS, POSTERITY

"These fifty-gallon drums," he's telling me,
"Their water's radioactive two millenia. . . ."
It's breakfast at the artist's colony.
His paint-flecked sleeve is reaching for the ham.
His grant's not NEA, but AEC—
Devise a "semiotic," a symbol still readable
In A.D. 4,000, some ideogram for *deadly*.
"They'll stencil it in red on every barrel
They store. I'm working for posterity."
His studio's a cactus forest: six-foot exclamation points.
Thunderbolts and skulls like teetering stacks of heavy
Metal album covers. *"Hardest to paint
Are the simple things*, Cezanne said that, or someone
Like him. Just call me the goddamn toxic Cezanne."

SEAL IV.
THE ECCLESIASTICAL COMMISSION TO INVESTIGATE
THE RECEIPT OF THE STIGMATA BY MARY VAN HOOF,
MARQUETTE UNIV. HOSPITAL, 1952

Holy Week in a Psych Ward cell—her hands
And feet are bandaged, and she claims to feel

The scrape of thorns all night against her forehead.
The stenographer charts each ecstasy, and all
Sharp objects have been taken from her room.
Blood tests daily: stigmatic blood in theory should be iron-
Poor, its salt content low. Father Gray performs
His daily interrogatory. *How often does the Virgin*
Come to you? Is she, for example, right here
Before you in the room? What prophecies
Has she uttered in recent weeks? Is it true your father
Makes you sleep tied to a chair? Your mother—is she
Often hurt by him? Is it true he broke her collar
Bone? What sort of hairshirt did he make you wear?

SEAL V.
CATHEDRAL BUILDING: A PHOTO OF CHERNOBYL

Inside the reactor core, a zigzag pulse
Of light drilling through the wall's six-story crack.
The lead-robed worker turns to us, the camera flash
Reflected in his goggles, white-hot asterisks,
Exploding spiral galaxies. He'll die
Of thyroid cancer in a year or two,
But the work will last "at least a century,"
Slow retrieval of deadly debris, the crews
Stabbing trash in Dantescan gloom, like artisans
In an anti-matter Salisbury or Chartres.
They'll wreathe their labor in a concrete dome that's seven
Miles across, mausoleum of shattered atoms.
The lead-robed worker turns from us, descends
A stair. The camera hisses as the film rewinds.

SEAL VI.
AFTER THE FUNERAL

Inside the Bible on his bedside table
An address decades gone: ALBEE, S.D.,
And PROPERTY   R C   WOJAHN   P.F.C.
The *12 Steps* of A.A.: "Expect a Miracle,"

Embossed in Gothic lettering. The O_2 tanks
And tubes, a Kleenex box, his watches.
Bookmark at Revelation, verses scored with x's.
Now the trumpet blast. Now the lamb breaks
The Seventh Seal. And now The Wormwood Star,
"Like unto a torch," comes thundering from the sky
Beside his marginalia: "prophecy"—
With triple exclamation points. *Father,*
Where art thou as I call? Upon what journey
Didst thou embark, that such signs could point thy way?

Nominated by Linda Bierds, Mark Jarman

GUILT TRIP

by DAVID LEHMAN

from ANTIOCH REVIEW

Too much coffee. His mind was racing. Relief of tension:
Was fucking no more than this? Love no nobler than parking?
"She specialized in making him feel bad." He wanted her
Anyway. Something other than the law of mimetic desire
("I want you because he does") was at work. He had watched
Enough movies to understand: Vietnam was the product
Of bad grass, a paranoid trip on the IRT, and the garbage
Was growing, a living organism like the monster
In a Japanese movie, c. 1954. What a strange wonderful island
America was, a monument to impermanence and ocean foam.
Old people lived there, arguing noisily in slow elevators
Over 53 cents off for orange juice, minimum purchase $10.
The scar on her belly convinced him she was telling the truth.
He wanted her anyway. "How they could make a six-part
        documentary
About the Sixties, and never once mention the pill,
I don't understand," she said. "I have a better sense of humor
Than you do," said her seven-year-old son, "because I'm more
Serious than you are." He was right. In the fresh green breast
Of the new world, he had sought a compliant nipple. In time
The darkness would overcome him, sweet as the sweat of sex.
"I love you," he lied. "I love you, too," she replied,
Waking beside him in the morning, scaring him with her love.

Nominated by Lloyd Schwartz

SOMEBODY

fiction by REBECCA MCCLANAHAN

from THE KENYON REVIEW

HE IS NOT dying. If he were, they would not be in this mess. Doris pulls the pillow over her head.

"I'm dying! Help me. Somebody!" She is the only Somebody available, but there is nothing she can do. Her eyes feel sandy. She has already gone to him three times during the night.

The vibration begins again. He is kicking the metal bedpost. Where does he get the strength? "Somebody!" He doesn't call her name; she is The Woman Who Works Here.

On the way downstairs she ties the sash of her bathrobe. His room smells of urine although she put fresh sheets on at midnight. "What's wrong?" she says.

He stops kicking, slips a shrunken foot back under the covers. His voice is suddenly childlike and playful. "Is it snowing yet?"

"It's August."

"I heard the wind."

"It's August. It doesn't snow in August."

"We need to get the shovel." Now his voice turns guttural. "Is That Man still here? Tell him to get my car out." That Man is Herb, Doris's husband. But Herb has gone to pick up their daughter and granddaughter, who will be arriving for their annual visit tomorrow. *No, not tomorrow*, Doris is thinking. *Today.* It is almost light already.

"The car is fine. It's safe," she says. Doris's father is ninety-six. He has not driven in nineteen years.

"Have him check the antifreeze. Do you work here?"

"It's not snowing yet."

"Call me as soon as it starts."

"Just as soon as it starts. Do you need clean pajamas?" But he has turned over and is already snoring, safe in the knowledge that his '62 Chevy will not get stuck in the snow. Doris rolls him to the edge of the bed and slides the wet sheet from under him. She unsnaps the pajama bottoms, then decides to leave them on. Even after four years, it feels wrong to undress him while he's sleeping, so she simply folds a towel and lays it beneath him. She does not go back to bed, for he can sense when she falls asleep and that is when he will call again. In the den outside his room, she reclines the Naugahyde Lazy-Boy and closes her eyes.

The snowstorm has just begun, swirling high and dangerous, when she is awakened: clink, clink, his spoon hitting against the cereal bowl. Last week she finally took the pitcher from him after he spilled the milk three days in a row, and now he is punishing her. Hold on, she tells herself. The Elms will surely say yes. By next month he'll be there and I'll be able to sleep. I can have dinner with Herb, just the two of us, how long has that been? Or go to the library. Or sit in the living room without him screaming for us to get out of his house.

When she walks into the kitchen, the clinking stops. Now he's looking out the window. "I just don't understand it," he says.

"What?" Doris says to the refrigerator, because if she doesn't answer, he will keep saying it.

"How they get all those birds to look alike."

Four years ago she would have laughed. Maybe even two years ago. It's the kind of thing her father would have said to make her laugh. He was a funny man. He still says the same things, but they aren't funny anymore because they aren't on purpose.

A bus stops at the corner. He stands and moves toward the back door. That's when Doris sees he is naked from the waist down, but his hand is on the doorknob by the time she can stop him. She doesn't ask what in the hell he is doing, what in Christ's name does he think he's doing, a naked old man running outside to catch a bus. "It's too late, Dad. You've missed it."

The first two years he lived with them after Doris's mother died, he caught the bus every morning. He dressed himself in slacks and shoes, even socks that matched, and a cowboy string

225

tie over his plaid shirt. He slicked his wispy hair with tonic and
gathered all his bank statements. Every morning he caught the
7:47 and every evening returned on the 5:32. It was his job.
Within weeks everyone in town knew him. Doris found out what
he did by reading his datebook, a tiny Hallmark calendar she had
given him, the kind clerks throw into the bag when you buy a
birthday card. He had written down the basics, and knowing her
father as she did, Doris filled in the details. From 8:15 until 9:00
in good weather he sat on the bench in front of the courthouse
and read the newspaper, circling the names of editors he dis-
agreed with so he could write them a letter that night. When it
rained or snowed, he walked across the street to the Blue Pitcher
and ordered a cup of lemon water into which he poured three
packets of sugar and for which he left the waitress a nickel. When
the courthouse opened at 9:00, he was on the second row behind
the defendant, taking notes during the testimony and offering
them at recess to the lawyer whose side he had chosen. He used
the lunch break ("A waste of taxpayers' money!" he'd say over dinner. "Those judges and their two-hour lunches!") to visit each of
the three banks and the Savings & Loan where he had accounts.
Once a month he'd take his Social Security check, divide it four
ways, and deposit it equally in each bank. On the other days he'd
simply check on his balance, asking each teller to write it in his
book and update the interest, which rarely changed more than a
few cents. But not just any teller would do; he picked the youngest, prettiest tellers in each bank. Sometimes he took one or two
of them to lunch at the Blue Pitcher; he always ordered a grilled
cheese sandwich and a pickle. The first Christmas after her
mother died, Doris wrapped twenty-seven boxes of chocolate-
covered cherries (which her father had withdrawn money to buy)
and drove him to town, waiting outside the banks and the courthouse and the Blue Pitcher while he delivered the candy "to my
friends," as he called them. Christmas night a bleached blonde
who could not have been more than twenty-five knocked at the
front door and asked for him. "We have a date," she said, giggling. "For a movie." And Doris's father appeared, wearing a new
string tie and carrying the last box of chocolate-covered cherries.

When she finally gets him bathed and into his slacks, it is
nearly 9:00. Maybe he will sit in the chair for Donahue so she

can make the meat loaf for dinner. Her father likes Donahue, the way he stirs up arguments. Oh no, she thinks as she looks at the *TV Guide*—Lesbian nuns. Her father hates Catholics, and she doubts he knows gays exist. It will be question after question, she'll have no peace. So while he's not looking she pushes the mute button and tells him there's something wrong with the sound, does he just want to watch? He nods and she arranges the afghan on what is left of his lap.

Her hands are cold and greasy from the hamburger, and she has just added the egg when the phone rings. She rubs her hands on a paper towel and picks up the phone. "Hello?"

"Mrs. LeConte? This is Barbara Ludwig from The Elms." The Elms is the last possibility in town; the other three homes have refused him. "The committee met yesterday afternoon."

"I'm choking! Somebody!"

"Drink some water, I'm on the phone. Excuse me, go on," Doris says.

"We've decided not to take him. I'm sorry, but we can't risk it happening again." "It" was biting the nurse who had tried to cut his meat during Orientation Day last week. It had taken five stitches to sew up her hand. "Unless you want him on Hall C." No, Hall C was not an option for Doris: her father diapered and strapped to a wheelchair all day? "I'm sorry, Mrs. LeConte, but there are other homes in town."

Why is it after all these years she can only recall his cruelties? He never even spanked any of his children, and those other things she had witnessed as a child she later discovered weren't cruelties, but simple realities of farm life. The dead chicken tied to the dog's neck was for a reason—so the dog would be forced to smell his victim until the odor of rotting chicken sickened him. In the long run, this act would save other chickens. And when her father killed the old rooster, it was for its own good and for the good of the brood. The eggs were no longer being fertilized and if her father had simply introduced a new rooster, the old one would have been spurred to death or, if it gave up its territory without a fight, might have become mentally disturbed until it wasted away.

Doris is kneeling in the bathroom, scrubbing the floor with Clorox. She had left him for five minutes, just long enough to

227

run across the street to borrow baking powder for the biscuits. He had tried to get to the toilet in time and when he couldn't, had simply sat on the toilet lid and kicked off his soiled trousers and shorts. By the time she got back, feces were smeared across the toilet, on the tile, on the den carpet in the pattern of his shoe heels, and the upholstered chair where he now sits, once again naked below the waist except for the black shoes which hang from his hairless legs like the shoes of a ventriloquist's dummy. She cannot bear to love him anymore.

When she hears the garage door opener, she throws a towel over him and tries to help him to the bedroom for clean clothes. Last week the nurse weighed him—93 pounds—but he is dead-weight against her as they shuffle across the room, sinking with each step, his knees giving way beneath him.

Maddy comes from the bathroom, pulling up her Minnie Mouse tights. "Yuk! There's poo-poo in there," she says. In a hurry to get her father dressed, Doris forgot the soiled trousers which are still wadded on the floor beside the sink. What does a three-year-old, newly toilet-trained and proud of it, make of this?

"We'll be right out!" Doris says, guiding her father's legs into clean sweatpants. Sweats look ridiculous on old men, she thinks, but they're the only clean clothes left, time to do another washing. She sets the shoes aside; they'll have to be cleaned later. She remembers how her father used to scrape his rubber waders at the back door when he came in from the pasture. She slides his feet into slippers and lifts him from the chair.

When he sees his granddaughter Lindsey, he doesn't see his granddaughter Lindsey. He sees an attractive young woman who has come all this way to visit *him*. He shakes Doris from his arm as he walks across the room to greet her. "Hello, young lady," he says. "Do I know you?"

"That's Lindsey," Herb says, carrying a suitcase toward the stairs.

Doris's father glares at him, his eyes narrowing. "I didn't ask *you*."

"Hi, Grandpa." Lindsey kisses him on the cheek, bristly with gray whiskers. His electric shaver gave out a few days ago, and he won't let The People Who Work Here come near him with a razor. "Remember Maddy? Maddy, give Great-Grandpa a kiss."

"He smells funny," Maddy says and walks off, swinging a one-armed doll by the hair. Maddy likes to operate on her dolls; in her room at home is a lunch box full of extra body parts.

Doris kisses Herb on the lips. "I missed you," she says. His response is a pat on the shoulder and a tight smile. Doris hugs her daughter hard, feeling the muscular straight back. Doris wonders how *she* feels to Lindsey. Soft, probably. Soft and fat like grandmothers are supposed to feel.

"You know her?" Doris's father asks Lindsey.

Lindsey laughs. "Always a card, aren't you?" Then when she sees he is serious, she folds her arm around Doris and pulls her close like the couple in the Geritol commercial. "This is my mom," she says brightly. "I think I'll keep her."

Herb is at the door now, reaching for his golf hat. "Anyone for a walk before dinner?" he says.

"I'd rather make love to *her*."

At first Lindsey pretends not to hear her grandfather, who has moved toward her and is stroking her arm. Then she begins laughing. She stops when she sees the look in her father's face. Herb starts toward Lindsey, and Doris's father shoves out a scrawny arm. "She's not yours," he says.

"She is your *granddaughter!*" Herb screams. Maddy has rejoined the group, standing in the doorway. This is better than *Sesame Street*.

"Herb," Doris says, moving between them.

"It's okay," says Lindsey. She shakes a finger in her grandfather's face and, in the voice of a cartoon schoolmarm, scolds him. "We can't have that kind of behavior. Come on, Maddy. Let's go outside and swing."

Herb does not take the verdict from The Elms well. He and Doris do the dishes in silence while Lindsey bathes Maddy. He blames me, Doris thinks. After all, he's *my* father, not his. But as she wipes the counter, Herb comes up behind her and rubs her neck. She leans into him. They are in this together. *For richer or father*, she is thinking.

"I went to a funeral, but I don't know who the man was." Her father's voice is clear as a radio announcer's and although he is two rooms away, Doris can hear every word. He must have Lindsey cornered. Since his illness began three years ago, they haven't had many visitors.

"It was Lawrence, remember?" Doris says as she walks into the den.

"I'm talking to the lady," he says and turns his back on Doris. "I looked in the casket but couldn't make him out. I think I was at the wrong funeral."

Doris picks up the afghan which has fallen around his feet. "It was your son Lawrence. He died last year. He had cancer." Everyone dies of something, she thinks. She wraps the afghan around his shoulders, but he throws it to the floor.

"It's hot in here," he says. "You people keep it too damned hot." She feels her father's hands; they are cold as pennies. "I had a son once but he died when he was two. This man looked familiar, but I couldn't place him."

"That's right, Dad. One of your sons died as a child. But Lawrence was seventy-four." Of course, he'll never believe that. In his mind he is a young man. He refuses to use his senior citizen card, and even before he got sick he wouldn't go to Elderhostel or to the Wednesday night suppers at the retirement village. A bunch of old people, he said. Old white-haired women. *Like me*, Doris thinks.

"Mother's right," Lindsey says. "Lawrence was my uncle, so that makes him your son. I was at the funeral too."

He grabs the doily from the arm of the chair and begins to twist it. His eyes turn red, then fill, but he holds the tears there. "Yes, that's right," he says quietly. "I remember now." Parents should not outlive their children, Doris thinks.

The night Lawrence died, Doris had a dream. The whole family was in it—Mother, Dad, her dead brother Ranson she knew only through pictures, Lawrence, Herb, Lindsey, little Maddy herself. They were playing hide-and-seek on a summer evening much like this one. The moon and fireflies were just coming out and everyone was barefoot. Doris was It, standing at the big tree and counting to fifty while everyone fled for cover. When she opened her eyes it was black, the moon and stars gone, even the fireflies. She began to run, thrashing her arms wildly. Surely she would find them. She thought she heard someone breathing, but when she reached out, no one was there. Finally she found her way back to the big tree, but no one had tagged Home.

Maddy is beside Herb in the Lazy-Boy, flipping the pages of the worn Mother Goose book, the same one Herb used to read to Lindsey. No wonder kids have nightmares, Doris thinks. Rock-a-bye baby. Until the branch breaks, Jack cracks his head open, the Old Woman whips her shoe children, and Humpty Dumpty falls. Doris doesn't recall her father ever reading to her, although he did recite poems he'd memorized long before—Longfellow and Tennyson mostly. Sometimes when she goes in to check on him, he's speaking the poems to the dark, word for word.

During *Dallas* they keep the sound low. Maddy has fallen asleep across Herb's chest and although it's two hours past his bedtime, Doris's father is sitting erect on the edge of the couch, his veiny hands clenched.

"Come on, Dad." Doris moves toward him, but he slaps her hand away.

"I'm not going anywhere."

"It's 11:00."

"Come on, Grandpa," says Lindsey who has been nodding beside him, her feet tucked beneath a cotton robe. He ignores her and starts rubbing his knuckles, leaning farther forward.

"He's going to rape that child," he says.

Doris glances at the TV. But, no, it's just the weather report, the radar map blipping silently, showers in the midwest. Her father is staring straight at the snoring Herb.

"Help me, Lindsey. Let's get him to bed before he wakes everyone up." She used to hate it when people talked about her father in the third person, as if he weren't there, but now she understands: he *isn't* there. Lindsey suddenly realizes what her grandfather is saying.

"Don't be silly, Grandpa. That's Herb and Maddy." Her voice is maternal, the rhythms soothing like those of a clucking hen. "Let's all go to sleep."

"He'll get you too. I'm not moving." His body is rigid, the black shoes planted in the carpet. "How did he get in? Does he work here?" Yes, Doris thinks. We both work here. That's all we've done for four years.

Herb wakes himself with his own snoring. "Sorry," he says, and begins to stroke Maddy's hair. "Guess I dozed off. Showers tomorrow, huh?" He turns up the volume on the remote control.

"Let go of her." Doris's father spits out each word separately. Herb turns to Doris.

Her voice is toneless as a robot's. "He thinks you're going to rape the girls." Herb moves his hand from Maddy's hair and lowers the recliner to sitting position.

"Let's go to bed, Dad," Herb says calmly, but his mouth is tight. Suddenly Doris's father is up, his feet spread apart, fists cocked like pistols.

"Come near me, I'll kill you."

"Did you give him the pills?" Herb says to Doris.

"Two."

"I think they backfired."

"Get away from that child!" her father shouts. His breath is stale and he spits saliva with each word. Herb stands before him, eye to eye, silent. Doris can see the blood rising in his neck. Then suddenly Herb turns and walks toward the back door. The rape delusion has happened twice before, and Doris knows that as long as Herb stays in the house, her father will not budge.

The golf cap will shield Herb from nothing this August night, but by habit he grabs it on the way out. "Need anything?" he says. There is an all-night convenience store a few blocks away.

"Milk," Doris says, and as soon as the door is shut, the crisis is over. For now. Her father leans back onto the sofa, his rage buried somewhere in the cushions. He begins to whimper, and it takes both Lindsey and Doris to help him to bed. "I can't find Eartha," he keeps saying. "I've looked everywhere, but I can't find her."

Why couldn't it have been Mother who lived forever, Doris wonders. "We'll look for her tomorrow," she says as she pats him into bed.

As it turns out, Lindsey's visit wasn't a complete waste. For two days Doris's father seemed lucid. He didn't even repeat any stories except the one about the car. "It was my brother's '26 Ford. Brand new. I'd borrowed it for the weekend and was taking it back to him. Little Dorie'd been all over me, wanted to go too, but she had the croup and we thought she should stay in. She was a cute little thing, about like her," he said and pointed to Maddy. At this place in the story, Doris always left the room. She didn't want to hear the rest, although it was a happy ending, one

232

in which her father emerged as a hero in one of those miraculous feats scientists would later attribute to sudden increased adrenalin. What else could explain such a small man lifting the wheels of a car from the legs of a little girl? But lately what seems more miraculous to Doris is how a father could back a car over his daughter in the first place. And how that little girl would remember none of it, although her mother and brother would swear for years that it was true.

Lindsey decides to leave three days early—something about the house painters, she tells Doris. Herb has to wait until nearly noon, when his father-in-law finally falls asleep on the sofa, before he can load the luggage into the car. He's sleeping off last night's rampage—he tried to stab Herb with a dinner fork—and now Maddy thinks this is a game, tiptoeing past the troll, escaping from his dungeon. Doris wraps up tuna sandwiches and oatmeal cookies and pours a thermos of strong coffee for Herb. She imagines how it would be, a night in a motel somewhere, a night of rest and then the quiet drive back the next day, sipping coffee and watching the cornfields tick past, the green rows even and perfectly spaced. Herb kisses her cheek. "Lunchtime tomorrow," he says. "But don't wait if you get hungry."

All day, on and off, her father dozes. When she nudges him awake for dinner he pushes the baked ham away and begins quoting "The Lady of Shalott."

"You've got to eat," Doris says.

"Where's the pie?"

"You finished it at lunch."

"You ate it," he says. "Where are my cookies?" His hands slip in and out of the sofa cushions, searching. Sometimes when she changes his sheets she finds candy wrappers under his pillows. "Here they are," he says and breaks an Oreo apart, licking the white filling. He reaches for the remote control button and begins switching from one station to another, settling on a rerun of *Gilligan's Island*. Doris carries the tray back to the kitchen. As usual, she has made enough for an army. Still cooking for guests who never come—couples they used to play Canasta with, neighbors who'd drop by unexpectedly, the women from her sewing circle. She sits in semi-darkness and eats her dinner of ham, rice, green beans, and salad. The Oreos will keep him satisfied for a few minutes.

He has turned the volume up so high that Doris doesn't hear anything until the crash and the sound of glass shattering. By the time she gets to him he is lying at the bottom of the basement stairs, his hands clutching the cord of a broken lamp. Blood pours from a cut in his forehead.

"He got confused," she tells the nurse who signs them in at Emergency. "He thought it was the door to the bathroom." The nurse eyes Doris suspiciously and makes a mark on her clipboard. They wait in an adjoining room for a doctor while Doris holds a cold compress to the cut. After nearly an hour, a young intern with a receding hairline and a brusque manner, checks her father for bruises and cleans the cut. "These are for pain," he says as he hands Doris some pills. "They may make him disoriented. If he passes out, call me. He might have a reaction." Doris nods obediently.

It is nearly 10:00 when she gets him home and into his pajamas. The pills work instantly. As she positions the white pillow beneath his head, she thinks he has never looked so peaceful; maybe he'll sleep all night. He looks almost handsome in the pale light from the streetlamp, his arms crossed on his chest. He might be in his casket. She can almost imagine it. But his chest is rising, falling, rising effortlessly with each breath. Her arms ache. Her head aches. The backs of her legs ache. She thinks of taking one of the pills herself, but she'll need to be alert if he calls in the night. On the way to bed she props two chairs against the basement door, just in case.

Doris sinks into sleep like a corpse draped with chains and lowered into quicksand. Her last thought is of those bog people in England that archaeologists discovered thousands of years later, clothing and hair still in place, their skin leathery and perfectly preserved right down to the last scar. Hours later when she first hears the cry, her eyes will not open; are they weighted with coins? She tries to fit the cry into her dream, but there is no dream. But there *is* a cry, a whimper that begins as animal, shapeless in the distance, then forms itself slowly as it climbs the stairway toward her until by the time it reaches her bed, it is a human cry. "Somebody!" Then a gasp. One foot is off the bed now and its weight propels the other foot toward the floor where like a bat programmed for blind flight, her body aims for the door.

The cry descends the stairs just ahead of her. She follows it to the bathroom door and inside. Her father has fallen between the tank of the toilet and the wall. He lies twisted, his limbs folded in a pattern like origami. She stands in the doorway. These things happen all the time, old people fall during the night, it can't be helped. He had a reaction, the doctor will say. To the pain pills.

The cut on his forehead has opened and bright blood gathers in the hollow of his throat. She looks down at him. His eyes for a moment are the wild eyes of the fox she once saw him corner against the henhouse seconds before the bullet caught in its chest. She hesitates, then kneels beside him on the tile and un-knots the puzzle of his limbs. And as she lifts him to his feet, his heart is hammering against her.

Nominated by Carolyn Kizer

THE WRITERS' MODEL

fiction by MOLLY GILES

from SIDE SHOW

I'M OLD NOW but when I was young you could talk me into anything. I had an open mind. So when I saw the ad saying some professional writers needed an "adventurous girl" to "interview for fictional purposes," I was intrigued, especially when the ad said "by simply answering questions" I could "make an important contribution to American literature." I had always wanted to make an important contribution to something, so I dressed in my best suit and white gloves and showed up at the address listed in the paper.

I arrived on the hour at a dark basement in a bad part of town. Nobody answered when I knocked so I tried the door, which opened, and I stepped into the strangest room, like an interrogation cell in a jail, with one bare bulb in the middle of the ceiling and an empty chair waiting beneath it. A ring of silent people circled the chair. I caught the glint of their pens and pencils and saw the note pads open on their laps. All the note pads, I noticed, were blank. For some reason, that touched me. I straightened my hat, went to the chair, and sat down.

"Ask me anything," I said and the first writer said, "What is your body like?" I stared. I realized that all the writers were men and that many were dressed alike, in tweed jackets with leather patches on the sleeves. One by one they adjusted their horn rimmed glasses, lit their briar pipes, patted the Irish setters lying at their feet and looked at me as if they expected me to take my clothes off.

So I did. I am not shy and I already understood that to these writers I was neither woman nor human; I was an object. An *objet* (I comforted myself) *d'art*.

"Why are you smiling?" one writer asked, and I told my little joke as I took my jacket off and another said, his voice sharp, "Do you know French?" and I shrugged as I unbuttoned my blouse because everyone knows some French and then I stepped out of my skirt and for the rest of that first session there was nothing but scribbling and an occasional testy, "How about German? How about Greek?" from the back.

I didn't have to do many sittings stark naked after that; they had their notes to refer to, after all, and the small room was cold. It wasn't my body they had come for anyway, it was the questions—the questions and the answers I gave them. Many of them had seen a woman, touched a woman, had sex with a woman—many of them were married—but not many had ever really talked to a woman, and this was their chance.

How do you feel about your underpants?

Do you jiggle when you run?

What is it like to have someone inside you?

Does size matter?

What does orgasm feel like?

Those were the physical questions, some of them, though of course there were many more. Everything about breasts fascinated them but nursing—they did not care to hear about that—and very few asked about menstruation or childbirth. They all wanted to know about "the first time" and if I'd done it with women, or had it done to me as a child. Nymphomania intrigued them and they could not hide their disbelief when I said that neither I nor any of my girl friends knew anything about it. The other, non-physical questions were more varied but not really much more surprising:

Do you fish?

Do you dream?

Do you vote?

And, the one that made them all hold their breath:

Do you read?

At the break, many continued to write as they watched me sip my tea from a thermos, eat half my sandwich. They were allowed to smell my perfume and look through my purse. When I went to the toilet it was permitted for one or two of them to come with me and watch, take notes if they needed.

After the break a few presented me with "problems" they "had blocked" on—those were the words they used. You are about to be stoned for adultery: how do you feel? Your husband has run off with another woman: what do you do? Your brother is kidnapped, your daughter is raped, you are raped, there's a lion charging toward you, there's a corpse in your closet—easy stuff, most of it, nothing, I thought, to get blocked by. Sometimes they brought costumes for me—snake suits or nurse uniforms or frilled gingham aprons—depending on what kind of character they were trying to depict—and they would ask me to act out a fight scene with a lover, or improvise a suicide note, or pose with a whip, or pretend to go crazy—and all that was easy too.

The only part of the job that was not easy was Free Form Time—the five minutes reserved at the end of each session for me to talk about the things that I'd been thinking about during the week. I had so much I wanted to talk about, big things like Truth, War, Luck, and Honor and of course a lot of little things too: my fear of white horses, the way a bowl of apples looked in the moonlight, the shoes I'd had to return because they were too tight. But the writers were always tired by this time and cranky as children. Some swallowed yawns, others openly doodled, many just leashed their dogs and left. I saw I was not holding their attention and I had to fight the temptation to start making things up. If I'm not careful, I thought in a panic, I will turn into a writer myself.

Looking back I see it was an easy job in many ways. The men were lonely and ignorant, but they were educable, I thought, and I took pride in helping them, however slightly, understand others. When I saw that a few female characters based on me were being called "real" and "rounded" in the book reviews, I was, frankly, flattered. But when I read the books themselves I felt sick. For nothing had changed. The women in these books were the same as they'd always been—the same saints, sluts, and sorry set of psychotics that I had been reading about all my life. Where were their passions? Their generous hearts? Where had I failed?

The writers' questions began to tire me, that same one, week after week, about the underpants, and I decided to quit before I became what they saw. With the money I'd saved I finished

238

school and since then I've been a milliner, a chef, a sandcastle architect. I've run child-care centers and nursing homes. I put up wallpaper one autumn in Australia, worked the vineyards in Brittany, clocked bicycle races in Houston. I've always been drawn to the odd job, in every sense of that phrase, and I wasn't too surprised to see a space ship land in my back yard last night. The little man who got out looked familiar, with his domed forehead and hard hurt stare. He had come a long way, he said, to study someone like me. And much as I'd like to see Mars, I picked up the shot gun and marched him right off my porch. Some things can't be studied, I told him, and there is no one like me.

Nominated by Dorianne Laux

WHITE HUNTER

by DIANE JOHNSON

from THE THREEPENNY REVIEW

AT FIRST IT had seemed okay, morally speaking, to have come. For J. to have come, at least. In my mind doctors were exempt, like the Red Cross, could go places other people boycotted and protested. It was understood they were there to help people. As for me, since I had no serious excuse for being there—no journalistic mission, no relatives—my own presence in South Africa couldn't be justified apart from my role as J.'s companion. But I could be there as a witness. My role was to know. So that when the Jeep driver who had been taking us around the game park, a gentlemanly kid in shorts and army boots, did, on the third day, suddenly say, "They are more like animals than people, you know," I was there to hear it. "The natives here are," he continued. "The African. He even smells different. You can't teach him anything. He is like a child, he can't plan ahead. You give him a sack of peas and tell him it has to last him for the winter, it will be gone in a week all the same, then he will come back to you for more." I had been glad I was there to hear it. Forever after I would know, in discussions about South Africa, that the things that were said about the white people were true: they did despise and hate the blacks and talk insensitively. At least the Afrikaaners did. In Capetown we had met many concerned, white English-speaking people, usually in the Jewish community, who were working for change. If nothing else, the traveler learns that things are rarely morally obvious.

This driver, Dirk, had only spoken out after three days. Before that the talk had been, with J., of birds, of the hundreds of species, and of the big animals we were seeing. Only after three days did he speak his mind, but now I knew his mind, the mind of South Africa. It reminded me of nothing so much as the mind of America, insofar as I had known the mind of America when I was little, about ten, in my small town, and people had said the same things about Indians—Native Americans—about how they couldn't plan ahead, couldn't drink, couldn't be trusted to look after themselves, couldn't be trusted period.

The little lodge we had stayed in also reminded me of my childhood, of camping in national parks built by the CCC, with the same dusty paths and green paint, the rangers wearing the same clothes as this young man, and the flag on its pole, and the faded map in its glass case, the families in their cars, with guidebooks and thermos bottles. The families were all white here, of course, but then they had been all white in my childhood too, families in their Chevys, children sitting in the dusk on the logs around the campfire area, unpacking their dolls. In America you could get out of your car. Here in South Africa a rather exciting air of menace and fortification was conveyed by the closing of the gates at dusk, and by the signs telling people to stay in their cars. The children in such an atmosphere, of course, stayed in the cars, or safely inside the lodge. Blond children, sturdy blond overweight parents—these the Afrikaaners—and the English-speaking families, large-toothed and thin-legged in shorts, with binoculars.

The gates of this compound were shut each night against wild animals, not against the natives. J. and I had remarked on the general absence of anxiety in South Africa, the lack of security checks and metal detectors on the plane flying up here from Johannesburg. Across my mind the newsreels of the Sixties: the marches and German shepherds and whips, the fat man called Bull, men in helmets and epaulets and boots, and shadow-like black children skipping, and the mothers and fathers singing, and preachers walking among them, and the mood of elation.

We were here by mistake. J. had been invited to visit a black hospital in one of the Homelands, when, with five days left on our immutable airline tickets, our passage to that area was cancelled. De Boerck had suggested a few days of game-watching instead, first in the Kruger National Park, and then in an adjacent, private hotel, luxuriously run by a fellow he knew. These

241

changes in our plans had put J. in a bad mood; he would rather have stayed in Tanzania; alternatively, there was a meeting in Nairobi he should have gone to. He does not support changes in plan very well.

Still, I couldn't shake off the feeling that I was in America, and couldn't stop thinking there ought to be a lesson in that, if I could think what it was. I had been feeling like this the day before yesterday in the Land Rover, but then had seen a giraffe. There had been no giraffes in Mississippi. This was another land, of rhino and elephant. The Mississippi marchers were a caramel color, handsome and sturdy, but here in the shadows the blackness of the Africans was different. The thinness of their limbs and the glint of their eyes—like coins against the purple blackness of their skin—made them seem unrelated to the Americans. Here the people wound their bodies in beautiful striped cloth, and the slowness of their steps, and the swaying gait was African, not American.

Contrasting with the serious, austere, Boy Scout-like atmosphere of the Kruger National Park, the Simba Private Hotel and Game Reserve was cozy, overdecorated with "tasteful" faded chintzes and hunting trophies and prints, photos of the famous people who had stayed there. I recognized Jerry Lewis holding a pair of antlers. Jalousies shaded a broad lobby where fans swirled slowly on the ceiling, and the stuffed heads were hung of members of all the species of animal J. and I had met, and coatracks made of their antlers—the twisted spirals, the forked, the branched, these menacing appendages which had been rather unconvincing on the mild-eyed living creatures who had bounded away from our vehicles on their tiny hooves. It was unbearable to look at the walls here.

The White Hunter, as I thought of him—the owner and friend of De Boerck—was an Englishman named Reeves, with a hale, alcoholic manner, stocky form, arms and legs (in shorts) covered with a mat of curly reddish hair, and something behind his eyes not so drunk as he seemed. The place was run on the lines of a European hotel; you sat at the same table for breakfast and dinner, and said good morning to all the other guests. Then there were game drives or game walks—these last by special arrangement, lunch, more game drives and game walks, and "sundowners" by the river, when you were meant to drink gin and watch the animals gather down by the river, if they did. The animals were not so abundant here as in Tanzania, and the atmosphere was different. Where they had roamed in their numbers in Tanzania, here they were prized like valuable freaks, with a carnival of people depending on them—the drivers of the smart vans, the uniformed blacks who erected gaily scalloped canopies over the lunch area and spread the cloths on the folding tables brought out into the bush, the cooks, the boys who carried sturdy pikes to protect the guests on the game walks, or to give the illusion that they needed protection.

Where the gentle Tanzanians were reading tracts by their leader Nyerere, and asking themselves what their attitude to the bourgeois should be, South Africa was the last stand of colonial privilege. Ian, the driver, was a good-looking Rhodesian, recently demobilized after some years as a mercenary in Mozambique. This romantic profession had left traces on his handsome face— rugged squint-lines and scars of sunburns. He was a white soldier of Africa who seemed to feel that his present duty—driving American ladies in a Jeep, with only an Uzi to hand—was about as dangerous as anything else he had done. When he allowed us to alight, to stand for a while concealed in a blind of thatch and bamboo, he stood alertly with the rifle in his arms. No game, however, menaced us. He granted us a short walk through the jungle underbrush, he walking in front. I was glad at last to walk. To be in Africa, like being in Alaska, is to be confined in some kind of motor vehicle every minute of every day. Ian told us of the misery of Mozambique, the wandering women and dead babies, the endless dust. "Poor bloody bastards, they think they want freedom, there's not a place in Africa where the black man is better off than right here," he said.

"Of course the animals are protected," he said, adding in a lower tone, "though we might take someone hunting from time to time, by special arrangement." That would be his real job, I supposed, clandestine hunting trips with rich Americans or Germans. Looking at Ian's Uzi, I thought of Americans shooting buffalo from the trains moving west across the American plains and leaving their corpses where they fell. I thought of those rednecks in Florida who teach their children to hunt and kill baby deer.

"What do you hunt?" J. asked Ian.

243

"Well, antelope, that sort of thing," he said, looking off into the underbrush, his tone unconvincing. He has killed elephants and lions, I thought. I imagined them loading tusks of contraband ivory in the night. What if your child grew up to be a mercenary? There was something of the gentleman about his accent, not as harshly South African as some, the vowels a little more English, an occasional complicated word betraying an elaborate education somewhere along the line.

From the grounds of the Simba Private Hotel and Game Preserve, Ian drove us back into the Kruger National Park. All the vegetation around here was more equatorial, lush and ferny than the land farther north. The trees had soft, inviting leaves instead of the thorns of the Tanzanian trees, and flowers and trailing vines laced the branches overhead. A single tree groaned, half bent beneath the weight of an immense orchid plant in bloom, its petals of white and orange making it seem as if a million butterflies had landed in it. An African tree orchid, Ian said, was a rare, protected species. He said he hadn't realized there was one nearby.

At dinner, J. and I were almost alone in the dining room, except for the glass eyes of the glowering beasts whose stuffed expressions of perpetual ferocity I had found unsettling at breakfast. The White Hunter himself sat at a corner table talking to a woman with blond hair vaguely wiglike in its brightness. The White Hunter did not look at her, but instead scanned the room with his sanpaku eyes. Sanpaku is the word I had read somewhere to describe the kind of eyes in which you see the white below as well as above and to the side of the iris. It is a sign of bad health and can be remedied by eating brown rice. The bright-haired woman drank her Pym's cup, clutching it with both red-fingernailed hands. From the bar, we could hear the light laughter of a group of men. Black waiters in white jackets gave an air of seriousness to the bringing of pea soup, salad, a roast that seemed to have been boiled and tasted gamey, raising apprehensions about which sort of animal, among those pitiably decapitated creatures nailed on the wall, it had been.

We smiled at a couple like ourselves, a man and woman our age, and I marveled at how other women can turn themselves out—nails, coils of hair arranged with a maximum of intention—

in the wilds of Africa. I have seen them do it anywhere. It means caring enough to lug a hair dryer along, or giving up the sight-seeing of the afternoon to make an appointment with a hair-dresser. Plenty of women are like that. My hair straggled, still damp from the shower, and my arm was spotted with mosquito bites, reminding me of my arms and ankles as a child—mosquitoes and the dreaded chiggers. In the meantime I had al-most forgotten, until now, how it was to have a body all bitten and covered with sores, even though most of the people in Africa do, and India, and wherever you were on any of several subcon-tinents. Here we dutifully took our chloroquine and hoped for the best.

As I was thinking about insect bites, the waiter's hands sud-denly intruded across our plates in white gloves, like the hands of a mime. In Spain we had had dinner once in a private house where the servants wore white gloves like this, a fastidiousness that had seemed a little disagreeable, implying the dirtiness of hands. And here it seemed to mean, no black hands, only white hands, are touching your food.

"Buffalo or maybe wild pig," J. said of the meat.

After dessert, the waiters detached from their brackets the tiki-torches that lighted the patio, and carried them nearer to the musicians who were gathering at one end of the dining room. From the direction of the kitchen a procession of women entered into the circle of light, and the drums adopted a pronouncedly African beat, excited and jungley, trying to suggest exhilarating savagery tattooed from village to village on hollow logs and gourd marimbas.

The women had brightly colored kangas knotted around their waists and were topless. The flickering light of the torches, like the dappled light of an African forest, cast stripes and spots of shadow across their naked breasts. They were light-colored or darkest black, were small and stocky or tall, willowy Ethiopians, and their breasts were all different—small, low, high, flat, pen-dulous, it was like a plastic surgeon's book of choices. One woman had the voluptuous fat breasts of a stripper and another a mere protrusion of nipple. The nipples were black against lighter skin or small, like the spots on cats.

These women began to dance, a dance consisting of standing in one place and bouncing up and down on first one and then the other foot, half bending and extending their knees, while making small dog-paddling motions with their arms in time to the drum music, which imperceptibly quickened. The compelling feature of the dance was simply breasts, jiggling up, down, up, down, to the drumbeat, faster and faster.

Now I noticed that these same women were the chambermaids during the day, recycled as danseuses. There was the girl who had made our bed this morning. Her expression was bored, or, more likely, tired. It was terrible to think that the poor girl, tired after the day, had to take her clothes off and jiggle up and down for tourists. I could hardly bear this, nor could I turn away. In the middle of this strange misery, J. stood up and tugged at my elbow. His look and the set of his shoulders expressed either his disgust at this exploitation of tired cleaning women made to bare their breasts for tourists at the end of a long day; disgust of the management's idea of us, tourists and Americans, thinking we would want to see the breasts of poor African chambermaids; or maybe just boredom. I had never before walked out of anything, not even a movie, am compelled by temperament to sit transfixed until the bitter end of whatever it is. My heart pounded with excited indignation and relief as I followed J. out.

We heard footsteps behind us on the stair. I still felt irrational fear, as if, having seen something shameful or illicit, we would be pounced on or pierced from behind, as the tigers in India pounce on men in the forest. When I turned at the top of the stairs, I saw it was the Hunter himself.

"Not our cup of tea," J. said.

"I know," the Hunter said, smiling, serenely ignoring or mis-understanding this remark. "What about me?—I have to look at it every night. Sometimes it drives me mad." J. stared at him frostily enough, but must have decided it would be pointless to continue.

In the night I woke up hearing low voices coming from the compound parking lot, with the sound of wheels on gravel. I went to the window. There was no moon, and in the absolute blackness I could not see and so went back to sleep. In the morning we made ready to leave. A young boy carried our suitcases, and J. had gone into the lobby to pay the bill. As I wandered out into the driveway, I noticed that a truck which had stood by the flowerbeds behind the garages last night was now parked in a slightly different place, and something lay in the back, covered by a tarp. My heart contracted with fear to see this ominous shape, the size of a large animal. It was just the size of a lion or a cheetah, could even be a zebra. I walked closer, pretending, in case anyone saw me, to be looking at a bird who rustled in the hedge.

The manner in which the thing was covered made it obvious that it was contraband. I steeled myself against the sight of the glassy dead eyes of a lion, or some other creature I had so recently admired in life. Or a cache of ivory, perhaps. When I thought the porter was looking the other way, I reached out and lifted the corner of the tarpaulin. Underneath was the tree orchid, pried off its support during the night. Were they going to sell it? Transplant it here? I was both relieved that it wasn't a dead animal and indignant that some other living thing had been despoiled.

I was overcome, however, by irresistible desire. I could, by reaching out my hand, break off two rhizomes, enough to propagate. Of course I wouldn't do it—you'd have to smuggle it into the United States, for one thing. "No plant material," said the signs in Customs. I hesitated. I remembered a time when, unable to finish the lobster served on a flight from Cancun, I had wrapped it in my napkin and put it in the carry-on, thinking we would eat it for supper. Then J., with the carry-on, had been apprehended by the Customs officers and dragged away as censoriously as they might have dragged the most desperate drug-smuggler.

When I realized that J. had seen me looking at the flowers, I knew he would be thinking of that. On the other hand, the memory of the bright blossoms filled me with covetousness. Two little segments would never be noticed in my purse, rescued from the evil White Hunter's despicable and illegal designs.

Armed with this defiant, self-justifying argument, I detached the two segments and put them in my purse, and went back to the washroom in the lobby to moisten some tissue to fold around the broken ends.

But I told myself this would be my last wicked act. If J. objected, I would explain that I knew I shouldn't do it, but that I was at the end of my rope about people. That was the feeling this place gave you. The feeling welled up, in the ladies' room, that people were hopeless. Widespread travel encourages deepest misanthropy. People kill each other and innocent creatures, they plunder the trees and burn the grasses. Who could countenance the savagery of their killing, the vulgarity of their lusts? The arrogance of the idea of hunting, the selfish brutality? The force of these emotions overcame me. I was tired of travel and wished to live a simple life among flowers—stolen orchids—and animals. A woman cannot do much, but I could become a friend of the sad dogs owned by feeble old people I saw in the streets, being dragged along on leashes, underfed. I would befriend cats, like a mad old cat lady, and grow orchids and African violets and live to myself.

The tree-orchid did live for a time on a piece of bark in my kitchen. How I nourished it, consulted books, fed, watered, withheld water, misted, and cherished it. It put out a little root, but then a brown rot began to consume its leaves, and, over a week, ate them away.

Nominated by Kristina McGrath, Sigrid Nunez

DEAF POEM

by TESS GALLAGHER

from MOON CROSSING BRIDGE (Graywolf Press) and
PASSAGES NORTH

Don't read this one out loud. It isn't
to be heard, not even in the sonic zones
of the mind should it trip the word "explosion"
and detonate in the silent room. My love
needs a few words that stay out of
the mouth and vocal cords. No vibrations, please.
He needs to put his soul's freshly inhuman capacity
into scattering himself deeper into
the forest. It's part of the plan that birds
will eat the markings. It's okay. He's not coming
that way again. He likes it where he is. Or if he
doesn't, I can't know anything about it. Let
the birds sing. He always liked to hear them
any time of day. But let this poem meet
its deafness. It pays attention another way, like he
doesn't when I bow my head and press my forehead
in the swollen delusion of love's power to
manifest across distance the gladness that joined us.

Wherever he is he still knows I have two feet
and one of them is broken from dancing.
He'd come to me if he could. It's nice to be sure
of something when speaking of the dead. Sometimes
I forget what I'm doing and call out to him. It's me! How
could you go off like that? Just as things were

getting good. I'm petulant, reminding him of his promise
to take me in a sleigh pulled by horses
with bells. He looks back in the dream—the way
a violin might glance across a room at its bow
about to be used for kindling. He doesn't
try to stop anything. Not the dancing. Not the deafness
of my poems when they arrive like a sack of wet
stones. Yes, he can step back into life just long enough
for eternity to catch hold, until one of us
is able to watch and to write the deaf poem,
a poem missing even the language
it is unwritten in.

Nominated by Henry Carlile, Louise Glück, Arthur Smith

FORREST IN THE TREES

fiction by DENNIS LOY JOHNSON

from PLOUGHSHARES

I SAW MY FIRST ghost when I was nine years old, only I didn't know it was a ghost at the time. This was on the Great Plains, in South Dakota, I think, on our way to the Black Hills. I was with my mother, my three-year-old sister, Lillie, and my new step-father, Forrest Bender, who was a Sioux Indian. He had stopped the car—in his careful way, making sure the trailer was well off the road—so he could read a historical marker, one of the small cast-iron plaques the federal government places on the sides of interstates. This was something Forrest was forever doing, he couldn't let even one go by, and my mother was beginning to resent it more and more.

"We can have lunch here," he offered, wading out into the grass and waving his arms around him.

"We'll never get there at this rate," my mother said.

Forrest dropped his arms to his sides and stared off into the distance. "Sometimes the journey is as important as the destination," he said solemnly.

"Who said that?" she snapped at him.

He looked back at her, puzzled, then a smile took over his face. "I did," he said. "Just now."

"Oh, please," my mother said. "Spare me."

We all knew what she thought. Her use of the phrase had taken on new significance since the time—just a few weeks before—when she'd found a bottle of whiskey he'd stashed in the trunk, in the spare-tire wheel well.

251

But he wandered off in the other direction, to the plaque. "On this site in April of 1876 a train of 82 Conestoga wagons from Harrisburg, Pennsylvania, was attacked by a Sioux war party," Forrest read out to us. "All 228 settlers were killed in what has become known as the Pettibone Massacre."

"Cripes," my mother said. "The perfect place for a picnic." She was anxious to get to Seattle, where she was going to start a new job, working as an administrator at a drug rehabilitation center. It had been her idea that, for the sake of Lillie and me, we stop at some historical landmarks along the way—Mt. Rushmore and Yellowstone, in particular—to make up for the fact that we would be out of school (pre-school, in Lillie's case). But my mother hadn't counted on Forrest's diligence.

"This is some real American hist'ry," he told her now. I was beginning to like the singsong of his speech, the way he pronounced *Amur'can*. He slapped his belly and let out a war whoop. "*Hoka hey!*" he said. In the vast, open space his voice seemed to carry off and disappear. "*Hoka hey! My people.*"

"Look, Cochise," my mother said, "let's just eat before there's another massacre in this place." Lillie and I looked at each other, knowing our mother was nearing the end of her patience. We'd moved around a lot when it was just the three of us, going from rental to rental, neighborhood to neighborhood. It always seemed to make my mother a nervous wreck, but this was worse than usual. Her weird sense of humor was leaving her; she'd dropped her nicknames for us, stopped calling us Disney-man and Lillie-Belle. She was becoming more and more stern and jittery and tight-lipped the farther we got from St. Paul, which we'd never left before.

She reached into the Corvair—even then it seemed a hundred years old—and yanked out the old army blanket she always kept in the back seat, then strutted off into the grass at the roadside. "Walt, get the cooler from the trunk," she told me as she unfurled the blanket and spread it out on the grass.

"I'll get it," Forrest said, starting towards the car.

"I told Walter to do it," my mother said.

"It's okay," he said to me, stopping to ruffle my hair with his pudgy fingers. "Go sit with your mother."

"I told Walter," my mother repeated.

Forrest's fingers stopped in place on my head, then fell down to my shoulder as he must have realized my mother's suspicions. Through my T-shirt I could feel the roughness of his hand, from his last job digging ditches for a pipe-laying outfit. "Okay, okay," he said. He handed me the keys then went over to where my mother sat on the blanket and sat down cross-legged next to her with a sheepish smile.

I climbed over the hitch where the boxy U-Haul was connected to the car. It held all our possessions. After my mother's giant yard sale, we didn't have much to move. Forrest was tickling Lillie and her laughter peeled across the grass as I brought the cooler to my mother.

Forrest pulled himself up and plopped Lillie in place on the blanket while my mother distributed lunch. Nobody said anything more as we sat there and ate our sandwiches. The silence seemed sudden. There were no other cars on the highway. There was only the sound of our chewing, and then, eventually, of the wind rustling the grass, and the trill of an occasional killdeer as they shot up from the thickets along the roadside, their long tails pluming behind.

"They look like arrows," Forrest eventually said. He said this as if talking to himself, the way he did, like a narrator to an unseen audience. He leaned toward me, but spoke out toward the grassland rolling to the horizon. "Imagine a blanket of arrows, flying out of the clouds of dust, the *wasichus* shooting back into the clouds. That was all they could do."

"What's wazychoos?" Lillie asked him.

Forrest smiled and mussed her hair. "White people," he told her. "Prob'ly a whole bunch of blon' blockheads, like in Minnesota."

I looked at the tall grass around us and tried to imagine the people from St. Paul there, with wagons and horses, and maybe hats.

Forrest said, "They wou'n't have been able to kill them all like that, though, with the wagons like a fort. They would have had to charge into them—screaming like banshees—and then killed them by hand, with hatchets and clubs. Then they would have sliced the tops of their heads off, for the scalps. Little babies, too."

"For God's sake," said my mother, slapping her half-eaten sandwich down on its cellophane wrapper. "That's it." She grabbed up the remains of her sandwich and threw it into the cooler. "Let's go." She stood and snatched what was left of Lillie's sandwich, then mine, and threw them into the cooler, too. Then she stormed back to the car with Lillie in tow.

Forrest pulled his attention back and looked after her. He seemed unperturbed. "It's this place," he confided to me. "She feels it. When something like that happens, it leaves something behind. Fear and killing . . . it leaves something in the ground. There are spirits here."

I looked around again. I remember thinking I could hear a pounding, like a heartbeat, a muffled drumbeat like a TV sound track when the Indians appear on the ridge. I could sense them, just beyond the crest of grass, coming at any minute to cut the top of our heads off. There was a sudden thump and I leapt to my feet, ready to run. Then I realized it was only my mother, slamming her car door.

Still, I kept a keen eye on the rising wave of grass and stuck close to Forrest as I waited nervously for him to collect our things. "What did they look like?" I asked him, scanning the horizon expectantly.

Forrest, on his knees, calmly finished packing the cooler and put it under his arm. Then he stood next to me and paused to look out at the hummock of grass.

"They weren't very han'some," he said, "not like in movies. They were mos'ly naked, and greasy. They looked silly sitting on their little ponies with their legs sticking out. Some of them were fat."

He handed me the cooler and squatted down to gather up the blanket.

"Like you?" I asked as I turned and stumbled in my hurry to get back to the car. I thought Forrest was right behind me.

He laughed and I turned to see he was still standing off in the grass. "Maybe," he said. He flapped the blanket in the air to clean it off. "Prob'ly. Sure, like me," and he laughed again.

I stood nervously by the open trunk and watched him: a short, thick man with slick hair in a ponytail and skin that was dark against his khaki work shirt, standing out in the waving grass and the clear air flapping a blanket. But my eyes kept drifting past him, not really seeing him; they were worrying, instead, the verge of grass.

My mother stuck her head out the window. "Close the trunk," she told me.

I felt relieved when we drove away from that place, and watched the land slip away out the window as we accelerated, like we were making a getaway. Along the roadside, a killdeer shot out of the grass and fell back again, like an expended arrow.

When we'd left St. Paul, we'd stopped in the Minneapolis suburbs to say goodbye to my uncle Seth and his family. Uncle Seth was my mother's older brother, and on that visit I remember noticing for the first time how much he looked and acted like my mother. Everyone had always said how much alike they were, but no matter how hard I looked I'd never been able to see it before. Observing it, finally, it felt like learning something, something about science, a subject I was having trouble with in school. It was like getting my eyes to work better, my senses becoming more adult, like when I'd finally come to understand what my mother meant when she asked me if something tasted salty, or sweet or sour.

It made me wonder about my own sister, too, as I watched Lillie in the backyard. I was trying to follow my mother's directions to keep her from getting into trouble with Uncle Seth's two boys, who were five and six and wild. My mother called them "Irish twins," a joke I didn't understand but knew was directed at Uncle Seth's schoolteacher wife, Colleen.

I took the opportunity to try and teach Lillie some more of the expressions I'd picked up at school, all the while wondering if we mirrored each other, too, without knowing it. I wanted to see her mimicking me, up close. I liked the idea of this. So I tried to teach her to say, "No way, José." But Lillie wouldn't pay attention, she kept trying to pull away to chase after Uncle Seth's boys. I would grab her and pull her back, but she kept coughing in my face and giving me a hard time.

When I saw Uncle Seth and my mother go off on the side together, just before we were supposed to leave, I'd abandoned Lillie to spy on them, hiding nearby behind one of the elm trees, dead from the blight. Lillie scooted off happily, her pudgy little legs and arms churning, her coughs coming like small barks as she raced madly after my cousins. Uncle Seth glanced at Forrest—who was off in the driveway checking the fluids in the car—as if to make sure he was out of earshot. I stared at my mother and tried to imagine her with short hair and a deeper voice, in a flannel shirt and work boots like Uncle Seth.

"Kat, this is crazy," I heard Uncle Seth say to her.

"No it's not," she said back. "Nothing's ever worked for me here. I've got to start over again."

"But you're driving clear across the country."

"A new place, a new start," my mother said. "And it's a good job."

"It's a depressing job," Uncle Seth said. "And what is this guy?" He nodded off toward where Forrest was visible, bent under the hood of the car. "Practice? Another one of your projects?" Uncle Seth knew my mother had met Forrest at the soup kitchen. She was a volunteer. He was on line.

"How dare you—" my mother said.

"You married him so quickly, you don't even know him. He's a drunkard. You want him around the kids like that?"

"Don't you tell me how to raise my children," my mother said, tucking her chin down, her voice seeming to get quieter and hotter at the same time. "He's had some bad luck, just like I have. We're both trying to make a change. I know what I'm doing."

Uncle Seth tucked his chin down, too. "This is no change," he said, "except that you're gonna be a thousand miles away from your family and friends. Sure, you've got a job, but what about him? Believe me, Kat, this guy is no change."

"I know what I'm doing," my mother said again, turning on her heel and moving off to scoop up Lillie as she came speeding by. Lillie's legs kept churning for a moment, like a toy whose wheels keep spinning when you lift it off the floor. My mother slung her over one hip and went and stood next to Forrest, who straightened up from the car and put an arm around her. He gave my mother a squeeze, then took Lillie and lifted her up onto his shoulders.

Lillie grabbed his ponytail and held it so it stuck up from his head, splayed like a feather.

"Ready?" Forrest asked my mother.

Lillie dropped Forrest's ponytail, grabbed his collar like reins, and kicked at him with her little sneakers. "Giddy-up!" she said. "Giddy-yup, giddy-yup! Ride 'em, cowboy!"

Uncle Seth wandered over slowly, examining the ground, then he studied the car. He kicked a tire, rubbed a hand on the fender. Then he turned to face my mother and shrugged. Both of them dropped their shoulders and then moved to each other and hugged tightly. I watched from behind the dead elm, my cheek pressed against the bark, until they called me.

That night, when we finally set up camp in the Badlands National Park, I thought how my mother was right about Forrest. He had led to a change. For one thing, there was no school anymore. We were living in a tent now, cooking over fires. This had been Forrest's idea. He said that this was a cheaper way to travel than staying in motels, and my mother had seemed relieved both at his thriftiness, and at finding out he was right. The rangers at the National Parks charged us only a few dollars to pitch the tent we'd borrowed from Uncle Seth, and the campgrounds had bathrooms with running water.

My mother's tension seemed to let up a bit as we cooked hot dogs over a fire and then sat there to stay warm. It was early autumn and the nights were getting chilly. "Oh boy," she said. "Wilderness family."

Forrest loved it. "I haven't done this in years!" he said, looking around and stretching his arms out as if searching for something to embrace. He had been brought up in South Dakota, on the reservation. "I'm seven-eighths," he'd said when he told us about it. I didn't know what he meant by this, but math was another subject I didn't like so I didn't ask. Instead, over dinner I got him to tell Lillie and me stories about his ancestors, particularly about Crazy Horse. "Ah, *Tasunke Witco*," Forrest said. "He was my gran'father."

"Right," said my mother, laughing. "And my great-grandparents came over on the Mayflower."

"They did?" Forrest said.

"Squanto!" I said, surprised to find something from school coming in handy.

"Squanto was a pretty good guy," Forrest said. "But those Pilgrims put one over on him. He should not have trusted them. Crazy Horse would have slaughtered them."

My mother's mouth fell open, then she buried her head in her hands.

"What's slottered?" Lillie asked.

"He would have cut out their hearts," Forrest calmly explained.

"Oh," said Lillie, giving a precocious nod, as if this made complete sense to her.

My mother shook her head and looked up at the sky. "Must we?" she asked the stars. Then she lowered her gaze back to Forrest. "She's already sick. Do you have to keep her up all night with nightmares?"

Lillie had kept up her coughing all day long. She was always sick, it seemed to me.

"I'll go get the blankets from the car," Forrest said. He got up, unwinding in one fluid motion—Forrest was not a man without grace—and went to the car. He was gone a long time. Lillie and I sat looking into the fire while my mother snapped a twig to pieces.

When Forrest came back he wrapped a blanket around Lillie and stroked her hair for a moment, tucking it into the blanket and making her giggle. Then he brought the rest of the blankets into the tent. My mother got up and went in after him, pulling the flap closed, and I could hear the fevered murmur of her voice, scolding him.

"I want more stories," Lillie said.

I looked off at the strange shapes of the hills across the open space of the campground. The limestone formations circling us on one side were getting darker against the deepening blue of the sky. On the other side of us, the flat plain stretched off to a range of distant mountains. The first stars twinkled along their edges. Even as a kid, I knew this was a beautiful sight, and that the single lone billboard—placed out beyond what must have been the boundary of the park and lit up by a row of small spotlights— was some sort of desecration. It was for a private campground, and camp was spelled with a K. This bothered me. Spelling was one thing I was good at.

"I don't think so," I told Lillie. "Shut up."

After the Badlands, Forrest drove us off the main highway so we could pass through the reservation where he'd been born.

"Maybe I'll see somebody who remembers me," he told my mother.

She was still irritable. "I thought you were a boy when you left," she said.

"I was," he said. "But you never know what will come back to you."

Off the interstate, the two-lane blacktop passed through a clutter of billboards for things like "The World's Biggest General Store Only 86 Miles," or the "Bear in the Lodge Truck Stop With Real Buffalo Burgers." One said, "Go Back You Missed the Petrified Gardens!"

Then the billboards stopped and Forrest told us we were on the reservation. We passed a few farmhouses and some trailers with long, rust-pocked cars parked haphazardly in the dirt around them. Eventually, we stopped seeing any more signs of civilization at all, save for utility poles and fencing. Mostly it was just mile after mile of rolling, yellow-tipped grass.

Then we passed a lean man walking the other way along the shoulder. Forrest honked the horn and the man waved. Lillie and I hung out the side window and waved back until he was out of sight. Then we drove for miles more of empty grassland, until my mother said, "My God, We haven't passed a thing! That man must be walking for miles!"

"That's what you do here," Forrest said.

Eventually, we came upon a white clapboard church with a steeple, set far back off the road, and then some houses and another trailer or two, and then finally we came upon a sign for gas and a grocery store. We pulled off the road and into the lot, where there were several clumps of men standing around next to a scattering of pickups and old American cars, big and white and dirty, like the bellies of washed-up boats.

"You go and get some cough s'urp for Lillie," Forrest told my mother, "and some pop. I'll ask for directions."

"This won't take long," my mother said.

"Okay," said Forrest.

She took Lillie and me into the store and stopped just inside the door to get her bearings. I noticed the women working the bank of cash registers. They looked like white women but they had dark hair. I stared at them, trying to figure out if they were Indians or not, until my mother took my hand, and Lillie's, too, and pulled us away. We wandered down one aisle, then up another. Lillie wasn't paying attention, and when my mother paused to examine a tall stack of soup cans, Lillie walked into the back of her legs. An old woman, hunched up and wearing an unnecessarily heavy down vest, stopped as she was passing us to finger Lillie's curly blond hair. "Very pretty," she told my mother, smiling. "Your children are very good-looking."

My mother gave the woman a look of momentary confusion, then thanked her primly and took up our hands again. We passed what looked like entire families, women and children and grandparents, shopping together. They all nodded and smiled at us, then returned to carefully studying packages before placing them in their carts or back on the shelves.

When we came out Forrest was standing next to some old-fashioned gas pumps with glass bubbles on top. There were three or four men with him, wearing ragged straw cowboy hats and dirty denim clothes. They were passing a bottle in a greasy sack back and forth and laughing. One of them, an old man with fat round cheeks, kept touching Forrest, putting a hand on his arm, then taking it away, then putting it back again as they talked and laughed.

"We're ready," my mother called to Forrest from the car.

"Okay," he said, then nodded at the men and came over and got back in the car with us. He was still chuckling over something to himself.

He started the car, but before we could pull away the man who had been touching Forrest came up and leaned down into his open window. He smelled funny and had a few long black hairs coming out of the smooth skin around each end of his mouth. He was smiling, and it made the hairs stick out.

"Maybe you have a dollar you could give me," he said to Forrest.

Forrest looked at my mother, who looked like she was about to speak, but no words came out. Then she looked down and around herself, shifting as she searched the seat for her purse.

But Forrest turned back to the man and said, "We don't really have it to spare."

"You sure?" the man asked. His head was nearly completely in the car. His eyes were shining and looked like they were brimming with water. "One dollar?"

My mother stopped her rustling and stared at the man in the window.

"Sorry," Forrest said.

"It's all right," the man said. He held the greasy sack out to Forrest.

"No thanks," Forrest said.

"You sure?" the man asked. A grin took over Forrest's face, as if in spite of himself, and the man laughed. "Happy journey," he said. Then he stepped back, smiling, and gave us a wave as we pulled away.

"Boy," said my mother.

"He knew me," Forrest said. "He knew my father. He called him Chief. 'Chief Bender.'" Forrest laughed. "I told him my father was gone and he said, 'Then you are Chief now.'" He slapped a hand on my mother's thigh and turned his head to all of us. "You can just call me Forrest, though," he told us.

Back on the road, my mother was silent, staring out the window pensively as the wind whipped her hair around her face. Lillie was asleep next to me with her mouth open. Forrest was humming happily, and he would point out things and comment on them to me in whispers. Even though our picnic stop had scared me a little, I was anxious for him to bring us to another place with ghosts. I sat up and stared closely at anything he pointed out, my head going all the way around and back to Forrest as we passed it. It was like it was just him and me for a while.

But we didn't pass any more of the little iron historical markers. Instead, the reservation's highway signs were all homemade, green with hand-painted white letters in obvious imitation of the signs on the interstate. But these signs were wooden, and few and far between. There were just enough of them to tell you how far away from something you were, or how far you had to go to get someplace.

When we did, finally, pass a few historical markers, these, too, were Indian versions: they were billboard-sized, huge sheets of plywood completely covered with long passages of small, cramped words. But Forrest didn't stop to read them. "I know what they say," he told me whenever we passed one, and then he would recite the history of the place, what had happened there, who had died.

261

"Red Cloud died in that house," he pointed out once, when we passed an old, ornate Victorian-style house half-hidden in a clump of pine and willow trees. "He was a very old man. He died all alone. He was a great chief, he won many battles, but the other Indians di'n't trust him because in the end he was frien'ly with the *wasichus*."

I felt a tingle, as I had on our picnic, like it wasn't hard to imagine something still there but not quite visible, like there was an old Indian—I saw him in a chief's headdress, wrapped in a blanket, for some reason—lurking in that lonely stand of trees.

In between the signs, Forrest continued his breathy whistling or humming. My mother had kept her silence since the grocery store, and it began to seem strange. Good mood or bad, my mother was famous for always keeping up a determined stream of talk. She would even tell you what she was thinking, going on at length about simple errands, or her complex plans for the future. "I'm thinking we ought to do this or that next, Disney-man," she'd announce, and then she'd go on to explain it all in detail. Even when she seemed to have nothing on her mind, like when I'd find her staring out a window, she would feel the need to explain. "In my mind, I've gone to California," she'd say.

But she was silent now, lost in thought, and Forrest began to notice it, too. His music grew quieter, as if he didn't want to disturb her. After a while, I got bored, so I woke up Lillie and tried to teach her to say, "Give me some skin, man," and to put her hand out flat and let me slide my palm across hers. But she was irritable. She thought I was going to give her an Indian sunburn, which was something I'd done to her when she was little; I'd take her wrist and hold it in place with one hand and twist her forearm with my other hand until I'd worked the skin red and she was squirming. I hadn't done this to her since Forrest came around, though. I sensed it was one of the things I shouldn't do around him, like talking about my real father. But Lillie didn't trust me, so she started coughing in my face again. I didn't like to teach her these things in front of anyone, anyway, because sometimes my mother would whack me for it and say, "Cut it." So eventually we got quiet, too.

When we passed a sign with an arrow saying "Wounded Knee," we were all surprised when my mother suddenly spoke.

262

"Let's go to that," she said. It was the first thing she'd said since the grocery store.

Forrest slowed down and looked at her. "You sure?" he asked.

She looked at him. "Yes," she said. "I've heard about that place." She turned around in her seat and mussed my hair, then sat back and put her hand casually on Forrest's shoulder. She looked back out the window and said, "Maybe it'll be educational."

Forrest shrugged, and when we got to the exit he maneuvered the car carefully off the highway. The side road followed a small, deep-set, churning river, and the flat land dipped down with it. We were suddenly in rolling country that had been hidden from us. The river cut into a deep ravine, and we passed over it on a bridge made of wood and iron. It ended next to another big homemade historical marker. One road met another there, bending off in either direction, but Forrest pulled up next to the sign and stopped. Across the way was a hill, on top of which was a lonely church and a graveyard. It seemed like we were the only ones around for miles.

"This is it," Forrest said.

My mother seemed surprised, and she looked at Forrest the same way I did as I asked, "No souvenir stand?"

"Nope," Forrest said.

When I think about that place now, I remember it as being early morning and gray, with fog creeping from the riverbank to collect along the foot of the hill and reach its ghostly tendrils up the sides, the tombstones seeming to lift up out of it. But Lillie, who claims she remembers things from the cradle, tells me it was midday and the sun was shining hot.

My mother got out and stood in the dirt, reading the sign, which had so much to say the words were continued on the back. I stood next to her and counted three misspellings before Forrest called to us to follow him up the hill. "Come on," he said. "You can see it all from up here."

Dreaming about it now, I see myself quiet and spooked, but I also remember complaining that I wanted a soda until my mother finally got annoyed and shushed me in a sudden burst of anger. Then she withdrew, going off to weave slowly and seemingly aimlessly through the headstones. Forrest trailed her with Lillie in his arms, her legs wrapped around his waist.

There were photographs on the markers, and I was surprised to see these weren't the graves of warriors with feather bonnets. The photos were mostly of people in what looked like school portraits, or young men posed in modern military uniforms.

"My God," my mother said after a while, "they all look so young!" I saw her lips moving slightly as she drifted along, calculating. Then she stopped short. "The average age is about twenty-eight!" she said to Forrest. And this was another moment of tasting sweet and sour: the first time I was ever precisely conscious of my mother having an age. She was twenty-eight, too.

I didn't know at the time how old Forrest was—he seemed ageless, as old as my mother yet at the same time older, much older. But he didn't seem at all daunted by her discovery. His lopsided smile was in place and he seemed as cheerful as ever. "Yes," he said. "I am an old man, by Indian stan'ards."

Perhaps because I had become absolutely desperate for soda, this place did not evoke the ghosts for me of our picnic on the prairie, nor of Red Cloud hidden in the willows. It was a disappointment, and it bothers me now that I don't remember it more clearly. It only comes back to me in bits and pieces: I remember my mother reading out some names—"Ann T. Respects Nothing," "Asa Walks Away"—and I have a vague recollection of Forrest squatting down with a blade of grass in his teeth, the white church looming behind him as he told us about the first Indians who had died there. He told us about the soldiers across the ravine with Gatling guns, and Lillie said, "What's catlinks?" But that's about it. At the time, there were no ghosts for me there.

My dreams now are scattered and colored by a wishfulness that I'd been more perceptive then. My most vivid memory is of being a little surprised that my mother did not scold Forrest when he described all the dead children in the snow, their blood a satin blanket beneath them; instead she thwacked me on the shoulder when I interrupted him to complain of my thirst.

And when we got back in the car and drove off, she looked out the window and rubbed her hands over her bare arms as if she had a chill.

For once, Forrest was silent, too, and his silence was even more unusual than my mother's, and in that way it gradually came to me that something had happened and that I had missed it. It would be left for me to ask Lillie about, years later. It would be left for me to dream about later. Maybe my mother was thinking about the children in the snow. Maybe she was thinking about the calm way Forrest could tell such a horrible story. I turned to look out the back window, but all I could see was the big, dull box of our possessions trailing along behind us, pulling on us whenever we tried to ascend a rise in the land, pulling on us like a great weight.

It wasn't until we were in the Black Hills that the sense of something foreboding returned, and I could hear the Indian sound track again, and imagine them, stray and feathered and on horseback, in the pines on the rocky slopes. The tingling returned as the road unreeled, twisting and curving back through the switchbacks. There were bursts of houses and signs and places to stop, but they would disappear in moments and we would find ourselves climbing and winding our way through untouched and rugged landscape, being watched.

When we passed a sign saying "Crazy Horse Monument," it seemed to confirm my feelings.

"Forrest!" I shouted, lurching forward in the back seat to grab his shoulder.

My mother, who had been dozing fitfully, roused up and said, "Huh? What?"

"It's nothing," Forrest said to both of us.

"But Crazy Horse!" I said, baffled as to why he was driving past the exit.

"It's nothing," he said, more to my mother than to me. "There is nothing to see."

My mother was craning back over her shoulder, trying to read the sign from the back.

"It said Crazy Horse!" I told her.

"It's just a mountain the Indians are trying to carve up to look like Crazy Horse," Forrest explained. "Like the whites did with Moun' Rushmore."

"You're kidding," my mother said.

"No," Forrest said. "They've been working on it since before I was born. But it only looks like a moun'ain that's been blow'd up." He shook his head and smiled. "Bunch of dumb Indians," he said. "They can't figure out how to blow up a moun'ain like the white man." He chuckled, a low sound deep in his chest.

"But—" I started.

"God," said my mother, straightening her frazzled hair. "No whining."

"Trust me," said Forrest. "It's nothing. Crazy Horse woul'n't like it." His shining black eyes smiled at me in the rearview.

But whether it was Crazy Horse or a blown-up mountain, both sounded like something I wanted to see. I couldn't understand why Forrest would stop at every one of the little iron historical plaques, where there was never anything except grass, and not at a place where there was actually something to see. I folded my arms and slipped into a funk in the back seat.

The car moved slower and slower as we climbed up into the hills. We kept passing signs for Mt. Rushmore, but it never seemed to be arriving. My mother kept shifting in her seat and sighing. "This is taking forever," she said. Lillie was coughing, saying, "How much longer?"

In my mood, I decided to contribute. "I have to go to the bathroom," I said.

"Don't start," my mother snapped back over her shoulder.

"I'm not starting," I told her.

"Yes you are, you're starting," she said.

"Are we almost there?" Lillie asked.

My mother twisted in her seat to face us. "Now look, you two—" she said.

Forrest clucked his tongue.

She turned to him like she was going to snap at him, too, but he merely nodded, indicating something in the corner of the windshield: the colossal head of George Washington had suddenly appeared through a crease in the mountains.

"Holy cow!" my mother said.

George Washington vanished as quickly as he'd appeared. The road circled the foot of a mountain, then cleared it, and suddenly, rising majestically before us, was another mountain on which we could see all four gigantic heads—Washington, Jefferson, Roosevelt, and Lincoln—carved into the sheer rock face. They were skirted by a wash of granite rubble left when they'd been blasted out: a clean, gray apron of stone trimmed in pine. A perfectly white cloud drifted beyond in crystal blue sky. It was an amazing sight.

"Wow!" I said, all thoughts of mood and ghosts gone. "Cool!"

Forrest was chuckling. "The white man," he said, "they know how to blow up a moun'ain."

When we got there we parked and made our way to the gate, unable to take our eyes off the sight—except for Lillie, who was whining in my mother's arms. But my mother paid no heed, she was transfixed, although after Forrest paid the entrance fee she did manage to mutter, "So expensive . . ." under her breath.

"I'm hungry!" Lillie complained.

"Shush, baby," my mother cooed, barely distracted.

"I'm very hungry!" Lillie persisted.

"What are you hungry for?" my mother asked.

"I need candy," Lillie said.

"Oh," my mother said. "No you don't." So Lillie coughed wetly in her ear. My mother wiped it off unconsciously and resumed her trance, staring off through the enormous windows of the visitor's center as we moved toward the outside viewing area.

When we got there I had to thump at my mother's side to get her attention. I wanted some quarters for the binocular machines.

She dug out some change mechanically, and I slipped in a coin, but it took me a few minutes to figure out how to work the viewer. My mother and Forrest were no help at all as they stood there in stunned wonderment. But it seemed like as soon as the viewer whirred to life, my mother was pressing up next to me. "Let me see," she said.

I pushed her back without taking my eyes from the lenses. "Wow!" I said. "Can we go up there?" I was imagining climbing around on Lincoln's nose.

My mother gave me a firmer nudge and took over the machine, shifting Lillie onto her hip.

"I don't think so," Forrest said.

"I need candy!" Lillie said, whacking the side of my mother's head as she tried to look through the eyepiece.

"Shush!" my mother scolded out of the side of her mouth.

Then one of my teachings came back to me: "You're garbage!" Lillie shouted in my mother's ear. I cringed as I waited for my mother to figure out where Lillie'd gotten this.

But she just put Lillie down on the flagstones and clung to the binoculars with both hands.

"This is really something," she said. Lillie was pounding on her thigh.

It began to seem like we were standing there forever. My mother just couldn't get over it. She fed quarter after quarter into the machine as Forrest stood at her side with his arms across his chest. When a busload of tourists flooded the viewing area, I found my attention drifting to them, to the fact that they were all wearing jackets but also shorts, as if willing it to be hotter and more vacationlike than it was.

Lillie kept pounding my mother's thigh with her little balled-up fists, and when she started crying my mother reluctantly pulled away from the machine and lifted Lillie up into her arms. Some big kid with glasses immediately took over the binoculars.

We made our way back through the building, heading through the cafeteria to return to the car and feed Lillie. But by then Lillie was wailing. She was so worked up she couldn't form words, she just pointed at the food stand and mumbled gibberish like a baby. My mother patted her back and murmured, "It's too expensive, baby. There's food in the car. Just hold on a few more minutes."

"Maybe if we eat here it will satisfy her," Forrest said behind me.

"What?" said my mother, turning to him. She put Lillie down with an *umph*. "We can't spend our money in these places."

"I want to go to Deadwood," I said, annoyed that Lillie was getting her way. We'd seen signs for the place and I recognized the name from TV. I thought we might be able to catch a gunfight. "You promised," I reminded my mother.

"I'll go get the food from the car," Forrest said.

My mother looked at him. "No you won't—" she began.

"It's okay," he said. "I'll be right back."

I was being ignored, standing between them while they talked over my head. "Hey," I said, poking at my mother. "What about Deadwood?"

Suddenly Lillie let loose a blood-curdling scream and everybody at the tables turned around and looked at us.

"I'll be right back," Forrest said, and he was gone.

My mother gave a sigh but quickly turned to the sobbing Lillie. "Lillie-Belle, shhh," she said, squatting down to rub her back. "We're gonna eat in a minute, baby."

"Mom!" I said.

She turned on me. "Hush, just hush!" she commanded.

Lillie immediately started screaming at the lapse in attention. "You're garbage! You're garbage!" she shouted.

My mother recognized it this time and gave me a withering look. "I'm gonna brain you," she said. Then she grabbed Lillie by the shoulders and shook her. "You, too! Now stop it this minute!"

Lillie whimpered but quieted down, and my mother led us to an empty table. "You better not go back on your promise," I muttered.

"Enough!" my mother said. She started yanking napkins from the dispenser and slapping them down around the table like place mats.

When Forrest finally came back he seemed as mellow as ever. But in her anger, my mother's suspicions flared up again. "Better?" she said sarcastically.

Forrest was bustling around the table, giving us all sandwiches. He stopped in confusion. "Huh?" he said.

"What about Deadwood?" I asked, folding my arms, ignoring my sandwich.

"Sure," Forrest said distractedly. "We'll go there."

"No," my mother said. Lillie had folded her arms, too, and was refusing to touch her sandwich. My mother had to take it and place it in her hand.

"What?" I said. "That's not fair!"

Forrest nodded carefully. "Yes," he said. "We may never pass through here again."

Lillie slapped her sandwich back down on the napkin.

My mother went stiff for an instant. "Don't *you* start," she said to the table in general. Then she picked Lillie's sandwich back up.

"I'm not starting," Forrest said. "Hey," he said, "when we get to Seattle, we're going to be rich." He laughed and waved an arm over his head. "We'll be flying everyplace!"

My mother pried open Lillie's fingers and jammed the sandwich back into her hand. "Oh really?" she said. "You gonna get a job, too?"

Forrest's eyes went wide and he blinked. "Sure," he said. His smile was sad for a moment, then he seemed to snap back. "I'll

269

get a job building bridges. They must have bridges in Seattle. Only Indians are dumb enough to build bridges."

My mother snorted. "You're afraid of heights," she said.

"What about Deadwood?" I asked.

"I said no!" my mother said. "We've got to start making time! I've got a job to get to!"

"Don't worry," Forrest said. "I'll find something."

"But Mom—" I started.

Lillie slapped her sandwich down again and there was an explosion of lettuce.

My mother fell back in her chair and blew her hair from her face. "God help me," she said.

"I'll find something," Forrest said again, staring vacantly at his sandwich.

"I don't care anymore," my mother said. She sank back into the passenger seat and waved a hand of dismissal in front of her face. Forrest took it as a sign that he should drive us farther up into the mountains to Deadwood.

But when we got there, there wasn't much to see. The saloons looked fake and there were no cowboys or gunslingers, only a crowd of tourists. We walked along the sidewalks for a few minutes, my disappointment growing deeper and deeper that it didn't look like it did on TV. My mother stayed a few feet behind us, sunglasses hiding her eyes, arms folded tight.

We had come to a stop on the edge of town and were staring off at a small mound holding a desultory cemetery that was obscured by signs saying things like "The ORIGINAL Boot Hill" and "Visit the Final Resting Places of Famous Shoot-Out Victims," when a man wearing shorts and knee-high black socks came up to Forrest. Forrest had been staring off with a hand shading his eyes from the sun, and he was confused when the man said, "Pardon me, do you work here?"

Forrest thought about it for a minute and said, "Well, I work wherever I can."

"Oh, for God's sake," my mother said, stepping up. Her big, black sunglasses flashed in the sun. "Of course he doesn't work here."

The man looked surprised, then annoyed.

"Just get away from us," my mother said in disgust. She put one hand on my back and the other on Lillie's and steered us directly back to the car. Forrest followed quietly.

After that, he began to drive relentlessly, spiraling down out of the mountains and hauling us out into the flat twilight. He didn't even stop when we saw a huge thunderstorm on the distant horizon. Nobody said a word as we watched the curtain of darkness, rent by sheets of lightning, moving toward us, and it looked fearful all the way. When it was upon us, Forrest had to slow the car down to a crawl. But it swept over us quickly, a swift pounding of the car, then moved off to the other horizon as we drove on, accelerating into the following night.

I was tired. I could actually feel it in my legs, a muscular tension and numbness from being cramped in the car, and a weariness, too, from all the walking around. The long day of tourism became a jumble of sensations, with each place becoming confused with another until they virtually blocked each other out. In the void, the excitement of the trip had worn off; I couldn't figure out why we were doing this anymore, and I gradually found myself thinking about home, actually remembering us there as we were before Forrest, visualizing it vividly, like seeing ghosts of ourselves. "We should go back," I wanted to say.

In the dark, we couldn't find any national parks, and eventually we had to settle for a private campground somewhere in Wyoming, a small place with spotty grass and clumps of slender, wind-bent juniper saplings. It was crowded with trailers and RVs and station wagons, and the bathrooms had no showers and were a long way off.

We pitched the tent between two silvered trailers, working by the light cast through their small, awninged windows. When we were done my mother plopped down on the ground, exhausted.

Forrest gathered sticks for a fire. "If you want to go and wash up, I'll watch the kids," he said to the shadows where my mother sat.

"Really?" her voice said dryly. It was another moment where we all thought about what Forrest had hidden in the car trunk that one time.

271

He looked down into the pile of twigs. "Honest Injun," he said quietly.

The pause that followed reminded me of when my mother used to smoke, and she would stave off anger by tossing down her cigarette and grinding it into the dirt for a long, slow moment. "We're not going to Yellowstone tomorrow," she said. "No more stops." Then she got up and left.

Forrest stared after her, then shifted his gaze to the car. I felt compelled to speak. "Tell us a story," I said.

He turned to me almost gratefully and folded himself down to sit cross-legged by the pile of twigs.

"What do you want to hear?" he asked. Then he reached over and gathered up Lillie, who was sitting next to him, half-asleep. He cradled her gently in his arms.

I wanted him to just toss her in the tent. "Anything," I said. "Crazy Horse?"

"Hmmm, *Tasunke Witco* ..." he said. "Your mother doesn't like me to tell you stories about Crazy Horse."

"Well, what Indians are going to be next to him?" I asked. I was thinking about the blown-up mountain, thinking it was going to be an Indian version of Mt. Rushmore.

Forrest knew what I meant. "Oh, just Crazy Horse. But you are right. There should be many Indians next to him. Red Cloud. Sitting Bull, for sure."

"Are you related to him?" I asked. "Chief Sitting Bull?"

"No," Forrest said. "I wish I was. But I know a good story about him." Lillie murmured in her sleep. Forrest rocked her. The lights of the trailer next to us had gone out and Forrest seemed to have forgotten about starting a fire. It was just the two of us, sitting in the dark.

"He wasn't really a chief, he was . . . *wichasha wakon*—a holy man, what you call a medicine man. But his medicine was very powerful, and the whites were afraid of him. Even when he surrendered, they made him live apart from the other Indians, in a lit'le hut out by a river. He lived there with his wife, and some trick ponies Buffalo Bill had given him. They would dance when they heard a tom-tom. But the other Indians wanted to be with Sitting Bull, so they went out to the river, too. The whites decided they had to put Sitting Bull in jail, so they sent some soldiers out there to get him. The Indians di'n't understand, they

272

gathered around Sitting Bull, and one of the soldiers got scared and he shot Sitting Bull. Bang! Bang! *Tatanka Yotake* fell down, dead, and then all his horses started dancing. The Indians and the soldiers got very scared. They thought Sitting Bull's spirit was in the horses."

"What happened then?" I asked.

"Hell broke loose," Forrest said simply. "There were more massacres, broken treaties, much blood—"

My mother stepped out of the darkness and I nearly jumped out of my skin.

"Jesus Christ, Mom!" I shouted. The words leapt out of me.

In one stride she stepped over to me and slapped me hard across the face. She'd never hit me like that before.

"Don't you ever talk like that to me!" she said.

I couldn't help it, I started to cry.

Forrest's whole body flinched, as if he'd been hit, and it woke up Lillie. She started to cry when she heard me, and her wailing seemed to fill the camp.

My mother spun around to face Forrest. "What are you doing to my children?" she said. His mouth opened in surprise. "Telling them these horrible stories!" she said. And then, to my utter surprise, she buried her face in her hands and started to cry, too. "I've got a job to get to," she sobbed.

Forrest stood but was uncertain whether to move to my mother or not.

"I'm sorry, Katrina," he said, but my mother just stood there sobbing.

"I'll take the kids to clean up," he offered, and when my mother still didn't react, he stretched a hand out to me. "Come," he said, and he led us away from my mother.

We made our way through the dark campground, the crickets throbbing the only sound. We spent a long time in the washroom. Forrest seemed to be lost in thought as he carefully washed Lillie's face, tucking her hair back and cleaning behind her ears. She was sniffling, half-asleep and cranky in his hands, but eventually he managed to soothe her. When he was done he held her by the shoulders, propped on the edge of the sink, and smiled at her. "She'll be all right," he said. "Tomorrow she'll be in Seattle." I wasn't sure if he meant Lillie or my mother, but I was relieved to hear that we were almost there.

273

We walked slowly back through the camp, but when we got within sight of our tent, Forrest stopped and said, "Wait." My mother had started the fire, and she was sitting there staring into it. "In here," Forrest said, gently pulling Lillie and me into a nearby clutch of juniper saplings so my mother wouldn't see us. We stood there a long time, and I wasn't sure what we were doing. I looked up at Forrest—framed in a headdress of dark, rustling leaves—trying to figure this out. His gaze was fixed on my mother.

She didn't move, she just stared into the fire, until Forrest put Lillie down and told us to go to her.

When Lillie and I walked up to the fire, hand in hand, my mother looked up with red eyes, then gathered us both in her arms in a sudden rush, like we'd been away from her for a much longer time. She hugged us, then held us at arm's length and looked at us, eyes brimming. She held us for a long moment before she seemed to realize we'd walked up alone.

She looked off the way we'd come. The stand of thin trees was thick in the liquid darkness.

"Forrest?" she said. "Forrest?"

Forrest never came out of the trees. We waited, my mother standing and staring at the dark, until finally she gathered us up and we went into the tent to sleep. "He's probably just taking one of his midnight walks," she said nervously.

In the morning we couldn't find him. My mother stopped me from asking anyone if they'd seen him, but we walked around the campsite for a long time looking. At first, my mother seemed dazed, but by the time she threw open the door of the empty washroom she was angry and determined. She strode directly back to the tent, and we began to pack up. When she tossed Forrest's rolled-up sleeping bag in the trunk, I saw her pause for a moment, and the angry look left her face. She stared at the spare-tire wheel well, and I wondered momentarily if there had ever been a bottle of whiskey there. But my mother's still gaze seemed to be searching for more than that. Then the look switched off and she closed the trunk. She drove us the rest of the way, straight through to Seattle.

She remained that way for a long time, tight-lipped and determined, before she revived somewhat, coming around to something like her old self. Her new job helped, I think, as it was busy and filled with more responsibility than any job she'd ever had before. I was in my new school, and Lillie was being watched during the days by an elderly neighbor. The trip, surprisingly, quickly began to fade from my memory, to shift from dulled recollection to something I rarely thought about in the hubbub of starting over.

We went on with our lives. We never talked about Forrest. In my own thoughts, I barely even tried to guess at why he'd disappeared. There had been so much tension, and then we moved so quickly after he left us. It seemed to make a kind of sense, as if he'd meant to offer relief somehow. After a while, it seemed like it had always been, before Forrest, and it was quite some time— months—before I would notice the sound of my mother crying at night. In the mornings, though, she would seem herself. Eventually, I stopped hearing her in the darkness, until one morning I came down to find her in her bathrobe, staring out the kitchen window. When she saw me, she smiled. "In my mind, I've gone to California, Disney-man," she said.

And over the years, the clear recollection of Forrest faded from me. I could no longer precisely find his face in the ocean of my memory; he became a jumble of images, like the trip itself. I was happy, years later, when my job with the government took me over some of those same highways, because I wanted to place the memories of that time in sequence. I thought that was the only way they would add up to something. I'm not sure if I've done that, though, or merely remembered things in an order that my grown-up knowledge of American geography tells me must be so. It could be that my memory is not true.

Still, I have tried to verify it as best I can, to get out of my memory what I can. In a motel room one night, I found the story of Sitting Bull's murder in a book. The book was written by a white man, like myself, perhaps wishful, like myself. The book's version was slightly different from Forrest's, and now I'm no longer certain which details are Forrest's, and which are the book's. Sometimes, when I think of that story, I find I have substituted Forrest's face for Sitting Bull's: it is Forrest's horses who are dancing.

And on the endless hours of American highways, that is the way my mind works, *remembering* things as if they were interior movies, remembering the things, even, that I didn't participate in; remembering things long past as if they were still going on. The people of my life play all the parts in flickering images, dreamlike images, as I stare off at the grass. Passing stands of trees, I imagine Forrest in there, like Red Cloud, staring out at me. Passing meadows, I see him—for moments oh so fleeting—waving his blanket, signaling the ghosts.

I search for control, when the tingling comes up, but still, I stop at every historical marker.

Nominated by Susan Moon, Ploughshares

THE PARAKEET AND THE CAT

fiction by SCOTT BRADFIELD

from CONJUNCTIONS

"BEING YOURSELF IS NEVER a very easy row to hoe," Sid said, nibbling sourly at a bit of unidentifiable root or mulch. "Being the only stray parakeet in a drab world filled with cackling hive-minded pigeons, sparrows, black crows and pheromone-splashed finches can be a pretty dismal experience indeed. Especially if you're all alone. Especially if you're at all like me, and inclined to be pretty morose at the drop of a hat *any*way."

Without a doubt, winter was the hardest season. In winter, even the leaves abandoned you, while all the anxious birds you were just getting to know on the high wires departed precipitously for warm, ancestral climes—places with mythic, irreproachable names like Capistrano, Szechwan, São Paulo, Bengal. Other birds never told you where they were going, how long it took to get there, or even invited you along for the ride. They seemed to think that if *they* had a perfectly nice location picked out for the off-season, *every*body did.

"It's sort of like being all dressed up with no place to go," Sid told the ducks at his local pond. "I mean, my hormones have shifted into superdrive. My blood's beating with procreation and heat. And not only can't I find any girl parakeets, I can't even find the goddamn continent of Australia." The ducks were an addled, pudgy lot, filled with ambitionless quacks and broad steamy flatulence, fattened by white breads and popcorn dispensed by local children and senior citizens. They sat and jiggled their rumps in sparse blue patches of the partially frozen pond. Snow was everywhere. Winter was pretty indisputable now.

"God*damn* it's cold," the ducks honked and chattered. "Jesus fucking Christ it's *cold* cold cold. We're freezing our collective little butts off out here."

Ducks might be self-involved, Sid thought, but they were still a lot better than no company at all. If you kept close to ducks, you might pick up stray bits of cracker or information now and again, or be alerted by the emergency squawks that proclaimed wolf-peer or weasel-crouch. The winter world was a hazardous and forlorn place, and you could use all the friends you could get. Buses and planes and whirling frisbees and crackling power cables, children with rocks and slingshots and BB guns and pocketknives. The wide world was filled with angular objects that were always rushing toward you without any regard for personal space or decorum. Not to mention the ruder angularities of solitude and exile. Not to mention hunger, sadness, constitutional ennui or even just the bloody weather.

Sid had possessed a home of his own once. A tidy gilded cage with newsprinted linoleum, plastic ladders, bells on wires, bright sexy mirrors and occasional leafy treats of damp lettuce and hard, biteable carrot. Beyond the cage, as ominous as history, stretched a lofty universe of massive walls and furniture and convergent ceilings inhabited by gargantuan creatures with glistening forests of hair and long fat fingers. These gargantuan creatures were always poking these fat fingers at you, and making you sit on them. They whistled and kissed, or made tisky chittering noises, as if *they* were really the parakeets and you too damn stupid to tell otherwise.

"You think you're Mister Big Shot when you've got it all," Sid told the ducks, who were nibbling a waterproof, oily substance into their feathers with irritable little huffs and snaps. "Food, water, a warm place to go to the bathroom—that's all you care about. You happily climb the plastic ladder, or happily ping the bell, or happily chat yourself up in the flashing happy mirror all day long and everybody's happy, because that's what you're sup*posed* to do, that's the life you're sup*posed* to live. Happy happy happy days, all the happy goddamn day long, happy little morons just pissing your happy lives away in some stupid cage. I mean, you *think* you're living your own life and all, but you're not *really*. You're just living the life that's expected from you. That's why you're in a cage, after all. That's why you're getting all that free food."

Sometimes, when Sid was feeling especially bitter and over-reflective, he paced back and forth on a sturdy branch that over-looked the most duck-populous rim of pond. He took quick bites out of the twigs and leaves and flung them hastily over one shoulder, like forsaken illusions. "Then one day you get sick, just a little head cold, and *you're* not worried. But the gargantuan people outside aren't so optimistic, and want to know what happens to you *then*? Want to know where this happy little free ride takes you for a happy spin *now*? Into the trash can, that's where. Right into the smelly old happy trash basket, whether you like it or not."

When Sid stood at the farthest, thinnest extreme of branch, he could feel the faint vegetable pulse of the tree between his toes, he could see the widest horizons of frosty blue pond and white winter sky. "Boy, I'll remember *that* day as long as I live. I'm totally headachy and miserable. I'm coughing up phlegm like it's going out of style. I'm feeling too weak to keep my perch, see, so I drop down to the bottom of the cage for a few succinct winks. I guess while I was sleeping, the gargantuan people gave the cage a few exploratory thumps—I think I remember that much. But I was too tired to react. I just wanted to take this long nap at the bottom of the cage, and the very next thing I know, *bingo!* I'm digging my way out of a newspaper-padded shoe box in the trash can outdoors. I'm sick as a dog. I'm so pissed off I can't see straight. I mean, suddenly there's all this *space* everywhere, loads and loads of *space*, fat and white and dense with dimensions I've never noticed before. The always. The indescribable. The *everything*. I just wandered and wandered, and before long I stumble across you guys, and this nice blue pond you've got for yourselves. The rest, as they say, is history."

Though the ducks might sit and listen to Sid for a while, absently preening one another and snapping at fleas, eventually they grew impatient and irascible. They got up and waddled about self-importantly.

"He's *such* a bore," the ducks complained loudly, flapping in Sid's general direction. "Talk talk talk—*that's* all he does. And want to know how often the subject of ducks comes up? Zero times, that's how many. In fact, we're beginning to suspect this guy doesn't have any interesting duck stories to tell *whatsoever!*"

Being as the odds against his ever running across a female of his own species were something like thirteen trillion to one, spring didn't offer much promise for Sid. This made winters especially hard, especially while the snow fell and icy winds knocked you about. Spring was the sort of dream you had to dream *with* somebody, and Sid was beginning to feel this particular dream was one he would never successfully dream at all.

"Have you even *seen* any girl parakeets?" Sid asked whenever he encountered random sparrows or blackbirds. Usually they were strays who had suffered recent illnesses or injuries, their eyes clarified by wild, dispirited memories of flocks that had long abandoned them. "I mean, they don't even have to be that cute or anything—I don't mind. And if you haven't seen any girl parakeets, how about Australia? It's like this really big vast yellow place—a continent-sized island, in fact. I don't think it's the sort of place you'd ever forget about once you'd seen it. *I* never saw it, and I dream about it every night."

Sid's dreams of Australia were filled with bounding orange prehistoric-looking creatures and black, canny aborigines who hurled hatcheted boomerangs and fired poison darts from blowguns. Brilliant clouds of parakeets swarmed in the bright sky, crying out Sid's name, wheeling and singing songs about an ever-imminent spring which would surely last forever. Whenever Sid awoke on his cold branch he could still hear those distant parakeets singing. Then he took one glance around the frigid, lens-like pond he knew. It was only the routine squawking of ducks. Ducks and ducks and ducks of them.

"Look at Screwy!" they cried (for the ducks were eternally ragging one another, like old maiden sisters). "He's trying to eat another gum wrapper!"

"And look—here comes Big Bubba Duck. And boy, does he ever look pissed off at Harriet!"

Raging with secret, genetic industry, Sid spent entire days chewing things up. Branches and leaves and nuts, punching through their knotty, fibrous tissues with his sharp hooked beak.

"This is what I do," Sid told the ducks, flinging bits of wood and pulp everywhere like a miniature buzz saw. "I'm a wood borer. I bore wood." When Sid wasn't talking to the ducks, he was tearing everything within reach into splintery little pieces. Day after day, hour after hour, sometimes even late into the night when he couldn't sleep.

"I'm a wood borer," Sid proclaimed edgily, his eyes wide with something like panic. "Wood boring just happens to be one of those things I do really, really well."

One day, after a particularly dense snowfall, a cat arrived at the pond, bringing with it a murky, hematic odor of cynicism and unease.

"Hey there, you guys," the cat said, maintaining a polite distance. The cat was gray, and sat itself smugly on a large gray rock. "Boy, are you ever an attractive-looking bunch of ducks! Seriously, I'm really impressed. I never even suspected ducks *came* as good-looking as you guys, or halfway near as intelligent, either. I guess that just goes to show me, doesn't it? I guess that just goes to show that I don't know that much about ducks after all."

At first, the ducks glided off warily into the cold trembling pond, pretending not to be bothered, but never taking their eyes off the cat for one moment, either.

"I'll tell you something, guys," the cat continued, in a voice as gentle and intrepid as desire. "I just came from the city, and you don't have any idea how lucky you've got it out here. What a nightmare. What a cesspool of smog and urine and crime and poverty they've constructed for themselves in the city, boy. Dog eat dog, cat eat cat, cars running *every*body over without so much as a hi or a how-de-do. Bang crash roar crash bang—I've had enough city life to last me a few thousand centuries or so. Which brings me, of course, to why I've decided to move out here to the woods with you guys. Fresh air, sunshine, plenty of exercise. And of course a *strictly* monitored vegetarian diet from now on. I'm taking charge of my life, boy, and taking it on the road. Call me an outlaw, if you wish; call me a rebel. But I'm tired of living the life society *tells* me to live. I'm finally going to live *my* life for *my* self, thank you very much. Come hell or high water."

While his smooth voice wetly purred, the cat licked his stubby, retractile claws and groomed his long twitchy whiskers, as if

281

dressing himself for church. Then, giving the ducks a last fond look over his shoulder, he rested his head on the large gray rock and fell indefensibly asleep.

"Frankly, I don't think you ducks are exactly the brightest flock of fowl I've ever come across in my rude travels," Sid said, perched high atop a thin, bouyant willow. "We're talking a fat gray cat now, and that means cat with a capital C A T, and I can't believe I'm having to actually spell it *out* to you guys. Cats are what you call notoriously fond of fowl, fowl being you ducks and me both. We're like this cat's dream of a main meal, and I don't care what he says about wildlife solidarity, or karma, or pantheism, or even free will. That cat wants to eat us alive. He wants to chew our flesh and rip our blood vessels into stringy pasta. But he wants to play with us first. He wants to tease us and cut us and watch us die slow. That's because *he's* a cat, and *we're* what you call fowl. Am I going too fast for you guys or what?"

With the arrival of the cat's sedulous gray voice, a cloud of drift and complacency began to descend over the tiny duck pond. The ducks took longer naps on the bank, and didn't squawk so much, or flap, or flirt, or battle. They wandered off aimlessly into the high reeds and bushes, snapping up bits of worm and seed, cuddling with their ducklings and gazing up at the slow riot of white, hypnotic clouds and mist. It was as if everyone had suddenly ceased dreaming all at once, Sid thought. It was as if expectation didn't persist here anymore, or incandescence, or passion, or blood. Across the pond's cold glaring logic, the only heat was the large gray cat's heat, the only voice was the large gray cat's voice, the only burn and lungy whisper and modular red pulse was the cat's, the cat's, the cat's, the cat's.

"*Carpe diem,*" the cat said. "Seize the day, live for the moment, enjoy it all while you still can. As long as you've got your health, you've got *everything*." When the cat wasn't sleeping, he was speaking his low voice across the pond, a voice which the steely surface of water seemed to reflect and amplify, like light or temperature. "Sleep and eat and make love and party, party, party till the cows come home. Why live for tomorrow when tomorrow may never come? History, genetics, philosophy, evolution, teleology and math—that's the world of the city, pals. That's the world of machinery, concrete, hypermarts, petroleum and death. We, on the other hand, are in and of nature. We make our own rules, define our own characters and attitudes and laws. You may be ducks, and I may be a cat, but that doesn't mean we can't also be really good friends. I'm actually a pretty thoughtful and sincere individual—once you get to know me, that is. Everybody likes me, everybody trusts me. Everybody perhaps with the exception of my little pal, the parakeet. Isn't that right?" the cat said, peering up into the acute angles of sunlight that intersected the jostling willow like spiritual traffic. "Isn't that right, little pal?"

That's right, Sid thought firmly to himself, refusing to allow the cat even a glance or a whisper. He didn't want to grant the cat any responses that could be woven into luminous spells of innuendo, gossip and misdirection. He didn't want his best thoughts and intentions to be mistranslated into catlike purposes.

And just to clarify the matter a little more precisely, Sid thought, I don't happen to trust you one single little bit.

"Did anybody ever tell you that you have really beautiful plumage?" the cat said, and began licking his knobby paws again, his thick tongue snagging every so often against a stray indication of claw.

I know, Sid thought, staring off resolutely at a distant mountain. My plumage is quite exceptionally beautiful indeed.

Just about the time of the first slow thaw, Sid went for a flight around the pond and discovered the partially devoured remains of a duck concealed behind a copse of blueberries. Flies converged there, and an odor of bad meat and disintegration. Initially Sid felt a moment of giddy, electric self-displacement, as if suddenly confronted by his own reflection in some twisted mirror. The sky seemed closer, the wind harder, the ice colder. Then, with an involuntary jolt of panic, Sid leapt flying into the brilliant white sky.

"It was Screwy," Sid told the other ducks back at the pond. "And just the way I always said it would be. Lungs, kidneys, liver, brains—that cat even chewed the spleen out of him. We got to stick together, now. We got to keep alert, assign guard duties and group leaders. We got to remain calm and, *what*ever happens, stay the hell out of the high brush. Women—keep your ducklings in line. Guys—sharpen your bills against that sandy rock over there. This is war, this is Jericho, this is the Final

Battle. Evil has come to our pond, and it's snoozing away on that big gray rock over there. Evil has come to our pond in the form of a cat, and that cat wants *all* of us for its next breakfast."

"Evil?" the cat sighed, reaching out with its front paws for a hard, slow stretch. "Isn't that a bit much, really? Aren't we all part of the same food chain, aren't we all equal in the eyes of Mother Nature? Don't go getting all moralistic on me, Mr. Parakeet. Ducks die in this hasty world of ours, and so do cats—that's the law of flesh. And Screwy, if you remember, was not a particularly astute duck. If you stop and think about it for one moment, you might realize that Screwy could have been eaten by just about *any*body. So don't go blaming me because of my species, pal. My species may be feline, but my heart is true, and I only wish all of you—ducks and parakeets alike—nothing but the best health, the longest lives, the happiest dreams. And now, if you don't mind," the cat said, resting his chin on his paws, "I think I'll get back to my own happy dreams for a while."

"Quack quack," said the addled ducks, milling about in a dispirited feathery batch. "Screwy is no longer a duck, the cat is no longer a cat. Parakeets and cats disregard ducks altogether, and only talk about abstractions like Evil and Law and Society and War. This is a little too complicated. This is a little too obtuse. Let's do like the cat does, and take ourselves a nice long nap. Let's all take a nap and dream of fat, meaty flies in our mouths, and a world filled with nothing but other happy, happy ducks."

Sid began keeping meticulous census on the extinguishing flock. Fifty-seven, fifty-six, fifty-four, forty. Thirty-nine, thirty-seven, thirty-one, twenty-five. He couldn't always locate them after they disappeared, but he could quickly sense the general attitude of cool and unworried disaffection that possessed the pond's addled survivors like some sort of inoculation. The survivors rarely looked at one another anymore, or exhibited any signs of affection. They allowed their ducklings to wander off unprotected into the high brush, they didn't eat as much as usual, they grew thin, spotty and slightly diarrheic. Sometimes they slept, or drifted aimlessly on the thawing pond among wide broken platforms of ice, or just strolled aimlessly in circles on the bank, snapping at indistinguishable pebbles and insects. It was as if the ducks had surrendered to a force far greater than themselves, a force which permitted them to nap, disregard, wander, delude, demagnify and concede. The world's escalating reality was making the ducks more and more conjectural and abstract. Soon the bank and brush surrounding the pond were littered with splintery duck bones, broken duck bills and moist forlorn puddles of bloody duck feathers.

"They don't listen to a word I say," Sid complained to himself out loud. "It's like I'm talking to myself. It's like we don't even speak the same language anymore."

"They do what nature tells them," the cat said wisely, sharpening his claws against the base of Sid's willow. "That's why they're at peace with themselves, that's why they can sleep and nap and rest. They realize that the universe is just this big blazing oven, burning entire planets for fuel, driving into the long black spaces all alone without any proper destination in mind. Ducks aren't smart enough to trouble themselves with things like morality or justice—and that's where they're one up on you and me. Heaven's a dream they'll dream *after* this life, and not before. Why don't you try it yourself, pal? Why don't you just take it easy and go with the flow? We all die, we all suffer, none of our dreams hold. It's not necessarily bad, or evil, or tragic, or sad. Just look around you—the ice sparkles, the bare trees sway. Winter's a pretty beautiful season, if you give it half a chance. As long as you've got a nice thick coat to keep you warm."

Every night, Sid grew feverish with bad dreams and black reflections. He tried to stay awake and watch the cat, who never seemed to abandon the perimeter of gray rock. He could see the cat's luminous green eyes in the darkness, eyes that watched him while he drifted away into near-deliriums, lulled by the cat's ceaseless gray voice.

"Come down out of the tree," the cat whispered. "Come down and take a bath in the pond. It's not so painful once you know, it's not so scary once you're taken by its teeth. It can even be a very sensual experience, or at least so I've heard. You won't be lonely anymore. You won't suffer. You won't live dreams that always disappoint, you won't feel hope that always flees, you won't know love that always lies."

Sid began to lose his formidable appetite; he stopped trying to rally the ducks into assuming tactical deployments and responsibilities; he even stopped boring wood. He sat in the high willow all day long simply trying to stay awake, drifting into reveries and naps, awakening with a galvanic thrill whenever he smelled the cat in the tree and looked down.

"I just thought I'd come up and visit for a little while," the cat said, attached to the willow's trunk by four alert paws. "Do you mind if I come up just a little further? Oh, okay. But maybe later? Maybe later in the week?" And then, with a casual glance over his shoulder, the cat retreated backwards down the trunk of the tree again, his long tail twitching, his fat rump writhing with a slow, almost erotic beat.

What *could* you count on in life? Sid wondered. Loneliness, predation, crepuscular scurryings, agony and death and the cold comfort of abstractions? The ducks in the pond continued to dwindle and nap. Twenty-three, nineteen, eighteen, twelve. Winter, Sid thought. Cold and very white.

"What's it all about?" Sid asked himself out loud, half asleep, nearly submerged by his own watery dejection. "What's it all mean?"

"Nothing," the cat whispered. "Or at least nothing that matters."

"Who really cares?" Sid asked. "Who's there to hold you in the night, or hear you cry? Who's there to tell you it'll all be better in the morning?"

"Nobody," the cat whispered. "Nobody, nowhere."

"Why's it worth doing, then? Why should I struggle? Why should I even try anymore?"

"You shouldn't," the cat whispered, out there in the darkness. "You shouldn't struggle, you shouldn't try. Just come down out of the tree, pal. Come down here with me and *I'll* take care of you. We're similar sorts of people, you and me. We're different from everybody else. *We* belong *together*."

At night now Sid could hear the cat boldly taking the ducks and unashamedly eating them. The ducks hardly made any fuss at all anymore, or emitted any sounds. There was just the rushed guttural purr of the cat, and the wet sound of meat in his throat.

Night and annihilation were everywhere. All day long the fat gray cat slept on the large gray rock.

Sid knew he couldn't last; he knew he'd have to surrender eventually.

286

"First rule: I don't want to be cut," Sid said. "I don't want to be bitten, or tortured, or flayed. I want to go with dignity. Then, afterwards, I don't care what happens. That's just my material substance, that's not my *me*. But I know I can't do it alone. I'm too scared. I know I'll chicken out at the last moment. That's why I need *you*."

"Don't be frightened," the cat said, gazing placidly at Sid in the high branches. "Of course I'll do anything *I* can to help."

They embarked one morning after a cold rain. The high dark clouds were just beginning to break apart. On the bank, a small remaining band of thin, desultory ducks slept together fitfully in the shadow of the large gray rock, wheezing and dreaming. First, the cat waded alone into the pond and winced.

"The water's pretty cold," the cat said. "But I've got a nice thick coat, so I don't mind."

As the cat began to paddle, Sid leapt weakly from the willow and landed on the cat's fat behind.

"I want to go out there," Sid said. "To the island."

The island contained a few leafless trees and one broken, abandoned children's fortress cobbled together with planks of wood and old orange crates. Everything seemed misty and uncertain to Sid that morning. He had not slept properly in weeks. He couldn't keep his meals down. He knew what he had to do, but he didn't feel any desperation about it, or sadness, or urgency. He simply knew he was too tired to go on living with the way things were. He had to get it over with while he still had the strength.

"Anywhere you'd like," the cat said agreeably, looking at Sid over his shoulder, his body coiled and alert beneath the water like an assumption.

"I always thought drowning was the best way to go," Sid said distantly, watching the island approach, counting his reflections in the rippled water. "I always thought it would be just like falling asleep."

"I'm sure it's very peaceful," the cat said. "I mean, but in the long run, of course, it doesn't really matter *how* you go, does it?" The cat's eyes were sly half-crescents, void and messageless, like signals from outer space. "It just matters *that* you go, and with as little pain as possible—that's *my* philosophy. I mean, the only people death really affects are the loved ones left behind—and you're not exactly leaving the world very crowded in *those* departments, pal. Or are you?"

"No," Sid said. "I guess not."

"Death's pretty much overrated, when you get right down to it," the cat said, his voice expanding across the pond with a curt gray clarity. "I don't think death's any more inscrutable than life, really. It's not destination, or conclusion, or loss. I think of it more as translation—a reintegration of the furious self into the selfless, eternally mundane process of *living*, grinding on and on and on. Not truth. Not justice. Not morality or law. And certainly not individuals like us, pal. Individuals don't mean very much compared to the eternal burning engines of the night. Space and planetary explosions and famine and floods and madness and war. I guess I'm what you'd have to call a pantheistic sort of cat, being as I believe—oh my."

They were only a few yards from the brink of the island, and the cat had come to an abrupt halt in the water.

"What's that?"

There was something brittle about the cat's voice now, something tentative and uncatlike.

"What's what?" Sid asked and, with a succinct flurry of wings, transferred himself to a gnarl of a drifting branch.

The cat was squinting with concentration, his chin partially submerged beneath the lid of water. "I seem to have one of my feet caught in something."

"Reach down with your other foot," Sid said. Sid was feeling dreamy and sad. Nothing broke the corrugated surface of the pond except the earnest, conspiratorial figures of parakeet and cat.

"Yes," the cat said. "If I just . . . Oh, that's not it. Now I've got my other foot caught, too."

"They're what the ducks call slipweeds," Sid said, "because they never give you the slip. I realize it doesn't make sense calling them slipweeds—but then, go figure ducks. I don't know if you've noticed, but ducks never swim near this island. Ducks keep to the other side of the pond entirely."

"Oh my," the cat said. The cat's eyes were suddenly wider. He spat out trickles of water that rilled into his mouth. "This is a bit dire, isn't it?"

288

"Maybe for you," Sid said.

"Listen," the cat said, "maybe if you came over here a little closer. . ."

"Fat chance," Sid said. "A snowball's chance in hell."

"You don't like me very much, do you?" The cat was beginning to struggle and kick a little, like a fish on a line. "I think you're being very unfair. For a cat, you know, I'm actually a pretty nice guy."

"I'm sure you are," Sid said, his own voice enveloping him like a dream. He was trying to keep his eyes open. He was trying not to fall asleep. "I'm sure you're a perfect saint—for a cat, that is."

"Oh hell," the cat said, and then, with a sudden twist and a plash, his round black snout vanished beneath the surface of water like a midnight vision overcome by harsh, irrefutable sunlight.

Sid was too exhausted to fly. He floated on the knobby branch for hours, hearing the secret rhythm of waves, the moist interior warmth of planets, pausing occasionally to take a sweet sip of water, or ponder his own imponderable reflection in the brightly lidded pond.

"Maybe the cat was right about destinations," Sid thought, drifting in and out of sleep as the branch rocked, rocked him. "Maybe, in fact, destinations are places we never get to. Love, home, safety, death. Heaven and marriage and family and hell. Maybe they're just notions of permanence we've invented in order to protect ourselves from the general impermanence of life itself. Maybe the universe *is* an oven. Maybe life really *is* without meaning. But maybe, just *may*be, these aren't reasons to give up life, but only reasons to enjoy and appreciate it more. Maybe we don't ever get anywhere, or find what we want, or know anything utterly. But maybe that means we can stop punishing ourselves so much, too. Just getting up every day and doing the best job we can—maybe *that's* the most we can ever expect from life. Doing the best job we can every day, and then being kind to ourselves afterwards."

By the time Sid's branch reached shore it was late afternoon, and Sid took himself a little bath. He nibbled damp neglected crumbs from the sand, and felt a tiny kernel of strength blossom in his heart and face. Everything about the waning sunlight seemed slightly richer, warmer, bluer and more real than it had

289

that morning. In the shade of the large gray rock, even the frazzled ducks were beginning to stir a little. Sid couldn't help feeling momentarily pleased with himself.

"Hey, cat!" Sid called out over his shoulder, brushing the water from his wings with a little swagger.

As if in response, a few trembling bubbles surfaced from the blue pond.

"Screw you, *pal!*" Sid said, and then, just as suddenly, he realized.

Completely out of the blue, Spring had begun.

Nominated by Conjunctions

HOMAGE TO THE RUNNER: BLOODY BRAIN WORK

by MARVIN BELL

from AMERICAN POETRY REVIEW

WRITING POETRY is a way of life, not a career.

Ray Mullen, potter and painter, on his retirement from teaching: "No matter what you make, you can't buy a day of your life."

Word comes from eastern Long Island that another of my favorite former teachers has died.

Mike, and Mike's brother, Perry, whose card identifies him as "the P-Man," have come to haul away some bedsprings, the heavy bank teller's machine that Jason and friends pushed up the driveway into the carport a decade ago, and some metal storage shelves from Sears that were our first bookcases. Perry spots my wooden wagon and wants to buy it to fix it up. The sides are missing, but ok. Dorothy tells him the story of how I got the wagon, how I fell as a small child and split open my head and had to go to the doctor for stitches and how after that I wouldn't get a haircut because all I knew is that someone in a white coat wanted to do something to my head. So my father gave Johnny-the-Barber a red wagon with which to tempt me on my way home from school. Dorothy tells Perry the story in the hope that the story will go with the wagon, and of course she's right: material things are not a life but evidence of a life.

And Mike's brother says, "Every kid ought to have a wagon that has a story attached to it. When I was a kid, I had a disease that was dissolving my hip joint. I had to be in a body cast for thirteen months. So my father bought me a little metal wagon and my sister used to pull me around the trailer park. One day we got too wild and I fell out and broke the body cast, so they had to take me back to the hospital and I had to have it done all over again."

Mike will have to come back to take away my radio equipment, from the days when I was W2IDK. Amateur radio was a way of life, not a career. This was before transistors replaced tubes and technology made single sideband sound normal. Before that, a voice on single sideband (which takes half as much room on the dial as a normal modulated voice signal), sounded like Donald Duck. On Field Day, we'd put up tents, string antennas and mount beams, fix up places to sleep and to cook, start up the generators and stay on the air for two days to test our ability in emergencies. "Hams" were strange people then, oddballs who knew something and who shared their information generously but who didn't care if others heard about them or not. The "shack" (an attic) where I first heard the mysteries of short wave and code belonged to W2EBT. "Two Eggs, Bacon & Toast," he called himself, and "Elderly, Bald & Toothless." The shack in the woods where I built my first transmitter, a twenty-watt piezoelectric crystal-controlled oscillator, and power supply belonged to the reclusive W2OQI ("Two Ossified Queer Indians"), who showed me how, and I caught a ride to radio club meetings with W2FCH (Herbert Snell, who called himself "Two Females Chasing Herbie").

Now I sometimes wander out to the cliffs at Fort Worden, outside Port Townsend, Washington, where in June the local hams still set up for Field Day. But now they use TV and fax machines, their transmitters are tiny, their beam antennas don't have to go up on trees to fall over, and they eat and sleep in campers and trailers. When Mike wants to, he can take away my Lysco 600-watt transmitter, my HQ129X receiver, which came from the radio room of a Coast Guard boat, my Vibroflex key with its repeating dot mechanism, and the rest of it. I see the c.w. operators at Field Day using their monokeys, which have repeating dot and dash mechanisms both, with the result that their "fists" have no personalities. I learned plenty from my time as a ham radio operator, but I'm glad I didn't stay to be overcome by technical gee-whiz and the comforts of home.

And Mike can take away my photo enlarger and the rest of the darkroom equipment. Those were great days, the days of Aaron Siskind and Harry Callahan and Ansel Adams and Robert Heinecken and Nathan Lyons and Walter Chappell and Henry Holmes Smith and Van Deren Coke and the young Jerry Uelsmann and Clarence John Laughlin and Art Sinsabaugh and Minor White and a whole generation of hot young photographers gathered around Minor at the Rochester Institute of Technology and around Siskind and Callahan at the Institute of Design in Chicago. I met some of these photographers while attending Alfred University, and others when I lived in Syracuse and Rochester and still others when I lived in Chicago. This, too, was a community, and creative photography was a way of life, not a career. Nowadays photography is taught in most art departments. For a while, even after I stopped photographing, I'd be asked to visit photography classes. But the students wanted to talk about photography, while I thought we should talk about pictures, and then when they put up their pictures most of the things they hung were related to photographs as rendering is to drawing. These weren't art, they were technique. These weren't compositions, they were symbolic records. The students would resist whenever I suggested they put aside their 35-mm. direct viewfinder cameras and start using cameras with ground glass viewfinders so that they could learn about light and composition. They took photographs that were literary illustrations. They were earnest students on a career track, and they didn't, wouldn't, and couldn't understand. There continued to be many good photographer-artists at work in this country, but their images soon floated in a sea of images while viewers paused only for the sensationalistic.

As for my own photos, I let them go to seed. I was all set to print a portfolio of nudes—pieces of the body sculpted by light—for Margaret Randall's bilingual magazine out of Mexico, *El Corno Emplumado*, when I stopped photographing and printing. I had learned to see as a photographer, which was of more moment to me than producing pictures to frame. It was a way of life, not a career. All that remains on our walls from that time are

293

three images I made without the camera by printing paper "negatives" torn from the funnies: both sides of the page can be seen along with the dots (holes) in the screens then used to print newspaper graphics.

I haven't yet decided if I'm going to give away my cornet and trumpet. The cornet is a Bach handmade job, built before the Bach factory sold out to Conn, a horn which used to belong to Ned Mahoney, who sat second chair to James Burke, the virtuoso soloist with the Edwin Franko Goldman Band. Many a time my friend Roger and I sat in the front row at the Goldman Band concerts in New York City's Central Park with the score to that night's solo spread out on our laps. And the trumpet is an Olds Mendez with two triggers (to flatten the normally sharp tones when the first or third valves are pressed, though one can do this by lip). I used that horn to play Jeremiah Clarke's "Trumpet Voluntary" with Dan Clayton in black robes from the pulpit on Easter. Music was my introduction to artists and nighthawks. I don't think I have ever lost the feeling that late hours and creative expression go together. (I began this essay after midnight. It is now 3:30 a.m. What time will I quit to sleep?—About 6 a.m.) We horn players were a community. We tried to make money, but there wasn't much to be made, so it had to be a way of life for most of us, not a career. Yes, my music teacher hoped I'd go to music school, but the idea was to become a teacher. The idea then was always first to earn a living and then to take private time for art.

I've seen Carl Fracassini recently, in New Mexico where he is retired. Frac was my pottery and drawing teacher, and he doesn't expect to live much longer. He asked me to pick some of his drawings to take home. He was a great teacher and a wonderful artist who lacked the pretensions of his colleagues—he preferred to cook and build and hunt and fish and make pots and drawings and create a community among his students—and so he never received the full measure of respect he deserved at the university. No matter to those of us who learned quality and community from him. Mike won't have to take away any pots. Except for a couple that Dorothy rescued, I broke them all when I gave up potting.

294

I visit a sophomore "core literature" class to observe one of my advisees. The teacher does her job well, and the class is alert, but these are students from "ordinary" backgrounds like mine—not the children of professionals but of workers and small business owners, probably raised largely without the benefits of special classes, private schools, foreign travel, or substantial home libraries. They lack the courage to be articulate, so they speak in an all-purpose colloquial flow designed to show how well they fit in rather than how they stand out: plenty of "you know's" and "I mean's" and "kind of's," lots of "like's" but no "as if's," all of their speech having a general quality of imprecision that nonetheless communicates what they wish to express so long as things remain simple. They seem to understand what they mean, but they never quite say it. Ultimately, as with imprecision in poetry, when the conversation grows more complex, they will be able to say neither what they understand nor what they do not understand. Most of the time, however, it won't make any difference.

In the poetry seminar, we have been reading Bishop and O'Hara, with Dugan and Jarrell on tap. Bishop comes up first. What a pleasure to read poetry bearing such precise powers of observation, such precision of language, and such careful and effective rhetorical emphasis, with the courage of open-faced and even-handed syntax, the courage of accessibility, the courage not to overwrite, the courage to have a viewpoint without faking a vision. The whole group feels it. This is one of those seminars in which, if the members of the class want to absorb new influences, I'm game. Bell's rules: (1) No one has to write a "good" poem; and (2) Teacher has to do the assignment too. The first time, we write poems after the fashion of Bishop or O'Hara. In fact, we write our own poems but under the flag of surrender to some aspect of another's poem. In a later meeting, I hand out a few poems by Neruda from an early book, *Residence on Earth*. Let's see if we can combine Bishop's reticence and observation with Neruda's abandon, Bishop's vertical thrust with Neruda's horizontal speed. What I don't say is that it doesn't matter whether or not one can actually do it, but only that the assigned influences and the deadline take the writer away from his or her self-absorption and self-importance, including *a priori* themes and agendas. Also, that the students give themselves permission to fail. And that they learn, eventually, the value of the arbitrary when it receives sufficient attention—but that is more complicated than needs be said.

A little Neruda goes a long way. I make a crack to the effect that our lives are filled with passion and physical detail, while in American poetry hysteria and anxiety often pass for passion, and filler takes the place of observation. I think to myself, but don't say aloud, that we have a band of poetry critics whose own prose styles naturally lead them to prefer overwriting of all kinds, which they may perhaps think is a signal of literary ambition.

During the core literature class, I wrote down, "Literature is for beginners." I was thinking about thinking. Because, for the poet, after all, poetry is the result, not the intention. Poetry is the residue of bloody brain work, the signal that a process has taken place that creates an emotional approach to thinking. All technique is subsumed in what we later call the "poetic" quality of the text. All the fame in the world is secondary to the epiphanic moment when the poem began to cohere. For the poet, the true consequence is the next poem: hence, a way of life, not a career.

Deby Groover, a potter and printmaker from Athens, Georgia, tells me over coffee that her first pottery teacher said to the class, "If you have any attachment to anything you make, then you better go ahead and break it now."

I don't have any heavy poetry equipment for Mike to haul away. I do plan to sell my papers and many of my books soon. I need to clear some space. Poetry has accumulated around me. I didn't set out to teach where I teach. I set out to earn a living, figuring I could write no matter what. I had a wonderful son at an early age and, when the marriage ended, I kept him with me. I had to make a living. I wouldn't have had it any other way. Still, when I was asked to return to the Writers' Workshop, I hesitated before saying yes. It was still a community then, a smaller community, finding its direction inside the community. Today, like other writing programs, it's heavy on visitors and events, with a decided emphasis on official reputations, and it thus takes its instructions from outside. Like other universities, mine now constantly measures its standing and judges its faculty in ways that

296

damage the community. In this dog-eat-dog economy, education, too, has become more of a career than a way of life.

My seminar students had dropped off but one poem to be xeroxed for class. I had mine: that made two. I was downhearted: hadn't they been able to become selfless enough, to improvise, to swing, to play, to relax, to get down, couldn't those who were wearing the emperor's new clothing shed it to believe in the referential possibilities of words, hadn't they seen the lesson of Bishop's poems and O'Hara's and Neruda's, absent the fawning criticism and the literary fighting for position that follows them, hadn't they understood that those three poets were finally just like them?

And then they came to class, which is held at our home, and Dorothy put out things to eat and drink, and we let some Tom Waits play as we gathered, and they had all written their poems after all and xeroxed them in time, and the freshness of their words and the emotional weight of their pretend-abandon made our group of poems written to deadline a better worksheet than they could expect in any of the sections of the graduate poetry workshop where their more "important" and "original" poems were to be discussed—the ones they made up from ambition and order and fancy talk—and some of them were saying that they were planning to put these poems on the worksheets for the other classes, and we said ok, next week it's all O'Hara and the week after that it will be all Bishop and then it will be Dugan, and once again the world was all right if it could provide this sort of opportunity for community and thought and high spirits with writing at the core.

Poetry is a way of life, not a career. A career means you solicit the powerful and the famous. A way of life means you live where you are with the people around you. A career means you become an authority. A way of life means you stay a student, even if you teach for a living. A career means your life increasingly comes from your art. A way of life means your art continues to arise from your life. Careerism feeds off of the theoretical, the fancified, the complicated, the coded, and the overwrought: all forms of psychological cowardice. A way of life is nourished by the practical, the unadorned, the complex, and a direct approach to the

297

mysterious. Obscurity is a celebrated path to nowhere, an affliction. For poetry to be a way of life in a referential world, it requires of us the courage of clarity—linear, syntactical and referential—which in no way compromises the great wildness of experience and imagination (think of Bishop, O'Hara, Neruda, Dugan, Jarrell . . .). The rewards for this courage and this surrender to influence (a form of community) and clarity are beyond career.

Which are you pursuing: a way of life or a career? The scent of literary careerism has never been stronger. Conversely, the need for each of us to find a way of life—to quote a Dugan poem, "personal life wrung from mass issues in a bloody time and lived out hiddenly"—has never been of more moment.

To most of my current and past students, thank you, wherever you are. To W2EBT and W2OQI and W2FCH, to my dead teachers and friends, to the last few who remember how it was in the arts, to those who still practice in secret or solitude, to Robert Heinecken on his impending retirement, to the sound of Miles Davis playing standards through a straight mute, to all those in my life with pizazz and humility whose lingo had the snap of reality and the metabolic shiver of deep feeling and who did not judge and compete but laughed a lot—my mortal indebtedness.

Nominated by Richard Jackson

KALA: SATURDAY NIGHT AT THE PAHALA THEATRE

by LOIS-ANN YAMANAKA

from PARNASSUS: POETRY IN REVIEW

I was shitting 'cause the theatre lady,
she own the store where us buy slush afterschool
and she know I only seventh grade
'cause her daughter our classmate, Nancy.
NNNAaannccy. The *one*—the one told us she had policeman
in the sixth grade. *Policeman.*
Fuzz, brah, fuzz. Yeah, you neva know?
The theatre lady is her *madda.*

She look at me *long* time
when she rip my ticket in half.
Then she give me one real long piece toilet paper
for wipe the soot from the sugar mill off my seat.
Last time you and me went,
she gave us small piece, rememba?
And when I went home, I wen' catch lickens
from my uncle 'cause my pants was all black.

Mugs walk first then Jimmy boy push my back part
for follow him. He walk close behind me.

All the old man sit in the last row.
I smell the tobacco they spit on the floor.
They laugh when I walk past
and say some words in Filipino.
I know they talking about me.
Jimmy boy push me again.

Of course neva have cartoons.
You stupid or what?
You neva seen one X-rated movie before?
Me too. Okay. No tell nobody, okay?
Had five cheerleaders 'cause the movie
was *Cheerleaders Growing Up.*
They all was haole
and they was on one picnic table
like the one we get at school.
They all was telling their stories.

Had one, her was call to the office
'cause she was one bad girl smoking cigarettes
in the bathroom. The fat, bolohead principal,
he make her all scared. He say he going to tell her fadda.
So the cheerleader, she all nuts, right?
He say he fix everything for her.
But he tell her
she no can tell nobody.

Then the teacher, he one man, he come in
the office. He wearing a suit with one tie.
The principal, he sweating already so he wipe his glasses.
The teacher, he one real worm.
He tie the cheerleader to a chair.
He tell her, *Don't be scared,*
and he gag her mouth.

Then the principal, he take off her shirt
and she crying. Her eyes all black underneath
from her eyeliner. Then he take off her bra
and the teacher suck her.
For *real.* I *saw* um.

Don't cry, he say *or we're going to have to tell
your father what you did*, the principal say.

Jimmy boy hand go on my leg
and he look at me long time.
I no look at him.
I must do that to you, he tell.
Mugs, he laugh and make his eyebrows go up and down
at Jimmy boy. *Me and Mugs, maybe.*
Come my house with us in the back by the shed,
he say. *I going do that to you.*

I try get up for buy popcorn or use the bathroom
or something. But Jimmy boy grab my wrist
and hold me down to the seat.
You sit right here, he tell.
So you can learn.
I shut my eyes.
Had four more cheerleaders.

Nominated by Parnassus: Poetry In Review

THE WATCHER

by EDWARD HIRSCH

from ANTAEUS

LEOPARDI IN ROME, 1823

He could not decide if the city at dusk
was the furnace of gods
                              or the oven of man,
but he was there nonetheless, like an afterthought.

What was the world but an interminable afternoon
where sunlight smouldered
                              and scorched the rooftops
and heat clung to the skulls of churches?

Oracles lay prostrate in the blue dust
and shadows wandered aimlessly
                              between the ruins.
Things that were once known were now lost.

He examined porticoes, columns, doorways
leading nowhere. Monuments
                              to crumbling deities.
One-armed soldiers. Statues with broken genitalia.

A temple where vestal virgins were slaughtered
for letting the sacred fire
                              flicker and die out.
If only someone remembered how to light it . . .

No one spoke to him on his daily outings—
a hunchback going blind,
                              a walking sepulcher
climbing up and down the library stairs.

He was like a ghost radiating through fog.
And he was an eternal
                              connoisseur of absences,
of tedious late afternoons in empty piazzas

and overheated nights in cramped apartments.
He heard clocks tolling
                              from his bedroom at night
and felt the dull thud of the hours passing.

He watched a full moon lingering behind clouds
and saw a terrifying vacuum
                              sealed up around him
like air strangled in the lungs of a tunnel.

Nothingness: the vacancies between stars,
the barrenness of a hilltop
                              overlooking the arches,
the silence of a past that no longer exists.

Infinity: the distance beyond distances,
an impalpable unborn space
                              glittering beyond time,
the bountiful emptiness of everything.

Nominated by Michael Collier, Sherod Santos, Arthur Smith

A HUNGER ARTIST BY FRANZ KAFKA: A STORY

fiction by DANIEL STERN

from THE PARIS REVIEW

> *We don't have time enough to be ourselves.*
> *All we have time for is to be happy.*
> —Camus
>
> *We don't have time enough to be ourselves or*
> *to be happy. All we have time enough for is*
> *our work. And not enough for that. That's*
> *what counts!*
> —Brandauer

Brandauer had Tuna Fish for lunch every day of the nine years I knew him. Sometimes on rye toast, sometimes on white bread, sometimes with a Coke, sometimes with a small glass of milk. Not a full-size glass: the half sizes kids drink from. It took him about twelve minutes and he was ready to go back to work.

We met the year my second book was published—the one written with vanishing ink. I was also working as a rep for a production company which specialized in the fancy avant-garde commercials which were then in style. That was the year applause began to come to Brandauer, late and sudden. When it grew to a crescendo a few years later, while nothing much was happening in what we laughingly called my literary career, he felt a statement was called for. "Don't get too excited," he said. "And don't envy me. Coming at this time in my life, these honors are like rocks falling on my head." He was fifty-six, tall and lean as a panther. A grizzled Jewish Panther of the writing jungle. I didn't believe his disclaimer then; nobody did. Later it was another matter.

This late-bloomed success was the main reason we met. Brand-auer had come out of his cage, for a time. This never-photographed, never-interviewed, slowly famous, invisible comic artist of rigor and denial had actually agreed to teach a course at a Creative Writing Workshop. And, as if one wonder were not enough, he also agreed to be interviewed.

The setting for these extraordinary events was to be a small but serious Writers Conference near Seattle. Having been tapped by *The Paris Review* to do the long-refused interview, I sat in on his class. The fortunate few were early, without doubt a first for *them*, notebooks out, necks craned upwards—Brandauer was six feet tall and thin and looked a little like Abraham Lincoln if Abra-ham Lincoln had been of eastern European Jewish descent.

Everyone sitting around the long oval table waited, watching this man who had emerged from a dozen years at hard labor in solitary confinement, five in the Sheepshead Bay section of Brooklyn and seven in Genoa, Italy, learning, as one critic wrote, to make sen-tences walk, dance and sing. There were three well-documented years in France, as well, where he'd lived in a stone house on a hill in a tiny perched village near Avignon. But there too he had mostly stayed in his stone room, performing his self-appointed task as the ballet master of the modern English sentence.

That's right—no wife, no children, all sorts of friends, but no family who could claim time away from his mission. Or so every-one thought at the time. Given this well-publicized first surfac-ing, the class's expectations were naturally high. If Brandauer knew this, he wasn't letting on. He picked up the small, green-covered book of stories by Kafka and began to read " 'A Hunger Artist,' a story by Franz Kafka. *During these last decades the in-terest in professional fasting has markedly diminished . . . At one time the whole town took a lively interest in the Hunger Artist. It used to pay very well to stage such great performances under one's own management, but today that is quite impossible. We live in a different world now.*" In a short time it became terribly and comically clear that all Brandauer would teach, in what was advertised as his Creative Writing Workshop, was one fourteen-page story by Kafka. No student self-expression, no handing in of manuscripts to be criticized by the classmates, no memorialized encouraging comments scribbled in the margins by the Master.

What he did give to the students was an eloquent overview of a story about a man whose art was fasting; who practiced it in a cage, setting world records for taking little food sometimes, no food other times, for days, weeks and finally many years—on his own and later in a circus. For a time, since the art of fasting itself had a large audience, he was famous, successful—even as his ribs stuck through his skin. Later, the art falls out of fashion and the hunger artist dies, by now, utterly forgotten. Into his cage they put a young panther; they bring him the food he likes . . . *and the joy of life streamed with such ardent passion from his throat . . .*"

The kids were stunned. When Brandauer read the end in which the dying Hunger Artist whispers to the Overseer that the audience should not admire his fasting . . . *Because I have to fast, I can't help it.* And explains, finally, *Because* . . . and here Brandauer hunched down and spoke the Artist's last words in a hoarse whisper, . . . *I couldn't find the food I liked. If I had found it, believe me, I should have made no fuss and stuffed myself like you or anyone else.*

He was a smash. The young people all around me were applauding, thrilled. They had clearly forgotten, in the excitement of the moment, that Brandauer had not even read a story of his own, let alone one of theirs; had not told them how they should write or even how he wrote, himself, except by implication. It was a subtle, allusive, brilliant performance. Several faculty members had invited themselves in, stood in the back, and they were going wild, too. The single exception was the striking young woman who sat next to me, shoving impatient hands through her long red hair. She never took her eyes off Brandauer. Either she was extraordinarily fair or her exquisite face was pale with some emotion I couldn't figure out. Actually, she looked the way people in books might look when "pale with anger."

While she stared at him and I stared at her, Brandauer made it clear but not pleasant to the students that *all* he would deal with was the way the story was made. No fancy hermaneutics; just how something is made.

"Look how Kafka has the audience *itself* take an active part in the Hunger Artist's dramatic fasting presentation. There are casual onlookers in front of his cage, but there are also *relays of permanent watchers selected by the public—usually butchers,*

306

Kafka tells us—and they are to watch to make sure the Artist doesn't have some resource to secret nourishment. With two words, *usually butchers*, Kafka introduces humor into this grim business."

"Critics," one student called out.

Brandauer paused; he patted a pencil against the wire frame of his eyeglasses. He did not look at the waiting student. He smiled, as at a private joke. Then he proceeded: "Later, however," he said, "just before the end, not only is he not being scrutinized, but no one even notices the starving Hunger Artist; he's hidden beneath layers of straw, until an Overseer notices what seems to be an empty cage and pokes around until he discovers the artist almost dead from his fast." So much for interpretations and analogies.

Brandauer must have sensed the restlessness, almost a confusion in the air. "This is the way we will work, here," he said, bending over the table on which lay the text. Tall and skinny he arched his back, one half of a pair of parentheses, and explained that the only way he knew to learn to write was to read. So, in the remaining sessions they would read and reread and reread again this small story by Kafka. "We will reinvent this strange little story by one of the strangest writers who ever lived—and then you'll go on to invent your own, that's what counts. I'm sorry if you expected more or different. I can't give more or different. This is the only way I know." It was the first time I heard that phrase from him—"that's what counts." It was not the last.

Outside, on the slippery steps of the conference hall, Brandauer and I made arrangements to meet for the interview. The inevitable Seattle drizzle huddled us under umbrellas. I scribbled his address.

"Come at four. We'll do two hours, then I've invited some people for dinner."

"I'll bring the wine."

"Don't bring anything. I have a bottle."

Suddenly there was a presence between our two umbrellas. The young girl with the angry gaze, my classroom neighbor, stood there. She had forgotten her umbrella but had brought the gaze, intact.

"Professor Brandauer . . ." she said.

"*Mister*," he said. "I don't profess anything. I'm just a writer."

She pushed a bundle of manuscripts towards him. It was dauntingly large enough to be secured by a fat rubber band. Water streamed down her forehead past large blue, unblinking eyes. I couldn't help thinking she looked like a water nymph in some Bernini fountain in Rome; a beauty.

"Can I lend you my umbrella," Brandauer said, an old-fashioned gentleman. He was carefully not looking at the papers she held.

"No." she said, "You can read my stories."

"They're going to be soaking wet." He moved to bring her into the protected circle but she moved away, impatient.

"I came up from Newport News . . ." She paused as if searching for the strongest argument she could make. Indeed, I would have guessed even further south than Virginia, going by the music below the rage in the words. ". . . just to get your comments on my stories."

"You heard what I . . ."

"*This is my life*, Mister Brandauer," she said. "I have read everything you've . . ."

"Only four books," he murmured. But anger had made her deaf to Brandauer's mild irony.

". . . and I didn't come all this soaking way to hear what's his name. I came to hear what you think about my—my—" I was afraid she was going to say her life, again; I'd seen Brandauer sort of wince the first time.

"What's *your* name," Brandauer said.

"Penelope Anne Golden. You *will* read me, then."

I was impressed by the "read me." She couldn't have been more than twenty-four and she already felt there was a "me" to read.

"It wouldn't be f-f-f-fair to the others. Th-th-th-that's what counts."

It was the first time I'd heard him stammer. He owned one; but like the rest of his inventory, he used it sparingly.

"I don't give a damn about the others," Penelope Anne Golden said. "I came here for you!" She licked the rain from her lips while her stone glance stayed on Brandauer's face.

"Miss Golden, you don't understand . . ."

"*I don't have to,*" she said and backing off a little, threw the rubber-band-bound sheaf of papers at Brandauer. She threw it underhand, a softball throw and Brandauer had to drop his umbrella to catch it. He stood there, like a statue of himself, Penelope Anne Golden's life in his hands, rain blinding his eyeglasses.

What I remember most about that first evening at the tiny apartment Brandauer had rented in downtown Seattle was how lavishly we three dinner guests poured out conversation, laughter and information. The other two were two professors of American Studies—married to each other and Brandauer's work. We shared the subtle feeling of being the three people in the world, that night, privileged to be in the presence. I entertained us all with a re-creation of the scene in the rain with the lovely southern rebel. That started a sort of anarchic evening of excessive laughter and noisy talk; not the sort of wildness Brandauer was used to.

Before the others arrived, he had carefully measured out his steps around the little folding table, setting down the napkins, measuring the distance between knife and plate, neatly parsing out everything else: the wine in the small, over-decorated, hardware-store glasses, the lean anecdotes he told, the Chicken Casserole he'd cooked, the portion sizes just enough, no more, no less.

He was so serious! When he joined in the joke telling with a story about a Japanese businessman returning home from a trip to an unfaithful wife who had slept with a Jewish man, we laughed and Brandauer laughed. But by departing for a moment from his habitual grave bearing, he gave the joking weight. He was like a Japanese visitor, without the language, trying to join in a light-heartedness he did not quite understand but longed to experience.

During dinner he continued to measure out the food and wine as if we were marooned on a desert island and had to be sure the rations would last. He'd told me, "I have a bottle," and that's exactly what he had, one bottle of wine for the four of us, not a drop more. You felt he didn't understand why anyone would want more was enough. And what was enough was clear. His conversation, too, was carefully proportioned—he spoke in short, clear, ironic phrases with not one stammer. And, at one point, when the laughter and noisy commentary got out of hand, loud and boisterous, Brandauer pounded his hand on the table for quiet. A God of large and small universes, he was accustomed to being able to control them; a master of where to place the period, he got his quiet along with a certain astonishment.

309

About halfway through the interview session before dinner, he suddenly said, "That girl . . . what did you think?"

"I think you're on the spot," I said, "You and Kafka, both. She's one of those tough southern cookies. She expected personal attention and you gave her Kafka."

"I like her intensity," he said. And he quoted Yeats to me— something about lust and rage attending old age . . . I said, "How old are you?"

"How much do you weigh?" he said. He'd watched me settle and resettle myself on the couch as I fiddled with the tape recorder. He watched everybody and everything, better at asking than answering questions.

"Too damned much."

And I told him how my second marriage had broken up because in one of my cycles of voracious overeating, I had reached over to my wife's plate, at the Peking Gardens, and started eating from it. Everyone else at the table thought it was mildly amusing, a weird little action. To *her* it meant the marriage was over, it meant I didn't give a damn about anybody or anything except my own hopeless hungers.

"Second wife? You're pretty young."

"I'm on my third."

"Sounds like courses in a meal."

"This is my life we're talking, here," I said. "Don't turn it into another Brandauer metaphor."

"*My life,*" he murmured "That's what Penelope Anne said. Everybody seems to have this *life* they own." He said it mournfully. I didn't know him well enough to say, it wasn't like a car you bought or didn't buy—that he, too, must own a life. But it wasn't that clear.

We finished the interview a few days later and I left Seattle to go back to New York, looking for my next job and some fresh ways to patch up the various tears my marriage had developed. I left without finding out what happened to Penelope Anne Golden and her rain-soaked plea for personal literary attention.

I did not see Brandauer again for a year and a half. He was back in his lair, making sentences with which to make stories and making stories in which to nest his sentences. I was busy running around looking for some happiness. I was always able to find *some,* so I could never either renounce the habit or conquer it. I started a magazine designed to appeal to the restless paperback publishing industry, for a time, then did Public Relations for a Ballet Company that spun off from the American Ballet Theater. You get the idea; things that kept me busy that could never be confused with a real career.

Brandauer wrote a letter: "I read your first novel *Skydancer.* It is strongly imagined and seriously comic—but is insufficiently crafted so the spirit dies halfway through, leaving the reader with a big chunk of inanimate flesh to deal with. Perhaps you are too scattered to give your craft enough attention. All these different activities." He closed his unexpected letter with a typical Brandauer trick: two quotations without their sources. *Don't forget*, he wrote, *"Life isn't everything." And in any case, "It's best seen through a single window." This last—that's what counts.*

What the hell did he want? He certainly did not think I could follow him into the compression of despairing images into wildly comic characters which, during these next years, made him as famous as Beckett or Malamud—to whom, along with Kafka, he was most often compared. Or into his solitude to become a saint of art. Him and his "that's what counts"—counting up our ever-lasting pluses and minuses. And what the hell would he do with the sum if he finally arrived at it? In the language of his youth his speed was seventy-eight, mine was thirty-three and a third and often a whirring, laser-spun CD. But I loved his songs. My affection was not unrequited: He invited me to join him at a Writer's Conference at the University of Arizona in June.

I arrived in Tucson by a series of disastrously late planes. Which is why I missed Brandauer's class and drove up to find him standing, surrounded by students in a shimmer of sunshine. I got out of my car and a wall of shaking heat hit my face. Brandauer was the only one who wore a jacket and tie, and he sweated passionately everywhere you could see: his shirt collar wet and limp, his blue tie smeared and wet, his handkerchief mopping eyes and half-bald forehead.

The group thinned out and there was Brandauer with the Angry Young Woman of a year ago: Penelope What-ever-her-name-was. It was the Seattle tableau all over, but instead of rain a monstrous, debilitating fried egg of a sun.

I was so startled to see her that I slowed my approach. I watched them through a shimmering horizon-haze of crackling, dry heat. It was like a mirage must be, except it didn't look pleasant.

"You're just changing names and places, Penny," I hear Brandauer say. "Sometimes the imagination needs a push."

My God, I thought in that hallucinatory hot wind, a year later and they're still arguing. Though I did note the "Penny." The argument, and who knew what else, had become personal.

"*You* need a push," she said. "Get you out of your damned Kafka-land."

They began to walk. I followed, not wanting to interrupt.

"I'm not telling you how or what to do. But a series of sexual encounters do not make a work of fiction."

"That's because I'm a woman. How about D. H. Lawrence?"

"How about sitting in the shade? I'm fainting from the heat."

"Pricks are okay but Cunts are not proper literary material, is that it?" It was the precise moment to interrupt. Now or never and just in time. Between the two of us we got Brandauer into my air-conditioned Toyota. Tucson in June at 11:30 AM: Heat stroke was not unthinkable. We put him to bed in the air-conditioned studio apartment rented for him by the university.

"I should never have come out," he said. "I can't handle you p-p-p-p-people."

I was surprised, again, by the stammer; surprised, too, that he included *me* in his soft, exhausted impeachment.

"Okay," Penny said. "He's right." She paused to soak up her second margarita. "My youth is so full of weird sex stuff that I can't make head or tail out of it. But writing stories is the only way I know to get it all straight—if I don't then I'm cooked."

"Right now, *he's* cooked," I said. "And what do you mean your youth?"

"I'm twenty-four, honey. In Virginia twenty-four is a mature woman." It came out *woeman*. And, in spite of that lovely, lofty white brow and bright red lips, her "honey" was so strongly flavored it shriveled my scrotum.

I took refuge in questions of fact. "How did you get Brandauer to comment on your stories? He was so firm about what he would and wouldn't do in the class."

312

"He insisted I drop out of the class." Penny said. "Dis-enroll."

I swear I had guessed the answer in advance; I was getting to know Brandauer in spite of himself.

"It was the only way to be fair to the others, he said. I became an auditor and he'd read my stories and go over them with me over lunch."

"Tuna Fish," I said. "Every day."

"How did you know?"

"So you won."

"I lost," she said miserably. "I wanted to exorcise my crazy adolescence by turning it into fiction. He poisoned my hope." She was something. No one I knew but Penny could have said, with a straight face, *He poisoned my hope.* She rummaged in a giant tote bag and out came a notebook. "Here's what he said—it was so awful I had to write it down." She read, like a schoolgirl reciting a lesson, *Art is not ecology. We don't need to conserve the life you've lived and lost—we need a new life from you . . . one you can imagine but probably can't have. We want imagination not biography. That's what counts.*

She threw the book down and then surprised me by dropping her head on folded arms. For a full minute she wept. I didn't know what to do so I reached across the table and touched her cheek. My hand came away wet. It felt too intimate. But it stopped the flood. She flared up again: "So I said, *How about Proust?* And he said, *How about you?*"

"Why do you care what he thinks so much?" I said hopelessly.

"Because he knows. You know how he's always saying about this or that—that's what counts? Well, sometimes I think he really knows what counts, that he has that gift. I didn't mean what I said about Pricks and Cunts and all that. He's not full of shit. He may be the only one who's not." Over a Tex-Mex dinner ordered on impulse I tried to distract her. No use.

"How do you make a living in between Brandauer encounters?" I asked.

"Sell books in a little store downtown Newport News. That's where I first found him."

"Him?"

"His books. When I heard he was going to teach—I grabbed my stories and lit out for the territory. But he wouldn't teach. Just talk about this one crazy story." She poured a ton of ketchup

313

over everything and laughed. "Dug my own grave." she said. "You're a kind man to listen to my troubles." She spoke with that formal prose southerners seem to be born with.

Later we were less formal. I was too close to her, and she was a melange of smells; some kind of flowery perfume on her neck, fragrant gin on her breath and ketchup on her fingers. Also, the wide blue eyes made things pretty skittish. Except for Brandauer. We'd made the mistake of calling to make sure he wasn't dead of heat stroke. He wasn't, but then he knew Penny and I were together and it smelled like a betrayal. The night's mission was aborted.

Already I could hear him saying: *"Her eyes—you wanted to make love to her because of her wide, beautiful eyes—is that a person, a human being, their eyes, wide or close together? A human being as parts?"* The Brandauer eye went right to the heart of things. Butcher of values, he left no fat on issues—only the hearts of matters were good enough for him to sell. He respected his customers. Okay, call them his readers. Call them the audience.

Finally, I understood Brandauer's exasperated stammering wrap-up of Penny and me: *I should never have left. I can't handle you p-p-p-p-people* . . . I didn't like it, but I understood it. Coming out into the world had left the poor bastard open to everybody from Penny and her all-important "life" to writing groupies from all over. There was one young man whose name had been Wilbur Jonas until he became a convert to Orthodox Judaism. He changed his name to Chaim and brought his unfinished novel all the way from the wealth of Shaker Heights, Cleveland, by bus, to Fargo, North Dakota, to hear Brandauer talk about "A Hunger Artist." He had converted from Jewish Middle-class Agnosticism to Orthodoxy. His beard was so long he looked like his own great-grandfather. Brandauer gave him special attention. He treated him as if he were some sort of sacred monster.

We were *all* his problems. I who wanted to devour all the life and time there was, and was unable to learn the mysterious Brandauer alchemy of making caterpillars out of butterflies, questions out of answers; Chaim, who wanted to find the Talmudic tradition in new fiction; Penny and the other Pennys who were busy with the sacred matters of personal experience which drew his contempt.

Sometimes I got sick of him.

314

"What's so special about your buddy the shtetl kid," I said, irritated. "The Rabbi Nachman of Cleveland. He wouldn't even eat your Tuna Fish, brought his own food? *You* don't believe that stuff," I said, "Why do you give that kid so much leeway?"

"I like Chaim," he said. "I like his choice of names. It affirms Life."

I shrugged. "He wants to bomb Arabs. Some affirmer of life."

"He's fervent," Brandauer said. "That's what counts."

Those years of his coming out were my pendulum years. I swung like a pendulum from Diet Centers to eating binges, from reducing farms to Food City, no doubt making a shambles of my endocrinological system. Jobs were the same. Like Tarzan on his vines I swung my way through the jungle of employment, never staying put very long.

Women, too, were included in this cycle of appetites. At least two of them had wonderfully adhesive skin, that is they stuck to my life. Others had skin as smooth as a mind without memory and soon became part of the past. One of them, Sybil, became my fourth wife. I wanted Brandauer to be the Best Man but I was afraid he already was, and skipped the invitation.

One November, at a conference in Fargo, North Dakota, Brandauer told me, "You're a feverish man. A cooler temperature would be more productive." I allowed myself an intimate moment with the Master.

"The fever is not the problem," I said. And I tried to make him understand how it was always the matter at hand, whatever it was, which heated me up—a lovely woman who promised understanding and pleasure, not necessarily in that order; a *poulet à l'estragon avec moutarde et endives;* and that fine literary moment when the word *and* joins the actions of two characters perfectly. All were equal in me.

Brandauer gazed at me in spectacled despair. His silhouette seemed more fragile than ever; his cheeks were sinking inwards, signs of age or loss of weight, I couldn't tell.

"That's only good for somebody who's going to live forever," he said. "I haven't met one yet. The rest of us have to choose."

"How about a walk," I said, desperately.

"This is North Dakota. It's five degrees outside."

"Ah," I said. "Yes. As usual I forgot."

The following summer we met at the Bennington Conference. I was in my brief phase of smoking good cigars—delicious, slow-smoking, fragrant Panatelas made by Upmann in Havana, shipped, legally, to Switzerland to a man named Gross, who then shipped them to me, illegally, in a box marked *Swiss Cigars: Gift Under Twenty-five Dollars*.

"Is it worth all that trouble," Brandauer asked.

"Absolutely."

"I think maybe the trouble is part of the pleasure. It makes a big deal out of a small joy."

To throw him off the scent I told him about Hemingway's comment that you had to plan your pleasures, work at them, otherwise they wouldn't happen. Everything else will happen anyway, work, obligations, but not pleasures, unless you planned for them.

I leaned back satisfied with having scored. Brandauer stood up, said, "It goes vice versa, too," and went home to his desk. As if to prove him right, I wasted that entire day in pointless phone calls, switching vacation plans while he wrote a page and a half.

A couple of years later I was asked to fill in at the last minute, at a winter Conference in Boulder, Colorado. I was working at a new job: Writer/Producer of trailers for Monster Movies. You know, bite-sized smorgasbords designed to make children and certain minority groups—the primary monster-lovers—hungry for the movie itself. I needed the money to pay for Alimony. The Divorce from Sybil had turned into the usual horror movie and I'd put on thirty pounds out of misery.

But Brandauer was going to be in Boulder, so I cleared my schedule. When I arrived, there he was, small, green-covered Modern Library edition of the *Selected Kafka* stories in hand.

In the interim he had won the Pulitzer Prize for his *Collected Stories* and a National Book Award for a new novel. The novels were getting shorter and shorter. You could hardly tell them from the stories, which were also getting smaller. I was eager to see him. But more eager to have *him* see *me*. I'd just dropped forty-seven pounds at the Pritikin Center in Florida. It had cost all my extra cash—but I was proud of the exhibition of will.

There was a foot of snow everywhere. We met for lunch in some Western Inn-type place with a fireplace, and a moosehead

316

on the wall. They featured Steaks and Venison, but I knew what Brandauer was up for. I took perverse pleasure in ordering even less. What's less than Tuna Fish on white toast and a cup of black coffee? It wasn't easy, but I scrounged up an assorted vegetable plate. That got his attention. But he made no comment.

"I brought you a present," I told him. "It's a poem. I wrote it on eight hundred calories a day, at Pritikin. It's called: 'The Hunger Artist.'"

It was a long son of a bitch but he seemed to pay special attention to the last two stanzas.

> *Out of the fleshly fabrication*
> *Appears an honesty of skin.*
> *In the hungry, human situation*
> *The gotten grace is always thin.*
>
> *The body less than fills the eye,*
> *The flesh, a tissue shield.*
> *Bare bones beneath a cannibal sky:*
> *Shape is fate revealed.*

"It's not 'The Hunger Artist,' it's 'A Hunger Artist.'" He folded the gift-poem carefully in four parts and put it in his wallet. "The article is crucial. He's a special case."

Not a word about my poem, a poem as personal to me as my gut.

We stormed the snow, a blast of white wind in our faces, and walked to the parking lot. I had to shout to be heard.

"Okay," I said, off-balance as only he could throw me off, "*The—A—*My God . . . I've heard you read that story in eight cities to students dying to learn how to write their own stories . . ."

"Are you finished with your new book?"

"No—I've been gearing up for this new job. And the divorce took it out of me."

"Ah," he said. There was nothing more devastating than a Brandauer. "Ah."

"Do you like making these commercials you work at?"

As if confessing something shameful I said: "I do, yes. It's fun, it's easy and it's good money."

317

He fiddled with the lock to his car.

"It may be frozen," I said. "Let me try."

He paused a long time and said, "I could never handle the world the way you do." This did not sound as if he admired me for it, believe me. Irritably, I said, "I think *you* do it much better. The world handles me, not vice versa. I'm always playing catch-up with money and women."

"Thanks for the poem," he said.

Before I could reply with something properly bitter, the snowy shape of Penelope Anne Golden made its way through a blast of white wet. She wore a hooded parka; the hood made her look like one of those figures in a medieval print: All she needed was a scythe.

I figured we were finished so I backed away as she approached. I watched them from the safety of my warming car. She was gesticulating wildly, Brandauer stood there like a prisoner being accused of various crimes. Every few moments he shrugged. I don't think he said anything. Clearly, he still had not treated her "life" the way she wished.

I started the car and Penelope was standing outside knocking on the window. She spat a mouthful of snow at me. When I rolled the window down she stuck her sweet snowy face in and kissed me. It was an angry kiss, more like a bite.

"Do y'all want to make love to me?" she asked.

It was such a crazed moment that I thought the "y'all" meant both of us—me and poor soaked Brandauer hunching himself into his Volkswagen. But it was nothing so fancy. He must have said something about her stories that got her southern rage going and I was handy. Her mouth had a soft, wet give that was tempting. But over her shoulder I saw Brandauer struggling to start his frozen car and all I could do was shake my head from side to side.

"Fuck you," she said and stumbled away in the snow.

The next day, in class, Brandauer read the last line of my poem: *Shape is fate revealed.*

"What the hell was that?" I said, afterwards.

"It seemed appropriate."

"You're too damned appropriate, Brandauer," I said. "That line makes no sense without the rest of the poem."

"Too bad," he said. "You gave it to me. It's mine now. And I gave it to the class. Remember it's *A* not *The*. By the way, you look terrific with your new shape. Maybe now you can make do with less all around."

I said nothing about yesterday's craziness in the snow with Penelope. He said even less.

A few months later *Time* magazine got wind of Brandauer's cross-country number. It was oddball enough to get their attention. This shy master suddenly zipping around the country teaching writing students using only a fourteen-page story about a strange custom of fasting as an art form. And, of course, Kafka was the perfect writer to refer to without having to read him. Everybody knows what you mean when you talk about Kafka, don't they?

When they called me, the researcher said they'd gotten my name from a Ms. Penelope Anne Golden. I thought, She doesn't know the rules of the game, and I eased them off the phone. Naturally they confused Brandauer with the Hunger Artist in the story. And naturally they called it *The* Hunger Artist, losing Brandauer's precious *A*.

Reading the piece made me think about our singular friendship. What a match! Brandauer owned a natural dignity and carried himself with such care that it bordered on the mysterious. He had the patience of someone enrolled in a religious order for life whose faith had never been shaken. Myself, I had a gift for clowning and an attention span of about a minute and a half. He was at home with order; I was companion to confusion. His arena of pleasures was narrow, carefully attended to. Mine was indiscriminate, loose (with significant exceptions such as ignoring Penelope Anne's sexual invitation). And, strangest of all, he insisted on taking me seriously; something I could never quite manage. We were a comic pairing, a Mutt and Jeff of the writing life.

The comedy ended abruptly in Miami. There was a woman at his bedside, tall, European looking, her dress a little too long, all in gray. She fluttered off the instant I arrived.

". . . who told you . . . ?"

"Don't talk."

"Isn't it crazy dying *here?* Did you see those foolish-looking palm trees on the way from the airport? This is not a serious place."

He was bringing his own seriousness with him, hooked up to all the usual hi-tech medical paraphernalia, a Frankenstein monster of unexpected disaster.

319

"The food is terrible here."

"Hospitals," I said stupidly.

"It's Tuna Fish every day for lunch. Awful."

He didn't seem to know he was making his own deathbed comedy. Maybe they gave him Tuna Fish because someone told them it was his lifelong lunch.

Brandauer gestured for me to bend closer. His chest wind was not blowing with its usual strength.

"Chaim . . ."

"No, I'm . . ."

"I know, I know." He was irritated at his lapse—confusing me with his Orthodox Jewish disciple. He wanted order, as usual, not confusion.

"I envy the p-p-p-p-p- . . ." It was the longest, most painful stammer I'd ever heard from him. I waited while he struggled. Finally the word arrived: ". . . panther!" We were back to topic A. Or topic K. Relieved and exhausted by the effort he added, "I envy him—just a little," and sneaked in a quick little smile. "That girl, Penelope . . . you slept with her?"

"No," I said too quickly.

"Ah," he said. "Too bad."

I was starved. In the gray hospital cafeteria I drank some chemical coffee and ate a cardboard croissant. The pale bird of a woman who had been at Brandauer's bedside sat down next to me.

"No intrusion meant," she said. "But you're a friend of my husband's, are you not?"

She spoke with a foreign accent and sounded like a translation and that was how I learned the whole secret subtext of Brandauer's story, a wife and a son kept hidden in Italy all those years. Her name was Francesca and her son was Mauro. She was content, she quickly made it clear, to be Brandauer's background story. Her son had been left with friends in Genoa. But she'd sought me out because she wanted the world to know that her husband was honest and responsible and had always taken care of them even during his long absences.

"What can I do?" I asked.

What came through at last was that, to her, I was Brandauer's friend the journalist. He must have shown her the Interview in *The Paris Review*, so many years ago.

320

"Tell me," I said, "did he have this heart problem for a long time?"

"He found out about nine years ago," she said. "His whole family had the heart—but his started then."

"I see." I don't know what I saw, but nine years ago was when he'd left his little room to start teaching.

"And you will tell how he was good and a good father, too. Not just a writer. You will write about this for the world."

I was too exhausted to set her straight, too miserable at how awfully ill, white of face and starved Brandauer looked. Yes, I would tell the whole world, I said, I would tell how fine and honest he was. What the hell! The comedy of misunderstanding had begun with a generation of students excitedly greeting Brandauer and, instead, getting Kafka. Let it end—if it was ending—with a redundant, foolish promise. I had no means of addressing any large public to tell them about this man who was indeed, so fine and honest that he sometimes seemed a visitor from a different place. She kissed me on the cheek and left an odor of dried flowers, vaguely foreign.

"What I couldn't tell Penny was . . ." He started on this as soon as I was at his bedside again, as if we'd been talking all along. ". . . she couldn't see it . . . that putting it together was the main thing . . . all the big chunks of life she had . . . all the struggles, the pleasures . . . you need a line, I told her . . . a line of words . . . just like a poet you need a line . . . then the people and the lives and what they do to each other . . . then they can go into the line and find their beat . . . But . . ."

"Listen," I said. "How do you feel? Do you want the nurse?"

I waited. He seemed to have forgotten I was there. Then, very softly:

". . . *Enough . . . and not one bit more. That's what counts.*" He laughed. It was like a cough with an edge of amusement. "*And then, even a little less.*"

"Isn't that what you've been telling *me* all this time?" I felt like an idiot dealing myself in. It seemed to me that he nodded.

"But don't forget," I said. "For the panther, enough is a whole lot of bloody meat."

Brandauer smiled. "Did I tell you how I envied the p-p-p-p- . . ."

This time I interrupted and supplied the word. "Yes, the panther," I said. It sounded impatient and mean spirited. I felt badly that I had not let him finish his own stammer and I began a burst of words. "I've always loved the double ending: when the Hunger Artist dies after whispering that the public should not admire him: . . . *I have to fast, I can't help it. . . . I couldn't find the food I liked. If I had found it, believe me, I would have made no fuss and stuffed myself like you or anyone else . . .*" I was weirdly proud at being able to quote so much from memory. Foolishly, as if that meant I understood it, understood Brandauer, our confused friendship, my eternally unfinished life.

"Then they clear out the cage," I went on, "And put in the young panther. *The food he liked was brought to him without hesitation by the attendants . . . his noble body, furnished almost to the bursting point with all that it needed seemed to carry freedom around with it, too . . .*" I was quoting more and more, in desperation, watching Brandauer fade away from me on the rumpled pillow. After all the years of his classes it was like a final examination I'd suddenly set for myself. I spoke the ending.

"*Somewhere in his jaws it seemed to lurk; and the joy of life streamed with such ardent passion from his throat that for the onlookers it was not easy to stand the shock of it. But they braced themselves, crowded round the cage and did not want ever to move away.*"

"Bravo, my friend," Brandauer said, although I'd done nothing more than quote the published ending. Perhaps I'd passed.

"I wonder," he said, "If panthers have heart attacks . . . all that red meat . . ." At the corner of my eye I saw his wife start to move towards us.

"Listen," he said, already fainter.

"Yes . . ."

"That thing you wrote—the gift—a poem about dieting . . ."

"Yes."

"Well," Brandauer paused and a shadow of an old smile showed up on his lips. "It doesn't matter so much what you eat," he said. "*What matters is what eats you. That's what . . .*" Apparently he could not manage the last *counts*; the last summation left hanging in the empty hospital air. He grew silent and the silence became sleep and the sleep became death but not until the next morning while I was turning my rented Ford onto its side at the entrance to the freeway.

"What did he mean, that stuff about the Panther?" Penny asked.

"Who, Kafka?" I was in a teasing mood. My ribs had stopped aching, though they were still strapped. The cuts on my forehead had healed. I'd survived.

"Brandauer, I mean," she said. "You know damned well."

"I think the talk about the Panther was for himself," I told her. "There was something else for you and a few things for me."

She laughed. Not an angry note in her scale these days. "He's preaching at me from beyond the you-know-what."

"Talking, maybe—preaching, no!"

I was determined to be serious for as long as possible, determined to hold out for as long as possible against the white dress, the soft skin, the shining pearls sliding across the summer suntan, the sweet citrus scent of perfume. I told her what Brandauer had said about the trick of just enough and no more—about the line of words, though I couldn't get it exactly as he'd said it.

We were in Middletown, Connecticut in July, a hot and sticky time in the Connecticut River Valley. The Wesleyan Writer's Conference, like so many, was scheduled for a hellish time of the year. I'd called her to deliver Brandauer's message and to ask her if she was still coming to the Conference even though our original reason for enrolling was now cremated, the ashes buried in a cemetery in Italy.

And here we were, wearing our name tags but skipping the standard get-acquainted cocktail party in favor of our own dinner. We sat at the bar waiting for a table and I told her about the accident, about the turbaned Doctor Singh at the Emergency Room, about how he had ignored my Brandauer grief and blamed the crash on vertigo and weakness due to my crazy up-and-down dieting.

Tonight, I said, was definitely to be up. The place I'd picked was famous for its lamb, its fresh vegetables and its strawberry soufflé dessert which had to be ordered hours before dinner. I'd done that and with it a rich '79 Chateau LaLagune.

"No Hunger Artist you," Penny said. "Do you think he knew you'd hunt me up and deliver his last words?"

"I don't know. He didn't have too much breath left and he knew it. He was just getting all sorts of stuff out. Last Chance Saloon stuff."

323

"I kept thinking he'd drop that damned story. Pay attention to something else. It doesn't matter anymore." She laughed. "God, we fought it out in rain and heat and snow."

"What *were* you two fighting about?"

"I thought I knew—I wanted him to pay attention to me and my life—my love affairs in purple prose . . . yes, I know that's what they were, now . . . I wanted him to love my stories as if they were parts of my body, of my self. Then, when that didn't happen and he stuck to his guns about making me imagine everything as if it was new, then I wanted him to love me and my body as if we were my writing. But he wouldn't do that, either. All he would do was tell me to cool out my prose, cool out my life . . . cool . . . God!"

"Was that about when you asked me if I wanted to make love to you in a blizzard in North Dakota or somewhere? I figured that for a ricochet."

"Did I do that?" It was the first time I'd ever seen the southern steamroller embarrassed. I did not remind her about the "Fuck you" that had followed. "I was so pissed off I told *Time* magazine all sorts of bullshit about him."

"I noticed."

"There's too much air-conditioning in here," she said. But the maître d' quickly rescued her from embarrassment and chill.

Dinner was phenomenal—the lamb pink and juicy and the soufflé hot and runny. Her big theory came out over the coffee.

"If you hadn't called me I would have dug *you* up."

"Oh?"

"I had to tell you what I'd figured out about Brandauer. When I found out about the heart attack it threw me. When I stopped crying I read the full obit and a light bulb went off." She leaned over the debris of dinner, intent in the old way, almost angry again. "*He knew he was going to die,*" she said. "The paper said he'd had a history of heart trouble for almost a decade. It explains everything."

She was in no mood for my interruption or disclaimer. "His picking that particular story and living the way he did, the way he gave only the minimum necessary to life, and *everything* to writing."

"Because he knew his clock was ticking so fast, you mean?"

324

"Don't forget," she said solemnly, "The only piece that you could call furniture in the Hunger Artist's cage was a clock."

"My God," I said. "You're picking up where he left off."

"That's why Brandauer kept teaching that story. It was his anthem." She wiped some pink from her lips, soufflé or lipstick I couldn't tell.

"That's not all," she said.

"Hold it," I said. "He could just as easily have gone the other way. You know—live all you can—that Henry James stuff . . . seize the *carpe* . . . *carpe* the *diem* . . ."

"Ha, ha," she said. "Listen, I've got something I want to read to you." I'd never read or heard anything she'd written. She pulled out some crumpled papers and over the coffee cups and bread crumbs she read this:

Krakauer: a story

Word was out that Krakauer was leaving his cage. After fourteen years of writing private astonishments, he was going into the public world to teach. This was an event worthy of comment in media as disparate as *The New York Times Magazine* (with its oddly inappropriate ads of young women in their sensual underwear) and *Critical Inquiry*, with its puritanically ordered columns of dense text.

Would he teach hermaneutics and literature—the Real Stuff—or just Creative Writing, the Fake Stuff? Would he be skinny, emaciated from years of isolation in Genoa, making and remaking sentences, *The New York Times* wondered? Would he be distracted from the larger concerns of The Academy by the sophomoric demands of students, *Critical Inquiry* wondered?

On a spring day in Seattle, the mystery was dispelled. That first morning Krakauer met with a crowded class of students still wet behind the ears with Seattle rain.

"I will not read any student's stories," he announced, this wraith from the lost land of language. "Instead, I will read 'A Hunger Artist by Franz Kafka.' "

Muted exclamations of pain and thwarted personal ambition. One pale young woman felt her chance at a new life slipping away.

Krakauer was firm. He began to read . . .

It was too damned good; the sentences supple and simple. Better than what I've written here. Tougher, more condensed, cooler; less tangled with the ego of a narrative voice.

"Hey," I said. "I haven't read your other stuff. But you seem to have cooled out. It's very strong, so far."

"I know," she said folding the papers back into her bag. "It's just the beginning."

I decided that such an expansive dinner deserved a cigar and we moved to the terrace.

"Do you mind if I smoke this?"

"Go on. My Daddy smoked cigars."

I touched Penny's cheek and rubbed my hand gently downwards, to see if anything had changed between us. She closed those enormous eyes for a flick of the lids. Her tongue licked a raspberry seed from her upper lip. A tick of time but it told me enough.

"Well," I said. "I guess it's just us, now."

A long sigh, then a grin. "I miss him," she said. "Even more than when he was here."

Melancholy laughter from both of us.

I put my arm around her shoulder and she collapsed against me. I had a story to finish on my desk, that night. It could wait.

In the morning I woke with my head on Penny's gently moving stomach. I felt satisfied and hungry and strange. The night before we'd been a kind of solution for each other. Now it was morning and we could start the natural process of becoming problems for each other. What would we do now with our bodies, our minds, our stories? How would we deal with each other—our anxieties, our appetites? *It doesn't matter what you eat . . . It matters what eats you . . . That's what . . .*

Penny stirred. She got up and went to the bathroom. When she came out I watched her while she performed a morning stretch, warm and lean. Conventional southern young woman that she was, she'd worn a white nightgown to bed, like a bride. The sun shone behind her through the bathroom window and I saw her shape revealed through the fabric of her nightgown, her parted legs an elegant V with curly pubic hair, perfectly clear, infinitely mysterious. My desire for her was urgent and stupid, without thought. I had no wish to read her stories, to encounter previous lovers. I wanted to be Opus One. I made love to her as if I wanted to get her inside myself, not the other way around. The exertion stung my strapped ribs and reminded me of my brush with highway death following my final brush with Brandauer. But holding Penny afterwards made me feel safe for the moment. I noticed, for the first time, that her right eye sort of wandered. Fresh details; she would be my newest unfinished story.

Immediately after, she was back at her idée fixe. She sat up straight. "Now, in the morning light," she said, "do you see how it explains everything? He *knew* he was going to die."

I kissed her lips; a faint flavor of raspberry from the night before. "You mean unlike the rest of us."

"Come on. You know what I mean."

"No," I said, implacable, remembering the jaws of the Panther.

Nominated by Len Roberts, Joyce Carol Oates, M. D. Elevitch, Robert Phillips

THE SUN, THE RAIN

fiction by MARIE SHEPPARD WILLIAMS

from THE AMERICAN VOICE

for Wren

ROSEALICE CAME to us off the street.

Who is "us"? We are an agency for the rehabilitation and employment of blind people. There are other kinds of handicapped people working here in addition to blind folks: deaf people, people who do not speak or who have speech impediments, Hmong refugees we were asked to take in because they do not speak our language yet; people with brain tumors, people who are what is called retarded, people with cancer, epilepsy, cerebral palsy, whatever: people broken, ill, crazy, or otherwise deviated in any one of a hundred ways from the golden, sound-limbed, competitive standard that we say in this country is normal.

All of these people are supposed to come to us by referral, from the State Office for the Blind, or the Department of Vocational Rehabilitation, or some other such agency. The reason they are supposed to be referred, instead of just coming in by themselves, is that we need a lot of preparation to be sure we are doing the right and best thing in each case rather than just dishing out spontaneous good will: we need eye reports, medical reports, psychologicals, authorizations, work histories, Individual Written Rehabilitation Plans, etc., etc. The human services professional, in spite of the high place we accord him or her, theoretically cannot—if you judge by our systems—be trusted any farther than you can spit.

Since we need all this paper to keep us on the right track, there must of course be someone to send it to us; therefore we need referring agencies.

328

Well, but nothing is easy these days; I guess you know that. I mean, you live in "these days" too. You are normal, or you say you are, but even so you need a lot of paperwork to make it through. Things are not simple any more. Maybe there are just too many of us now for simplicity.

Me and Vange figure that we own this agency. We are social workers. If you know any social workers, you will know that they all tend to think that they secretly run things, that the people who ostensibly have the power couldn't get along without them. Vange—short for Evangeline Josephine, and named for two dead aunts—has been here for nearly twenty-five years, me for only ten, but I am Vange's boss. This is hard for people to figure: Vange is so much smarter than I am, why isn't she the boss? Because that's the way it is, that's why. I have the right paperwork.

People are people, though, they simply will not or cannot be orderly, follow the rules all the time, and so sometimes handicapped people come into our sheltered workshop without any paperwork. Social Service is constantly bitching about this. As a matter of fact, I am the head of Social Service: what the hell is going on here? I say to Marlin Jenkins, the workshop director. Why did you let this person start working without coming through Social Service? Well, Marlin will say, but we didn't know: he didn't tell us that he was legally blind. Or epileptic. Or crazy. Whatever.

Sometimes we advertise for sighted people in the newspapers, or put a sign in our front window: some percentage of our jobs do require sight. We hire these people without any credentials at all: off the street. That is what Off the Street means: that people just decide to ask us for work on their own initiative. And Rosealice came in one day off the street. Our window sign said Clerical Help Wanted, and she walked in and said she typed eighty-five words a minute, and that's how we got her. If Jack the Ripper could type eighty-five wpm, we'd have hired him too.

Upstairs (in the Rehabilitation Center, which is supported financially in part by the sheltered shop) we heard about her before we saw her.

They've got a very strange new typist downstairs in the Production Office, Vange said one day. She types eighty-five words a minute error-free. Her name is Rosealice.

Rosealice? I said. One word? Like you said it? Rozallis?

Right, said Vange. Ro-Zallis.

What an odd name, I said. I never heard that name before.

Well, she's an odd person, said Vange. Maybe she has an odd name because she's an odd person.

Anybody who can type eighty-five words a minute error-free in this building is odd all right, I said.

I made up a reason to go down and see Rosealice. We are like a small town here, or a family; all of us are intensely interested in anything unusual that is going on anywhere in the building. So I took some stuff to be typed and went downstairs and asked Jan— the production coordinator—if I could use her new typist: Annette is snowed under upstairs, I told her.

Jan said it was ok to use Rosealice.

Take it in and tell her I said it was all right, she said. It might take you a little while to explain to her just how you want it, though. She's kind of different, Jan said.

So I carried my stuff into the room next to Jan's office, where the typewriter was banging away so fast it was almost a steady noise instead of your usual plock-plock-plock. Hi, I said: you must be Rosealice, I'm Joan Shepherd, I work upstairs in the Rehab Center, how are you, welcome, I'm real glad you're here: well, you know, all the things I would say to anybody new. I mean, you can't scare me with "different"; listen, we are practically immune to "different" here; we have, you might say, built up a tolerance.

The typewriter stopped. Brown eyes in a large, pale, square face looked up dazed from the copy. H-hello: she said. Her mouth bent into a stiff parody of a smile. Hello, I said again. Do you like it here so far? I said. I l-love it here, she said: everyone is so kind here. I am very hap-happy here. She spoke very fast, the words came out like bullets, and her stammer was like bullets too. Her eyes homed in on mine and locked. I felt like I'd been shot dead center. Honestly. Jesus: what an impact she had on me. Well, and you don't expect that, do you? I mean, people just don't look at other people like that.

And there was a problem all right. That became clear right away. It was like she couldn't hear me; really, literally, not hear;

330

though she wasn't deaf or anything like that. And she was very scared. I had to tell her the same things over and over, and even then she didn't get it. Finally—I don't claim this was inspiration, actually it was more like despair—I took a pen and sort of drew on the copy the form I wanted the final product to have. And that she understood.

Oh! she said, and her face cleared a little, the awful concentration lessened for a second. *I see!* And she took a pen and the copy, and I stayed with her while she read the thing aloud all the way through—hesitating and stuttering in fear, but stubborn, my god, intense—and she wrote over my neat little penciled corrections with the heavy black pen; she wrote large, bold, black. And then she typed it up absolutely perfectly, with a perfectly even touch. It was beautiful—and listen, she did it faster than the speed of light practically.

She's visual, I told everybody; that's the thing, she is absolutely and totally visual. You just have to show her, draw it for her, and then she's ok.

It wasn't that simple, of course, but that was the heart of it.

She didn't get on well with Jan. Rumors kept drifting up, mostly via Vange.

Jan says she doesn't think Rosealice will make it in the Production Office, Vange said one day.

You're kidding, I said: we get somebody at last who can type eighty-five words a minute, and Jan thinks she won't make it? You've got to be kidding.

Well, that's it, said Vange. She can only type, she can't do anything else. Jan needs somebody who can do all sorts of things, filing and all the rest of it, not just typing.

My god, I said, how silly can you get? *Jan* can do the other things. This agency *needs* a typist who can do 85 words a minute; I mean, *desperately.*

Well, yes, Vange said. But another thing is, Jan can't stand her. There's something too strange about her. Jan is thinking that if she doesn't work out as a typist, maybe they could use her on one of the assembly jobs in the workshop.

My god, I said: when we need a typist so badly, they'll take one like that and put her on *assembly?*

Well, said Vange. There's nothing wrong with assembly. And she likes it here. If Jan can't use her . . . .

That's not the goddamn point! I said.

You know, I was furious. I simply can't stand waste. I am very efficient, very compulsive.

Well, in the end I saved her for typing. She's upstairs with us now, at the desk by the dictaphone. She's up to ninety-five wpm, and climbing. And she has learned braille by sight. She does most of the brailling now for our blind staff members and board members. She learned braille faster than anyone ever did before in our experience: well, I knew she would, she is a natural, her eye-hand coordination is fantastic.

And she loves brailling. She learned it just in time to meet the demands of our eight new blind board members who insist upon having everything, I mean *everything*, in braille; well, but you know, it's right that they should have it, isn't it? It's just that before Rosealice, we simply couldn't keep up with it.

I really think that in a manner of speaking God sent her to us. She is so useful to us. She answers our needs perfectly. And we answer hers. Perfectly.

Rosealice is a large woman, heavy, strong, built like a long-shoreman, like a stevedore. On the job she had just before she came to us—we only know a little about this, Rosealice doesn't tell us much about herself—she did some sort of clerical work on a loading dock. They made her lift heavy things, she says. She didn't like it. Her face grows dark and tense when we ask her about that job.

Her breasts are large and pendulous nearly to her waist. We speculate on whether or not she wears a bra. Kelly, the executive director's beautiful, thin secretary, makes jokes about Rosealice's breasts. She *can't* wear a bra, says Kelly. There's no bra anywhere made in a shape like that. Unless it's for, you know, like a *cow* . . .

But she *must* wear one, I say. She's so conventional. She's not the kind of person not to wear a *bra* . . .

Christ, what am I saying?—I am for god's sake the manager here.

Let's just not discuss this, ladies, I say.

332

Kelly has a kind heart, though; she is kind to Rosealice. In fact, all the secretaries are nice to her. I have made this happen. I have explained Rosealice to the secretaries, explained that she is different, and how she is different. I have, you could say, sold her to them: well, though, this is my job, selling people to other people. And to themselves. Listen—I will say—underneath what I concede is a grisly exterior, there is a poet, a flower, a really lovely person . . .

Rosealice did things at first that nearly blew the whole project. Annette came into my office one day to talk to me about it. She sat at my desk with her hands folded primly in her lap, looking the picture of the perfect secretary.

Um, she said. I really like Rosealice.

Out with it, I said: how can you like her? She's awful.

Well, not *awful*, said Annette. Not exactly.

Her hands began to twist together.

Oh, come on, Annette, I said: of course she's awful. I think you and Jennifer are doing a wonderful job to put up with her at all.

Well, there *is* a problem, said Annette: two problems, in fact. Two main problems . . .

Ok. I said. What are the problems.

Well, said Annette. She keeps asking questions. She asks things that she knows already. She asks about everything, every other minute. Sometimes she even asks the same question over and over. Me and Jennifer can't get our work done, she's driving us crazy asking questions.

She's afraid, I said. I'll fix it. What else.

She coughs, said Annette. She's got a terrible cold and she won't stay home and she coughs and spits into this handkerchief, and it is all wrinkled and dirty and it's making us feel sick . . .

Oh, I said. Yes. That's harder.

Can you make her stop? said Annette.

Oh, yes, certainly, I said. I can do that.

So I talked to Rosealice. Vange and I talked to her together, actually. We told her that we liked her: if that was a lie, it was meant well. We said that she was doing a great job. We told her that we really wanted her to be able to stay with us. We told her that there were certain ways in which she would have to change if she was to stay.

Oh, I w-want to stay, said Rosealice: I know you girls will tell me what I have to do so that I c-can s-stay . . .

So we told her, and we laid down some rules. You must not speak to Annette and Jennifer *at all*. For a while. We will be your supervisors; you must come to us. You must not ask questions when you know the answers: *you do know the answers, you are intelligent*. You must go across the hall to the bathroom when you have to cough. This is what the world wants of you. Conform or forget it.

I am intelligent, she said. Smiling grimly, concentrating. And nodding. Getting her head around it.

I must not speak to Annette and Jennifer.

I must come to you. Or Vange.

I must go into the bathroom to cough.

Well, it sounds bad. I know it. But it was necessary. Dammit. And right. And we meant well—God sees the heart. And she thanked us; listen, she practically blessed us. You girls are my guardian angels: she said.

Anyway, it worked; she stopped asking so many questions and she coughed in the bathroom.

Were her feelings hurt? Annette asked me.

No, I said. Not at all.

What did she say?

Well, she thanked us, I said: she was grateful. Really, it's ok, Annette.

I feel so bad about it, said Annette.

Darling Annette, not twenty years old: with your heart-shaped face and serious smile.

You don't need to, I said.

I don't understand, said Annette: I'd be so hurt.

There was also the question of the "highwaters." For a long time, Rosealice wore her polyester pants hemmed up with about eight-inch hems, so that the pants were six or seven inches shorter than was fashionable.

The secretaries appealed to me: Joan, they said, can't you convince her to stop wearing those highwaters?

For heaven's sake, I said. What do you want from me? I made her stop coughing. I made her stop asking so many questions . . .

I felt really irritated about this.

Besides, I said: what have the highwaters got to do with her *job*?

Nothing, I guess, Annette said. But they make her look different. They make her, I mean, she doesn't *fit in* . . .

Fitting in, apparently, is important. And the secretaries are right—it isn't the quirky mind, or the agonized face, or the heavy worker's body—it's the highwaters.

Vange says: The thing is, the secretaries are right, the highwaters, I don't know how it works, they make her look retarded.

What is going on here? Vange loves the retarded people, why does she worry that the highwaters make Rosealice look retarded?

Well, maybe it is this: that Rosealice is too close to what *we* are. The retarded people are obviously totally different from us, we do not have to acknowledge relationship to them. Could that be it? Isn't that obvious?

Her face: I didn't really tell you much about her face. And now that I've thought of it, what can I say? Well, it is a large face. Square. Worn: she is only two years older than I am, she is fifty-one, I know this because I have reviewed the paperwork on her; but her face is terribly marked by whatever her life has been. It is a strong face, pale, with no makeup. The large features are not intrinsically ugly, but there is an effect of ugliness. This face is twisted and squeezed inward at all times in what appears to be an agony of tension and uncertainty; it never relaxes, it varies only between tension and more tension. This is true even when she types or brailles: both things she loves doing.

When she smiles, it is worse. Her smile is a crucifixion: she seems to be in terrible pain when she smiles. The skin of her face is very tight and shiny. The smile breaks it into planes and lines, and whatever light there is slides from plane to plane on her face like little lightning. Why: the smile itself is like a dreadful light.

She says she is happy. She says so all the time. She keeps saying it. To anyone who asks. Or who will listen.

And—this is a strange thing—I believe that she *is* happy; it is not a lie. She is not deluded.

She *is* happy; she really is happy, I said to Patsy Aaron, our tutor in the Rehabilitation Center.

Yes, said Patsy, I think you're right. I think she is happy. But there's something else wrong: with me: her happiness makes me want to cry.

* * *

A few weeks after Rosealice came, Vange and I gave a Tupperware party. You know about Tupperware, I assume; is there anyone reading who doesn't know about Tupperware? Well, but years ago I didn't know about Watergate until it was almost over—maybe there is someone out there who finds it as difficult to keep track of this civilization as I do. "Civilization" is the focal word here: not knowing about Tupperware is an anti-cultural position.

Well: so then: Tupperware. Tupperware is a ritual of this culture. Sort of like Social Security. Tupperware is important: a focus for a ceremonial gathering together of people who do not especially want to be together so that they may buy—at a rather high price—an excellent plastic product that they basically do not need and do not want. People are told when they are invited that they don't have to buy this product; however, it is a strong and renegade individual who can hold onto an intention not to buy. Dessert is served, and coffee. There is a saleswoman present who demonstrates the plastic product and takes orders. I have never heard of a male Tupperware salesperson; and I don't know that there has ever been a Tupperware party for men. Fundamentally, it is a female rite.

You get something at a Tupperware party that is not in the description of what happens. I think you get a guarantee of commonality: we're all in this together, and we are all alike: there are no outsiders here.

Well, Vange and I are students, undeclared, of civilization and its peculiarities; so when we observed that the workshop people were at one point feeling left out of things, we hit upon the idea of a Tupperware party to bring back a feeling of community. We invited all the blind women in the workshop; plus those from other departments: otherwise who would the workshop people feel community *with*? We invited our own department of course—Social Service—and everyone who had any remote connection with Social Service, the Intake people from the Rehab Center, for example; and the tutor, Patsy, who doesn't exactly belong any place in particular and who might very well feel left out too; and all the secretaries from everywhere in the building because hardly anybody ever considers them. That's how Rosealice happened to come: she got lumped in with the secretaries.

336

When it came right down to it, we invited fifty-two people: a simply monstrous Tupperware party. Well, but only thirty-nine actually came: thank God, says Vange.

Patsy Aaron was sitting next to Rosealice in a big circle—actually a double circle, there were so many of us—around Vange's living room at the Tupperware party. I overheard a conversation between Patsy and Rosealice: clear, between the words of other conversations, you know how this will happen sometimes in a crowd, one thread will suddenly emerge as separate from the whole, and all the rest will seem muted.

Rosealice: I think this is wonderful don't you just w-wonderful?

Patsy: The party, you mean?

Rosealice: Yes I think it's so w-wonderful that we are here that Vange asked us to come here Vange is wonderful. Rosealice's voice is tense and urgent and happy: she speaks in a stuttering loud monotone.

Patsy: Yes, Vange is a nice person.

Patsy's voice is light and intelligent, as always.

Rosealice: Oh no Vange is *wonderful*, everything is *wonderful*, everyone is *wonderful*, just *wonderful*.

Patsy: (laughing) Well, I don't know about *everything*. I don't know about *everyone* . . .

Rosealice: Oh—yes: everything. I think we all have so many reasons to be happy. For example, we have the s-sun, the sun shines, and I think that's so wonderful, and we have the rain . . .

I decided to rescue, that is after all part of my business, rescuing: Listen, Patsy, I yelled across three other people: don't sweat it. The sun will probably fall out of the sky tomorrow . . .

Patsy: laughing: in relief: Oh, *right!* We don't have to be happy after all, terrific, tomorrow the sun will fall . . .

Across three people I saw uncertainty in Rosealice's face. Oh, no, she said: the sun will still be there tomorrow . . .

I was ashamed. Yes. I was. I do have a capacity for shame.

But listen, what else could I have done? Could I have let Patsy sit alone confronting this dreadful heresy, that we should be happy *because we have the sun?*

The next day Patsy came to see me in my office.

337

How did Rosealice get like that? she said. I mean, you're a therapist, you ought to know.

Oh, sure, I said: I ought to know. She's crazy, I said: that should be obvious.

Yes, but, the awful part of it is, the thing is, she's *right*. Said Patsy. She's right and we're wrong.

Oh, well, yes, I said: that is certainly true. Absolutely. (Ha-ha. I am in my sarcastic mode.)

Patsy: I mean, we *should* be happy, we *do* have reasons to be happy.

But we're not, I said.

No we're not, said Patsy.

And that's normal, I said. What we are is ok. What she is is not ok.

But that's terrible, said Patsy. That's so sad.

Me: Oh, yes. That's terrible. That's sad. Oh, yes.

How did she get like that? Patsy's question. Well, I don't know; Patsy thinks I ought to know but I don't. I can make some guesses. Vange makes wilder guesses than I do: there's incest there, she says darkly.

I make something up for the secretaries, I convince them of what I do not know.

You know, I say to Annette, really terrible things have to happen to people to make them like Rosealice is, we don't know what happened to Rosealice, and we probably never will know, but the thing is, if we are kind to her she will be happy here: and she's worth it, she's so useful to us, nobody works harder, or better. And I guess we can stand it to have one happy person here.

The fact is: Annette says: the truth is. She gropes for the words. Finally: I couldn't get along without her now, she says. I don't know what I would do without her now.

We get clues. Not very many. A few: startling.

One morning I was humming something when I went into the secretarial area.

Are you happy today? said Rosealice to me: You must be happy today.

Happy? I said: Certainly not. (*You take that back immediately:* is the thought in my mind.) What makes you think so?

You're hum-humming, says Rosealice. Her voice is cracking with anxiety.

I think that one over. I believe you're right, I say. I feel surprised. An answer occurs to me: I believe it must be because it's Tuesday, I say: I have always liked Tuesdays.

She jumps on this enthusiastically, like a dog onto a wonderful bone: Oh! she says. Oh! I have always liked Tuesdays too!

Is that so? I say. I am paging through a book of records. The paperwork here is driving me absolutely up the wall: it seems to be increasing geometrically lately.

Oh! Yes! she says. In fact I wrote a song about Tuesday when I was a little girl, it went like this, *On Tuesday . . . a bear ate . . . my . . . brother . . .*

She sings it: a simple delicate complicated melody.

I look at her. I don't very often look right at her, it might burn my eyes I think. Jesus, I say: that's a great song, Rosealice, I could have written that song. When I was a little girl.

I can remember being a little girl; but the concept is strange to me in relation to Rosealice. She could not have been a little girl, it is out of the question.

When Rosealice had worked for us for thirty days, she was—as all of us are upon completion of thirty days of work—inducted into full status at the agency via the ceremony called Getting Onto the Insurance Plan.

I gave her the plastic Blue Cross card that signified her initiation.

Here you are, Rosealice, I said. Keep this in your billfold and then if you get taken to a hospital or something you've got it.

What is it, she said. Taking it from me and turning it over and over in her fingers.

It's a card that says you are covered by the agency's insurance plan, I said. When you work here for thirty days you get onto the insurance plan.

Insurance plan, she said.

Yes, I said, you know, when you get sick now you don't have to pay for it if you go to a doctor: You're covered. Eighty percent.

I'm covered, she said. She sounded scared.

I took a deep breath. Covered, I said, means that you are in our health insurance plan, you're a member of it. Like the rest of us.

Are you a member, she said.

Yes, I said.

Oh well then I guess it's all right if you are a member too, she said. Is Vange a member.

Vange too, I said.

Oh then it's all right, she said.

Yes, it's all right, I said.

I told Vange about it afterward. I don't think she knew what insurance is, I said: listen, Vange, is that possible, that she didn't know that? My goodness, said Vange. My word.

I ride the same bus with Vange coming to work every morning. The 7:41 a.m. 4J bus. This bus picks me up practically right in front of my house and drops me off across the street from the agency. I get to work about one minute before 8 a.m., the official starting time, which is about as perfect as you can get. I could drive, but taking the bus is so easy. Obviously, as a manager, I could come in late, but I don't; I am much too neurotic for that. Well, I am scared, you see; this college master's degree and this manager's job came on top of too many insecurities for me ever (apparently) to feel that the degree *and* the job were anything but accidents.

The 7:41 is almost, but not quite, as convenient for Vange: she walks a block and a half from her home on Aldrich Avenue S. to ride it.

Sometimes Rosealice gets onto our bus at Lake Street. I believe she takes another bus from St. Paul; I have that impression. I have never actually asked her, though.

Vange and I sit in the front seat that adjoins a long seat to make an L shape along the side of the bus right up to the front door. Whenever Rosealice sees us she plunks down right by us on the long seat. Always. If the nearest place is taken, she stands by us, grabbing a hand hold.

W-well, hello there! she says. Shouts, actually. Rosealice always talks in a very loud voice.

Hello, Rosealice, we say distantly, hoping everyone will notice the dismissal in our voices.

Rosealice chatters on and on. She says the same things again and again.

H-hello.

H-how are you girls?

Isn't it a, isn't it a, lovely day?

Have you, have you, have you—*staccato, well I told you before, like bullets*—read any good books lately? (Yes, honestly.)

Isn't it a lovely day?

Etc. Etc.

Vange and I (by tacit agreement, it is not spoken or arranged) decide to sit farther back on the bus. Rosealice never sees us back there. I suspect her eyesight is not very good.

We both feel guilty as hell.

Why are we doing this, Vange? I say. When we feel so guilty about it.

I know, says Vange.

But why, I say.

Well, we are avoiding a scene on the bus, says Vange. We are being thoughtful of our fellow riders.

Sure, I say.

She's too different, says Vange: We can't stand her.

But we like her, I say.

Oh yes, says Vange. Liking is one thing. Conversation on the bus is another. Knowing her is another.

Not *like*, I said. *Love*. I *love* her. Don't I?

Yes, I think so, says Vange.

Why, I say.

She means something important to you, says Vange.

When I see her typing upstairs in the morning, I feel happy, I say. It's like walking into the sunlight to hear the sound of her typewriter. Honest to god.

Maybe she's my happiness, I say.

Maybe she's my sun.

Maybe, says Vange.

I told you before, Vange laughs at me.

She's certainly your responsibility, says Vange: you saved her.

When we go by the secretarial area now, we can hear the sound of Rosealice's typewriter banging away. It does not sound like the other typewriters. Well, the other typists, as it happens, do not want to be typists. They want to be: social workers, counselors, managers, recreation directors. They are discontent with what

341

they are; they want to be something more, something other. They are in a way full of envy; they envy us, the social workers, etc.

Rosealice likes being a typist; she says she does. Oh I love typing, she says; when we ask her. What about brailling? I ask her. Well, brailling too: she says. Which do you like best, brailling or typing? I ask her. Well, both: she says: I like them both. I have upset her a little, though: when I asked her to choose. Her forehead creases in an anxious frown. She finds her solution, and the cloud clears: I like about half of each, she says. Every day.

The sound of Rosealice's typewriter is a happy, tearing-along, going lickety-split, rhythm, music sound.

She's very lucky, says Vange.

How so? I say.

She really likes to type, says Vange. She really loves it. She has found her niche. It's a pleasure to walk by and hear that sound.

I tell Rosealice that. Vange says it gives her pleasure to hear the sound of your typewriter: I say to Rosealice.

Oh, I love to type: says Rosealice. It makes me happy to type: she says.

Yes, I say, that's what I'm saying. It is very clear when you type that you love doing it. It makes us all feel happy too, that you are happy.

I just love to type, says Rosealice firmly. Her smile, that agonized cracking of the tense mask, hurts me. I go away. She goes back to her typing. The sound is happy again. Tap-tap-tap. Hap-hap-hap. Tappy-tappy-tappy. Blessed are the: how does it go? For they shall see God? Or something. Wow. This track could take you anywhere. You could trip out on this: I could. Nevertheless, I do not want to be a typist. I do not want to be what I am, though, either. If you give me my heart's dearest desire, whatever that might be, I think probably I will not want it after all.

Rosealice dresses kind of funny. I told you about the highwaters. Well, there are other things. Sitting and typing and brailling and being happy, she is getting fatter. Her winter coat—which seems to be made of good wool, it has a good label, Peck and Peck, we can see the label when she hangs the coat in the secretaries' closet—her coat does not close anymore across her big body, her huge breasts.

She wears a strange hat. It is a child's hat, I think.

One afternoon she rides the same bus with me and Vange going home. It is a cold day. I am sitting at the front of the bus and Vange is next to me, on the inside of the double seat. Large Rosealice is looming over us. Rosealice wants to stay by us, she holds onto a pole by us. The bus gets crowded, people have to push past Rosealice to get on at all. She will not move back. She carries a purse and a black metal lunch box such as a manual laborer might carry. She has an awful time juggling the purse and the lunch box and the pole, the hands that type so capably are clumsy in this operation. She is wearing the coat that will not close, and her funny hat.

It's very cold today, she says. Smiles eagerly. Breathes audibly. We are communicating, the smile says: isn't it wonderful?

Mm, I say: Cold, yes. My tone is discouraging, I feel. I do not want to communicate.

I am not cold, though, she says: I have my hat on.

Mm, I say.

My warm, furry hat, she says.

Mm-hm, I say.

She *will* tell me, though. I cannot stop this thing she wants to tell me.

It makes me look like a kitten, she says.

I look at her. The hat is a hood or bonnet that ties under her chin. There is a wreath of fur that goes around her face. Her large white face smiles and simpers inside the wreath of yellow-tan fur.

Maybe a lion, I say. *Maybe a werewolf, I think*. I feel grim. I am always grim at the end of a day. I do not like my job. I want to be a hardware sales clerk or something. Maybe a mail sorter at the post office. But this hat idea somehow interests me, I am attracted by it.

No, a kitten, she says. A nice little kitten. She nestles her face coyly into the fur ring. She bridles and preens. Smiles. Nestles. I am a kit-kitten, she says.

So. This big, strong, white-faced typist-braillist is a kitten. I shrink down a little inside my coat. I am embarrassed.

She babbles on: I am a kitten, I am . . .

All the other people on the bus are watching, listening.

Listen, suddenly I want to tell you, the fact is, I personally am a giraffe. No listen, I really mean it: *I am a giraffe*. In my imag-

343

ination, I can hook into giraffeness. I have always known this. Did she buy the hat because she knew she was a kitten? She did. Oh, yes. I know this.

Thank you for telling me, Rosealice, I say.

To hell with the other people.

But I do not tell Rosealice that I am a giraffe.

* * *

In a way, though, you know, I can after all see her as a little girl. When I try. I can see her under a tree: in a garden. The sun is shining. There are flowers all around. There is a stocky, plump, black-haired, brown-eyed, happy and strange little girl. She is about six years old, I think. She is singing: *On . . . Tuesday . . . a bear ate . . . etc.* She is touching the flowers and speaking to them. She is addressing the sun; well, she knows the sun, she is an intimate acquaintance of the sun. There is always a boy present, the boy is older. The boy is cruel, he hates the little girl. He teases her; always. Nyah, nyah, nyah, nyah-nyah-nyah, he taunts her. You are fat. You are ugly. He pulls flowers from their stems. He tears them apart. He throws them at her. Fix them, he says. She tries; but who can fix a flower? She is crying. You are stupid, he says. Then he gets tired of his game. He runs away.

Actually I am making this up. All I can really see is a little black-haired girl sitting in a garden. Under a tree. And the sun is always shining. Or else it is raining.

I suppose I should confess: there are things I know in myself that are involved in the way I feel about Rosealice. I understand about the typing, for example. It has always seemed to me that if I could only find the one thing I liked, really *liked,* to do, that then I would be happy. And I am clear on this: that the thing does not have to be big or important. What I envision when I think about this is building little houses out of toothpicks: I do not mean that I actually want to do this, I only mean that it would be all right to want to do this. There would be no moral lack involved in wanting to build little houses out of toothpicks instead of wanting, for example, to be a doctor or a politician— just to pick out at random a couple of important ambitions. Other people could choose to be doctors; in my imagining, being a doctor would be every bit as good as building little houses out of toothpicks. But—and this is the point—it would be no better. There would be no value attached. Only happiness, if you could call that a value: happiness would be the value. Are you happy? would be the question.

I notice that I have inadvertently hit toothpick-house-building rather hard. I wouldn't want you to get the idea that I really want to do that. It is just a metaphor. A symbol. Whatever. Actually, I think that particular thing wouldn't suit me; I think I would get tired of that pretty quickly.

Do you know the idea of the God's Fool? This idea runs all through the literature and myth of western civilization; maybe through every other civilization's literature and myth too, I wouldn't know about that. But the God's Fool is sort of a happy simpleton: he goes his own way. He (or she, obviously it can be a woman too, like for example St. Therese, whom they called The Little Flower, I am named for her, Joan Therese, my given name is), anyway, the God's Fool smiles a lot. He never judges the rest of us: I expect he thinks we are rather wonderful. But he himself is humble; he is not in any way conceited about his own gifts, whatever they may be. He is usually intent, this simpleton, upon some task which is pretty much beside the point.

I guess the juggler of Notre Dame was a God's Fool; juggling balls in front of a statue for the glory of God, my word. My goodness. Francis of Assisi: he must have been one of them. Candide. The Fool in the Tarot. Blake. Albert Einstein? Johnny Appleseed? Why not? (Do you remember the song we used to sing when we were children about Johnny Appleseed? Something like this: *The Lord is good to me . . . and so I thank the Lord . . . For giving me . . . the things I need . . . the sun, the rain . . . and the appleseed . . .*)

Listen: this is an important question: could typing be something a God's Fool would do?

Once I had a notion at the back of my mind that *I* ought to end up as a God's Fool, was meant to be one. Do you think you can choose such things? The problem with the idea of being a God's Fool, though, is basically a socio-economic one: I mean, who ever heard of a God's Fool owning a house and a car and a color TV, or

345

working as a manager? I guess it's hopeless, this secret notion of what I was meant to be? Well, why do I ask you—of course it's hopeless. I am as bad as Rosealice with my questions.

What do you think, Vange? I asked one day. Do you think a person can choose to be a God's Fool?

I don't see why not, said Vange. What do you want to know for? Why are we discussing this?

Do you think I could be one?

No way, said Vange.

Why not?

Well, she said: for one thing, you lack humility. For another thing, you have too much money.

I guess that's true, I said. Both of those things are true.

I know Vange thinks I am getting a little peculiar. I catch her looking at me funny every once in a while. Well, Vange loves me, you know. She wouldn't want me to go off the deep end or anything, or do anything that was actually going to hurt me.

She has nothing to worry about. Obviously. Since I lack humility and have money. And I am not about to take up the one and dump the other. Being a God's Fool or any other kind of fool is not an option, goddamit. I'm unhappy with the way things are, all right, but I'm not that unhappy. I'm no more unhappy than anybody else. Do you think? What do you think?

Annette meets me and Vange at the door as we come into the building one morning. She is very upset, she can hardly get her message out fast enough.

They're going to take Rosealice away from us, Joan! she says. Vange! You have to do something!

What in the world, I say. Vange says.

It's true, says Annette. Why, Annette is almost crying. She says: I got here early and Claude came up and told me.

Claude is the Director of the Rehab Center: maybe I told you that before.

That's crazy, I said. Why would they do that?

The new blind board members don't want her, Annette said. Because she's not blind. They think she should be blind. That's what Claude said.

346

Well. I was simply knocked over. Vange! I said. Do you know anything about this?

Vange always knows things ahead of time.

I did hear a rumor, she said.

Why didn't you tell me? I said. Yelled. God. I was so mad.

Rumors aren't always true, Vange said. Mostly things like this don't actually happen.

Is this one going to happen? I said.

I think so, says Vange.

No it's not, I say. I'll stop it somehow.

You have to tell her, says Annette. She is really crying now into her little white lace hankie. I can't tell her, she sobs.

She is not going, I say. I won't have to tell her. Nobody will have to tell her.

I put my arms around Annette. Don't cry, darling, I say. I'll fix it. Everything will be ok. You'll see.

But everything wasn't ok. I couldn't fix it. The blind board members won, and Rosealice had to be told that she couldn't braille and type for us any more. I told her. Like Vange said, she was my responsibility.

Do I have to leave here then? she asked.

You can go into assembly if you want to, I said. In the workshop. With your eye-hand coordination you'd probably make as much money there as here. Well. More. Probably.

Oh, thank you, said Rosealice: I don't have to leave you all. I can stay here.

Honestly. She didn't seem to care at all about the brailling and typing. It was—apparently—us that she loved.

Rosealice doesn't have to leave; but I am leaving. I can't stay here any more. I am going to go out and build toothpick houses. Well: I'm going to art school, is what I am really going to do. I suppose I can get some kind of part-time job. Or I can live on my savings. For a while.

I thought Rosealice would be upset when I told her I was leaving, and she was, but the news didn't kill her or anything. Will you come back to see us sometimes? she asked.

Probably, I said. (Though I am not the sort to come back, that is not my style.) But: Certainly, I said. I promise. Of course. Of course I will.

347

Well, then, that's all right, she said: Will Vange leave too?

No, Rosealice, Vange will stay, I said: Vange and I are not Siamese twins, we are not joined at the head or anything. I do lots of things that Vange doesn't do. And vice versa. Vange does lots of things I don't do.

I think of you together, said Rosealice.

Well, we are together, I said. Sometimes. Sometimes we are separate.

Oh, well, then, that's all right, Rosealice said. If Vange doesn't go. She smiled: that terrifying smile.

* * *

She's on assembly now. She went on before my scheduled time to leave. I was able to set that up anyway. Lose the war and win the battle. I should tell you that I've given the folks here six weeks notice; well, you know, I've liked it here, even though I did complain a lot, and I thought I owed them that: six weeks notice. I thought, you know, that it would be hard to replace me. I thought I was terribly good at what I did.

Actually, there's talk of not replacing me at all.

I've seen Rosealice in the workshop every day since she went there. The line leader says she learned astonishingly fast: nobody faster, ever. She's up to $7.43 an hour already, which is more than she'd ever make upstairs as a typist.

Do you think you can be happy here, Rosealice? I say.

Oh, yes, she says. She stops twisting the little piece of wire on the object that she is assembling. She smiles, and her face breaks again into that mass of shiny planes and the light from the overhead fluorescent bounces and slides off the planes and lines of her face. I'm ter-terribly happy, she says. The people here are all so n-nice. Mr. Jenkins is so nice. And V-Vange comes.

You know, I'm jealous. Just a little. She was mine before and now she isn't. You know? I mean, I'm glad for her, but I'm also just a tiny, *teeny* bit jealous. But I forgive myself. I was only human after all, I say to myself. There, there, dear: I say. To myself.

I'm going to art school. I guess I told you that. When I leave. After art school, who knows? You never know about human beings. They can surprise you.

348

I figure I'll have to cut back some while I'm in school. I probably won't be able to afford to drive the car, for example; when you really sit down and figure it out, cars turn out to be terribly expensive. Maybe I'll just simplify things; and I already know a lot about getting around on buses. So maybe I'll get rid of the car altogether one of these days. One of these fine days when the sun is shining. Or when it's raining.

Nominated by Maxine Kumin

TWO CITIES:
ON THE *ILIAD*

by SUZANNE GARDINIER

from THE KENYON REVIEW

> And, through the palace, mothers wild with fright
> Ran to and fro or clung to doors and kissed them.
>
> VERGIL, *Aeneid*
> (Fitzgerald)

Far FROM FISHING, far from the cutting of timber to build, far from hunting and from the raising of stone walls, far from the tending of flocks, far from plowing and irrigation and the buzzing of flies over pails of spring milk, far from the washing of clothes and the weaving of cloth and the tending of children—as Simone Weil put it, far from hot baths—the action of the *Iliad* takes place. It takes place also far from us in time; but as Homer's similes lock together the gaffing of a fish and the spearing of a man, flies over milk and soldiers over a corpse, Robert Fagles in his recent translation (1990) holds us very close to Troy and its blood-soaked plain and will not let us go.

Homer's audience is not made up of soldiers; the similes are for its benefit, so that someone who knows what a dazed fawn is may also know what twelve young men dragged from a river are, hands bound behind their backs, to be thrown on a funeral pyre in pieces. The listeners seem almost a different species from the soldiers; it takes many of them to lift the lethal boundary stones that the poem's heroes heft one-handed. The story is sung around civil fires, where listeners bound together by words host the spirits of men who have no use for words, who have nothing but contempt for them. At the poem's center is the walled city of Troy, where the public square and the fortress meet and disappear into each other; it is the realm of women, of old men, of cowards, of children, of those who are weak as the listeners are weak. Of what happens in this realm the poem gives only glimpses: a man fled from battle to make love; a child recoiling from his father dressed for war; a woman weaving as slave women prepare her husband's bath, who hears screaming and drops her shuttle. The poet's steady gaze is fixed not here but on the plain and waters outside the city, and on the bodies of the young men who make their province there—on their necks, nipples, flanks, teeth, eyes, wrists, cheeks, on what becomes of all of these as they make each other die. What Elaine Scarry (74) calls "the question of how the road of injury can end up in the town of freedom" is never asked here; this is not the poem of the town but of the road, not of oaths or principles or governance, not even of death and the shadow it casts over the living, but of bodies and their openings by weapons, of the butchery of men. From this the poet's gaze never wavers, and about this he never lies.

Is this our beginning? An epic is an ancestor; is this ours? If so, the choice is one among many, as we choose among our ancestors the one from whom we will claim descent. As a nation of speakers of Indo-European languages, we could as easily claim the young *Mahabharata* and its *Bhagavad-Gita;* in tribute to the Afro-Asiatic strand of our Judeo-Christian heritage, we might claim the *Book of Job,* or the *Epic of Gilgamesh,* whose origins precede the *Iliad's* by a thousand years. As residents of the Western Hemisphere, we might claim the Mayan *Popul Vuh,* or some yet-unknit Nahuatl sequence—or the Delaware Big House Ceremony set down, or the Mohawk Ritual of Condolence, or the story of the peace made among the Five Nations of the Iroquois. As residents of the United States, we might claim *Leaves of Grass*—or sew together and claim the folk tales and songs with the story of the survival of slavery in them, as the Finns made their *Kalevala* in the last century from what peasants remembered.

By content, the *Iliad* is not the epic of slaves, nor of those who hold the earth sacred, nor of those who value the words of women or children, nor of those who deeply value words at all,

351

as sacred vessels, as anything more than the ritual preludes to battle. It is the epic of soldiers, and of the cultures whose central places have been occupied by them. It is the epic of cultures whose sense of connection to a universe that is whole has been broken, whose peace is the interval between wars. As such, it is clearly one of our ancestors, whether we hold this country's sword of power or live at its point. Whether or not it is this one among all the others to whom we will pledge allegiance remains to be seen.

Some indication of the allegiances of this translator is offered in his preface; he thanks his collaborator and comrade, Bernard Knox (who provides the sixty-page introduction and explanatory notes) and describes their shared manuscript, his typescript ringed by his friend's notes, as "a battle-map": "The vulnerable lines at the center are shored up by a combat-tested ally, whose squads reinforce the weakest sectors and who deciphers Homer's order of the day and tells a raw recruit what war—the movements of armies and the sentiments of soldiers—is all about. And more, what tragedy—in this, the first tragedy—really means" (xii). Later, the translator to whom Fagles owes most, Robert Fitzgerald, advises him to "fit on your greaves and swordbelt and face the moil or the melee" (xii). The drudging work of this moil is, of course, killing; here Fagles reverses Homer's strategy, giving us not the civilian to stand for the military but the other way around. Homer's joinings open the heart to grief and truth; Fagles's reversals, in his preface, allow the truth of what he describes to be obfuscated, and the way to grief to be blocked. In comparing the task of translation to the work of killing, so that we may better understand, Fagles makes assumptions about his audience that Homer does not, and allies himself with the point of view of particular elements in the poem rather than with that of the poem as a whole. He and Knox are not Astyanax and Andromache, son and grieving, knowing mother, nor Hector and Priam, son and grieving father—nor allied with Thersites who is beaten for speaking against kings, nor with Polydamas who counsels retreat and excels at trading words. They are soldiers in the field together; Knox in his turn quotes Robert E. Lee's thoughts on war at Fredericksburg—"It is well that it is so terrible, or we should grow too fond of it"—and says that "it is just as sentimental to pretend that war does not have its monstrous ugliness as it is to deny that it has its own strange and fatal beauty, a power, which can call out in men resources of endurance, courage and self-sacrifice that peacetime, to our sorrow and loss, can rarely command" (29). The two together establish themselves as brothers within the world of war, deploring it faults and praising its virtues, and address themselves to other initiate brothers. In these statements, unlike Homer's poem itself, there is remarkably little grief; in allying themselves with the poem's heroes, these two share the heroes' central tragedy: they cannot comprehend the plain realities before them, the emotional significance of the countless preventable horrors, because they bear hearts that refuse to break.

The strength of this translation comes from just this armed, unbroken heart, honestly revealing itself, in partnership with Homer's text. Its voice is not lofty or stately or elegant; it is not, in Knox's words on the poem itself, "august, authoritative . . . a vision of life fixed forever in forms that seem to have been molded by gods rather than men" (12). Its timbre has less in common with gods' speech or the mournful human voice than with the ring of bronze weapons against each other; its vocabulary has less in common with the diction of canonical classics than with the lexicon of modern war.

Here is Richmond Lattimore's version, from 1951, of the fighting just before Patroclus enters the battle and is killed:

It was around his ship that now Achaians and Trojans
cut each other down at close quarters, nor any longer
had patience for the volleys exchanged from blows and javelins
but stood up close against each other, matching their fury,
and fought their battle with sharp hatchets and axes, with great
swords and with leaf-headed pikes, and many magnificent
swords were scattered along the ground, black-thonged,
   heavy-hilted,
sometimes dropping from the hands, some glancing from
   shoulders
of men as they fought, so the ground ran black with blood.
(15.707–715)

Here is the Fagles of 1990:

Now churning around that ship Achaeans and Trojans
hacked each other at close range. No more war at a distance,

353

waiting to take the long flights of spears and arrows—
they stood there man-to-man and matched their fury,
killing each other now with hatchets, battle-axes,
big swords, two-edged spears, and many a blade,
magnificent, heavy-hilted and thonged in black
lay strewn on the ground—some dropped from hands,
some fell as the fighters' shoulder straps were cut—
and the earth ran black with blood. (15.820–829)

Fagles's lines are rhythmically made and broken; there is never a sense of shoehorning a cumbersome Greek meaning into a protesting English shoe. Yet he is literal, plain, in tribute to Homer's great vivid plainness: Lattimore's "cut each other down" becomes "hacked each other," "fought their battle" becomes "killing each other," and "patience for the volleys exchanged from blows and javelins" becomes "waiting to take the long flights of spears and arrows," making the meeting of bodies and weapons much more clear.

This plain music is again evident in the chapter titles Fagles chooses: his fine ear makes Fitzgerald's "Assembly and Muster of the Armies" into "The Great Gathering of Armies," while his insistence on the literal makes Book One, "Quarrel, Oath, and Promise," into "The Rage of Achilles," and the later "A Ship Fired, a Tide Turned" into "Patroclus Fights and Dies." Both the music—this version is made to be read aloud—and the plainness of the diction bring the poem close to us, in this time; Fagles's use of the vocabulary of modern, mechanized war brings it closer still.

What Lattimore calls "the wearisome burden of hatred" (21.385–386) and Fitzgerald "heavy and harsh strife" (21.299), Fagles calls "total war" (21.437), while Lattimore's Paris calls to Diomedes "You are hit, and my arrow flew not in vain" (11.380) and Fitzgerald's "Hit you are, and hard! / No wasted shot, that!" (11.332–333), Fagles's shouts "Now you're hit—no wasted shot, my winging arrow! / But would to god I'd hit you deep in the guts / and ripped your life away!" (11.447–449). The "no wasted shot" seems a tribute to Fitzgerald, one of many; but crowding the rest of the text are units and battalions, trenches and breastworks, and Hector in his desperation saying not "Ah me!" (Lattimore, 22.99) or "Here I am badly caught" (Fitzgerald, 22.119) but "No way out" (22.118). There is terror in Fagles's faithful ren-

354

dering of Homer's literal descriptions; there is more terror in the juxtaposition of Homer's song and the stripped modern voice singing it. This terror is clearest in one word, repeated at intervals throughout the translation: "nonstop." No other word embodies the horror of modern war more completely: its seeming bureaucratic neutrality, its emotional remove from the place where bodies are opened, the cobbled euphemistic flatness of the official stories told about it, the sickening mechanical steadiness of its continuance. Nowhere else are the stories of Auschwitz and Hiroshima—our agony still bears the names of cities—told more succinctly. Where Lattimore writes, "But swift Achilleus kept unremittingly after Hektor, / chasing him" (22.188–189), and Fitzgerald "Great Akhilleus, hard on Hektor's heels, / kept after him" (22.222–223), Fagles writes, "And swift Achilles kept on coursing Hector, nonstop" (22.224). Here the terror is compounded by that "coursing"; the words have all of Homer's pitiless, equitable literalness, and are at the same time completely empty of whatever spiritual meaning Homer's meter and diction may have carried. There is no protest in them, no hint of another world where such things do not happen, no heroic behavior, and there is not grief. "Nonstop" is part of the vocabulary of what Robert Jay Lifton has called "doubling," meaning "the division of the self into two functioning wholes, so that a part-self acts as an entire self." (196) In this realm the Nazi doctors were able to do their work, and the creators of the atomic bomb to do theirs; in this realm we may use martial metaphors without smelling blood, or support the bombing of distant populations, or keep functioning without continuous, conscious alarm in a world that may no longer need a nuclear war to bring about its own rapid destruction. Fagles's voice speaks its unbroken heart in a language both true to Homer and near and familiar to us; in making clear its own emptiness, it sounds the echo that is the consequence of its division: the echo of the ghost presence of what it has lost.

*

When he left, I found, in front of his chair,
a bloody rag, part of the dressing,
a rag to be thrown straight into the garbage;

355

and I put it to my lips
and kept it there a long while—
the blood of love against my lips.

C. P. Cavafy, "The Bandaged Shoulder"

When the *Iliad* begins, the Achaeans and the Trojans have
been at war ten years; but in Homer's version no one has de-
serted, no maimed men walk among the bickering heroes, no one
speaks gibberish or not at all or wakes sweating from nightmare
sleep. It was Gandhi's insight that two fighting men may seem
opposed, but are also in fundamental agreement, about the rituals and methods of what they enact together. The soldiers of both
sides on the plain of wheat and blood make a society of their
own, exclusively composed of young men; the old men and
women and children of Achaea are years and miles away, while
those of Troy remain within its walls and constitute its identity:
late in the poem, Polydamas warns that Achilles "will fight for
our wives, for Troy itself!" (18.306). Each member of the society
of soldiers has received the training required for membership,
reinforced by ten years of practice; one of its cardinal principles
demands the steeling of the human emotions that arise in the acts
of killing, of witnessing killing, and of risking being killed oneself.
This is what a soldier must learn; and in this poem, being a soldier is synonymous with being a man. In spite of such careful
training and reinforcement, fear and disgust and despair well up
in even the bravest fighters; the cry raised to call them back, to
re-enact that steeling, is "Be men, my friends! Discipline fill your
hearts!" (15.651).

At first it seems as if it is men and women who are so rigidly separated from each other; the soldiers' favorite taunt is "woman," and
men who walk more comfortably in the town than on the plain,
like Paris, are held in contempt. But Paris makes it clear that the
separation is not primarily between men and women, but between the true soldiers and all others, who will not undergo the
requisite steeling. As Helen's face is applied to a war for land and
trade, to hide its purpose, and the face of Chryses' daughter with
no name applied to the murderous quarrel of the kings, so is a
woman's face applied to the conflict between these two cities: between the values and customs of peace and the values and customs of war.

It is not only women, Achaean and Trojan, who stand outside the battlefield; the fathers of Achilles and Hector are as far from the central action of the poem as are Hector's mother and his wife. Even the soldiers themselves bear this mutinous civil sister in their bodies; the exhortation "Be men!" is intended to extinguish her. Near his death, Hector describes himself as "stripped of defenses like a woman / once I have loosed the armor off my body" (22.149–150). This sister is linked both to cowardice and to nourishing, sentient life; Achilles has within him the largest quantity of what in the poem is called courage, and also the deepest affinity with death. "Let him submit to me!" Agamemnon demands; "Only the god of death / is so relentless" (9.189–190). For most of the poem he is divided even from his own army, imprisoned in his solitary rage; his great triumph, the killing that will keep his name forever on his people's lips, is a suicide. As he dies, Hector wears Achilles' armor, stripped from the corpse of Patroclus. Made of polished brass, it gleams; Achilles can see his own face in it. His mother's prophecy has made it clear that Hector's death and his own are inseparable; yet he proceeds, to win a glory that may somehow provide a connection that will not be destroyed. Shakespeare's Henry V promised his soldiers that their names would be "familiar in his mouth / as household words"; but the method Achilles uses to create a bond with this world of households serves only to sunder it.

All the soldiers share this sundering, enemies or not; even the word "enemies" is inadequate here. Who are enemies: Hector and his wife, whose purposes could not be more opposed? Hector and Patroclus, who become each other? Hector and Achilles, who are described, here in Fagles's words so directly, with the language of lovers? "No way to parley with that man—not now—" Hector says in his last hours, despairing of the civil realm of diplomacy, long since forsaken, "not from behind some oak or rock to whisper, / like a boy and a young girl, lovers' secrets / a boy and girl might whisper to each other. . ." (22.151–154); later he taunts Achilles to dodge "*my* brazen spear— / I wish you'd bury it in your body to the hilt." [An age ago Achilles stormed of Agamemnon's theft of Briseis, "Well *let* him bed her now— / enjoy her to the hilt!" (9.407–408)] Hector calls to his phantom brother Deiphobus, who is not there. Achilles, "scanning his splendid body—where to pierce it best?" (22.378), tears him at the unprotected throat, the tender, vulnerable bridge connecting head and heart, separating them, re-enacting the mutilation he has inflicted on himself, the one which each of the poem's soldiers has inflicted and endured.

Patroclus has killed Sarpedon and planted his foot on the fallen man's chest to withdraw his spear, in the churning of the struggle to possess the corpse; scarcely later, it is Patroclus whose corpse is struggled over, and Hector who plants his foot on the fallen man's chest, and scarcely later Hector who has fallen, wearing the armor of the man he killed and of the man who kills him. The element of suicide appears again and again in the repeated gestures and changes of costume. As Simone Weil translated it, "Ares is equitable, he kills those who kill" (163); these exchanges insist also that those who kill, kill themselves.

*

There are voices in the *Iliad* we do not hear at length, and faces we do not see, or glimpse only briefly: those of the people who bind the battle wounds; those of the slaves in Troy and in the Achaean camp; and those of women, who may also be the nurses and the slaves, who are ignored, derided, raped, and given as prizes in athletic contests. Also scarcely heard is the voice of the child each soldier has murdered, who lives on under his armor, who cannot kill or die without shrinking and weeping, who began in the civil realm Hector's mother begs him back to by showing him her breast. The city these silent ones constitute is that of the dance, of true politics, of love; in the poem, this city is given a place for itself only in the images on Achilles' shield. Clausewitz said that "War is a continuation of politics by other means"; the *Iliad* in Robert Fagles's hands makes more clear than it has ever been that the polis was first a fortress, and that what we know as politics is a continuation of war.

And he forged on the shield two noble cities filled
with mortal men. With weddings and wedding feasts in one
and under glowing torches they brought forth the brides
from the women's chambers, marching through the streets
while choir on choir the wedding song rose high
and the young men came dancing, whirling round in rings

358

and among them the flutes and harps kept up their stirring call—
women rushed to the doors and each stood moved with wonder.
  (18.572–579)

These are the doors—beautiful, protective, full of human care—
that the Trojan women will kiss in their terror, as they are torn
apart with axes and wrenched from their sockets. The *Iliad* says
little of the doors, or of the women who kiss them, as we who
claim the *Iliad* as an ancestor say little of them now, fresh from
our latest spate of killing, nurturing yet another generation of
boys who play with swords, who cannot kiss each other, and girls
who hesitate at the edges of the guarded public realm. When the
silence surrounding this other city is broken, it may first be with
a message to the smoking din of its counterpart. It may begin like
the note French photographer Alain Keler saw written on the
glass face of a coffin in San Salvador; in the coffin was a woman
killed by the army in a massacre of peaceful demonstrators. As
the photographer watched, a woman wrote, "I love you. I will
never forget you. I will tell my daughter about you when she is
old enough to understand" (126).

WORKS CITED

Cavafy, C. P. *Collected Poems*. Trans. Edmund Keeley and Philip
  Sherrard. Ed. George Savidis. Princeton: Princeton UP, 1975.
Fagles, Robert, trans. and ed. *The Iliad*, with introduction and
  notes by Bernard Knox. N.Y.: Viking, 1990.
Fitzgerald, Robert, trans. and ed. *The Iliad*. Chicago: U of Chi-
  cago P, 1951.
Keler, Alain. *War Torn*. Ed. Susan Vermazen. N.Y.: Pantheon,
  1984.
Lattimore, Richmond, trans. and ed. *The Iliad*. N.Y.: Anchor/
  Doubleday, 1974.
Lifton, Robert Jay. "Doubling: The Faustian Bargain." *The Fu-
  ture of Immortality*. N.Y.: Basic Books, 1987.
Scarry, Elaine. *The Body in Pain*. Oxford: Oxford UP, 1985.
Weil, Simone. *The Simone Weil Reader*. Ed. George A. Panichas.
  N.Y.: David McKay Co., 1977.

*Nominated by Henri Cole, Jane Cooper, Campbell McGrath, Kristina McGrath,
Sigrid Nunez*

SLEEP APNEA

by MARK COX

from NEW ENGLAND REVIEW

3 A.M. will always be the long hall
of the hospital's sleep disorder wing:
every blemish waxed over, encased,

like my father's paperweight of fishing flies—
each twisted bit of hair preserved within glass.
I will always be half-naked, the mane of wires

looped over my shoulder and bunched in my hand,
as if I've just been ripped
from the dash of a submarine—

those copper connectors
and colorful, plastic-coated conductors sprung
necessarily from flesh.

In the john at The Daily Planet (a bistro
in Burlington, VT), there's a poster of Boris Karloff
on the *Frankenstein* set: he's completely made up—

scars highlighted, each ghastly node and unnaturalness in view—
but he's drinking tea or coffee—his left pinky extended—
and smoking a cigarette. Me, I just snore

and occasionally stop breathing in my sleep,
so that I die six or seven times during the first two hours—

no big deal. But I've been thinking about that crown

of electrodes, the mask through which they fed me air—
I've been thinking about the deep bell-helmeted mummy walk
I do beneath the surface of my life.

The endless horizontal mine shaft of the hall
promised linoleum, a bathroom, and if lucky,
a tiny geyser of water that would arc to me

out of nowhere and back. Fish nosing through seaweed—
that's the emblem for my dreaming;
the little fake castle, painted badly, and bound

for the bottom of the aquarium; the multi-colored gravels,
too perfect, no matter how randomly spread. I won't ever
hold my head quite the same way again—

the weight of the wires will always be with me.
So that even that echo of Old Testament rhetoric
seems imprinted:

Cox translated into graphics; Cox, the video game;
Cox, whom the technicians say
says *shit* in his sleep.

Nominated by Tony Hoagland, Kent Nelson, Gordon Weaver

GINZA SAMBA

by ROBERT PINSKY

from TRIQUARTERLY

A monosyllabic European called Sax
Invents a horn, walla whirledy wah, a kind of twisted
Brazen clarinet, but with its column of vibrating
Air shaped not in a cylinder but in a cone
Widening ever outward and bawaah spouting
Infinitely upward through an upturned
Swollen golden bell rimmed
Like a gloxinia flowering
In Sax's Belgian imagination

And in the unfathomable matrix
Of mothers and fathers as a genius graven
Humming into the cells of the body
Or saved cupped in the resonating grail
Of memory changed and exchanged
As in the trading of brasses,
Pearls and ivory, calicos and slaves,
Laborers and girls, two

Cousins in a royal family
Of Niger known as the Birds or Hawks.
In Christendom one cousin's child
Becomes a "favorite negro" ennobled
By decree of the Czar and founds
A great family, a line of generals,
Dandies and courtiers including the poet

Pushkin, killed in a duel concerning
His wife's honor, while the other cousin sails
In the belly of a slaveship to the port
Of Baltimore where she is raped
And dies in childbirth, but the infant
Will marry a Seminole and in the next
Chorus of time their child fathers
A great Hawk or Bird, with many followers
Among them this great-grandchild of the Jewish
Manager of a Pushkin estate, blowing

His American breath out into the wiggly
Tune uncurling its triplets and sixteenths—the Ginza
Samba of breath and brass, the reed
Vibrating as a valve, the aether, the unimaginable
Wires and circuits of an ingenious box
Here in my room in this house built
A hundred years ago while I was elsewhere:

It is like falling in love, the atavistic
Imperative of some one
Voice or face—the skill, the copper filament,
The golden bellful of notes twirling through
Their invisible element from
Rio to Tokyo and back again gathering
Speed in the variations as they tunnel
The twin haunted labyrinths of stirrup
And anvil echoing here in the hearkening
Instrument of my skull.

Nominated by Michael Collier, Lloyd Schwartz, C. K. Williams

BENJAMIN CLAIRE, NORTH DAKOTA TRADESMAN, WRITES TO THE PRESIDENT OF THE UNITED STATES

fiction by BARRY LOPEZ

from THE NORTH AMERICAN REVIEW

Cathay, North Dakota
June 18th

Dear Mr. President,

In the wake of my brother's murder, I have been approached by the television networks and several cable news shows and have been urged to tell my side of what has happened here. I have declined to appear. I regard their interest in my views as insincere and their cordiality as false, the impulse of voyeurs.

I know they have approached you as well, and that you have been not so much cooperative with them as clever.

They are impatient with me in view of "the size of the story." When the Department of the Navy or the Justice Department issues yet another clarifying statement, they entreat with me

364

again, as though my earlier refusals had never occurred. Even if I were not opposed to this invasion of privacy, or to their speculation about my brother's motives, I would not want to become involved with these people. They represent to me a powerful and aimless lust, and I think it must finally do us and all of them harm.

They are not interested in this tragedy, Mr. President. They want to tailor what has happened out here, to make a weighted drama of it all. In the early days they waded into crowds and handed people small American flags to wave. They created embarrassment and manufactured argument by quoting opinionated but uninformed people. You joust easily with them. You manipulate them; and none of us is the wiser for it.

When I phoned a few weeks ago, it was, I felt, in the not naïve belief that we might be able to diffuse some of the anger my brother's actions have provoked. I had hoped we might issue a joint statement, one in which we acknowledged my brother's troubled heart and mind and perhaps, in some way, even the wrongfulness of his act, but in which we also praised the independence of his voice, and in which you expressed a willingness to address the issues that grieved him. I had imagined this might occur for two reasons—your sorrow over the way he was murdered and, to be blunt, your political instinct. The nation is exasperated by the insincerity and inattentiveness of powerful people. It is stupefied from too much entertainment and alarmed at its destiny. A political man, speaking tellingly and honestly, might ease people's fears and gather their support.

It is unfortunate that the man who handed you the phone did not have me on hold when he said, by way of identifying me, "the farm nut with the flying navy." I knew then we were going to have a hard time finding grounds for a conversation. I would not be the first to tell you, I suspect, that your glad-handing way with me, right then, only made me suspicious. A simple apology would have been so much better. And then you talked on as if I were a constituent, someone who might vote for you. We had no real conversation. You spoke without hearing, reminding me of the duties of a citizen as though I were a good but disobedient child. What you said was only remotely connected to our trouble. And then you said, as if you needed my sympathy for the tedium of your life, that you had to return to dinner with a power-boat racing champion and his fiancée.

I am writing you out of a sense of the civic duty you like to praise. And because I believe in the power of written thought to gradually and clearly illuminate, even across a gulf such as the one between us. It is possible to reflect on what is written down. I hope, then, that you will recognize here a way to dispel the rancor, the unrest that persists in this situation.

You could begin by offering your voice at least, if not the help of law enforcement officers, to halt the violence still being directed against my brother's farm. And you could heed his plea and act in the interests of people in every country fearful about the physical health of the planet and anxious about food. You and your aides believe that technology and business acumen together can turn our food shortages around. You've asked for the nation's understanding while limits on toxicity levels at fertilizer and pesticide manufacturing plants are temporarily suspended and while wildlife refuges are opened to the grazing of stock, explaining that these regulations will be reimposed and the refuges completely restored, "as soon as we get over the hump."

I cannot imagine that you think the nation believes you. This is more unbelievable, really, than that news of environmental ruin is rarely reported, and never in any depth in our papers. This sort of news—heavy metals pollution, soil erosion, radiation leaks—slides away from us in a few days. We can't dwell on it. We seek the distraction that you, frankly, are such a master of, with your limited short wars in distant countries and your promotion of attractive people and ideas.

If you mean to heal us, truly, you need to know more clearly what my brother did, and then review in your own mind what happened to him afterward and how you are going to act.

My brother left his farm here before dawn on March 14th and drove through in four days to San Diego. As is now known, I think, to every family in America, on the morning of March 19th he went aboard the aircraft carrier *Enterprise*, representing himself as an assistant to the Secretary of the Navy. So convincing were the letter and orders he handed the ship's commanding officer that the captain complied immediately with his request to evacuate the ship, so it could be swept and cleared of explosives secreted there by terrorists.

In some reports it is stressed that there was a naval team of demolition and electronics experts accompanying my brother, but this wasn't the case. I believe my brother acted entirely on his own, from beginning to end. He disembarked the *Enterprise* with the captain and his staff, then informed them that two Navy SEAL teams would come aboard to search out the explosives. He determined that all eight of the ship's reactors were being shut down and then directed the captain to have the docks cleared. He asked him to have a skeleton crew ready to reboard the ship with the SEAL teams. You have access to the papers my brother handed the captain. In the captain's defense, from what I've seen in the news magazines, you must agree that nothing could have looked more official, more pointedly military in its wording and reasoning, than that set of orders.

I have no idea where my brother got them, or whether he might have prepared them himself.

It is not true that my brother carried a sidearm or that he was dressed in a naval uniform at the time. He wore a tan, cotton suit, a blue dress shirt with a dark knit tie and dark brown lace shoes. (I know you see no humor here, but I had to smile when I read that the captain's staff thought my unassuming brother "self-assured, well-spoken, and succinct in his directives.")

While the captain's staff began assembling a skeleton crew and military police began clearing the docks, my brother excused himself from the captain's presence and was not seen again.

What my brother then did with the *Enterprise*, I cannot explain, nor do I wish to try; but I will tell you that I have no doubt at all that he caused the ship to rise into the air. When we were young I twice saw him do similar things. Once he raised a dog house six feet off the ground and got it to remain there for about half an hour. And one afternoon he caused a tractor, a John Deere 5020 weighing about seven tons, to rise from the ground, and then he proceeded to have it turn over in a series of slow somersaults and then to turn pirouettes on one rear tire, ten feet off the ground, before setting it back down.

From descriptions I have read, the *Enterprise* rose in a regal manner, with water cascading from its hull in enormous draperies, until it was about a thousand feet above the docks, over which it cast a huge shadow. It angled slowly north, rolling slightly to port as it did, and when pointed northeast began to gather speed, hardly apparent at first, until it was making something like forty-five knots. Its bronze props were rigid, motionless. If you looked through binoculars, I'm told, you could see the Tom Cats and Intruders and F/A-18s on the flight deck rising and falling irregularly in the headwinds.

We are all aware, now, that the ship followed my brother back to North Dakota, and that the military assault teams that landed on it were unable to change its course or to bring it any closer to the ground. But I must say it hasn't been stressed enough, in the light of what was to happen to my brother and others, that nothing aboard the ship had been disturbed, no hazardous condition created, that the commandos removed all sensitive documents (none of which was missing), locked the ship down, and flew all the aircraft aboard away.

During those four days, from March 19th to March 22nd, you and your military advisors settled quickly on an extraterrestrial explanation. You related portions of an Air Force report which you said documented extraterrestrial surveillance sorties into the Earth's atmosphere. And you reported that American fighter pilots had lost their lives in dogfights with alien space ships. I know it was a profound embarrassment, and infuriating, when my brother announced that he had removed the *Enterprise* from the San Diego naval base, acting as a private citizen, and that for the time being he was going to leave it floating in the sky several thousand feet above his farm. And when he said he had no demands to make, no indictments he wished to set forth, that he only wished people would ponder that huge ship, I understand that you became so angry you threw a model of the *Enterprise* to the floor.

I'm sorry you were so disturbed, but I do not find it necessary to defend my brother in this. He knew enough about modern life to realize that without such a remarkable incident no one would pay any attention. I believe it just occurred to him one day to create a kind of harmless disturbance with a certain scale to it.

You did not seem to notice when you flew out here in April the great whimsy of that ship turning in the summer sky. Cumulus clouds scudded by. The *Enterprise* would career slowly until its flight deck was visible from the ground, then roll back. Or over a period of time it would rise up to a point of balance on its prow.

Birds perched on it. Daredevil pilots tried to land on it before they were driven away by military gunships.

Curiously, for those first few days, the ship's lolling in the air seemed to have the effect my brother wanted. It was such a strange and ludicrous thing, it made people wonder what they had been thinking about, what was important to them. North Dakota was a fine place for it, too, seeming to so many to be so far from anywhere, a distant stage. And although I know you were irritated by it, I think you must agree that in that serious but also carnival-like atmosphere of the first few days, the hours were intensely, even delightfully human. Proponents of extraterrestrial theories preached their gospel before this "proof." High school bands played the national anthem and "Onward Christian Soldiers," even Taps, as though the *Enterprise* were just home from battle. Environmentalists cast the ship as a beached whale in a theatrical skit. It was all quite innocent and healthy, Mr. President. It did not turn dark until a contingent—we are told—from the Aryan Nation arrived. They picketed the theatrical production. They spoke of "the Lord's vengeance," an idea I could not understand, and of a lack of respect for military history. They harangued a group of women from Minneapolis conducting a peace vigil. In the violence that quickly followed—and we will be years straightening it all out—twelve people were killed and seventeen seriously wounded. They were shot by federal and state police and by military personnel. You showed no sympathy at all for the dead—which I thought appalling, as not a single one was armed.

You could so easily have diffused the violence. You should have seen the menace gathering, as soon as it became apparent what my brother had done, that he had actually stolen a ship of war. But by your silence, if you will excuse me, you seemed to encourage and even sanction the violence. It was a time that called for intelligence and leadership, even a sense of humor; you gave us only grimness and anger, and a fractured speech about the importance of national defense and the price of freedom.

During those early days, when the *Enterprise* rode through the air over California and Nevada, plunging ahead as if in heavy seas, its flags and standards snapping smartly, the wind whistling in so many different keys around it, no one noticed that the ship halted each evening where my brother stopped in nondescript motels—at Spanish Fork in Utah, in Maurine, South Dakota. No

369

one connected my brother with the ship until it had hung in the sky above his farm outside Pettibone for three days, and in response to a question from a newspaper reporter he said why it was there.

You will make up your own mind about whom to prosecute, whom to demote and court-martial, whom to bill for the expenses various agencies have incurred. (Your Department of Justice has informed me, as though it would be on my mind, that I may not write about the incident for profit. I don't mean to be difficult, but will they be sending a similar letter to the network producers?) And you will determine how to shape to your political advantage what has taken place. I don't argue with any of this. I am aware of the ironies of modern life. But I would ask you to consider that in your public assessment of my brother as "a man sadly misguided," "a foolish and violent enemy of his own countrymen," and in your judgment of his act as "a complete perversion of the patriotic instinct," you may be wrong. My brother was a wheat and rye and soybean farmer, a man respectful of all around him; when he was murdered in the city jail in Carrington, he died, in my view, a patriot. I would ask you to think heavily on this.

How can you be so certain of his motive, his meaning, when I as his brother, the person he was closest to in all his life, cannot tell you clearly what he was doing, what he intended? (Indeed, with the *U.S.S. Enterprise* still ranging loose over the northern plains while you pursue ways to secure it, how can any of us be certain of a position?) I can tell you these things about my brother. He used to say, "Soil conservation is the most elementary form of national defense." He was quoting the writer Wendell Berry, of whose work he was fond. He knew that the thought and effort we as a country were putting into the conservation of soil was as nothing compared to our effort to discover ways of havoc through military research. He worked his place with the devotion of an Amish farmer. He lived where he farmed. He was kind and generous in all his dealings. And until quite recently he was not inclined to public comment. I know in recent years, after the dioxin devastation in Atlanta and outside Modesto, and with the headlong way the country has gone in search of distractions, that he wanted to speak out. He was not particularly articulate,

370

but I believe he thought if he could get this warship out of its harbor and hung in the sky, people would talk and something good, something sane and imaginative, would surface.

Do you think he was right, Mr. President? I am hopeful you'll want to know. I am hopeful you'll take the time you are accustomed to granting even minor celebrities and put it to these thoughts. That you will ask the North Dakota State Police to enforce the laws of trespass against those who continue to burn what is left of my brother's farm. That you will condemn publicly those who encourage violence and then revel in their duty to violently suppress it. That you will call on the farm experts whose names my brother enumerated in public before he was killed and ask them how it's going, not with agribusiness and shortages and futures but with the soil itself, the blood and the flesh, from whence all the rest.

I forgive you much. The difference between us is that you have a power I do not. You have an ability to rectify, to redirect and galvanize, which I do not. You can give a hope I cannot. I resent this, but I accept it. I ask you to put aside your indignation over the disrespect you believe my brother showed a naval ship, which was for him a symbol of financial corruption, corporate malfeasance, and the country's infatuation with "moral" force, its belligerent pursuit of black and white positions. Put aside your indignation, and consider how to turn this incident to human advantage.

I cannot threaten you, nor do I wish to. I cannot demand of you. You are beyond all this. I can only write down what I think, and depend on you to find the wisdom to act. In the meantime, I remain suspended, a different, certainly, but no less credulous man than my brother.

Very sincerely,
Benjamin Claire

Nominated by Mary Peterson

VAN

by DAVID RATTRAY

from HOW I BECAME ONE OF THE INVISIBLE [SEMIOTEXT(E)]

IN THE SPRING of 1957 some cronies and I had a supper club in the dining room of the Green Lantern, an inn on the edge of Hanover, New Hampshire, where I was a student in my senior year at Dartmouth. One evening I had drunk a lot of wine over my meal when someone began telling about a new member of the ski team who was presently holed up in a sleeping bag on a mattress, sick with flu, in the team's sleeping quarters on the top floor of College Hall. It would seem that this 19-year-old NROTC scholarship jock was actually a poet.

I got up and went straight over to College Hall.

The object of my curiosity was dead to the world when I arrived. I turned on the light, a bare bulb in the ceiling, and shook him, asking what he had done with the church key.

I opened a couple of aged-in-the-wood India Pale Ales, which in those days came in a tall, thin, green bottle, and assured my new acquaintance, Alden Van Buskirk, or Van for short—he was still blinking and rubbing his eyes in bewilderment—that the strong ale was bound to bring relief. I was only sorry not to have been able to mull it for him, with cinnamon, nutmeg, peppercorns, sugar, rum—the sovereign grippe remedy.

I noticed Van was reading Whitman, Eliot, Hart Crane. Also Dylan Thomas. Had he read Pound, or Rilke, or Mallarmé? He shook his head. Nope. Homer? Yeah. Virgil? Mmm . . . A mellifluous bore. One ancient that he really dug was Ovid. Talk about a Book of Changes, we have one: Ovid's *Metamorphoses*.

372

Van sat up cross-legged on the floor, shedding the sleeping bag, and lit a Camel. I noticed his fingertips like my own were both tobacco and ink stained. He had nothing on his pale, skinny, hairless body but a pair of also ink-stained jockey shorts. Although the room was warm, there were goose pimples on his arms. He tried to blow a smoke ring, but sneezed. "Bless you," I intoned.

"Fountain pens leak," he informed me..

That summer I went abroad, and for the next three years we did not communicate. Early in the spring of 1960, when Van was about to graduate, I returned to Dartmouth, and we met again, this time thanks to a reading of works by Rilke and John Wieners that had been organized by Jack Hirschman, than an instructor in the English Department, whose first book of poems, *A Correspondence of Americans,* was at the printer's when we met. From him Van had first learned of the new poets who were springing up in Boston, New York, and San Francisco, outside Academe and in opposition to all that Eisenhower America stood for.

The almost slight teenager that Van had been when we first met had filled out to a not quite stocky yet powerfully built man. There was a jaundiced pallor to his face whose formerly prominent cheekbones were lost in an unhealthy puffiness, a moon-faced look quite out of character. His pale blue eyes were bloodshot. He made a crack about drinking. Drinking had nothing to do with it. He had been sick for about a year. His mother had had leukemia. When she died, he had a dream that he would go next and, soon after, the first in a series of spells in which the urine darkened from mahogany to black, or "Coca Cola," as he put it, while he suffered paroxysms of vomiting till there was nothing left to bring up but bile. After a day or two in the hospital, with transfusions and I.V. feeding, he would return to normal. It had happened several times. The black urine contained blood that had broken down and passed through the kidneys. His doctors had put him on high doses of cortisone steroids, which seemed to hold off the crises and speed recovery from them, but, he told me, the side effects were rugged. At one point the "little green pills" had made him see spaghetti-like worms coming out of walls. They lowered the dosage after that. Now he was okay, but the doctors still had no idea what was wrong. Although unable to confirm any of their speculations, they still inclined to a

373

"preleukemia" hypothesis. He shrugged. Maybe some weirdly toxic ski wax had gotten onto the sheath knife he had been using to cut salami.

This conversation took place on a warm afternoon in early spring, as Van and I were climbing from the still-frozen River at the foot of West Wheelock Street, along sidewalks rutted with thawing mud and slush, to a stone tower at the top of which, in a corner out of the wind, we paused in a sudden dazzle of raw sunlight. In his wrap-around sunglasses my companion looked like a racing car driver. The world has been under an evil spell for centuries, I explained. It was a revelation that I owed to a recent discovery of Antonin Artaud, who had died only a dozen years earlier. Reality, I assured Van, had nothing to do with the real world, which was in any case about to go up in flames. It turned out that he shared my apocalyptic expectations, except to him it seemed the world was already on fire. The Book of Revelation, Blake, Artaud, Jean Genet had all come down the chimney and were dancing in our heads.

The illness had caused Van to drop out of the NROTC. Great, I said. That made both of us draft-exempt. A year before in Paris, I confided, the daylight hours at the winter solstice had seemed to dwindle to no more than a couple in every twenty-four. It was a delusion, but I thought I was witnessing a final blackout. The sun would never return. Life would cease.

"When night doth meet with noon," Van interrupted, *"in dark conspiracy . . ."*

Huh?

"Keats," he informed me.

Right. I went on. Night after night, I awoke choking with asthma in the wee hours and burned mounds of Vesuvius Powder, a nostrum purchased from the pharmacy two doors away, inhaling the smoke through a paper funnel, which set off fits of sneezing and cleared the bronchial tubes. Then I would drink a cup of brandy and lie there waiting for the world to end. Early one morning I awoke on the floor with the feeling I had died. I had had a grand mal seizure. They put me on anti-convulsant medications. My draft status would have to be changed from 1-A to 4-F.

"Well, they won't be giving us any grief as draft dodgers," Van rejoined. "I was just about getting ready to leave the NROTC anyhow. No one in their right mind would be willing to fire shots in anger to defend this." With a sweeping gesture he took in the surrounding treetops and nearby clocktower of Baker Library gleaming golden in the late afternoon sun. To a casual observer we might at that moment have looked like nothing more than a couple of college boys sharing a cigarette.

We were fit for only one thing on the job market: teaching. Yet we recoiled from the prospect of joining a profession that seemed no better than a guild for the transmission of established values. The poetic vocation was a horse of another color. It was the call to a new, different way of seeing, of being, the call of Rilke's "Archaic Torso of Apollo": *You must change your life* . . .

Meanwhile, Van had accepted a fellowship at Washington U in Saint Louis as a means of postponing his entry onto the job market. I also was stalling. I had decided to spend a few months with my piano teacher at Dartmouth and immerse myself in a work that I believed held a key to the universe tucked away inside its dense and enigmatic fabric, Beethoven's Hammerklavier Sonata.

I was able to do this thanks to my mother, who had agreed to give me $100 a month until I became self-supporting. Although unhappy with the arrangement, she had acquiesced to it when I pointed out that her father had helped her when she was beginning as a writer in the early 1920s. He had paid her bills all the way to Outer Mongolia and back.

Nonetheless I told people that I was living on an income inherited from whaling ancestors. The latter were real enough; only the inheritance was imaginary. To Van, however, I admitted the truth. It came as no surprise. His own situation vis-à-vis Robert Van Buskirk, Sr. was similar. Both recently bereaved, our respective parents were terrified lest we end up as burdens to them, disgraceful failures. We resented their Philistine views and decided to ignore the old folks' existence except when it became necessary to block their oppressive, if well-meant schemes.

After graduation Van stayed on in Hanover so as to be within reach of the hospital. The home of a mutual friend happened to be vacant, and Van was invited to house-sit. I had a similar arrangement across the River in Norwich, where I had installed a piano. From his home in Rutland Van fetched an old car, a 1941 Buick convertible. He started dropping by in mid-afternoon, to improvise at the keyboard. He was a good musician. At the time I didn't give a hoot about jazz. He pretended to think I loved it.

375

On nice days we went to a swimming hole. Sunbathing on its margin, we read *Nightwood* out loud. We talked about drugs, which neither of us had ever taken.

I took a furlough from Beethoven. We went hiking in the White Mountains, wandering along ridges high above treeline from peak to peak for several days. One afternoon Van plunged into an icy pond from which one could see all the way from Maine in one direction to Lake Champlain in the other. He jumped up and down, shouting to me to come in. I shouted back that I'd rather stay dry.

Almost next door to where I was staying in Norwich was the 20-year-old Lisa Yeomans' house. Van and Lisa had met as teen-agers while skiing at Pico and had been seeing each other on and off ever since. Tall, fine-featured, blond, awkward, yet radiating adolescent grace, Lisa had a soft voice, observant eyes, sudden laughter. Van loved her and was always giving her advice.

One night he and I drove over to the Rutland State Fair. I was still young enough to see something like poetry in blue-collar America at play of a summer evening. Swarms of insects circled the arc lights. Van's dark-goggled face took on an eerie glow. His hair became the helmet of a humanoid alien. From his full, pale lips came a stream of sarcastic invective against the wasteful, exploitive, murderously hypocritical, witless, Leave-It-To-Beaver, Dairy Queen-slurping American way of life.

A week later Van lent me the Buick, and I went down to East Hampton for a few days at the beach. While I was there, he got deathly sick. Lisa phoned to tell me that he had been operated on to remove his spleen and might not live.

Van had just been moved from the recovery room to a private room when I arrived. Barely conscious, he asked me to read from John Wieners' *Hotel Wentley Poems*—the book was on the bed-side table. His fingers a waxy yellowish gray, he fiddled with an ice sliver, touching it to his lips. The sky outside the window was bright blue. I paused. "Don't stop," he urged.

A few days later Van was out of the hospital. Soon the only memento of the operation was a scar over his solar plexus. He groused some about an inability to concentrate or think clearly enough to write. I did not sympathize but told how Sinclair Lewis had once been invited to look in on a creative writing workshop. He was smashed, and boiled his exhortation down to one sentence. It went something like this: "You folks want to write, get out there and WRITE."

One morning early in September we took off in the '41 Buick. We buttoned the canvas top down and played the radio into the wind. Crossing the mountains, Van told of trout fishing with his dad when very young.

Over in New York State I dropped him off at a Thruway entrance and turned back to Saratoga Springs, where I was to spend the next two months at Yaddo, hard at work on a series of long poems that were as bad as they were ambitious.

Arriving in Saint Louis, Van found himself a furnished room on Waterman Street and registered for school. The student body consisted of several thousand airline stewardesses and crewcut types in shirts and ties. Van sauntered in in ink-stained khakis, a teeshirt full of holes, and bare feet in the filthiest tennis sneakers west of the Bowery. Some were drawn to him; others found him disturbing. He started writing me letters. (There was never a phone, so we never had a long-distance conversation.)

Checking in at the university clinic on September 20th, Van met a medical student named Jim Gaither, who was to solve the mystery of his disease. Gaither was about the same age as Van, and the two hit it off. Like their colleagues back East, the specialists at Washington University School of Medicine had posited an idiosyncratic preleukemia. Gaither was assigned to analyze test data and research the literature. Lacking background in hematology, he quailed at the prospect of the sophisticated blood work involved and decided to start with the urine, a simpler, more old-fashioned point of departure. The approach paid off. A finding of numerous fine, dark granules that stained blue in a potassium ferrocyanide solution sent Gaither to a recently devised diagnostic test for paroxysmal nocturnal hemoglobinuria, a blood disorder that had been observed in fewer than 200 cases since it was first described by the German hematologist Paul Strübing in 1882. The test turned out positive. A second acid hemolysis test using a normal person's serum was also positive. The diagnosis was established. From Gaither, Van learned that his prospects were not too good. One patient had survived with the disease for 20 years, however.

A few days after learning his diagnosis, Van wrote saying he was glad to know what he was up against inside himself, in the place where, as he put it, "all pursuits end. . ."

A letter written soon after hints at a feeling that something extraordinary would happen on Hallowe'en. Van had been staying up all night writing for several days. On the evening of October 31st, he went out for a drink and met a 30-year-old ex-convict named Johnny Sherrill, who was on parole and earning his living as a worker in a machine shop. The son of migrant fruitpickers— his part-American Indian mother also worked for a time as an artist for Disney Studios—Van's new acquaintance had spent the years since his teens drifting from state to state, scamming, jamming, pimping, gambling, doing time both for things he had done and things he hadn't. Johnny got along with the black guys in jail better than the whites. He identified with everything that had soul—gospel music, the blues, jazz, the rhythms of black speech, the witty verbal style, the subtleties and flourishes generally lacking in the language of their putative superiors on Tobacco Road.

Van had read Mezz Mezzrow, yet nothing could have prepared him for Johnny. The previous summer Van had reveled in Jean Genet's *Thief's Journal*. Now he was meeting someone who could have stepped straight out of its pages.

Van and Johnny left the bar and drove across the Mississippi to East Saint Louis, where at 4 A.M. in the riverbottom enclave of Brooklyn, Illinois, they stepped into a labyrinth of pink and blue neon, the Harlem Club, a palace of iniquity that might as well have sprung full-armed (indeed, bristling with weaponry) from the brow of Chester Himes.

The kid from Rutland had never seen anything like it. Here was a crowd of well-dressed, well-heeled, mainly black pleasure-seekers belonging to a culture having few points of contact with Middle America outside the used-car lot, the police station, and the hospital. Everywhere was a smell of strong spirits, perfume, marijuana, and tobacco, the strident beat of rhythm 'n' blues numbers such as "Quicksand" and "Soul Food."

Inside were several bars where you got your set-up by the half-pint bottle, with the mixer in a paper cup, and rooms where various legal and illegal games were in progress, as well as a little striptease theater, and yet another room with dancing. It was to this room that Johnny led the way through the crowd of drug dealers, pimps, hookers, and drag queens prowling the floor. Shortly before daybreak they were joined at their table by a red-haired transvestite who flirted shyly with Van.

By this time, Van was quite stoned. The idea of having sex with a boy was out of the question. However, what blew Van's mind was that he could not only sit still for such a flirtation, but open his heart to it and be deeply moved by what he saw and felt in the stranger's eyes, a love that to his amazement he found himself wholeheartedly accepting.

"I have seen a God," he wrote me the next day. Johnny had invited the transvestite to come with them but was softly rebuffed. She kissed Van goodbye, her lips barely touching his.

Upon reading his letter, I was put in mind of the lines from "Hermaphroditus" by Swinburne:

> Whosoever hath seen thee, being so fair,
> Two things turn all his life and blood to fire:
> A strong desire begot on great despair,
> A great despair cast out by strong desire . . .

It seemed as though fearing for his life had opened Van to love, any love, and maybe at this point the most impossible could be felt as the highest, and, because accepted though never consummated, as the love that casts out fear. The god he had glimpsed was none other than Eros, I supposed.

Van made plans to move in with Johnny, to buy a motorcycle. Christmas came. He spent part of the holidays with me in New York City, staying in an artist's loft on Second Avenue. One night I left him alone in the loft smoking some strong weed. I came back to find him all shook up. He had been crying, he wouldn't say why. Months later, the experience was evoked in a poem:

Last will and

If I die in sleep it will be in a convulsion whose "terror"
and "beauty" proved irresistible at last. I rise, the
quivering bud afraid to blossom.
It comes out of dreams where music,
color and objects interchange

but for their continual flame. It is within this flame-
flower I am drawn up sweating half awake and
horizontal. Spine arches in short
spasms. I see nothing above.
Darkness everywhere or are my eyes gone out?
Before now: I gave in to life and awoke
trembling—a coward.
But every time more rigid,
every time more pull, I
hurt with desire to
explode and vow no more retreats.
God wants to fuck me too,
and death will be my final lover.
I give her all.

With the New Year, Van returned to Saint Louis and the apartment he intended to share with Johnny. There was a newcomer
in Johnny's life, a 19-year-old prostitute named Carol. Carol and
Van fell for each other, and the two moved out, to a vast and
decrepit biracial hotel on Cabanne Street.

Here for a short time Carol's way of moving, talking, dancing,
making love became Van's. Carol referred to him as the professor
she was married to. One day they were chased by a gang of black
teenagers. This fit in with our mystique of the coming bloodbath.
To me he wrote:

> Young Negroes could purge the city here by bloodshed.
> That I was almost victim I applaud no less. Let all of
> it explode.

From my room in Hanover I also applauded, quoting to Van
from my translation of Stefan George's *Heliogabalus:*

> I chance while descending a marble stair
> Upon a headless corpse just halfway down—
> Oh my—my brother's blood congealing there.
> I merely lift my trailing purple gown . . .

Carol was eager to support him, Van said. He didn't want that;
he just wanted her to quit turning tricks:

I hurt to see her in black tights and leather jacket dancing out. I feel as if she is lost in some world of shining sewage, silver and gold, in a night I cannot enter or see . . .

Carol became in his words "the hieroglyph of my suffering." Then he was back in the hospital, this time with a hemolytic crisis precipitated by a bad dose of the clap. Upon leaving the hospital, he moved back to the white rooming house on Waterman Street where he had been in the fall. Carol begged him to come home to Cabanne Street. He refused.

While all this was going on, John F. Kennedy had been elected President and inaugurated, a development that meant nothing to any of us. Writing me soon after JFK's New Frontier speech, Van quoted a verse from the recently discovered *Gospel of Thomas:*

Jesus said: I have cast fire upon the world . . .

His old room on Waterman Street was occupied by a young woman student. A Florence Nightingale type, she took to waiting on Van. They were soon sleeping together, although he didn't really like her. He was now intensely aware of his deteriorating health. At times it filled him with rage, and he projected his nightmares onto the new housemate. Eventually she decamped.

Far from these upheavals in Hanover, I continued to prepare my Beethoven recital. We made a plan. In June, after the recital, I would drive out to Saint Louis in the Buick. We would proceed from there to Mexico.

While our letters discussed the coming trip, Van fell in love again. This time it was neither a transcendent vision as the divine stranger in the Harlem Club had been, nor a pink-heeled figment of the light fantastic, nor a nightmare phantom, but a reserved, extremely intelligent, ethereally pale, and entirely willing 19-year-old woman, Martha Muhs, a student at Washington U. Their love coincided with the coming of spring and was to continue for the rest of Van's life.

From a mail-order nursery in Texas I had obtained a boxful of peyote buttons and sent some to Van. A hilarious and touching letter reports on the rainy April day Van, Martha, and Johnny communed over the peyote.

381

On June 16 I drove west. Saint Louis was laid out flat in a heat wave when I got there. Van had moved into a huge new apartment with Johnny. Inside, Martha and her friend Jim Bryan were sitting fully clothed in a cold bath for relief from the heat, reading out loud from a story by Edgar Allan Poe. A horn honking in the street outside announced the coming of Johnny, who within moments was sharing a six-pack with Van and me. I was impressed. I found Johnny every bit as electrifying as Van had cracked him up to be.

My big moment came the next day, when someone wangled access to the university chapel organ. Pulling out all the stops for Van and his friends, I played the Hammerklavier finale.

Soon after that, Martha went home to Chicago. The two lovers took leave, promising to meet up in the fall. Van and I sat up all night reading Kerouac's *Dr. Sax* out loud. We began to prepare for Mexico.

Worried about the effect the trip was likely to have on Van's health, Johnny urged him not to go abroad. I paraphrased Beckett: "It's suicide to be abroad. But what is it to be at home? A lingering dissolution."

One morning toward the end of June we stepped over the border, having left the Buick in an El Paso parking lot. As we ground our teeth from the speed we had been ingesting ever since Saint Louis, the bus rattled over the sierras of Chihuahua heading south. Little did we know that we were passing through the very same region where a quarter-century earlier Antonin Artaud had witnessed the peyote dance.

A week later, we found ourselves facing the Pacific just north of the Guatemala frontier, outside a fishing port Van had chosen for its name: *Puerto Angel.* He had seen it on a map and said, "Let's go to Angel Port, man."

We had rented two open-air huts made of palm leaves on a hillside over the beach. From here Van wrote to Martha:

> *In the trees overhead vultures alight & sail off on black wings; jungle insects make electronic sounds and tiny lizards run around everywhere. The sea itself is the blue center of all this; its transparent azure shows thousands of strange fish drifting about—bright blue tiny fish, bigger black ones, goldtailed fish, barracuda;*

and even, 10 yards from shore, we saw an enormous
shark once about 10 feet long. The water is slightly
cooler than body temperature, the most delightful for
swimming I've ever found . . .

Our landlord was the police commander. The commander had
a safe full of narcotics given him in part payment for allowing the
CIA to use the port for mysterious operations a few months earlier, during the Bay of Pigs adventure, according to a local schoolteacher, a Castro sympathizer. I had no idea whether there was
any truth in the story, but did think the teacher somewhat nuts to
be saying such things to me, a stranger, and a gringo to boot, in
spite of my indiscreetly expressed opinion that Mao and Fidel
were the great men of the century. I had also chatted up the
postmaster on our arrival, telling him of our desire to stay for a
time at Puerto Angel and write; he had taken us to call on the
commander. Van's letter to Martha describes the scene:

El Señor Commandante (highest functionary in the
town, who is sheriff, etc., but, most important, the
Rent Collector) lives in the best house & has a moth-
like servant or lackey who hovers at his shoulder. He
looks like a William Burroughs figure—old, grey-
haired, with those transparent green glasses, a pistol in
his belt, high on junk all the time, very formal, re-
served, but junky-like in silences & gaze. The postmas-
ter explains that we are writers "with a great poetic
mission to fulfill here" and want a house at a precio
modesto. The Commander nods gravely at the former
statement as if he were accustomed to meeting such
personages, and brightens at the latter statement. Dave
& I look serious & poetical.

Actually, our tanned, beat appearance had led one new acquaintance to ask if we were merchant sailors. We hoped to make
some kind of a drug deal that would permit us to live off the
proceeds for a year or so. We were also hoping to write wonderful stuff right there in Puerto Angel.

One evening we saw what looked like a bright star moving in a
steady straight line across the twilit sky over the ocean. Van

383

pointed it out and informed me it was Sputnik. He went on to say that he liked the idea of metamorphosis because change is the law of life, whereas permanence suggests spiritual as well as physical death, both of which are also strongly suggested by the idea of closeness with another person.

Bored and peevish, we got new clothes and took to visiting a bordello owned by the commander. Van had been warned by his doctors not to get the clap, so he outfitted himself with condoms, setting off a minor stir.

The commander had a treasure that fascinated us, an ancient Mixtec jade statuette of a seated figure with a human face surmounted by a jaguar mask. This, the commander said, related to the teaching that each person's soul splits off amoeba-like into two souls at a key moment during the as-yet-unborn individual's earthward descent from the stars, and that the duplicate thus produced comes in the shape of an animal, bird, insect, or plant spirit that accompanies one throughout life like a twin. Van remarked on the similarity between this teaching and a certain Gnostic doctrine.

"With my eyes of light, I see my Twin," the commander quoted.

"The last words of Mani," Van exclaimed.

"Indeed," the commander answered. "Spoken while he was being flayed alive by the King of Persia."

I became fearful. According to an entry in my notebook:

> *Van gets skinnier and skinnier, yet it's impossible to think of him as being sick with a fatal illness. I doubt that any of the locals suspect. As we stepped out of the commander's doorway earlier today, I got a glimpse of him framed in pale afternoon sky, the rainbow-striped blazer loose about his shoulders, arms out because of the heat, his brown neck and thin shoulders forming an improbably jaunty angle, an effect completed by pegged slacks of olive-colored silk and a brand-new pair of dark brown ankle-strapped Argentino boots.*

One day we helped the commander perform an experiment on his *mozo*, the "mothlike" retainer Van had spoken of to Martha. The commander had found out that we had brought a few tabs of acid with us. He had two girls from the casino pin the little fellow while I dropped a tab in his mouth and poured in some tequila to wash it down. The commander was eager to observe the effects of lysergic acid first-hand. Later that afternoon he made a speech to us about Heaven and its impossibly desirable blue body, the sky.

Van began to wonder what sort of experiments might be in store for us, if we were lucky enough not to get ambushed by the *mozo* with a machete.

At length we bought a handgun from the Commander and embarked on a hare-brained scheme to hijack a small cache of high-grade bricks that I had gotten a line on in Nochistlán, a pueblo fifty miles north of Oaxaca, where there had been an earthquake weeks before, and people were crossing the still-open fissures on planks thrown casually across.

Here we hit a snag. In Van's words to Martha: "We broke into the biggest narcotics ring in Mexico by mistake and were nearly murdered."

We managed to escape in a rented truck we had left near the highway outside Nochistlán. One week later we smuggled a pound and a half of marijuana into the United States taped to our torsos and legs.

We recovered the Buick and started for California. En route Van got sick. We just made it to San Francisco General Emergency. After a few days he was better, but I had become terrified he would die, and wanted to hang onto him so he wouldn't vanish. This infuriated him. "Dave's suddenly following me everywhere in San Francisco, feeling put down every time I go out alone, adopting my ideas," he wrote to Martha. I began to imagine that an act of concentrated willpower might bring him back. My presence became insufferable.

Bad things kept happening. One day we were out driving in the Buick with the top down. Van's college friend John Ceely, who had just moved to the Bay area, was at the wheel. We'd been smoking some of the Mexican grass back at the apartment where Larry, another college friend of Van's, was putting him up temporarily. (I'd just settled in a Chinese boarding house on the edge of North Beach and was stoned all the time on paregoric I had gotten a doctor to prescribe for the dysentery that had followed me back from Mexico.) Van was in the front seat, next to John. I was alone in the back. As we swung onto the approach to a bridge, I hunched over and lit a joint I had brought with me. After a deep drag which I held in as long as possible before letting it out in a paroxysm of coughing, I stood up in the wind, toking at the joint held between my thumb and forefinger, flaunting it. Then I started screaming at the top of my lungs.

"Be cool! Sit down!" Van shouted, glaring angrily, adding in a stage whisper loud enough not to be lost in the airstream: "I'm holding!" I kept on yelling. I can't remember what the words were, if any. After a few seconds I sat back down, my face covered with tears. When I woke up I was alone in the car, its canvas top up, parked outside Larry's house. I had passed out and slept I had no idea how long. I wanted to go straight back to my Chinese boarding house, but instead trudged to the door and rang the bell to be let in. Climbing the stairs, I realized I hated Van.

A week later, walking through North Beach, we encountered posters reproducing a painting of a little girl ragamuffin with huge eyes, in a gloomy landscape like a bad children's book illustration. There was something irritating about those big dark eyes. You just knew the emotion they were supposed to convey was fake. There was a gratuitous perversity as well that repelled me.

"What on earth are they?" I exclaimed as we passed a cluster of them around a boarded-up doorway.

"They're Keanes," Van replied in an acid drawl.

"Oh no!" I said.

"Oh yes!" he replied.

"No," I insisted. "There's nothing keen about it, it's kitsch . . ."

This led to another bad moment. Van told me he welcomed Keanes as one more ingredient, like Dairy Queens and Montovani records, of the coming in fact already arriving Garbage Apocalypse. He said my European esthetic standards simply didn't apply to the reality of America. As he droned on about Apocalypse and American reality, another sad-eyed waif loomed up at arm's length. I reached out to rip it down.

"For Christ's sake," he interjected. "Let it alone!" We walked on in silence.

A few days after that we exchanged some more bitter words. I decided to leave.

I hitchhiked to Saint Louis and moved in with Johnny. Johnny now had a steady named Freddie Quinn. Freddie's girlfriend Nackie and I got together briefly. Van's letters to me resumed.

Freddie was pregnant. (Six months later, when the baby was born, it was a boy; they named him Alden, after Van.)

In September, during the Cuban missile crisis, we read about ourselves in the *Saint Louis Post-Dispatch* as unidentified "marijuana operators" on whose trail the police were in hot pursuit. Eventually I grew uneasy and hitchhiked back to New York.

In between ever-lengthening hospital stays, now at the U Cal Medical Center, Van took an apartment in Oakland with John Ceely. Here he wrote poems representing in his words "the last vision, the last light & my last body consumed."

Toward the end of November, after Van had been in the hospital for a month or more, John informed me that Van was running dangerously high fevers and because of clots in the extremities his toes were gray and there were red splotches on his arms, neck, and face. "Probably you've wondered," John wrote, "if you ought to come out and see him. What good would it do?"

I took peyote and had a vision of Van with tubes in him on a hospital bed, yet somehow also outside time in a heightened, eternal here-and-now state that the peyote made me feel was one in which everything in the universe past, present, and future is alive and simultaneous. From the experience I made a poem and sent it to Van. It now seemed to me that every word we exchanged had a special weight, and the power to cross immeasurable distance.

Postcards from him came every few days. He was going to be out soon. We were going to share a place in Hoboken. He had heard from Dave Haselwood of Auerhahn Press that John Wieners was in New York, writing great things. He was reading Melville's *Pierre*. He had a reservation for a flight arriving December 18th at Newark Airport.

On the morning of December 11th, my sister knocked at the door where I was staying to tell me someone had phoned with the news that Van had died the night before.

Nominated by Genie Chipps

387

SHELTER

by BRUCE WEIGL

from AMERICAN POETRY REVIEW

I need some cover tonight from the dark.
I need some shelter from the wings
who beat my head into memory
where my sister sleeps
in the small upstairs bedroom
among the crucifixes and dried palm leaves,
among the lavender smell
of our grandmother's
Sunday black silk dress
in her house where we've come as a family
after church,
the brothers of Belgrade
and the wives from across the river
which is called the river of blood.

In the crowded kitchen,
below my sleeping sister
a beautiful dandelion salad
waits like a bouquet
with blood sausage on a plate
and black bread and dark wine
and the aunts and uncles
and their children in their orbits
and the language
rough and thick on my tongue
when I try to say the words
because the air is suddenly wronged.

My grandfather swears too loud.
His brothers only laugh.
The women shush them all, Eat,
eat they say across the room
but something's cut too deep this time
and the children are pushed
with grace towards the porch and backyard,

and from behind the tree of drunken plums
I watch my grandfather
wave his pistol in the air
and his brothers reach for it
as in a frieze
and the shot explode
through the low ceiling
through the bedroom floor
where my sister sleeps and lives on.
I need some shelter tonight.
I need the sleeping hands to waken once again.

Nominated by Stuart Dybek, Kenneth Gangemi, Reginald Gibbons, Paul Zimmer

CHANGE MY EVIL WAYS

by DAVID RIVARD

from NEW ENGLAND REVIEW

Some days it is my one inescapable wish to live
alone, nameless, unfathomable, a drifter
or unemployed
alien. That afternoon I had gone
to watch a movie in which each of us appears
to have found shelter beside a grove
of scorched date palms, in an adobe ranchero or old
Air Stream trailer, the water bills unpaid,
irrigation pipes rusted. The valves are lashed
so tight we have to drink cheap red wine & scheme a kidnapping
as we drive a dusty sway-backed station wagon
in from town. And if we wear short skirts
and mud-splattered jeans, well, after all,
the only appropriate disguises for our selves
are our selves—the so-often baffled,
the raffish & untutored, insinuators of storm,
storm painted over our lips or speckling gray
a three-day beard.
I believe some days we might tell anyone anything.
Including everything that sounds more guilty
than we can afford to become, especially
how she slaps him
while wearing a faded orange T-shirt. Or
even how we speak warily,
treacherously, to the dying.
But should I tell how you either have faith or you've

got unfaith, when it is myself
I am usually
competing with, & too often made misgiving about?
And the rain here hardly ever seeks to be
rain, but who needs any acquaintance
with that fact?
        And there is evidently no one
to whom I can confess that I only want
everything to happen faster, that I meant to tamper with
the minutes, the second hand, as they swept
the clock face, so as to be dragged
forward to a time when I am a stranger
to everything but trust. I'm sorry. It was
the way she slapped him, inexcusably
beautiful, sororal. But then
the movie was over. I found myself walking
in Cambridge, & on the Common
there were some conga players, as well as the guys
with xylophones & fingerpianos & tambourines.
Have you ever seen minnows
flopping from shallow to shallow, doing somersaults?
The drummers' hands were pale fish,
like guppies thrashing the light
in a clear plastic bag, as blurred as children
careening in the careening mercuric blue dusk of August
around lawn sprinklers. Dulse wavering! Hair shook out
while somebody dances.
Some days it isn't a life
alone I need but one that supplies the luxury
of forgiveness. It was a day like
that, luckily.
Past the tobacconist's, a kid sang
his song about changing my evil ways, & strummed three-chord
blues, plugged into a boom box
that lay at his side like
a wolfhound, no, more like a hellhound. And I put my ear
close to his snout.
And I listened much too carefully.

Nominated by Tony Hoagland

THE LADDER: ROGER VAIL'S PHOTO OF A ROCKFACE IN THE CARRARA (ITALY) MARBLE QUARRIES

by DENNIS SCHMITZ

from FIELD

Imagine a world so heavy
that even the sun is squeezed dark!
As this photo imagines the world,
all light is pinched
out onto three toothed cables that saw the world

horizontal. Only the photo's tiny
ladder (lower right), so small
that maybe it's only the genetic imprint
of a ladder is the way

up out of the blackness.
Imagine what it takes to make this world,
imagine so much of everything—
tractors, BIC pens, Spandexed teen flesh—
so much of everything that it crushes

itself homogeneous & to go on being human
means to want pain,
to suffer so many sawcuts for the sake

of beauty! Forty-two years ago,
when the two county cops
dragged an Iowa limestone quarry
pool for Billy Thiel's body,
I watched the sun
on the wet trawling cable saw up through
the blackness all that muggy Labor Day,
the cop boat dividing the world

into the boat-width strips.
Swim? God, no, I'd never swim there,
but every day afterward I put
a toe down, dropped a coin,
my sister's doll's arm, something human,

until all of me was in the blackness.
Now I know I'm balanced on a ladder of humans,
blackness to my chin.
I can only intuit all of those under me,

sway as they sway—
there must be a man under the man
whose shoulders I'm standing on.
Over the blackness, two cops, inquisitors, row.
The fat one (I see only his outline)

bends out of the john-boat to me—
"do you abjure," he whispers,
"do you abjure?"

Nominated by Walter Pavlich

THE PILGRIM VIRGIN

fiction by JOSEPH MAIOLO

from SHENANDOAH

WHEN FATHER ED said he didn't "really want the damned thing," Victor was a bit shocked and, in some nostalgic way, even disappointed. Still, he made himself sound objective: "Then why bring it in?"

"The bishop, Vic." Father Ed coughed. "Too much sentiment behind it. He'd be in bigger trouble trying to block it."

The subject, over drinks in Father Ed's study, was the imminent visitation of The International Pilgrim Virgin, a statue of Mary in a queen's crown, "blessed by Pope Pius XII in 1947 for the promulgation of Fatima's message," Victor read in the brochure. Sponsored by the Blue Army of Our Lady of Fatima, The Daughters of Isabella, Centurions of the Holy Rood, and of course The Legion of Mary and Knights of Columbus, the statue would return to the United States following its "historic Round-The-World Flight" and after a tour in the east would come to Minnesota for a month-long pilgrimage in towns throughout the Diocese of Crookston. Not only were "rivers of graces" released wherever it was taken; all types of miracles had been attributed to it, from the instant recovery of the sick to the reconciliation of hostile countries. And now Our Lady of the Lake Catholic Church, in Birch Lake, was scheduled to receive and display the miraculous statue on Sunday, June 6.

"D-Day," Father Ed called it.

"It says here that the official escort's going to explain the message of Fatima," Victor said. "Didn't the Pope do that some time ago?" He thought it had to do with world peace, but it couldn't have been that. And while he knew that there had been a visitation by Mary at Fatima, he'd forgotten where it was, France or Portugal.

"It was supposed to be revealed some time in the '60s," Father Ed said, "but the Pope soft-pedaled it. He had enough trouble at the time without trying to explain old miracles. Frankly, I think it showed what he thought of it."

Feigning a what-the-hell tone, Victor said, "What harm can it do?"

"Open all that up again!" Father Ed said. "It's taken years to live her down."

Ed had read everything, even books that didn't sell very well: essays by South American priests, diaries by over-the-wall nuns, philosophy by Lutherans, civil-disobedience tracts by renegade priests, even poetry. Victor, on the other hand, in trying to keep up on the modern church, was struggling over the latest bestseller by the famous priest-novelist—"the lay priest," Ed called him. But Ed was always ready with a quip; that's what Vic liked about him. He drank crème de menthe, hated bingo, and said half-seriously that visiting the sick was a drag.

So while Ed smoked and joked—"let's go fishing on Pilgrim Virginia Day, or get sicker"—Vic took most of Ed's opinions as his own. But then Ed went too far. "The ignorant must have their opiate," he said. "Oh, not in the Marxist sense. Trot out the B.V.M. to keep the old idolaters happy." Vic didn't say anything— it was that green syrup Ed drank—but he didn't like it. There were still within him old, warm feelings about the other time and those who'd believed in all that.

Vic's father had told him many stories about when he was a boy up in Hallock, especially about Saint Patty's Catholic Cabin on Holy Cinder Blocks and its priest. No meek shepherd, Father Patrick Flynn rode herd on them all like a straw boss on a cattle drive. From not very high up on the meager altar, he chanted in Latin, burned incense, consecrated the Host and elevated shiny chalices and the golden, gaudy monstrance. In summer, he set up tents for Bible school; at harvest time, he frequently said morning Mass with no one present but an acolyte and the Lord. He transformed the church into a European chapel at Christmas and

395

sang endless glories to the Christ Child. Half deaf, he once gave an Easter homily on the season of rebirth, as a pair of hogs, in their wallow under the church, copulated noisily; when he finished and a portable phonograph played a scratchy recording of the *Hallelujah Chorus*, the swinish squeals reached a level of joy that finally even Father Flynn heard.

Raising his own children in the true faith had been a matter of grave importance to Victor's father; Vic's mother, a Norwegian Lutheran, had been required to sign a pledge binding her to support her husband's obligations. Father Flynn gradually turned the church into a cozy little log chapel where Victor was baptized, made his first Confession and Communion, and struggled with his Latin as an altar boy. So Victor accumulated some of his own stories about the priest, ever older and more hard of hearing, especially in the confessional. While the few girls in the parish waited their turn or knelt saying their penance, Father Flynn roared to the boys in what they called the black box: "You did *what* to yourself? *How* many times?"

But he was a master of the Mass and its liturgy. The Latin trilled off his Celtic tongue, even at Low Mass, in an ethereal vibrato that called up sinning and salvation, music and magic, dryads and leprechauns, as legions of tiny angels flew from the candle flames, bearing aloft the old Irishman's shimmering *r*'s. Liberated of the necessity of actually *hearing* the responses, he must only have been keying to their rhythm, which made young Vic's own execrable Latin all but superfluous. He thought of himself more as a kind of straight-man chanter; and once, alone with Father Flynn on the altar at early-morning Mass, with only one soul lost in penitence in a back pew and the priest moving about deftly as a stage player, Vic inadvertently tested his theory. In a spontaneous burst of superhuman daring and brilliant, though accidental, rebellion, instead of the usual *Et cum spiritu tuo* in response to Father Flynn's "*Dominus vobiscum*," he solemnly intoned: "Eat my weenie you're too old." The old boy never missed a beat.

The liturgical play carried on every morning in Hallock, then later in Birch Lake, was to Vic, even when he was making fun, the center of the universal plan; it signified that there *was* a plan. Later, after the Second Vatican Council, when it was going, then gone, he began to think of the Mass fondly as "the old show," and often recalled his mornings with a kindly old priest they had left behind in Hallock, not the crotchety taskmaster Father Flynn had remained. The last thing he had said, Vic remembered, was, "Don't go off and forget everything Holy Mother Church has taught you."

They didn't. For Vic's Confirmation—they'd been in Birch Lake for some time by then—he'd chosen Joseph, his grandmother's father's name, as his patron saint. They'd had a grand old show at the old Our Lady of the Lake; then family and friends gathered at their house. Vic was dressed for the occasion and feeling elegant and full of grace as he said to himself many times his "new" name: Victor Anthony Joseph Anderson. After the eating and the yard games, he went with his grandmother to a clearing within a cluster of bushes, wildflowers all around, where after she'd moved in with them she'd had Victor's father install a statue of the Holy Mother. She told him how proud she was of him, and there she told him a thrilling story about when she was a girl in the old country.

Then there were all those gray years when everything seemed to conspire to demand opposition not just to the old show but to everything old. It seemed that everybody, priests included, were relieved at having the burden of an ancient language lifted from their busy lives. They wanted messages, not mysteries. He sometimes thought they would have founded a new Church around "Have a Nice Day" if it was sewn onto a burlap banner. But he had to fight off such cynicism. He was a businessman; he knew better than to oppose a large majority, and most of them customers. But he needed a dose of mystery every now and then.

He was hanging on to his faith by a wing and a literal prayer. During the Protestant-like services he had taken to reciting silently old Latin responses. With Irene and the children dutifully beside him, he had settled into a grudging acceptance of Father Ed's witty, cough-wracked sermons, illustrated with equal parts television and literary allusions and tempered with a tone that, should he sound too dogmatic, amounted to an apology.

The statue might have been what a young Knight of Columbus—who had inherited his father's sword and uniform—could have given allegiance to. But it was too late for that. He could not even march in the annual parade with the other

397

Knights without feeling like a clown. Not since the time, shortly after his marriage, when he had walked proudly down the aisle of the old Our Lady and caught the look on Irene's face as he passed by her standing in the pew. She'd joked that night—"I thought the church was being invaded when I saw the drawn swords"—and being a young groom he'd laughed, too. "They do an awful lot of good, I know," she said, "but why do they dress like—like gentleman warriors?" He knew she meant *you*, not *they.* She was gasping for breath when she came to the hats. "They're shaped like mantel clocks, like Napoleon's. But aren't they wearing them ninety degrees off?" She didn't wait for an answer. "And that—that growth on them!" She grabbed her chest, panting. "It's not a plume, really; it's—it's"—she blew out so loud she spit a little on him—"it's plumage!" Then, *he* grabbed her chest, and they made tender, passionate love. "My—oh, my holy Knight!" she'd said in his ear. "I don't care what you wear." Still, he had felt shame throughout the next twenty years whenever he thought of that day.

The young bride, raised a Protestant, had become a rapier-sharp critic on such as pilgrim virgins, and virgins. Once, she'd left in Vic's underwear drawer a woman's magazine article about the Latin male's preoccupation with the "cult of the pristine woman." Which, since he and young Marco were the only males in town even slightly Latin, caught him completely off guard, showing as it did a side to Irene he'd never known was there. And which caused him a great deal of uneasiness on the occasional Sunday when the Church gave lip-service to Mary and what the enlightened women were showing to be mere cant, invented by Rome to keep them in what Rome considered to be their rightful place. "And not just the kitchen," Irene said. "The bedroom. Virgin to baby machine, overnight."

Victor could not fly in the face of all that, and he had no desire to. He agreed with Irene that he must do what he could to keep the statue from coming to town—"Sounds like a carnival," he'd said, "or Santa Claus"—but it wasn't much, or not enough; and so as Ed suggested after all the jokes, and as Victor finally agreed, they might just as well try to get through the ordeal with as little controversy as they could. It was a one-shot deal, at worst.

When Victor told Irene, she rolled her eyes and sighed. "Maybe a boycott would be in order."

398

"Oh, come on, now," Victor said. "If Ed, who doesn't even believe in the Assumption, can get through it, why can't we?"

"We? I have no intention of being in church that day. Wasn't that one of those infallible assumptions?"

He ignored the joke. "And the kids?"

But she didn't answer that. She looked skeptically WASPish as she said, "I suppose she—it—bleeds. Don't they usually?"

He laughed with her at that, even adding a gibe of his own. "With just two Latins in town, maybe we'll only get a couple of tears." But in the back of his mind was the scene of the young nun in the movie a few years ago, who had bled from apparently miraculous wounds before her Mother Superior and the atheistic psychiatrist, a chain-smoking woman who would not have admitted to a miracle if she had borne witness to one—which, obviously in the scene, she just had. During the young nun's trial for infanticide; in the numerous reviews of the movie; in the single, guarded discussion of it over pre-dinner cocktails with others in Birch Lake (a minor miracle of its own)—nowhere had anyone said what Victor finally exclaimed as he and Irene had picked up the subject on their way home: "But she had the *stigmata*, goddamnit!"

"Too bad we drew a Sunday," he said now, with some resentment. "The kids can't miss Mass."

Irene turned away. "I suppose not," she said, with forced resignation.

By the end of May, brought on by what amounted to Victor as an apocalyptic series of events, he had sunk into a spiritual torpor bordering on apostasy. For one thing, led by Jack Nordahl, who ultimately profited on all changes in town, there was a move to tear down the old elementary- and junior- and high-school buildings, both solid showcases on a square block near the edge of town. Generations had passed through their doors, but if Jack and the others had their way every kid in town would be bused to the new consolidated fortresses in the country. And there would be a shopping mall where the schools were.

At a meeting of the town council Victor had begun to object: "We already have—"

"You can always use another mall," Jack had said and laughed. And everybody had joined in.

399

So Vic, who hated confrontations, got out of that one by laughing with them and keeping quiet about what he had to say about demolishing the grand, old schools.

After a winter of meager snow and no spring rains, what was sure to be another long summer drought was setting in. The creek that ran through the back yard had already slowed to a trickle, laced occasionally with soap bubbles and an oil slick. After a short family vacation he had returned to find the three giant elms on the far side of the creek marked with red X's. A town crew had come later with chain saws and cut them down and ground the stumps to pulp. The lone silver birch in the front yard had brought out sickly, stunted leaves. And a church pew Victor had rescued from the old Our Lady and, after years on the enclosed porch, had put by the creek, had cracked and peeled, showing pine boards beneath oak veneer. He had never been a seeker of portents, but with the coming of The Pilgrim Virgin sending him on frequent mental journeys into the past, he had begun to find significance in such events.

On the day before the statue was to be displayed and honored, the Knights gathered at the church to practice the ceremony. Father Ed had left word that he had to be out of town for the practice but would be in church the next day to receive the statue below the altar and take over the ceremony from there. Vic laughed when he heard this from Irv Jameson.

"What's funny?" Irv said, wielding his sword. He was the only one who'd brought one.

"Oh, you know Ed," Elmer Schull said, "he's too young to care about Mary."

They formed the procession, using a small, rough litter Elmer had built from scrap lumber and a large doll one of the men had brought from home.

"She won't be here until tomorrow morning," Elmer said.

"How about the carrier?" Irv said. "We going to use that thing?"

Elmer laughed. "It's all coming tomorrow from Hallock. She's got her own authorized carrier."

As Vic saw in his head the old Hallock church, and Father Flynn, one of them said that the Bishop was coming.

On his way home he passed several yard sales and a carwash fund-raiser in the Presbyterian parking lot on the corner of his block. The loud, pulsing music ought to be against the law, he thought, as he waved to several teenagers. When he entered the house and closed the front door, the volume seemed not to diminish. He picked up the mail and went to the kitchen. The windows rattled, and he opened one to relieve the outside pressure of sound.

He always felt a keen anticipation of the mail, as if there might come at any time the message he would be called upon to spread. Instead, there was the usual stack of envelopes made to seem urgent, including a notice that he was a winner of millions, but nothing with a real stamp on it. When he threw them on the counter, the upper corner of one caught his eye: a blue-and-gold crucifix and the word CONGRATULATIONS!

He opened it and read the blue words: "My Dear Friend." He was not dreaming, the letter assured him; his "name appeared on a special list of people whom the Holy Land Fellowship regard as 'Miracle-Ready.' People who can really use a major Miracle in their life." He sighed and read on. "(A powerful Miracle Cross of Fatima is 'working' for you as of the date of this Certified Notice.)" He need only "activate the enclosed personal Miracle Card to receive . . . A TREASURE CHEST OF GENUINE DIAMONDS, EMERALDS, RUBIES AND SAPPHIRES. . . ." The Miracle Symbol of Fatima, a 24-carat gold crucifix, contained the Hallowed Earth of Fatima. There were testimonials from people identified by their initials. T. M. had received the Symbol one month, worn it to bingo the next, and won $10,000! B. B. proclaimed that "It happened so fast! Last Monday I see the notice about the Fatima Gold Cross and I send for it. Last Friday I receive it. Saturday I take it with me to the casino. Right away I win $2,570!"

Victor imagined a revolution in Las Vegas security: goons frisking gambling patrons for cross splinters and holy hairs. When he saw wallet cards for the Toll-Free Miracle Hot Line and an Unconditional Guarantee, he wadded it all up and stuffed it deep into the waste basket.

Where were the kids? They had work to do.

They were to shovel out the large mounds of wrinkled shavings left by the stump-pulping machine. Victor had ordered dirt to refill the holes; then they would seed and stake off the areas and

401

wait for a smoothing over of grass. If anything was going to grow this summer. When he tried to arouse an enterprising spirit in Marco by telling him he could bag the shavings and sell them for mulch, Marco said, "Who'd want it with a disease?" He thought of burning it, but that would take a permit. He'd just get somebody to haul it away.

He worked along with them for an hour or so, trying to make it fun by letting Nissa ride in the wheelbarrow on the return trips after dumping by the alley. But Kristi and Marco were closed off by their headsets, and they went about the work grudgingly, stopping altogether whenever Victor ceased making the effort to keep things going.

"Take off those earphones, and get to work!" he yelled. "I've tried to be reasonable, but enough's enough." He felt bad, though, as Marco stopped jousting with imaginary dragons and Kristi dragged about sourly. Setting her face, Nissa worked even harder. "Aren't you two ashamed to let your little sister outdo you?" he hollered. He couldn't help himself.

He walked to the ruined pew by the creek, intending to sit down, but the useful part was badly rotted. Only identical decorative portions in relief—an abbreviated Latin inscription in the quadrants of a rounded cross—remained reasonably intact on both ends of it. When Irene had asked him to move it from the porch, he should have refused. But he had thought it was solid and would hold up in any weather.

He went to the arched bridge and sat, letting his legs dangle. The music continued to blare, and he thought briefly that he could call down there and complain in a disguised voice. As he sat, gazing at the sluggard creek, several small fish floated by, belly-up. He knew that someone upstream had once dumped oil in it, and he had considered reporting it to the proper agency, but he'd have had to sign a complaint. And he had traced what had since become rather common soap bubbles to their source: a small, buried pipe which led to the house of one of his insureds.

At the end of the bridge he had set stones around the supports to shore them up against flooding, mortaring them over completely so that Kristi and Marco could scratch out their names with sticks, back when they would fish for hours for the big trout they said they'd seen. On a summer day they would lower cans on strings into the creek, as they talked about worms and bugs and all the things they were going to build with mud. Often he had hidden in the trees by the stone steps, filming them with the movie camera. He thought of the mallards which used to come every year to their yard, and he remembered when the kids had come running to the house, yelling that there was a tall bird by the bridge. Victor and Irene had gone out there in time to see a blue heron flapping its big wings slowly off down the stream bank.

He turned now to see them moving too silently among the pulp mounds, and he wondered where they had gone in so short a time—not the mallards nor the trout nor the big blue heron, but the little boy and girl who had haunted the bridge like trolls.

"Come here," he shouted amiably, waving his arm, and all three turned to him. But there was no look of relief or recognition on their faces, only that implacably feigned disregard for the voice of authority that had called and must be heeded. He smiled, to let them know that they could stop working, there was no urgency to his call. "Throw those instruments of torture down and come on over here, okay?"

Nissa began to dash for the bridge, but slowed to a walk when she must have sensed the reluctance of the other two, who gave pained looks at each other, dropped their shovels and met with a whisper.

"Come on. I just want you to sit with me for a while."

Now they really whispered, but Marco smiled, too. Vic put Nissa on his lap and motioned for Kristi and Marco to sit on either side of him. He didn't know quite what he was going to do or say. Kristi sighed abruptly. "What is it, Dad?" She made it sound as if he had gathered them there on the bridge to inform them that he hated the sight of them.

"Well, it's better than work, isn't it? Just sit here a minute. Okay?"

The minutes passed, and more, and he knew he could not occupy them for long that way. Finally, he said, "I want to tell you a story," and he heard the echo within him of his grandmother's voice long ago. He surprised himself by saying it, without having anything in mind. Marco began fidgeting, then distracting Nissa; Kristi swung her legs impatiently. He looked out at the winding creek bed. Rocks jutted dry tops like small tombstones above the paltry stream; branches clung to the bank like tangled snakes. And before he knew it he said, "When my grandmother was a girl about your age, Kristi, she used to go with other girls from her village into the mountains to gather wood." It was the story she had told him by her shrine, when he was a boy.

"Mountains?" Marco said.

"Back in the old country," Victor said. "She was slightly lame in one leg—you might remember her, Kristi—and one day when they were returning with large bundles of sticks balanced on their heads, she stopped to rest. The others usually waited for her, but they told her that day that they would go on and meet her at the shrine where they always stopped for a drink of water. Well, she rested for a while, and when she reached the shrine there was no one there."

"And why didn't they wait?" Kristi said, with impatience and what might have been some disappointment.

"Well, they were young girls, younger than you," he began delicately, "and they were anxious to get home before dark. It was a feast day to the village saint, and there was going to be singing and dancing in the *piazza*."

Nissa turned with a quizzical look.

"Not pizza," Marco said.

"It was an open place near the church where people could walk and visit each other," Victor said.

"Like the Presbyterian parking lot on the corner," Marco said, deadpan.

"Not exactly." Victor said, to Nissa, "But anyway, at the shrine she took the load of wood off her head and set it aside. Then she kneeled at the pool around the shrine and bent over and scooped the cool water with her hands."

Nissa said, "Why'd they have to go get wood?"

Victor started to explain that the villagers were poor and had only the wood to heat their hovels—he'd seen pictures of them—and to cook with year round, that all the chestnut trees had died. But if he did he would lose the other children, who had no patience with how hard it used to be. "They needed it to build fires," he said. "There wasn't any electricity or gas there."

He had reached that part of the story he remembered most vividly, the part most difficult to tell, for he had heard it with the belief of a child. *As she drank from her cupped hands, her long hair fell over her face and touched the water. She closed her eyes briefly, savoring the cool, sacred place. Tradition held that after*

*drinking she cross herself, look across the short distance of the
pool into the grotto where the wooden statue of Mary and the
infant Jesus had been harbored for wayfarers for over a century,
and say the* Magnificat. "My soul doth magnify the Lord," Victor
said, in a voice of old automatic reverence. ". . . From henceforth
all generations shall call me blessed." Again he surprised himself,
being able so thoroughly to recall the prayer, but it might have
been lost in the music. He didn't know, but he couldn't repeat it
in case it hadn't been. "Of course, she said it in Italian," he said.

"Is that the end?" Nissa said.

"No," Victor said, and they pulled in closer.

She felt that she was being watched before she raised her
head, he told them, and *as she looked below the earthen apse
where the spring poured, she heard above the trickle the slight
sound of hissing. She sensed a movement above, only a flicker,
from out of the bottom of the grotto; then she looked up slightly.
It took a moment for her to realize that what she saw was the
head of a serpent. It was looking at her. Its tongue came out,
wavering. She was fixed by its strange eyes and held her own
gaze as she recited aloud a*—he needed a special word—
"canticle," he said, knowing they wouldn't understand it; he
didn't himself, fully. And with the sound of the word he thought
of Sister Drought, Brother Sun, Lady Sorrow—all out of his lost
time as a believer in canticles and litanies and all that—and his
grief and disdain subsided.

"It was a series of short prayers," he said. "And while she was
saying them, the snake—it was huge—came out of the shrine
and went off into the woods."

They seemed moved. But he could not tell for sure, for if he
asked or talked on he would surely ruin the very thing that he, at
least, had felt. They took the shovels and went up the stone
steps, and he put the rake in the wheelbarrow and had rolled it
onto the bridge, when he heard a splash. Then several splashes.
Birds must be bathing upstream, he thought, as he stood watching from the bridge. Several otters, or whatever they were, came
chasing one another through the shallow water, darting onto the
banks, and back in. When they reached the deeper part beneath
the bridge, they dived and swam in circles. He called for the
children, but they had gone. And then the otters were gone, running across the little dam and on down the creek bed.

That night he awoke to an eerie sound in an otherwise quiet house, and to a spot of moonlight on the bed. He had heard the sound in his dream as if amplified and now perceived it as the breathing of his wife. He was turned away from her; exhaling against the pillow and his hands, he was aware of an odor as of something carbolic. He looked out the window at the ghostly birch, holding its crumpled leaves as if at a distasteful distance, and he realized that what he gave off in the night was the beginning fetor of age. He thought of the occasional weary look on Irene's face. If she had crossed the line of blooming, what region of decay must he, older by several years, have entered by now?

He lay there, daunted that he had not distinguished himself in any way that mattered. Having inherited the fruits of his father's hard-won enterprise, he had become a satisfied man of some privilege who received money for the guarantee that when bodies died, those still living would also get money. He had told the story of a young girl whose nerve, born of faith, had allowed her to look a serpent in the eye; inspired by the story as a boy, he had tried to re-tell it as somehow miraculous.

Tomorrow he was to come marching in gaudy regalia into an uninspiring church, its priest a critic of the sentimentally devout. *And where have all the old priests gone?* The young one who'd buried Vic's grandmother had, during the eulogy, referred to her shrines and such as her "bag of psychological tricks," as if with her passing there would be a new beginning, The New Church. *Math to religion: Sweep all that old shit under the rug, man, and let's get on with the times!* And indeed they had. He had tried to go along with it, but now he had reached that plane of equilibrium where he was not a believer and not a mover, not much of anything. He saw himself in not so many years as some hoary old fool with a dewlap who had let the urging of the moment pass him by. Why, he'd taken his souvenir pew and hadn't even objected publicly when they'd torn down the old Our Lady. He'd actually watched Elmer Scholl's crew demolish it, then participated in the breaking of ground for the new big, brick rambler. . . .

By God! They'd reformed the wrong things!

Latin, incense, the liturgy—they'd dismantled the Mass. And as soon as it was gone, the young began grooving on it, searching for it in other forms: Hinduism, gurus, maharishis, incense—in short, priests and ancient aromas to invoke mystery through ceremony. Sweep the miters, robes and jewels under the rug—all the rich and garish junk between the communicant and what was left of the—yes, he was still tied to the old show. But not with those trappings. The manger was a wooden trough, with straw! A chalice ought to be clay! But you couldn't bring it back, and surely not unadorned, anymore than you could republish an old book or release an old movie, not if you wanted crowds. Except for sentimentalists like him, once discarded, precious things, like old buildings, are forgotten by those who then go in search of them in other lands.

So changing back was hardly likely. What was needed was—he laughed—only a miracle. Just retrieve the old miracle hotline number. He fell asleep, then awoke. He would be justifiably shamed at church before his family if he went through with it as it was rehearsed. He lay sleeping and waking the rest of the night. By the time he reached over to turn off the ringing alarm clock, he knew what he would do.

He showered and shaved and, in his robe and slippers, made a small breakfast. When the others came to the table, Irene was dressed up.

"Did you decide to go?" he said.

She looked at Kristi. "It was decided for me."

"If Mom doesn't have to, we shouldn't," Kristi said.

"Yeah," Nissa said. Victor looked at her, and she put her face back in the funny papers.

"Yeah," Marco said, without looking up from the stack of advertisement supplements he was reading like a novel.

"I'm going," Victor said, "of course."

"I thought we could walk," Irene said, "but you're not ready."

"Why don't you go ahead and walk?" he said. "I still have to—"

"Dad doesn't want to be seen outside in his outfit," Marco said, drinking milk from the wooden goblet he'd bought on their vacation. "People might think he's the Caped Crusader."

Victor looked at him.

"I was only joking," Marco said.

"Better not do that this morning," Victor said. Then he rose. "I'll meet you after church," he added, and went upstairs.

While he was brushing his teeth, he heard a crash in the kitchen and Irene say, "Clean it up, fast. We have to go now."

He took the stairs two at a time to the attic, where he began digging through a large trunk. Among bell-bottom pants and a Nehru suit he found a pair of leather sandals, his pitiful attempt in the '60s to be "in." He kicked off his slippers and threw things out of the trunk, pausing at his graduation gown, still large enough but not right. He was looking for the monk's robe of tan homespun Irene had made for him some ten Halloweens ago, and found it hanging in the storage closet. He put it on and tied the rope belt and was ready to dash downstairs, when his old missal caught his eye. He grabbed it, thick and black as a small Bible; then hurrying down the stairs, he stopped at the landing.

He went to the window there and, feeling oddly naked, tucked the sandals under an arm and flipped the faded ribbon markers of the missal. He laughed bitterly, then felt the full urgency of what he was about to do and started for the kitchen. They'd probably think he'd gone mental, but when it was over he'd quit the Church, for good. One was about as good as another now anyway. Let Irene return to her own for the next twenty years, and take the children.

In the kitchen, surprised by its lightness, he took Marco's goblet from the counter. He rinsed it and dried it and turned to go to the coat closet, when he felt a sharp pain in his left foot and hopped on his right until his knee locked and he went to the floor. He had to let go of everything and now turned his foot to see a glass shard, like a small spear, in his sole. He pulled it out, then grasped his right foot, turning it inwardly until the knee popped into place. The goblet was broken into two neat halves, and he taped them together with clear tape, folded a paper towel under his bleeding foot and put on the sandals, picked up the missal, wrapped his cape around him and went to the car. He left the Napoleon hat and its plumage behind.

As he backed out of the driveway, the church bells began to ring. He drove the three blocks and parked near the front door of the church and got out, concealing the missal and goblet under his cape. The Knights were lined up in the narthex, he saw, as he opened the door a crack. Sashes, capes, swords—the obvious irony of their outfits was exceeded only by the sense of mission on their faces. Christian soldiers, they meant to bear the Queen of Heaven on this day. The litter-carriers jockeyed their load around to get into place, and he saw the frozen face of it, so familiar to him from all the pictures through the years of other Marys. He was startled at first that it was so large, but when he mentally subtracted the outsize crown on its head he was surprised that it was so much smaller than he thought it would be.

Irv Jameson said, "We can't wait anymore. Let's go," and when the front formation began to move through the church doors, Vic slipped inside. He had originally been assigned to trail the litter with drawn sword. He waited until those preceding the litter had gone, and as its four bearers moved with it to the doors he released his cape to the floor. He caught sight of the Bishop's miter, the crook of his staff, and began quaking slightly, then reached deep into himself. And came up with *Father Flynn, the girl his grandmother had been, the man his father had been, and for those hogs of love on that Easter morning long ago.*

He moved in behind Irv, who'd taken over his position, and as he did Irv turned. "For the love—!" He pointed his sword at him as if he meant to run him through, and in the confusion of the moment his absurd hat turned and fell a little.

It caused Vic to feel sorry for him. He felt pity for all of them, himself included, but there was no time for that. They were entering the church, and Vic shook him off. "Turn around!" he said in a harsh whisper. "And keep going." And when Irv did, straightening the hat, Vic pitied him all the more.

The wound in his foot hurt, and he limped slightly as he followed, last in his monk's robe and sandals. The singing had started—

> "Hai-il, Holy Queen, enthroned above,
> O, Ma-ri-a"—

and he joined in as he crossed the threshold into the church and all its light. The ushers stared at him, and he looked straight ahead, and up, fixing on the cross at the top of the bulbous crown on the statue. The glare hurt his eyes, and he blinked, holding the missal and wooden chalice to his chest, singing out,

> "Sa-al-ve, sa-al-ve, sa-al-ve, Re-gi-na,"

409

staring hard to keep from seeing to the sides. Thrilled to tears by the old hymn, he journeyed back to those mornings when he was just a boy on the altar with an old man making a miracle.

He picked up his step a bit, and looked around. Let them see me for what I am, he thought, as he continued joyfully with the second verse. And whatever that is, so be it.

Nominated by Shenandoah

CHRISTOPHER

by DIANE GLANCY

from NEW LETTERS

Har cume Christopher Columbus cumming ober t' waves.
Puff. Puff. He think he cume to the segund
part of urth.
His shups bump inter land at night
y hazé la señal dla cruz.
Hey Yndias. He say. *Hey Ermerica.*
He brang glaz beads & bells.
Luego se ayunto alli mucha gente dla Isla.
We think he god from skie. Yup. Yup. Wedu.
The blue oshen sprad like a table napkin by his shups.
Como el por ante todos toma
va como de hecho tomo possession dla dha.
Yaz. He say. *I take.*
Now whar find gold?
Our har like harsehair. He say.
He look our fish-tooth on spears. *Har har.* He laf.
Los reyes wand gold.
Gloria religion xpiana. Gloria Yndias. He say.
Y load his shups. Wedu.
Thar go Christopher. Huf. Huf.
Wid gold he own t' segund urth.
With gold he buy souls inter heben.

Nominated by William Stafford

COMPLAINT AGAINST THE ARSONIST

by STANLEY PLUMLY

from THE VIRGINIA QUARTERLY REVIEW

This pyrrhic fire the barn burned down and blew back
into the dust-weight of its carbon, that burned the air
flecked bright with it, above the wheat in flags,
the barn I spent the summer part-time painting, white
on white to purify the wood, the summer I wheeled ashes
in a foundry, working the aisles between castings
and the cutting edge of molds, ashes I had to hose down hard
like a dog pile of the intimate earth transformed. . . .
At night my arms would levitate like wings, a diamond
in each hand, the morning sun a low round furnace gold.

In those 18th-century English paintings alchemizing
ore, the ones with the dawn-like sunset reds and yellows
always rising, the silhouettes of buildings rising behind
the fires, the foundries are invisible, nothing but storms
the rain-gray horses are pulling the wagons from,
the night shifts ending, the pitch-black skies poised
like the weight of history above a pastoral—before Turner
and Constable and the oxygen-conversion of the landscape
into light—when the picture is still the reality of record,
heightened for effect, named for Coalbrookdale or Bedlam.

That night was industrial and animal, a burning-off of flesh,
the blue clouds' upward drifting like the longing of all clouds—

you had to stand there hours thinking what it was like,
this dying-off, this earth-transcending gift, the mind a
kind of angel sent ahead, since the suicide is to set the fire
and stay, to let it pull you in, like falling or flying,
since the men I worked among, the one who stayed,
had seen in fire what fire can do, if not this soaring
of a wind straight up, a living building all at once,
the blood screams breaking like electric lights

around the horse that came out stumbling, then soared.

Nominated by David Baker, Arthur Smith

SOMEWHERE ALONG THE LINE

by ANTLER

from THE SUN

What interested me most about gorillas
    when I first studied them
Was not that the males' penises are only
    two inches long,
But that gorillas shit and piss in their beds
    and don't leave to relieve themselves
        (though they build new beds every day),
Also they eat their feces, yes
    they eat their turds.
And this made me realize that we
    (somewhere along the line)
Decided we wouldn't shit and piss in our beds,
We agreed we wouldn't eat our shit
    or drink our piss,
That we would wear clothes
    and not go naked in public
        and not shit or piss in public
    and not jack off in public,
Not fuck or suck in public,
Not stick our fingers up our rear ends
    and smell them
        (even in the privacy
    of our own homes),

414

Or on meeting another of our kind
        sniff each other's cock and balls
                and cunt and asshole like a dog
        but shake hands like a man
And rather than pissing and shitting to mark
        our territory
We invented money
And rather than gathering food from plants
        we'd work to plant them raise them sell them
And rather than killing animals fish birds
        with our mouths and eating them
                raw and bloody
We'd hire others of our kind
        to kill them
                and cut them up in little pieces
        not with their mouths
                but with sharp knives in their hands,
And somewhere we decided rather than live in trees
        we'd kill them, cut them up in long pieces,
                build houses and live
        inside them while sitting in chairs
                made from them and write poems
        about them on paper made from them
                with a pencil made from them
        about somewhere along the line
                we decided to be different than
        gorillas and monkeys because
                our way of being was right
        because we were better
                than any other creature on Earth.

Nominated by Christine Zawadiwsky

415

THE LIFE OF THE BODY

fiction by TOBIAS WOLFF

from TRIQUARTERLY

WILEY GOT LONELY one night and drove to a bar in North Beach owned by a guy he used to teach with. He watched a basketball game and afterwards fell into conversation with the woman sitting next to him. She was a veterinarian. Her name was Kathleen. When Wiley said her name he laid on a bit of the Irish and she smiled at him. She had freckles and very green eyes, "Green as the fields of Erin," he told her, and she laughed, holding her head back and deciding—he could tell, he could see it happen—to let things take their course. She was a little drunk. She touched him as she talked, his wrist, his hand, once even his thigh, to drive a point home. Wiley agreed but he didn't hear what she was saying. There was a rushing sound in his ears.

The man Kathleen had come in with, a short, redfaced, bearded man in a safari jacket, held his glass with both hands and pondered it. He sometimes looked over at Kathleen, at her back. Then he looked at his glass again. Wiley wanted to keep everything friendly, so he leaned forward and stared at him until their eyes met, and then he lifted his glass in salute. The man gaped like a fish. He jabbed his finger at Wiley and yelled something unintelligible. Kathleen turned and took his arm. Then the bartender joined them. He was wiping his hands with a towel. He leaned over the bar and spoke to Kathleen and the short man in a soft voice while Wiley looked on encouragingly.

"That's the ticket," Wiley said. "Talk him down."

The short man jerked his arm away from Kathleen. Kathleen looked around at Wiley and said, "You keep your mouth shut."

The bartender nodded. "Please be quiet," he said.

"Now just a minute," Wiley said.

The bartender ignored him. He went on talking in that soft voice of his. Wiley couldn't follow everything he said, but he did hear words to the effect that he, Wiley, had been drinking hard all night and that they shouldn't take him too seriously.

"Whoa!" Wiley said. "Just hold on a second. I'm having a quiet conversation with my neighbor here, and all of a sudden Napoleon declares war. Why is that my fault?"

"Sir, I asked you to be quiet."

"You ought to cut him off," the short man said.

"I was about to."

"I don't believe this," Wiley said. "For your information, I happen to be a very old friend of Bob's."

"Mr. Lundgren isn't here tonight."

"I can see that. I have eyes. My point is, if Bob were here. . ." Wiley stopped. The three of them were looking at him as if he were a complete asshole, the little guy so superior he wasn't even mad anymore. Wiley had to admit, he sounded like one— dropping the name of a publican, for Christ's sake. A former algebra teacher. He said, "I have many friends in high places," trying to make a joke of it, but they didn't laugh or even smile, they thought he was serious. "Oh, relax," he said.

"I'm sure Mr. Lundgren will be happy to take care of your tab," the bartender said. "If you want to make a complaint he'll be in tomorrow afternoon."

"You can't be serious. Are you actually throwing me out?"

The bartender considered the question. Then he said, "Right now we're at the request stage."

"But this is ridiculous."

"You're free to leave under your own steam, sir, and I'd be much obliged if you did."

"This is absolutely incredible," Wiley said, more to himself than the bartender, in whose studied courtesy he did not fail to hear the possibility of competent violence. But he was damned if he was going to be hurried. He finished his drink and set the glass down. He slid off his stool, inclined his head toward Kathleen, gravely thanked her for the pleasure of her company. He crossed the room with perfect dignity and stepped outside, taking care that the door should not slam behind him.

417

A cold light rain was falling. Wiley stood under the awning and hopelessly waited for it to stop. From the place across the street he heard a woman laugh loudly; he thought of lipstick-stained teeth, a pink tongue licking off the creamy mustache left by a White Russian. He leaned in that direction, thrusting his head forward as he did when he caught certain smells in the breeze, curry, roasting coffee, baking bread. Wiley raised his jacket collar and pushed off up the hill, toward the garage where he'd left his car. When he reached the corner he stopped. He could not go home now, not like this. He could not allow this absurd picture of himself to survive in Kathleen's mind. It was important that she know the truth about him, and not go through life believing that he was some kind of mouthy lush who got tossed out of bars. Because he wasn't. Nothing like this had ever happened to him before.

He crossed the street and walked back downhill to the other bar. Two women were sitting in the corner with three men. The one Wiley had heard laughing was still at it. Whenever anybody said anything she cracked up. They were all in their fifties, tourists from the look of them, the only customers in the place. Wiley bought a whiskey and carried it to a table by the window where he could keep an eye on the bar he'd just been asked to leave.

Nothing like this had ever happened to him. He was an English teacher in a private high school. He lived alone. He didn't go to bars much and almost never drank whiskey. He liked good wine, knew something about it, but was wary of knowing too much. At night, after he'd prepared his classes, he drank wine and read nineteenth-century novels. He didn't like modern fiction, its narcissism, its moral timidity, its silence in the face of great wrongs. Wiley had started teaching to support himself while he wrote his doctoral thesis on Dickens, and then lost interest in scholarship as he began to sense the power he had over his students. They were still young enough that they had no investment in the lies the world told about itself; he could make a difference in the way they saw things.

Wiley read thick books late into the night and sometimes got only a few hours' sleep, but in nine years he had never missed a day of work; come morning he pushed himself out of bed just in time and drove to school still fumbling with his buttons, stomach empty, coffee sloshing in the cup between his knees.

Wiley didn't like living alone. He wanted to get married, had always assumed he would be married by now, but he'd had bad luck with women. The last one brushed him off after four months. Her name was Monique. She was a French teacher on exchange, a tall jaunty Parisian who humiliated the boys in her class by mimicking their oafish accents, and the girls by rendering them invisible to the boys. She wore dark glasses even when she went to movies. Her full red lips were habitually pursed. Wiley learned they were held thus in readiness not for passion, but scorn, at least where he was concerned. After Monique read *Catcher in the Rye* her dissatisfaction found a home in the word "phony." He never understood why she'd settled on him in the first place. Sometimes he thought it was for his language—he liked to talk, and talked well, and Monique was in the States to polish her English. But her reasons were a mystery; she dropped him cold without ever making them clear.

Wiley had finished two whiskeys and had just bought a third when Kathleen and the little guy came out of the bar. They stopped in the doorway and watched the rain, which was falling harder now. They stood well apart, not speaking, and watched the rain drip off the awning. After a time she looked into her purse, said something to him. He patted his jacket pockets. She rummaged in her purse again and then the two of them ducked their heads and set off up the hill. Wiley stood suddenly, knocking his chair over. He picked it up and left the bar.

He had to walk fast. It was an effort. His feet kept taking him from side to side. He bent forward, compelling them to follow. He reached the corner and shouted, "Kathleen!"

She was on the opposite corner. The man was a few steps ahead of her, leaning into the rain. They both stopped and looked over at Wiley. Wiley walked into the street and came toward them. He said, "I love you, Kathleen." He was surprised to hear himself say this, and then to say, as he stepped up on the curb, "Come home with me." She didn't look the way he remembered her, she looked older and very tired. He barely recognized her. He understood that he had no idea who she was. She put her hand to her mouth. Wiley couldn't tell whether she was shocked or afraid or what. Maybe she was laughing. He smiled foolishly, confused by his own presence here and by what he'd said, not sure what to say next. Then the little guy came past her and Wiley felt a blow on his cheek and his head snapped back, and right after that the wind went out of him in a whoosh and he folded up, clutching his stomach, unable to breathe or speak. There was another blow at the back of his knees and he fell forward onto the sidewalk. He saw a shoe coming at his face and tried to jerk his head away but it caught him just above the eye. He heard Kathleen screaming and the shoe hit him again on the mouth. He rolled away and covered his face with his hands. Kathleen kept screaming, *No Mike No Mike No Mike No*. Wiley could feel himself being kicked on his shoulders and back. It was a dull, faraway pain. It went on for a while, and then it stopped.

He lay where he was, not trusting the silence, afraid that by moving he would make it all start again. Finally he raised himself to his hands and knees. There was broken glass in the street, glittering on the wet asphalt, and to see it at just this angle, so close, so familiar, so perfectly a part of everything that had happened to him, was to feel utterly reduced; and he knew that he would never forget this, being on his knees with broken glass all around. The rain fell softly. He heard himself weeping, and stopped; it was a stagey, dishonest sound. His lower lip throbbed. He licked it; it was swollen, and tasted of salt and leather.

Wiley stood up. He steadied himself against the wall of a building. Two men came toward him, talking excitedly. He was afraid that they would stop to help him, ask him questions. What if they called the police? He had no excuse for his condition, no explanation. Wiley turned his face. The men walked past him as if he wasn't there, or as if he belonged there, in exactly that pose, as part of what they expected a street to look like.

Home. He had to get home. Wiley pushed away from the wall and started walking. He was surprised at how well he walked; his head was clear, his feet steady. He felt exuberant, even exultant, as if he'd gotten away with something. Light and easy. The feeling lasted through most of the drive home, and then it broke; by the time Wiley reached his apartment he was weak and cold, shaken with feverish trembling.

He went straight to the bathroom and turned on the light. His lower lip was split and bleeding, purplish in color, puffed up like a sausage. He had a cut over his left eyebrow and the skin above it was scraped raw all the way to his hairline. His chin was also scraped raw, and flecked with dirt. He could see a bruise beginning on his cheekbone. My God, he thought, looking at himself. He felt great tenderness for the person behind this lurid mask, as if it were not his face at all, but the face of a beaten child. He touched the hurt places. The raw skin clung to his fingertips.

Wiley took a long bath and tried to sleep, but whenever he closed his eyes he felt a malign presence in the room. In spite of the bath he still felt cold. He got up and looked at himself in the mirror again, hoping to find some change for the better. He inspected his face, then brewed a pot of coffee and spent the rest of the night at the kitchen table, staring blindly at a book and finally sleeping, slumped sideways in the chair, chin on his chest.

When the alarm went off Wiley roused himself and got ready for school. He couldn't think of a reason not to go except for embarrassment; given that others would have to cover his classes during their free time, this did not seem a very good reason. But he gave no consideration to what it would mean. When the first students saw him in the hallway and started quizzing him, he had no answers ready. One boy asked if he'd been mugged.

Wiley nodded, thinking that was basically true.

"Must have been a whole shitload of them."

"Well, not that many," Wiley said, and walked on. He went straight to his classroom instead of stopping off in the teachers' lounge, but he hadn't been at his desk five minutes before the principal came in. "Mr. Wiley," he said, "let's have a look at you." He walked up close and peered at Wiley's face. Students were filing in behind him, trying not to stare at Wiley as they took their seats. "What exactly happened?" the principal asked.

"I got mugged."

"Have you seen a doctor?"

"Not yet."

"You should. That's a prize set of bruises you've got there. Very nasty. Call the police?"

"No. I'm still in sort of a daze." Wiley said this in a low voice so the students wouldn't hear him.

Wiley's friend Mac stuck his head in the door. When he saw the principal he nodded coolly. "You O.K.?" he said to Wiley.

"I guess."

"I heard there were eight of them. Is that right, eight?"

"No." Wiley tried to smile but his face wouldn't let him. "Just two," he said. He couldn't admit to one, not with all this damage, but eight sounded like a movie.

"Two's enough," Mac said. "You O.K.?"

The principal said, "Just let me know if you want to go home. Seriously, now, Mr. Wiley—no heroics. I'm touched that you came in at all." He stopped at the door on his way out and turned to the students. "Be warned, ladies and gentlemen. What happened to Mr. Wiley is going to happen to your children. It will be a common occurrence. That's the kind of world they're going to live in if you don't do something to change it." He let his eyes pass slowly around the room the way he did at school assemblies. "The choice is yours," he said.

Mac applauded silently behind him.

After Mac and the principal left two boys got up and pretended to attack each other with kicks and chops, crying *Hai! Hai! Hai!* One of them drove the other to the back of the class, where he crashed to the floor and lay with his arms and legs twitching. Then the bell rang and they both went back to their desks.

This was a senior honors class. The students had been reading "Benito Cereno," one of Wiley's favorite stories, but he had trouble getting a discussion started because of the way they were looking at him. Finally he decided to give a straight lecture. He talked about Melville's exposure of the contradictions in human law, which claims to serve justice while it strengthens the hand of the property owner, even when that property is human. This was one of Wiley's pet subjects, the commodification of humanity. As he warmed to it he forgot the condition of his face and assumed his habitual patrol in front of the class, head bent, hands in his pockets, one eye cocked in a squint. He related this story to the last one they'd read, "Bartleby, the Scrivener," quoting with derisory, operatic exaggeration the well-intentioned narrator who cannot understand the truculence of a human being whom he has tried to turn into a Xerox machine. And this was not the voice of some reactionary fascist beast, Wiley said, jingling his keys and change as he paced the room—this was the voice of modern man; modern, enlightened, liberal man.

He had worked himself into that pitch of indignation where everything seemed clear to him, evil and good and all the sly imitations of good that lay in wait for the unwary pilgrim. At such

422

moments he forgot himself entirely. He became Scott Fitzgerald denouncing the foul dust that floated in Gatsby's wake, Jonathan Swift laying waste to bourgeois complacency by suggesting a crime so obscene it took your breath away, yet was still less obscene than the crimes ordinary people tolerated without a second thought.

And what happened to Bartleby, Wiley said, was only a hint of things to come. "Look at the multinationals!" he said. And then, not for the first time, he described the evolution of business-school theory to its logical conclusion, high-tech factories in the middle of foreign jungles where, behind razor-wire fences guarded by soldiers and dogs, tribesmen who had never seen a flush toilet were made to assemble fax machines and laptop computers. A million Bartlebys, a billion Bartlebys!

Wiley didn't have the documentation on these factories in the jungle, it was something someone had told him, but it made sense and was right in tune with the spirit of late twentieth-century capitalism; it sounded true enough to make him furious whenever he talked about it. He finished his lecture with only a few minutes to go before the bell. He felt very professional. It was no mean feat, getting his ass kicked at two in the morning and giving a dynamite lecture at nine. He asked his students if they had any questions. None of them did, at first. Wiley heard whispers. Then a girl raised her hand, shyly, almost as if she hoped he wouldn't notice. When Wiley called on her she looked at the boy across the aisle, Robbins, and said, "What color were they?"

Wiley did not understand the question. She looked over at Robbins again. Robbins said, "They were black, right?"

"Who?"

"The guys that jumped you."

Wiley felt his throat tighten. He'd always liked this boy and expected him to learn something in here, to think better thoughts than his FBI-agent father who griped to the principal about Wiley's reading list. Wiley leaned against the blackboard. "I don't know," he said.

"Yeah, right," Robbins said.

"I really don't think so," Wiley said. This sounded improbably vague even to him, so he added, "It was dark. I couldn't see them."

Robbins gave a great bark of laughter. Some of the other students laughed too, and then one of them hit a wild note and it sent everyone into a kind of fit. "Quiet!" Wiley said, but they kept laughing. They were beyond his reach, all he could do was stand there and wait for them to stop. Wiley had three black students in this class, two girls and a boy. They stared at their desks in exactly the same way, as if by agreement, though they were sitting in different parts of the room. At the beginning of the year they'd always sat together, but now they drifted from place to place like everyone else. They seemed to feel at home in his class. And that was what he wanted, he wanted this room to be a sanctuary, a place the rest of the world should be like. There was no other reason for him to be here.

The bell rang. Wiley sat down and rustled through some papers as the students, suddenly and strangely quiet, walked past his desk. Then he went to the office and told the principal he was going home after all. He was feeling terrible, he said.

He slept for a few hours. After he got up he looked through the veterinarians' listings in the yellow pages and found a Dr. Kathleen Newman on the staff of a clinic specializing in surgery on exotic pets. He called the clinic and asked for Dr. Newman. The man who answered said she was in a meeting, asked if it was an emergency.

"I'm afraid so," Wiley said. "It is sort of an emergency. Tell her," he said, "that Mr. Melville's cetacean has distemper."

Wiley spelled out cetacean for him.

And then a woman's voice was on the line. "Who is this, please?" It was her. But sharp, no fooling around. Wiley couldn't answer, he'd expected her to pick up his joke and now he didn't know how to begin. "Hello? Hello? Damn," she said, and hung up.

Wiley turned to the white pages. There was a Dr. K. P. Newman on Filbert Street. He wrote down the number and address.

Mac's wife Alice stopped by that afternoon with bread and salad. She had been a student in Wiley's honors class, and one of his favorites, a pale, slow-moving, thoughtful girl he would never have suspected of carrying on with a teacher, which showed how much he knew; she and Mac had been going strong ever since her junior year. They got married right after she graduated.

There was a scandal, and Mac almost lost his job, but somehow it never came to that. Wiley found the whole thing very confusing. He disapproved and was jealous; he felt as if Mac had made a fool of him somehow. But six years had passed since then.

Alice stopped inside the door and looked at Wiley's face. He saw that she was shocked to the point of tears.

"It'll mend," he told her.

"But why would anyone do that to you?"

"These things happen," he said.

"Well, they shouldn't."

She sent him back to the living room. Wiley lay on the couch and watched her through the kitchen doorway while she set the table and made lunch. He was happy having her to himself in his apartment, it was a wish of his. Alice didn't know he felt that way. When they went to bars she sat beside him and leaned her head on his shoulder. She took sips from his drinks. She liked to dance, and when she danced with Wiley she moved right up close, talking all the while about everyday things that somehow made their closeness respectable. At the end of a night out, when Mac and Alice drove Wiley home and came inside to call their sitter and drink a glass of wine, and then another, and Wiley began to read to them some high-minded passage from whatever novel he was caught up in, she would stretch out on the couch and rest her head in Wiley's lap while Mac looked on benignly from the easy chair. Wiley knew that he was supposed to feel honored by all this faith, but he resented it. Faith had become an imposition. It made light of his capacity for desire. Still, he put up with it because he didn't know what else to do.

Now Alice was slicing tomatoes at his kitchen counter. She had a flat-footed way of standing. Her hair was gathered in a bun, but loose strands of it hung in her face; she blew them away as she worked. She had gained weight over the years. She had gained too much weight, but Wiley liked the little tuck of flesh under her chin, and the plumpness of her hands.

She called him to the table. She was quiet and when she looked at him she looked quickly down again. Wiley did not think it was because of his banged-up face, but because they had never been alone before. In all her playfulness with him there was an element of performance, and now she didn't have Mac here to give it irony and keep it safe.

425

Finally she said, "Do you want some wine with this?"

"No. Thanks."

"Sure?"

He nodded.

She pointed her fork at the empty bottles lined against the wall. "Did you drink all those?"

"Over a period of time."

"Oh, great. I'm glad you didn't drink them all at once. Like what period of time are we talking about?"

Wiley thought about it. "I don't know. I don't keep track of every drink."

"That's the trouble with living alone," she said, as if she knew.

"I guess."

"So how come you didn't marry Monique, anyway?" She gave him a quick sidelong look.

"Monique? Come on. She would have laughed me out of town if I'd even mentioned the subject."

"I thought she was nuts about you."

He shook his head.

"Well, I sure thought she was."

"She wasn't."

"O.K., then, what about Lynn?"

"That was crazy, that whole thing with Lynn. I don't even want to talk about Lynn."

"She was pretty spoiled."

"It wasn't her fault. It just got crazy."

"I didn't like her. She was so sarcastic. I was glad when you split up." Alice bit into a piece of bread. "So who are you seeing now? Some married woman, I bet."

"Why would you think that?"

"We haven't met anyone since Monique. So. You must have somebody under wraps. The Dark Lady."

"I wish you wouldn't try to act sophisticated."

She colored but said nothing.

"Do you really think I'm conducting some great love affair?"

"I figured you must have somebody." She sounded bored. She was studying his face. "Boy, those guys really did a job on you, didn't they?"

Wiley moved his plate to one side. "There was just one," he said. "Short fellow. No bigger than a minute."

"Oh. Mac told me two. 'Two of our dusky brethren,' was what he said. Where did he get that stuff?"

"From me," Wiley said.

And then, because he trusted her and felt the need, he began to tell her what had really happened to him the night before. Alice listened without any disgust or pity that he could see. She seemed purely interested. Now and then she laughed, because in talking about it Wiley could not help but make his little disaster into a story, and telling stories, even those about loneliness and humiliation, naturally brought out the hambone and wag in him. He could see she was having a good time listening to him, that this was something different for her, and not what she'd expected when Mac asked her to look in on him. And she was hearing some straight talk. She didn't get that at home. Mac was good-hearted, but he was also a tomcat and a liar.

Wiley's way of telling stories about himself was to tell them as if they'd happened to someone else. And from that distance he could see that there was something to be laughed at in the spectacle of a man who energetically professed the examined life, the life of the spirit and the mind, getting drunk and brawling over strange women. Well, the body had a mind of its own. He told it like that, like his body had abducted him for its own low purposes, like he'd been lashed to the back of a foaming runaway horse hell-bent on dragging him through every degradation.

But it was not on the whole a funny story. When he told Alice what went on in his class that morning she shook her head and looked down at the table.

"I was speechless," he said. "I couldn't say a thing. We do *Native Son*, we do *Invisible Man*, I get them really talking, really thinking about all this stuff, and then I start a race riot in my own classroom."

"Maybe you should tell them the truth."

"Are you serious?"

"They'd respect you for it."

"Hah!"

"Well, they should."

"Come on, Alice."

"Some of them would. And they'd be the right ones."

Wiley shook his head. "It would get all over school. I'd get fired."

"That's true," Alice said. She rested her cheek on her hand. "Still."

"Still what?" When she didn't answer, he said, "All right, let's say I don't care about getting fired. I do, but let's just hypothetically say I go in there tomorrow and tell them everything, the works. You know what they'll think? They'll think I'm making it up—the second story, not the first. You know, out of bleeding-heart sentimentality, to make the black kids feel better. But what'll really happen, they'll end up feeling worse. Condescended to. Insulted. They'll think I'm lying to protect them, as if they were guilty. Everyone will think I'm lying."

Wiley could see her hesitate. Then she said, "But you won't be lying. You'll be telling the truth."

"Yes, but no one will know it!"

"You will. You will know it."

"Look. Alice." Wiley was angry now and impatient. He waited, and then spoke so that his anger would not show. He said, "I feel terrible. I can't even count all the things I've done wrong today. But I did them. They're done. If I try to undo them I'm going to make them worse. Not only for me, for those kids." This seemed logical to Wiley, and well and reasonably said.

"Maybe so." She was turning one of her rings nervously. She looked over at him and said, "Maybe I'm being simplistic, but I just don't see where telling the truth can be wrong. I always thought that's what you were there for."

Wiley had other arguments to make. That he was a teacher, and could not afford to gamble with his moral authority. That when the truth did more harm than a lie, you had to give the lie its due. That if other people had to suffer just so you could have a clean conscience you should accept your fallen condition and get on with it. They were good arguments, the very oil of adult life, but he said nothing. He was no fool, he knew what her answers would be, because after all they were his answers too. He simply couldn't act on them.

They sat there unhappily and then Alice got up and cleared the table. Wiley followed her to the kitchen. He stood in the doorway and watched her rinse the plates and stack them in the sink. When she finished she stayed leaning against the counter with her back to him. "Alice," he said. "Are you listening?"

She nodded.

"I shouldn't have dropped all this stuff on you. It's pretty confusing."

"I'm not confused."

He didn't answer.

"I have to go," she said.

He walked her to the door.

"I won't say anything to Mac," she told him.

"I know that. I trust you."

"What, trust me to keep secrets from my husband?" She laughed, not pleasantly. "Don't worry," she said. "I know how he is."

Wiley corrected essays the rest of the afternoon. He broke for dinner and then finished them off. It was a good batch, the best he'd had all year. They were on "Bartleby, the Scrivener." One of his students, a girl, had compared the situation to a marriage, with the narrator as the husband and Bartleby as the wife: "He looks at Bartleby the way men look at women, as if Bartleby has no other purpose on earth than to be of use to him." She bent the story around to fit her argument, but Wiley didn't mind. The essay was fresh and passionate. This particular girl wouldn't have thought to take such a view at the beginning of the year. Wiley was moved, and proud of her.

He recorded the grades in his book and then called the Filbert Street number of Dr. K. P. Newman. When she answered, he said, "It's me, Kathleen. From last night," he added.

"You," she said. "Where did you get my number?"

"Out of the phone book. I just wanted to set things straight."

"You called me before, didn't you?" she said. "You called me at work."

"Yes."

"I knew it. You didn't even say anything. You didn't even have the balls to give your own name."

"That was a joke," Wiley said.

"You're crazy. You call me again and I'll have the police on you."

"Wait, Kathleen. I need to see you."

"I don't need to see you."

"Wait. Please. Listen, Kathleen. I'm not like that, not like I seemed last night. Really, Kathleen. Last night was a series of misunderstandings. I just want to stop by for a minute or two, straighten everything out."

"What, you have my *address*?"

"It's in the book."

"Christ! I can't believe this! Don't even think about coming here. Mike's here," she said. "This time I won't stop him. I mean it."

"You aren't married to Mike."

"Who said?"

"You would have said if you were."

"So? What difference does that make?"

"It makes a difference."

"You're crazy."

"All I need is a few minutes to talk things over."

"I'm hanging up."

"Just a few minutes, Kathleen. That's all I'm asking. Then I'll leave, if you still want me to."

"Mike's here," she said. She was silent. Then, just before she hung up, she said, "Don't you ever call me at work again."

Wiley liked the sound of that; it meant she assumed a future for them.

Before he went out he looked himself over in the mirror. He wasn't pretty. But he could still talk. All he had to do was get her to listen. He'd keep saying her name. Kathleen. Say it in that moony broguish way she liked. Said that way, almost sung, her name had power over her; he had seen it last night, the willing girl blooming on the face of the woman, the girl ready for love. He would hit that note, and once he got her listening there was no telling what might happen, because all he really needed was words, and of words, Wiley knew, there was no end.

Nominated by David Jauss

POPULATION

by MARK HALLIDAY

from TASKER STREET (University of Massachusetts Press)

Isn't it nice that everyone has a grocery list
except the very poor you hear about occasionally
we all have a grocery list on the refrigerator door;
at any given time there are thirty million lists in America
that say BREAD. Isn't it nice
not to be alone in this. Sometimes
you visit someone's house for the first time
and you spot the list taped up on a kitchen cabinet
and you think Yes, we're all in this together.
TOILET PAPER. No getting around it.
Nice to think of us all
unwrapping the new rolls at once,
forty thousand of us at any given moment.

Orgasm, of course, being the most vivid example: imagine
an electrified map wired to every American bed:
those little lights popping
on both sides of the Great Divide,
popping to beat the band. But
we never beat the band: within an hour or day
we're horny again, or hungry, or burdened with waste.
But isn't it nice not to be alone in
any of it; nice to be not noticeably responsible,
acquitted eternally in the rituals of the tribe:
it's only human! It's only human and that's not much.

So, aren't you glad we have such advanced farm machinery,
futuristic fertilizers, half a billion chickens
almost ready to die. Here come the loaves of bread for us
thup thup thup thup for all of us thup thup thup
except maybe the very poor
thup thup
and man all the cattle we can fatten up man,
there's no stopping our steaks. And that's why
we can make babies galore, baby:
let's get on with it. Climb aboard.
Let's be affirmative here, let's be pro-life for God's sake
how can life be wrong?
People *need* people and the happiest people are
surrounded with friendly flesh.
If you have ten kids they'll be so sweet—
ten really sweet kids! Have twelve!
What if there were 48 pro baseball teams,
you could see a damn lot more games!

And in this fashion we get away
from tragedy. Because tragedy comes when someone
gets too special. Whereas,

if forty thousand kitchen counters
on any given Sunday night
have notes on them that say
I CAN'T TAKE IT ANY MORE
I'M GONE, DON'T TRY TO FIND ME
you can feel how *your* note is
no big thing in America,
so, no *horrible* heartbreak,
it's more like a TV episode,
you've seen this whole plot lots of times
and everybody gets by—
you feel better already—
everybody gets by
and it's nice. It's a people thing.
You've got to admit it's nice.

Nominated by Tony Hoagland, Lloyd Schwartz, David Wojahn

THE BUTCHER

fiction by MICHAEL BENDZELA

from NORTH AMERICAN REVIEW

I WOULD SNATCH A chicken off its perch and hold it upside down by its claws and stretch its neck out till it stopped flapping. I was still little, eight or nine, when my grandma showed me how to do it. I learned how to scald it so the feathers come off easy and to take a hatchet to its neck. I could gut it pretty good because I had little hands then which fit into the opening. I didn't need to be mean or cruel, just skillful and calm. The sadness of it was easy to get over.

I moved on to trout and largemouth bass, skinning them with pliers, filleting them with a hunting knife right near the lake, burying the remains in the woods. I picked off squirrels with my .22 and left their blood and entrails in washtubs. Later, when kids caught me dissecting a cat and ran away screaming, I gained a bad reputation. I had nothing against cats—they were always sick strays anyway—I was just curious to see how much they were like the squirrels and the fish and the chicken.

By the time I was a teenager, I had cut into just about every kind of animal you can find in the state, turning things inside out to look for I didn't know what, whatever I could find, I guess. I didn't raise hell or go out for sports or chase girls like other boys my age, I spent my time in the old tool room in the barn where I had set up a place I could keep things in, birds and snakes and mice put up in jars of an embalming solution I made myself, skunk and raccoon and woodchuck pelts mounted on a board and labeled. The other kids didn't get it, they'd come in to see what I was doing and laugh and look at each other. I dreamed at night of meeting other boys like me in the back of the barn, where I would pin them down on their backs until they smiled and gave up. Then I would pierce through that which kept our bodies a secret from each other. The boys would wiggle the way an earthworm wiggles between your fingers while you're baiting the hook.

When I turned sixteen I dropped out of school and got a job on a farm in the next town. I thought I knew how to handle a knife, so I just walked into the Gagnons' place and asked if they were looking for help. If you drove by their place you would never know what went on there, just a little barn off the road, the shingles weathered black and a lean-to just about fallen down, but if you drove out back you would see the old oildrums full of plastic bags bulging with guts and bones. Mr. Gagnon said he would try me out for a while and put his boy Rick in charge of me, and even though Rick said the job was a snap, he proceeded to show me just how much I didn't know.

Rick's father did most of the killing himself, but sometimes Rick helped him. The rest of us did the cutting. Some of Rick's sisters worked there, running the books and cleaning, mostly, but when it got busy in the fall they pitched in with the sawing and cutting and grinding. We would all line up at the long block table, drawing our knives on the wand to keep them sharp, and jaw and joke around while we portioned up lamb, venison, pork, even moose once. If someone made a bad joke Rick would say, Oh you really cut me up, but no one would laugh because it was old.

Rick let me learn on a buck he got that fall, which right away I thought was real nice of him. He told me how to make certain cuts and it made sense to me. I thought of it as being kind of like cleaning those squirrels, only blown up by a big magnifying glass. That moose we did—they were rare in our part of the state and hunted only by lottery—it was like a whole wall of meat and bone, a cavern, really, so you thought you could crawl up inside it on a frigid night and huddle it around you.

Business would wind down in winter, with deer season over and everyone's freezers stocked up for the holidays and the long haul till mud season, so I got to work alone with Rick. He was a few years older than I was and long out of school, so he put in full time while I usually took up the slack when someone on the crew had another job or kids to meet at home after school. Rick and I worked well together—we were both lefties. I cut with him for hours and told dirty jokes and watched the snake tattoo flex on his arm. We still had gutted deer hanging in big scarlet Vs in the cooler, a lot of work, but with Rick around time always seemed to go by too fast.

He wore the same faded jeans and thermal undershirt every day, but they were always clean when he came into the shop— the apron kept most of the gore off and he washed his clothes every couple of days. While he was showing me how to use the bandsaw I noticed that his fingernails were white as new moons. He always was shaved and he kept his wiry black hair slicked back. He wore biking boots, an old pair that he kept oiled, his jeans tucked into the tops of them, and whenever he walked away from me, all long-legged and butt flexing, I would have to look away. One day I was working along, cutting chops and trying to watch him out of the corner of my eye, when the blade ended up deep in the meat at the base of my hand near the thumb. I snatched my hand back and watched the blood just pour out, the pain increasing with each throb. Rick ran over and took me into the bathroom, where he fixed up a couple butterfly stitches and wrapped my hand in a towel to stop the bleeding. Then he gave me my first slug of whiskey and drove me in his truck to the hospital, a forty-minute drive away.

We didn't talk much, the towel slowly turning red along the way, then dark red, then dripping red. He got to watch as the doctor put the ten stitches in my hand.

On the way back, he said to me, We can't have you doing this all the time, now. I just smiled and looked at my bandage again. Then he said, Wastes too much gas.

I'd pop you if I didn't have this on, I said.

Promises, promises. All talk, no action.

Rick and I were wrapping cuts in wax-lined freezer wrap and taping them shut with masking tape and stamping the packages with the names of the cuts. It was wintry in the shop, even with the box stove in the office running wide open, and we were huddled together at the table, bumping arms and butts, elbowing each other to try to make each other mess up, cracking up. We were seeing who could wrap cuts the fastest. Rick's pile stacked up like presents under the Christmas tree, ugly presents, but with interesting shapes. I was falling behind in my wrapping because I couldn't stop laughing at the way he would toss yet another perfectly wrapped package onto his pile while mine kept coming out looking like someone had come along and opened them up and tried to tape them shut again.

What are we betting? he said. What do I get from you when I win?

I looked up at him. It hit me how we were alone in that shop and how when he grinned his eyes crinkled up and how his black eyebrows seemed to underline how good-looking he was. I had to look away.

What do you mean, *when?* I said.

We went through a whole bin of cuts and of course he had more packages in his pile. See, what'd I tell you, he said, taking the bin back to the cooler. I thought he would come right back with another bin full, but he was gone a long time. I finished boxing up what we'd done then went into the office to check the stove. I put a couple of more sticks in and put it in updraft then went to the cooler to see what Rick was up to.

I opened the dungeon-like door and called his name over the hum of the blower, but he didn't answer. I knew he had to be in there, so I went in and closed the door behind me. It wasn't very big, so if he was in there he had to have heard me calling him. I started to smile because I knew he was waiting for me.

I found him sitting in back with his apron off. He looked up at me while he was toking on a joint, and it was like he was looking right in and seeing for himself how I was feeling. Then he held the joint out to me and raised his eyebrows inquiringly.

All around us hung a few weeks' worth of work, the carcasses hanging as still as mountains in fog. I shivered and hugged myself. His father could walk in the barn at any time, yet he couldn't know Rick and I were in the cooler, the gasketed door sealing us off from the rest of the place. Rick blew out a cloud, and you couldn't tell whether it was smoke or fog. I took the joint from him and hit it.

Rick got up and began to pace and rub his hands together. In a few minutes my breath was coming fast and cloudy. I was breathing like a horse in winter. My eyes burned and my cheeks stung in the whistling cold. I looked at Rick and tried to swallow but couldn't.

You high yet, Bobby? he said.

I don't know.

You don't know? He came up to me with this stunned look on his face. You don't know? He poked me in the ribs and kept poking until he had me doubled-up against the wall.

Rick, man.

You don't know? Now he had both hands up under my shirt and they were icy cold as well as unbearably tickling. I dropped to my knees but I couldn't get away from his hands. He got on top of me, holding me down with his knee. I began to wail, but his rough, cold hand was right at my mouth, holding it in. I tried to turn my head away and arched my back, but he held me tightly by the jaw, his other hand still digging my ribs, his knee crushing my thigh. I was in tears now and didn't try to scream. He reached higher under my shirt, found my nipple, pinched it hard. I found flesh with my teeth and began to bite down—he let me.

During a cold snap that year Rick and I somehow ended up in his pickup, the back full of four-foot logs to weigh it down, up an abandoned road behind his father's farm. We got out with our pump-action shotguns and began stalking the scrub near the frozen brook. The wind blew needles into our faces and wreathed the base of each tree out there with a dune. The afternoon sun shone straight at our backs, our long blue shadows stretching out from our feet to the snowy distance. Rick was pissy that day for one reason or another. When he got like that I would just hang out with him and not say a word. He somehow made it clear that he was tolerating me. The fact was, since that time in the cooler in the shop, we were hung up on each other and we didn't know what to do about it.

We were having a bad day, and not because it was a bad day for hunting, though it was cold out. The weekend before, both of us got our limit in rabbits.

Rick was taller than me and could walk through the snow drifts quicker. He knew it, and kept ahead of me all day, acting like he didn't care if I could keep up with him. Somehow I knew that he knew he was tearing me up inside. I watched the back of his black-haired head all afternoon and all I could think of was raising my gun and pumping him full of shot. I was exhausted and hung my head during the whole hunt.

A rabbit began to dart back and forth up ahead of Rick. He fired twice and missed both times. Then he turned on a tree and emptied his magazine into it. Bark and wood chips exploded out and dirtied the snow all around the tree. The roar hurt my head. He got out all he couldn't say to me, then stalked back toward the truck with his gun. I trudged back through the snow with him, following in his tracks.

It was a little more relaxed once we got back to his dad's house. No one was home and we walked around in our wool socks, drinking coffee and smoking a joint. We had the kitchen stove cranked—you could hear the draft roaring up into the clear sky—and we had a window wide open so we could blow the smoke out into the cold. We still weren't talking, and being high seemed to lengthen and intensify our silence, and yet also to soften it and make it seem natural.

We went into the living room and sat wasted in front of the TV while the room slowly went dark. When the windows had all turned black, Rick pushed himself up out of his chair and said he had to go take a piss.

The TV show had ended and he hadn't come back yet. I got up and stretched my hands toward the ceiling, my blood looping through my body, then walked around the house, not making a sound in my wool socks.

I found him in the bathroom, standing shirtless at a sink full of steaming water, the mirror in front of him white with steam. My groin flinched as if from an attempted kick. Rick had a steel straight razor in his hands, his dad's antique one with the ivory handle.

He rubbed a hole into the steam on the glass in front of him and saw me there standing behind his shoulder in the mirror, and I saw that half of his face was lathered up.

You getting ready for bed already? I asked.

Rick just stood back and began stropping the razor on a strip of leather hanging near the sink. When he was done he looked up and his eyes touched mine in the mirror.

Come over here, he said.

I noticed he had the razor in his right hand. He reached up with his left to stretch out the skin of his cheek. I went up behind him, keeping my eyes on him in the mirror as the straight edge cut into the lather. With short, curving strokes of the razor, he shaved his cheek clean, the skin reddening slightly. He twisted his mouth to the side to work on his chin, then lifted it to scrape his neck, the steel making a singing, scratching sound the whole time. In a couple of downstrokes, the right half of his mustache disappeared. Perfect, no blood. We both stood there a moment, stoned, looking at his half-shaved face in the mirror.

He swished the razor in the hot water and put it aside to towel off the shaved half of his face. Then he picked up his dad's shaving brush, twirled it in the soapy mug, and began painting the other half of his face with it. He looked out at me from the mirror and for the first time almost smiled. When he was done soaping up he put the brush aside, then picked the razor back up and held it out to me behind his shoulder.

You try it now, he said.

I squeezed in beside him at the mirror. I leaned into the glass to look closely at my face. I passed my hand over my cheeks and chin—bare, almost fuzzless. I wasn't afraid of using a straight razor, I was just embarrassed at not having much to shave. I wasn't like him, who grew a black shadow on his face every day. I just shook my head.

Why not?

I can't.

What do you mean, you can't?

I don't have a beard yet.

He just breathed out and shook his head. Then he grabbed me by the wrist and put the pretty ivory handle between my fingers.

No, me, he said, I want you to shave me.

I just looked him up and down in the mirror and swallowed. Half his face in suds, the other half naked. Curly black hairs swirling up his chest right up to his neck. Nipples tiny, brown. The rest of him falling out of reach of the mirror.

Why? I said.

Because I want you to.

I turned the sparkling steel in my hand, stared at the trademark, *Boston, Mass.*

You ain't scared, are you?

No.

Then prove it. He stuck his chin out like he was daring me to hit him.

I turned and looked at him. I put my arm on his shoulder and leaned toward him until I could smell the soap. Using the small finger of my shaving hand, I turned his head ever so gently to the side.

I was shaking a little bit, but I never cut him. I had to swish some of the hair and soap off the razor, and as I did so I saw his Adam's apple moving up and down in the mirror. He glanced down to the side. I finished shaving his chin, then he made a long face so I could get at the hairs on his upper lip. Tears came to his eyes as I scraped the whiskers off. He smiled big at me when I was finished, like he was real proud of me. As I was cleaning off the razor in the now lukewarm water, he turned and put his hot mouth against my neck.

So that's how it was with Rick and me. He moved off his father's farm a little while later to live with his girlfriend. I quit the job at the shop because I wanted to go north and see what it was like. I wandered around, not doing much, driving trucks for a small logging company until I got laid off, laboring at construction sites. I never stayed put long enough to make many friends. I didn't know what I wanted.

When I wandered back home a few years later I didn't look Rick up and was sorry I didn't. He ended up killing himself, you see, so now I have to carry him around inside like scar tissue. I couldn't go to the funeral, I just couldn't. Everyone talked about how they just didn't get it, they never figured him for it, wasn't it a shame.

The only other time anything hurt me so bad was when I was twelve, when one night there was a knock at our door real late.

Who the hell's that? Dad said, and when he opened the door— Mom was afraid to—there was a guy standing out there with eyes like post holes. This horrible sound was coming in behind him.

It ran right out in front of me, the guy kept saying as we followed him out to the road.

Mom kept saying Oh my God and held her hands over her face. Dad told her to go back into the goddamn house and call the vet right away. The one remaining headlight on the guy's pickup was trained on our mare lying in the road, screaming, the glare poking right up into her open mouth. She looked all eyes and teeth. She looked like somebody else's horse. She kept trying to put herself upright on her front legs but kept falling back and screaming. All Dad and I could do was stroke her until the vet would arrive. She was breathing hard and moaning, like she used to do when she was foaling. She struggled, and one time she threw her head suddenly and almost caught me in the face.

Where the hell is he? Dad yelled. Mom said he was on his way, she had gotten him out of bed. Fuck it, Dad said, and ran back to the house for his rifle.

Nominated by Mary Peterson

COLEMAN VALLEY ROAD

by GERALD STERN

from BLACK WARRIOR REVIEW

This is where I had my sheep vision,
in the brown grass, under the stars.
I sat there shivering, fumbling with my paper,
losing tobacco. I was a spark at the most,
hanging on to my glasses, trying to hide
from the wind. This is how I bent

my head between my knees, the channels and veins
pumping wildly, one leg freezing, one leg
on fire. That is the saxophone
and those are the cymbals; when it gets up here
the roar of the waves is only a humming, a movement
back and forth, some sloshing we get used to.

That is my cello music and those are my headlights
making tunnels in the grass; those are
the clouds going down and those are the cliffs going out.
I am reaching up. I think I have
a carp's face, I have a round nose
and a large red eye and a ragged white moustache.

The strings are stretched across the sky; one note
is almost endless—pitiless I'd say
except for the slight sagging; one note is
like a voice, it almost has words, it sings
and sighs, it cracks with desire, it sobs with fatigue.
It is the loudest sound of all. A shrieking.

Nominated by Len Roberts

CLUMSY GUYS

by TOMAŽ ŠALAMUN

from WILLOW SPRINGS MAGAZINE

The woman is crying like a dragon because I'm a poet. No
wonder. Poetry is a sacred machine, a lackey of
an unknown deity who is killing as if by conveyor
belt. How many times I'd be
dead, if I hadn't kept cool, taken it easy and
been completely arrogant, so I can with my own instrument
blot my
wings out. Fly, fly ahead, sacred
object, that's not me, I am reading
The Times and drinking coffee with workers in blue
coveralls. They too could easily
kill themselves when they climb a pole and fix up
electricity. Sometimes they do. Poets frequently
kill themselves. They scribble on a piece of paper
I have been killed by too strong a word,
my vocabulary did this to me. So don't tell me these guys
aren't clumsy. You find them in all
professions. Any pedestrian can
kill himself if he doesn't know what
a crosswalk is.

                                    translated by Sonja Kravanja

nominated by Genie Chipps

AN ISLAND NOTEBOOK

by ALISON DEMING

from THE GEORGIA REVIEW

July 15

Today the water is glass, barely a ripple to disrupt the view so wide I swear the horizon describes the earth's great curve. The bay changes daily, its surface reworked by the wind and currents. It can be a dappled tweed, or riled up and spiked with whitecaps, or this liquid mercury so smooth and viscous a seiner cuts a gentle mile-long wake, one line of the V bending nearly into an S as it meets an opposing current. One could make a vocation of studying the patterns and find it less routine than most jobs. On the margin, Swallowtail Lighthouse turns its eye out into the dusk, scans back over the brush weir staked offshore below the spruce-topped cliffs. The structure is graceful and it works to catch the abundant herring which have made many islanders rich. On one of the adjacent even smaller islands there are three millionaires. I learned this from a birdwatcher I met there who had set down his tripod in the wild caraway to look for the puffins or razorbill auks which frequent the outlying rocks. He had once studied botany and knew the scientific names of several local species. An investment broker in St. John, who owns a share in The Mumps—a large double weir staked near the harbor—so I had reason to trust his authority on the matter.

In front of our cottage there's a road, for many years the only tarred one on fifteen miles of rock, spruce, and balsam. There are five villages strung along the eastern side of the island. Cars

444

race back and forth between them. Someone delivers an old rocking chair to his brother, brings her husband to work on the fisherman's wharf, calls at the nursing home or runs up to North Head to meet the ferry. I've wished for years the road wasn't there, since I come here to get calm and clear. But it's the compromise required to return year after year to just this view. And there are quiet places—almost everywhere else but the house is quiet enough that I can hear the breeze chafe the August-dry stalks of grass, water lick the rocks, or mackerel boil in shallow water as they are pursued toward shore by feeding dolphins. What I know of the place after thirty-five years of returning is that it engenders a state of mind like no other. The experience is a species in danger of being lost.

The first year I was eight, and my family had read a magazine article about budget vacations. The Finger Lakes. Cayman Islands. Grand Manan. Before that we'd gone for our two weeks to Nantucket and rented a house named Little Nest. My father fished for crabs in a tidal stream, and my mother indulged me by driving to the bayside where I could wade and collect the golden Pandora shells. My brother caught poison ivy, preferred the surf, and fought with someone every day—until he cried out for help, lodged up in a tree, a stick embedded in his eyeball. When that island got too crowded and too expensive (the two so often occur simultaneously), we went farther north. Going north simplifies things—fewer people, fewer industries, fewer comforts. I remember driving through an eternity of spruce, miles of it burned black and skeletal. I remember the car getting searched at the border and losing an hour. I remember having lunch across the street from a branch of the Hudson's Bay Company while we waited for the ferry to load our Studebaker with a sling and a winch. I remember knowing I was very far from home.

July 24

This morning Lester, my neighbor, shows up. It's his week off from Coastal Transport—the ferry terminal at North Head—so he has time for the side jobs that keep him equipped with a new pickup and ATV. Workers on the island answer to the schedule of season and tide. In June, men stitch twine onto the weir stakes;

445

July and August, they go out seining—do it at 3 A.M. if that's when the tide is right. By September, women clean smoked herring at the boning tables, pack ten pounds of the leathery strips in each wooden crate. At neap tide the unemployed pick periwinkles and dulse, an edible purple seaweed which is dried crisp in the sun. A few punch the clock of government jobs—fisheries, post office, liquor stores. And the ferry. But island time—work time—is a neighborly joke. If Lester says he'll be here next week to do the job, that means sometime in the next three months. Then, there he'll be—7 A.M.—leaning his ladder against the bedroom window of this poor, sleeping vacationer and singing like a meadowlark.

Today, replacing the cedar shingles on the south side of our cottage, he sets loose a handful of bats which have been nesting in the eaves. Fur plush as a seal's, little pink triangle of mouth rimmed with saw-blade teeth, legs doing double duty as stays in their wings. Brown skin silky, translucent. They shriek from the light, then fall dormant as if it's a toxin, scrambling lamely to hide under the heap of rotted shingles or slither under the sill into the cellar. As more tumble down from the staging, I scoop them onto a shingle and flick it to set them flying. They don't go far, falling drugged into the raspberry patch. "I'd kill them for you," says Lester, "except they eat their weight in black flies in a day." They keep screeching from their hiding places as I get near—the parents and some young ones, we figure, and they don't like the looks of me. Lester hammers and sings "Once more with feeling, then let's call it an afternoon."

The bats have lived here for generations—far longer than I've been coming. In the evening they'd wake up, zipping faster as the dark deepened, their flight patterns erratic and voracious. They drove my cat crazy. And they charmed one older couple who rented the cottage. Instead of cocktails, they had the bats at the end of the day, setting the porch chairs out on the lawn where they could watch them comb the air, the woman often walking among them, letting them swirl around her head. I hated to tell them that I'd evicted the tenants, but the shingling project left no choice. Leave the wood to rot, the process enhanced by composting batshit, or rout them out and repair. Their young have been raised here year after year. It's been a peaceful place, people in the house for only a few months. Every choice is a loss. I will miss them.

July 26

9:15 A.M. The phone rings. It's Ann. "We finally got our good day!" We agree on the 11:30 boat to White Head Island, a free mailboat that runs the half-hour passage; once a skow lashed to a seiner, it's now a proper ferry capable of carrying a dozen cars. The skow's gone and so is most of the white head—granite blasted out last summer to build a breakwater and extend the fishermen's harbor. In years to come tourists will ask why they call it White Head, and people will forget the reason. They'll call it Breakwater Island or Broken Head. At least here the progress is slow.

The smokehouses are working. Racks of glistening herring hang, dripping golden oil, the meat browning in the controlled heat of a sawdust fire. A few miles offshore a huge Russian factory ship, rumored to employ three hundred men on board, lies at anchor processing the catch through day and night, diesel exhaust clouding its air. There's no lack of market this year. We bike past the harbor to where the asphalt peters out into a gravel road, and from there to the great smile of an empty sand beach on the island's backside.

Ann and Mike are summer people. Recidivists like myself. Retirement and the physical concessions of aging haven't deterred them from loving the remote places. Every winter they camp in the Anza-Borrego desert, and summers they come here, Ann swimming daily into the ocean off one stony beach or another, though the water is chilled by the Labrador Current year round. It's her daily communion. Berrying is Mike's. He keels on arthritic legs, grazing into the patches with two containers slung by strings around his neck (one for wild raspberries, the other for gooseberries), wading into the sweetness that takes over the border zones between spruce woods and human habitation. He could die in the berries, I think, and it would be a short fall from there into timelessness. It's not greed that keeps him knee-deep in the tangled canes for days on end. Half the time he picks to give them away, going down to the fisherman's pier at evening and coming back with a whole flounder or pollock, next day repaying the

447

debt with a quart of red raspberries. Any bramble of the beauties is fair game, though sometimes a landowner barrels out to warn Mike he's on private land. And he'll say, "Well, gee, these berries are ready and no one's picking them. I'll give them to you—I just pick for the pleasure of picking." It's his meditation—centering on the moment of ripeness, here and here and here.

After a picnic lunch, Ann and I hike back to the bog lake to swim, our feet sponging into the deep sphagnum of the trail. The water is a clear, rusty tea—contaminated only with tannin, a clean vegetable compound, astringent, which closes skin wounds and invigorates the pores. The bog is a primeval place inhabited by carnivorous sundews, their spatulate leaves rimmed with red glandular hairs each topped with a bead of clear sap for enticing and trapping the prey. Minuscule orchids and pitcher plants.

Ann and I strip down, wade into the sandy mahogany muck until we can slip our whiteness into the perfect cool and glide to the center of the pond, floating on our backs to admire the fringe of cattail reeds that glistens on shore. Mike's gone off for the gooseberries which favor the gritty soil beside the gravel road.

July 29

I used to think I loved the island for its wildness—the transcendentalist's dream of a place so wild that by virtue of its wildness it's more civilized. Human culture here fascinates as much as nature, the way the place and its people are as much one thing as form and content in a painting by Paul Klee.

A woman moved here from Toronto after making documentaries, traveling to China and Russia, and stopping people on the streets of New York to ask what they dream about, what they wish for. A *farm*, so many of them said, and they could picture the color of the bedroom curtains.

Gleason Green, who at ninety-two can recite Robert Service poems and anonymous ballads. "That reminds me of a story," he says, stroking his palm, his eyes rolling up, the slurring cadence of his island accent a sweet transport back in time. "Some men came down from Newfoundland to sell fish. We asked them what their lives were like. Hard, they said. They traded seals for flour, sugar, and clothes." Then he ricochets off into another story—

"You know what a serenade is?"—telling how at a wedding party they used to blast off shotguns and dynamite caps outside the window. Once some guy blew his hand apart—but it was still a funny story. No elegy. Just the way it was. With a little encouragement, he tells how the Chrysler Corporation invited him to Detroit to tour the plant after he'd bought over three hundred motors for custom-built fishing boats. He used to make charter runs out to Kent and Machias Seal Islands, cooking up chowder and blueberry pie on board for the tourists. He earned a slot in *Reader's Digest*—"My Most Unforgettable Character." Twenty years later he still gets a few fan letters each month.

My father tells the story about a logging company coming to the island offering the men wages of $5 an hour, rain or shine, when they were lucky to make a dollar an hour for fishing. The company proposed to log off the island's balsam and spruce—a forest that sprawls over the majority of its interior. A meeting was called. The locals asked the company officials to give them half an hour alone in which to make their decision. Their answer—"If there's fish we'll catch them, and if there aren't we won't." The forest remains except for a few building lots, areas thinned out from harvesting weir stakes, and an unsightly gouge cut for the new airstrip which looks like a barber's mistake.

The airport is progress, of course, and the people wouldn't have allowed it unless they were certain it would benefit the island: provide a faster market for the salmon being raised in experimental aquaculture; lure back the Japanese market for sea urchins, beach dross which for a few years had turned into VCRs and Camaros; bring relatives home for the weekend and get the ailing off to medical care. Still, it's hard for anyone who's seen her hometown overtaken by malls, or his farm broken down into a trailer park—or worse, for its pretense of "value," a gaggle of condominiums—not to look on the airstrip with a fearful eye. Even the innkeepers agree they don't really want any more tourists.

The sling-and-winch car ferry to Grand Manan is gone. No doubt it was a deterrent to the more frivolous travelers, being a refitted mine sweeper from the Second World War. And to witness one's precious means of conveyance, loaded with the family's vacation cache, get hoisted by a derrick over the side of a pier was not everyone's idea of a relaxing getaway. The newer ramped vessel—

the *Grand Manan III*—instead of embarking from the genteel tourist town of St. Andrews, leaves the New Brunswick mainland from Black's Harbour. It's a working-class village, home of Connors' Brothers—The World's Largest Sardine Industry, or so boasts the only billboard in town. Identical cheap small houses, Connors' School, Connors' IGA, and most likely Connors' graveyard. There's no lunch counter here. Just a takeout trailer at the end of a dead-end road where travelers can buy strong tea and a greasy fish sandwich while waiting for the ferry to arrive. For those who live here, the landscape surrounding the town must offer consolation for the limits of daily life: the deep cove speaking of shelter at sea, as stands of balsam and blue spruce do on shore. The view out to the expanding channel and the uninhabited islets called The Wolves speaks the language of daydreams. Clusters of goldenrod harbor sleeping bees, apparently tranquilized by gorging on pollen.

Part of our family story about the place is that when you get on board and the ferry slips out into the channel, you leave your problems behind, see them drop away with the view of the mainland. This year, while the scenery fell into the distance, a woman twenty years younger than I came up the diamond-plate steel stairway from the car deck to the lounge, her unresponsive feet lifted one by one by her sister who walked behind and below. Two men lifted the wheelchair over a foot-high lip of steel until she was situated for the two-hour boat ride. I wondered, how did it happen, how long has she been that way, will she always remain so? How is it different to be young and have the body uncooperative, as opposed to being my father, who is struggling at eighty-four to recover from a major stroke? This new-formed constellation of nature, limitation, and decline all circling in my mind—this learning to live not with hope or despair but with what is. The obligation to survive.

August 1

Hiking the Red Trail from Whale Cove to Ashburton Head. I follow the cliff line, watching the cloud bank thicken and rile up the Bay. The wind carries the perfume of balsams, released when the bud caps are forced off by the pale fists of new growth. Tattered drapes of gray moss hang from the foggy evergreens. Below, fish schools swarm in the clear water, moving as birds do, as if with one mind, the shape of their society forming, deforming, and re-forming as fluidly as clouds or a symphony. I don't want to see a single person today. Want no human gabble to clutter my wave-lengths, want only to experience myself in relation to a place, to natural forces, to this molded sheet of paper the wasps have made—chewing up cellulose and spitting it out to build their hive. Handmade paper—the kind a few haiku could be penned on. I'm grateful for the invention of paper that allows me to chew experience and spit out a structure I can live with. But get a human being in the act and too often the enterprise inflates. I remember reading that a paper manufacturer once developed a fine-grade stationery by appropriating the muslin in which ancient mummies had been wrapped.

Fireweed. Boneset. Pearly everlasting. Wildflowers thriving in a pool of light opened by a fallen spruce. The trail is rough, the ground spongy. A matted heath. There are ancient plants—horsetails (tiny versions of a Carboniferous period tree) and delicate Indian pipes (waxy white saprophytes also known as ghost flowers). And somewhere in these woods there is no doubt a plant just evolving to which no one has affixed a name.

August 5

Saturday. 9 A.M. The Farmer's Market. A half-court lot with a rusted hoop, located between the old town hall and a closed movie theater—both now used mostly for rummage sales. Two pickups selling fresh garden produce, others selling hand-knit sweaters, quilts, framed color photos of the island, lemon-meringue tarts, oat-bran bread, and used books. I get my week's quota of greens, consider Ellmann's biography of Yeats and a collection of Leonard Cohen's poetry. A well-dressed couple sit on a prefab park bench stroking guitars and singing hymns. At the other end of the parking lot, Harry Green, a gaunt dulse-picker and winner of some backwater songwriter-of-the-year award, stands beside a display of cassettes, his expression ghostly intent while the tape plays out his life story.

451

Bud Brown, a rugged oak of a fisherman and childhood friend, gives me a nod. He says everything's gone downhill since the kids brought home a black cat two years ago—no herring in Brown's Weir, and the Maine Pearl Company which used to buy scales from him has shut down, overstocked, for the year. He doesn't even take his pumper out when they go to tend the weir. The Russian factory ship hasn't helped him. The Mumps is making millionaires. But the Mystery Weir isn't worth a trip out. Why do they call it that, I ask, because it's a mystery what they'll pull out of there? Could be, he says, or else it's a mystery how so many families have lived on it all these years. Ownership of the weirs, like the old whalers, is by shares. And while the method is ancient—handed down from the Micmac and Passamaquoddy who built brush traps along the shore—the expense is a risky contemporary proposition. A family can invest $20,000 in building a weir and make nothing for five years running. Then, if the herring run right and the market's good, in a day they can pay off the weir, the car, and the mortgage.

Bud thinks there are twice as many tourists this year and it will be worse with the new ferry next year. We agree that's terrible. I can complain. I'm not a "tourist." I'm "summer people," since I've been coming here long enough to have childhood memories of the place and since our family refuses to sell off the little strip of woods we own, though we don't lack offers. It's our small act of island preservation. We come here for the pleasure of repetition, regular as rising and falling tides.

Most people come here once. The worse come for a day, drive the length of the island, sleep over, notch their belts, and head north to bag Prince Edward and Cape Breton. It takes years to properly visit the place. To know which bog ponds are good for skinny-dipping, where the wild blueberries ripen earliest, where the first gooseberries and the last wild raspberries. It takes years to notice a singular gull—one that dives like a cormorant, showing an evolutionary anomaly which may change the future of its species, or the fool gull so aggressive it never eats, constantly chasing its flockmates away from the feast of a seine-net drawn on shore to be cleaned and repaired. It takes years of lying still on the bluff at Swallowtail to know that tourists come, wonder briefly over the view, and go. It's not worth the effort of feeling invaded. The island is like poetry: most people don't have time for it.

Before we had the cottage, we stayed at an inn called Rose Cottage, where several families took room and board. We ate in a big old-fashioned dining room with tablecloths, homemade rolls, and a crank-up telephone. A family from Toronto had a daughter my age and son my brother's. We kids could walk anywhere— down the road or the trails—and islanders treated us like something special, inviting us in for a handful of crispy dulse. Evenings we'd run like wildcats through the hallways until it was time to settle on the floor beside a stove-size radio through which we could almost hear episodes of "Boston Blackie." There were outings to remote islands, lobster parties on the beach, and hikes to the Hole in the Wall, the Southern Cross, and the Flock of Sheep—formations of rock which on the California coast would be so commonplace as to go unnoticed. Here each was remarkable and worthy of pilgrimage.

We too had our singular status, as summer people and as Americans. Everyone knew our names and told stories about the things we'd done together last summer. Our cachet increased with adolescence, the sexual economy being defined by limited supply and exaggerated demand. There were wild, scary teenage times—the flip side of the island's religious propriety and repression. In the fifties, liquor wasn't sold and drinking was considered immoral. Our parents would place an order with the purser on the ferry, who brought back the precious bottles from the mainland for the ritual cocktail hour. The islanders, in response to the prohibition, drank in the binge-and-purge style, tumbling into fierce bouts of booze when it was available. Teenagers made home brew out of grape juice and got sickly drunk at beach parties and backwoods deer camps. My brother ran with a wild crowd, managed to convince the parents that it was legal in Canada for a sixteen-year-old to drive without a license. He and his buddies careened for weeks, wrecked a car or two before the Mountie caught up with him.

Sex had the same trigger-happy danger to it. By thirteen the guys were randy and ready to go, quickly gearing up into a passion that was all horsepower and no brakes. For the girls it was different. Scared and aroused, we'd play the edges of desire until we came to a boundary we weren't ready to cross. One time some half-lit men picked up my friend and me to give us a ride home. One took me in the back seat and the others said, "Give her a hickey!" I didn't know what it was, only that it was bad for a girl to get one and that they thought it was funny to try. I felt the danger then, and later with guys I dated—men who I knew could force themselves on a woman. But there were others who would take you to see the sunset night after night, and together you'd watch the boundary between day and night melt away.

August 6

Sunday. Rain. From the table I watch the ferry float in through the fog like a celestial ship through a cloud, its foghorn sounding the way to port. The point where Swallowtail perches has melted into white, and the music of rain—percussion, woodwind, reed— plays through the cottage. Rain beads on the freshly painted deck outside my window. I find it a pleasure to catch up with the disrepair, with nature's disregard for human beings—manifest in the moss and the cross-members of the deck rail, the moisture lifting paint in flakes off the railing, window trims, and door. Every two years the deck needs repainting; fifteen years and the roof gets reshingled. These are the facts. Language and reflection answer facts the way repair answers disrepair. Paint seals the surface of wood—the old stuff drinking in the thick liquid until surface cells are too full to take in the sea mist and the rain.

August 10

White Head, again. This time with Garry, who's come from his summer workplace on Swan's Island, Maine. It's always special to have a first-time visitor to the island, touring with him the remote landmarks: Dark Harbour, Beech Hill, Seal Cove Beach, Hay Point—places with names that describe them. And the visitors are duly impressed. Twice when my parents brought friends here for a weekend, they left owning a house. (That was when the houses cost less than an economy car.) The only friends who bother coming up here are ones charmed by the discomforts—no reservations for the ferry, no swimmable beaches, no bars or resorts, a network of trails fit primarily for sheep, the occasional

454

scent of wild roses, the more common and rank perfume of smoked herring as the road descends into one quaint village or another.

Garry and I walk the gravel road back to the bog pond. Someone has left a dinghy with oars on a patch of marsh grass. No one in sight. Why leave the oars if the owner doesn't want others to take the boat across? On the far side we find a slapdash bench— just a bunch of driftwood lumber stacked up on a small sphagnum peninsula. We sit, take turns casting the copper wobbler into the circles that ripple out and intersect on the tea-dark surface. Whatever is feeding isn't interested in our bait, but we stay and talk about islands, nature, and God.

He's lived in Hawaii, traveled islands of the South Pacific, and tells how Jehovah's Witnesses propagated their seed on one tropical island, how the natives would dress up in Western clothes to go to church. Up here it seems the smaller the island, the more churches thrive on it. The people are susceptible, he says, because of their isolation. Yes, and they're opened to omnipotence by their exposure to ocean and sky. The danger of working at sea.

The cattails glisten and sway, silver edged in the sun, their brown torches leaning slightly into the north. We talk about his growing up in Florida, where children regularly drowned or died of snakebite. Swimming in a bog pond would have meant risking an encounter with water moccasins. Here in the north not much in nature is dangerous—a few mushrooms and spiders whose scale and scarcity are such that they don't make a child afraid to go out. Yet fishermen die here every winter, as one of them told us—a man we met one evening at the Whistle who had brought his mother to watch the sunset. His last time, the boat was out for forty-two straight hours, weather tipping the vessel so you could walk up its sides. It filled with waves. There was nothing to do but ride out the storm . . . and, in his case, quit fishing.

Another friend, Stanley Small, lost his arm in a wringer while fishing one winter off Sable Island. Nine men in a boat, stuck in the ice for five days—he said they'd laugh one minute and cry the next, and weren't ashamed to say so. Quitting, even for him, wasn't easy. He saw things out there he couldn't believe. A phalanx of whales migrating, cruising the surface side by side; you could have stepped off the boat and walked a mile on their backs, he said, if you could stand the stench of their blowholes. Porpoises, column after column, a mile and a half long, arcing and diving in unison like a synchronized half-time show. Dolphins hitching rides for two days by resting their tails against the bow. How many men did he know who were lost at sea? He'd stopped counting at fifty-eight.

The wind has come up. The bog pond is choppy, and we row into gusts that want to drift us down into the cattail rushes. G. sizes up the resistance, redirects the boat into the lee, and rows us in a parabolic curve around the sheltered shore. I love that he understands the water, wind, and currents, taking the long way around to make things easy. Others would try to plough straight through, fighting the obvious all the way. But he's a painter and he's used to looking for what others haven't seen.

August 12

Saturday. 6 P.M. The fisherman's wharf. A seiner chugs out toward Long Island. A swarm of small seabirds races back and forth six inches over the water, scanning for feed. A pickup rips down to the end of the wharf, speakers blasting. A party beginning, it looks like, on a purse seiner named Rolling Stone. Four other teenagers sit in a subcompact car and circle the joint. Down in the green kelp-ridden harbor, along the creosote pilings of the breakwater, beer bottles bob and herring or tinker mackerel meander. Saturday night begins, and all night I'll hear the scream of their cars, the bass line of their cassette players booming down the road. It's how they claim their piece of adulthood—with noise and wildness and speed. How many years of it before they'll be attending a church supper on Saturday nights—Baptist or Wesleyan for the populists, Anglican for the elite?

August 13

I wake up dreaming of riding horses with my daughter. Sunday. Another dazzling day. Thinking of nature and young women, their bodies commandeered by reproductive chemistry before they realize they're sexual beings, their need to feel the harmony and power of their relationship with nature. In the sun-slick ocean this morning, over east, I see a smudge. As it approaches, a shape. It looks like a tugboat hauling a smoke-stacked crate. Not until it's even with the bell buoy at Swallowtail does it turn broadside so that I see its size: an oil tanker or barge. Might as well carry a plague flag from its masthead. This is the summer the Exxon *Valdez* stepped up the course of evolution in Alaska. If that had happened here, the island would be finished. People couldn't fish for ten years. The cliffs would be slimed with black oil, carcasses battered into the rocks. And just yesterday some of us were proud to claim that oil tankers don't come into the Bay of Fundy. What is it doing here? A ship in trouble? Great. It lumbers, with its prehistoric cargo, toward port.

I drive down to the wharf to find out it's only the *Irving Seal*—a smaller tanker, maybe fifteen carlengths—making its regular benign delivery of fuel to the island. The tug maneuvers the steel hulk up to the breakwater. A tug has always seemed to me to be a friendly boat, stout and tough like a workhorse. This one sports a yellow and black stack, kelly-green railings, Canadian and corporate flags. She breathes hard and deep, puffs black, nestles the behemoth into her berth. A winch swings out to the pier, men wrench open the pipeline that runs along it up to the white storage tanks on the hill. The first thing you see when the ferry slides into port is that cluster of giant fuel tanks. I never thought before how much depends on them, by what risks the island has earned its comforts. An umbilicus is hoisted over, clamped on, and the island takes its nutrient.

A purse seiner dawdles into port, riding low, its hold full of pollock and cod. Out on the intertidal zone an old rusted storage tank catches my eye. I think I see a grubby long-hair crouched there, leaning to take in the morning news. It's just a tire and some rockweed, though it became for a moment an apparition of the kid who two years ago paddled a canoe out into the riptide, he and his buddy both ripped for the Saturday revels, and didn't come back.

August 18

Last hike of the summer. The trail to Indian Beach edges a precipitous wall of basalt several hundred feet high, volcanic rocks crumbling down to rubble at the base, leveling off to a beach of rounded stones heaped with drifted logs. The woods are dense. Blackberry canes arch over the trail. I eat a handful of the juicy explosions, gather more along the way. The island is fifteen miles long and five wide, its western side inaccessible from the water except by the wooden dory which is sturdy enough to grind up onto the stone beaches. One dirt road cuts across to Dark Harbour, the only substantial break in the massive wall that makes up the western side. Legend has it that even the native people who paddled over from the mainland found the island bleak and inhospitable, suitable only for foraging gull eggs and gathering eels. Their name for it, according to one historian, was inconsequential—*Munanouk*—meaning "island in the sea" as distinguished from lake island, river island, or hill island. The same name applied to a number of islands off the North Atlantic coast.

Someone has released pheasants and wild turkeys to roam and multiply in these woods, but I don't encounter them today. Forty years ago the men had hunts on the island—so many points for an eagle, crow, crane. It was sport. A guy would come grinning out of the backwoods—See what I've got—with the birds dangling from his belt by their claws. I overheard one of the old-timers tell the story—and this: not one of them today wouldn't want to live it again. Not one of them that doesn't regret what he did.

The woods are active with breezes and bees, fields of maidenhair ferns, red squirrels shinnying in and out of a hollow pine. The chuff of a deer's heavy breathing as it leaps out of harm's way. Giant beech trees—the climax species—each claiming a wide circle of the sparse forest light, starving out the alders or spruce that might start below. How these beings live, what they perceive, what this landscape has learned of geology and natural history, I can't know. I strain to fathom the place, as if it has an awareness of its own to convey that will settle somewhere like seeds in my consciousness, feeding me when I'm sickened with despair at the limits of my own nature or those I love.

The cliff softens, the trail switchbacks down to Indian Beach where a few dulse shacks are planted on grapefruit-sized stones. Nets stretch out for drying the purple weed on the heated stones. Spiders race in and out of the interstices, another unlikely niche inhabited by entrepreneurial creatures. The spines of an old weir stand the watch offshore. It's not solitude I experience when alone here, but connectedness—the seawater that links continents and inconsequential islands, the seawater working in all living cells.

August 20

My last afternoon. I walk down to the stone beach across the road in front of the cottage. Dozens of blue-spangled dragonflies: do they migrate like butterflies or go dormant in the cold? Rocks worn so that their history is bald—a red one streuseled with lime green, a tawny neapolitan, black ones etched with precise white lines, a lightweight fist of motley lava, purple rocks smooth as a plum. This time I walk south where the stones get bigger, grapefruit sized, but don't cease to be miraculous—conglomerates of purple and turquoise, swirls of pink and gray, some baked with nuggets of green. No matter how many times I've been down here, I still find a half-dozen rocks unlike any other I've seen, and I have to lug the things up the hill to marvel over. That painter who makes the hyperreal rocks—I think that his paintings, as true as they are, are a lie. Because that work was done by nature, the forge of the elements subjected to pressure and heat, *that* work has already been done and his mere copying, though accurate, is slight. The wonder is that these things exist with no help from the human hand. I gather a bowlful as if they are fruit. The annual harvest.

Sunlight fractures down through the broken clouds, local shafts singling out first the lighthouse, then the lumpy cliff where it sits, next the yellow Anglican church in the village, then humps of rockweed-covered boulders, then the makeshift bench where I sit. That lava. The melted, layered, folded rocks. Interbedded sedimentary strata. A fault line cuts through the Castalia Bank nearby, exposing the most varied rocks on the island. They make the earth appear young and in process. Is the land still rising up from the earth's viscous mantle? Rising up from beneath more slowly than it wears down from above? Or is this a settled topography revealing more of its history than its process—as a person's face tells a history. I'm thinking of a woman, superficially religious, who has aged with such torment grained into her. She suffered two abusive, alcoholic husbands, both of whom died prematurely. She

459

believes her reward will be in the hereafter, and that the degree to which she suffers in life will set the measure of her bliss to come, so she wears her anguish with pride. I know a man whose face shows the lines of happiness with which he wakes every morning, whether he has slept poorly or hasn't a dollar to his name. Or myself, whose emerging age lines are a squint between the eyebrows and the bridge of the nose, because I keep straining to see things more clearly. That's how history is made, right down to the brain cells which physically change to incorporate a new memory—part of the process of shaping and holding which all nature practices.

I have located myself for another year. Coming back here satisfies the part of me that's ancient, some shred of stuff in me that's been handed down from one DNA strand to another for eons, descended from the migratory flocks and tribes who knew how to read the planet without a map. The seal's head I've been noticing for hours again slips out of the water to watch me. I click and call, and it seems to respond with its attention. Maybe if I sit here every day it will come closer. More likely we'll both wander off to inspect something new and more interesting. Few creatures have the patience to try and tame a human being.

Nominated by Philip Booth, John Daniel.

MONDAY HER CAR WOULDN'T START

by BÁRBARA SELFRIDGE

from PLOUGHSHARES

MONDAY HER CAR wouldn't start and Anita spent all day renting-a-wreck and driving like crazy to the hospital two hours away, and at five she arrived, and at five her father wasn't dead.

(It was the carburetor, she found out later.)

At five Anita's father was only dying: a man so pumped with fluid he'd gained forty pounds, a kidney-less man who'd stopped smelling like himself. At five her father wasn't dead, only dying, and he knew who she was.

Anita, who works as a nurse, climbed into her father's hospital bed beside him, and her brother, who'd already said so many false goodbyes, left. Anita's mother was stuck: a wife of thirty-five years who could do nothing but crank up the bed, cranking it up, cranking it down again.

("Should I have divorced him?" Anita's mother had asked her children. "Do you despise me for staying with your father for all these years?")

At five Anita's father still knew her, but he was a man making faces: horrible faces, as if all the work of drawing air into his lungs must be done by his face. And Anita lay next to him, whispering: "Let go. This body doesn't work anymore. Let it go."

(Anita had married that fall, partly to give her father the one last party to host, partly to cover her bulletin board with pictures of him giving her away.)

Maybe at the end, in his brain, there wasn't enough oxygen to find comfort in an afterlife or to reconsider euthanasia. And maybe then, in his chest, there wasn't enough muscle to be his heart.

(The heart, they said at the autopsy, was no more than a blown-up paper bag, a paper bag trying to pump blood.)

At six thirty Anita asked the nurse for more morphine. "For the pain," she said, but she knew as the nurse gave it that morphine right then might cause death.

"Why are you doing this?!" Anita's father whispered, sounding angry and hurt, and not possibly knowing.

Five minutes later he was dead. Five minutes later it was six thirty-five and Anita was lying in a hospital bed next to a man she couldn't recognize, a dead man who neither looked nor smelled like her father.

(For weeks she wore her father's clothes. "Here, smell this," she said. "It still smells like my father.")

At six thirty-five it was over, unmistakably gone, but at five Anita's father wasn't dead, only dying, and he knew who she was.

Nominated by Susan Moon, Josip Novakovich, Alberto Alvaro Rios

FRENCH HORN

by ROBIN BEHN

from THE IOWA REVIEW

The name, you might think,
if you're twelve, and you know,
is like those kisses

someone will do to you
if you're lucky and remember
to let him. But how far down

your body will he go?
There's something like entrails
about all this gaggle of tubing

like a hospital i.v.
or how someone in the textbook
jailed up Cleopatra's hair.

And launching out of silence
to hit just the right note
is next to impossible, and so, in this, it is like

kisses, also. In public this thing
should wear a dress over its guts
like the girls who are good at it—one

especially, born
with no right hand.
But you have to put your hand *in*

to mute it, or let it
moan . . . What our bodies
were suited for was an

increasing mystery,
which may be why we envied
her efficient, perfect flipper,

which somehow worked best for this
as if the same template of wind
around whose body the brass tubes

had formed, had formed
her body, so she belonged more
to the horn than

the other way around.
We could see it carrying her home from school,
we could see its bell blooming

in her sweet broad face, and of course
it made us jealous, how she retained
1st chair, how the band leader doted

on her for whom the centuries of hounds
must have bounded,
after which had galloped

the lord's most velvet page
with his second, keyless, exterior, piercing
and definitely most heavenly curled brass throat.

What was he thinking, that one without the gun
whom all the guns charged after?
What was he saying in the back of his mouth

that narrowed and loosened
at will around the source of breath and made
the fall air need him? Was he that much like a woman

he needed one like her
as if to know himself by the slight
mammalian difference of his hand

stroking hers? We imagined
her sleep, where we thought she must have worn it,
(we worried, too, *If I die before I wake . . .*)

her right "hand" still lodged
in that brass extravagance with which
she'd be fit to shake heavenly hands;

and, on the pillow, like a receiver left dangling
in case a wayward god needed someone to confess to,
the trumpet-flower mouthpiece, open-ended

as the story in which a fox gets caught
doubling back to speak his peace
into her oiled body

which curves and flowers and over
the centuries develops three keys, three
left-handed means

that allow us to fast-forward in the one
stunning rip from deformity to grace
that opens, that is

the hunt.

Nominated by Lee Upton

IN THE JOHN DILLINGER MUSEUM

fiction by SUSAN NEVILLE

from SYCAMORE REVIEW

A MAN AND A WOMAN are walking down the street, and they pause in front of the John Dillinger Museum. Was this John Dillinger's house? the woman asks, and the man, who knows things, says no, that Dillinger was from up around Mooresville. But it doesn't matter, he says; to the right of the house is the Joan Crawford birdbath, and Joan never set foot in Indiana.

All up and down the street tourists are buying calico and ceramic ducks. Artists sit in retirement studios cranking out their visions of the surrounding hills. Centuries ago glaciers wrinkled up the land like the skin of a hound and left this hollow down somewhere near the belly for people to set up gift shops and amusements.

Behind the John Dillinger Museum a man in his 50s plays a guitar with no finish, and now and then he accompanies himself on the kazoo. He plays all day long for change. Earlier, the woman and the man sat on a bench eating ice cream and listening to him play. They left him a dollar. The guitar player lives for his music, in a camper behind the food store. In the mornings he practices and watches teenagers in shorts and thongs walk in and out of the store, sucking on thin-necked bottles of Coke. He is always in love but has never married. The woman is afraid her husband envies what he fancies is the man's much simpler life.

Next to the John Dillinger Museum is a toy shop. The owner dips a long stick into a bucket of soap suds. He makes bubbles as large

466

as a six-year-old. The bubbles are heavy and irregular with the weight of their own iridescent skins. They lumber and sag through the air and rise up right before their spark-filled burst. He can only make one bubble at a time. One creeps around the corner of the Museum and explodes near the woman's eyes. For a moment the air is filled with soapy glitter, like silky microscopic seeds.

So what say we go in the John Dillinger Museum? says the man, her husband who knows things. On a day like this? she wants to say. Spend it in a dark museum? She wants to keep walking toward dinner, a table in a light-filled window. But she can tell by the way he looks so hungrily at the picture of a wax Dillinger all laid out in the morgue that this trip is not a negotiable one. A spiral notepad and a pen are stuffed in the shirt pocket where her father, she remembers, kept his cigarettes.

The man's face is starting to wrinkle in that flat space in front of his ears. Time is passing quickly. His father's skin folded in the same way; she knows exactly what he'll look like twenty years from now. His skin is dark olive. Some of his ancestors were Mediterranean. He knows all about his ancestors. Her knowledge of the past stops with her grandparents; beyond that it's a primal fog. It seems to her that that's the way it should be. He's always trying to trace the tangled threads of personality back through generations.

It doesn't matter. Though she hates the thought of going inside the John Dillinger Museum, she'll go. She'll get through it some-how, all those wax faces staring at her all unblinking and unre-sponsive, the scary way they always seem to breathe if you stare at them for long, like her grandmother who winked at her from the coffin. Her mother said it must have been the very moment that her soul left her body. When you look at a human face, it should respond to you, not sit there silent and brooding as a tree.

Wax figures always look like dead people, she says to her hus-band, and he says yes, I guess that's why they're fascinating, like you want to pare the waxy crayon flesh with your fingers to see what's underneath.

They walk up on the porch and he stands there reading every work on the posters designed to attract him inside. "I could have spent hours; it was worth every penny"—a quote from some nameless woman in Cincinnati. She watches his lips move as he reads. "Offered without social or moral comment," another

467

poster says, "the Dillinger Museum is dedicated to the loss and sorrow on both sides of the law."

The Dillinger Museum is a barn-red house with white gingerbread trim, a good house for selling quilts or woven placemats. She turns around to look at the quaint street, the white picket fence they passed through. If it were up to her, she'd strip the house of its wax and fake blood and Joan Crawford birdbath and she'd put up a porch swing or a rocker, one of those kind where the twigs are soaked in water and then gently bent into shape, not forced or pounded. She would sit on this porch then and not read a word, just sit and watch the people stream by—every year a different clothing fad, every year a different purchase, but always the ice cream and the soft drinks and the lovers and the young families all weary from hiking, and the old couples holding hands. It seems to her that everywhere she looks there's a harmony, an intimacy she's lost or somehow never found: the comfort of families who are parts of the same whole, and they're the only two people who live in dissonance and grating, the daily misunderstandings which have led them here to the John Dillinger Museum where he wants to go in and she just wants to sit on the porch in a pure untinctured state, with all the worries and the differences between them boiled away so they'd always be as peaceful and alike as two glasses of distilled water. Now and then they'd clink at the hip in this bell-like ringing, and they'd pour their thoughts from one to the other and merge so completely you could never tell the difference between them. Instead, they're cups of liquid struck so hard from the outside that the circles travel inward, and refuse to touch.

I'll bet you could spend hours in here, her husband says, quoting the kindred spirit woman from Cincinnati, and he leads her through the door. A sign inside assures visitors that the machine guns behind glass are all reproductions, that the snub-nose 38 pointing straight at them in the wax Clyde's hand, Bonnie languishing on a chair at his feet, has no bullets, that even if you smashed the glass you couldn't shoot a soul.

A woman sits behind a bank teller's cage, bored as a zoo animal. She's in a bank no one would ever rob. She hands them a card for their money. No pictures, no food. There are four rooms. Children and people with weak hearts or other organs are advised to skip room three.

468

So, she says, this is the John Dillinger Museum. I guess if you live your life cruelly enough, someone will celebrate it.

I know, her husband says. Soon there'll be a Jim Jones Museum and a Charlie Manson Museum and a D. C. Stevenson Museum in among the apple butter shops.

Except that Dillinger wasn't really cruel, he adds, he was just a thief.

Oh, he was cruel, she thinks. Dillinger was a sharp metal edge pulling at the tight threads of the smooth Midwestern grid, hammering the strings of banks and homes like his own personal piano. He stole over a million dollars in fourteen months, a million 1930s dollars from families just trying to get by. Depression dollars. At least those families had someone specific and evil to blame for their suffering, she thinks. You could hate Dillinger, hate him clear through.

You can see why women loved him, she overhears a woman saying to the man she's with. Look at that dark hair, and those eyes.

Silly fool, she thinks, and she looks away from the woman and over at a yellowed poster on the wall. It states up front that this is not Dillinger's house but that he once robbed a grocery store an hour north. The sign also says that the TV movie is a pitiful poor excuse for a movie. The real truth about Dillinger, the sign says, is right here in this house.

Room One is small and cluttered with things. There are mirrors beside each window to make the room seem larger. Her own reflection takes her by surprise. The light is too gray. She looks older than she thought, and tired. So does her husband. She wants him to see what she sees. They'll never have another child. But he doesn't see himself; he's looking at the pictures of the white farm house that was Dillinger's childhood home. Dillinger's family stares back at her husband with that early Depression dust bowl seriousness. In every picture in her own photo album she and her husband have those giddy camera smiles. If their photos were ever on a wall like this with all the other families from this time and place, it would look like Eden—like a time of great tranquility and happiness.

Dillinger was a chubby child. His parents loved him, or so it seemed from the photographs. She doesn't understand why he couldn't leave well enough alone, take the fate his life had given

469

him. The poverty of that farmhouse couldn't be wished away. There was a straight line to follow between any two points. You don't just try to leap into some new dimension.

She looks around for something to pull her away from the thing she feels she's getting too close to—which is what?—Dillinger's childhood and the peaceful farm and the mother and the father, a glass case filled with wood and metal 1920s toys. Not his toys of course but the kind of toys he might have played with, and this the magazine he might have read, and this the brand of food he might have eaten, none of them adding up to the explosion of newsprint on the opposite wall screaming *robbery, robbery*, oh why did he have to bring her here on this sunny day to the John Dillinger Museum.

She looks out the window. A woman walks by outside in a yellow dress; behind her, a mother pushes a stroller. All these people walking by, not turning in the gate, with no idea what waits for them inside. Please hurry, she says to him, please. This room should only take a second to see. You could stand in the center and turn and see it all, but he pauses at each article, reads every word, wonders at each metal toy, each driftwood graying wooden block as though it were all a puzzle that his life depended on. If their lives were arranged in a house like this would it all make as little sense as this place did? Nothing could change the past, it's best to leave it all alone, and still he went back and back to it, trying to understand.

He won't write anything down, she knows, until after he's out of the building, and then he'll do it almost guiltily, as though it's something he's ashamed of. He'll continue talking to her, but he'll be lost in his own thoughts, and it will be hours before she can reclaim him. And in the morning, early, he'll be up there again in the spare bedroom, adding pages to that pile of typed pages that's been growing for months, thinking that the John Dillinger Museum could be the key to finally unlock all those miles and miles of solitary thoughts.

He looks over at her and smiles. He can tell she's bored or uncomfortable, and he tries hard to pretend that he thinks the museum is silly. He comments on the overwrought signs and the Dillinger t-shirts displayed in every room; he wants her to believe they're living in the same world still, though she knows he's gone already, flying out over some crevice like a spider with a

470

sticky thread, and she's the wall he wants to stay attached to, the hand holding the waving kite. Where do you go? she wants to shout at him. Why do you leave me here alone like this?

She takes his arm and feels the warmth of his blood; she wants to hear it speak to her. Are you there? Are you still with me?

They walk into Room Two. More wax figures. Ma Barker wears a purple coat. Except for the machine gun, she looks like anybody's mother. Carbines line the wall, this room an arsenal.

A waxy Pretty Boy Floyd stands with his back to a window. She could have seen him from outside, right from where they'd been sitting earlier, watching the guitar player.

This room is hot. It smells like candles. They should be sitting down to dinner now. She would have a glass of wine, clear as a diamond. It would be the two of them alone, the waiter faceless. They would watch the sun leave, the town get dusky dark. Firelight would glint on the white plates, on the yellow grain in the wooden floor. They would float there, alone, above a white tablecloth, the two of them, and when she looked at him she would know exactly who it was she was looking at. She realizes that she doesn't really trust him. She wants to trust him, but he's become complicated and moody and contradictory, and the harder he tries not to be, the worse it is. When he says that he loves her, she doesn't have any idea in the world what that means to him.

She looks down at the case beside her. Inside is a wooden gun carved out of the top board of a washtub. It's more clunky than the roughest toy. It's the gun, she reads, that Dillinger used to escape from the Lake County prison. It's the pride of the museum. Underneath it is a letter typed on yellow paper by Dillinger himself. It's long and chatty, and the ribbon needed changing.

Dear sis! Dillinger writes. *Here's the gun they thought was real!* he writes. The letter is filled with Ha! Ha!s like any ordinary boy's. *Keep it for me*, he tells his sister. *Twelve big prison guards locked up because of this wooden gun, ha ha. Look at it when you need a good laugh*, he says, *Ha! Ha! Love Johnny.*

It's a silly, childish gun. It shouldn't fool a soul. He must have been a magician; he had to believe in that wooden gun. He had to get the guards to see it in his face, to keep their eyes away from that splintery stick of wood in his hand.

Across the room, her husband leans so close to a case that she can see his breath on the glass. A handsome Dillinger stands

471

staring at him from the other side. Blue whiskers like flecks of metal in his pale face. Her husband's reflection floats above Dillinger's dark suit; Dillinger's hat rests on her husband's watery head. His hand reaches out toward the case and she's afraid she sees Dillinger's arm rising, and for a dizzy second it looks as though they're touching.

She runs from the room and feels her husband follow her. Only two more rooms, he says, his breath against her cheek. She won't look at him. He's a complete stranger to her. Nothing he can learn will bring their son back; there's nothing they can do. She wishes she were married to an accountant, a man who would leave for work on time in a three-piece suit, someone who remembered to record the checks, to pay the bills, a man whose loyalty is to the world that you can see, a man who would know how to deal with tragedy.

They wind up the narrow stairs. Photographs of the Midwest in the 30s line the stairwell. Hollow eyes, rusted gas tanks collapsing on themselves like cloth, barns falling from their own weight. Thirties honky tonk plays cheerfully on the loud speakers. Oh please come with me, she turns and whispers to him, and it's the young innocent boy she married that she says it to. The one who's been replaced by this private, suffering man. I'm here, he says, and he puts his hand on her shoulder, but he doesn't really see her.

I'm hungry, she says to him, just to hear her normal voice. Just two more rooms, he says, and she mentions a place down the street with fried chicken and biscuits, a place that's never changed in all the years they've been coming here, a place that smells, always, of sassafras tea.

There are warnings outside of Room Three. Don't come in! it says, if you're faint hearted. Go to Room Four! Her husband walks right in. The warning's not for her, she thinks, and she follows him inside.

There are pictures of the Biograph and of the woman who lured him in. This is the truth about John Dillinger, the poster says, not the movie truth. The lady in red? Her dress was really orange. The movie he went to see was a comedy. The woman wasn't his girlfriend, just an acquaintance who wanted $3000. Here are pictures of all the women he loved; the woman in orange wasn't one of them.

The honky tonk music fades out in this room, is replaced by the sound of gun fire and squealing tires. All the G-Men in the world stare out at her, and wait to gun Dillinger down.

She looks up at a clear plastic Invisible Man sculpture of Dillinger's head. A red plastic arrow is embedded in his cheek, underneath the eye. It won't be enough to see the body and the blood. This is how it will happen. This is the place that death will enter in.

She thinks of Dillinger's mother's face in the photographs downstairs. She wonders if she suffered for her son, if she thought of all the sons who suffered because of the child she'd given life to.

Oh, this room is the one she's waited for. This room is the way it should be. This room is the serious room, the moral room, the one that comes with warnings. It may have looked like excitement, the room cries, but after all the women and the drinking and the banks ripe and splitting open like a pod, and all the mothers in the world and all the fathers suffering for their sons and for their daughters, this is what it comes to in the end: Dillinger stone cold on a slab, crayon blood dripping eternally down his eternally contorted face, a facsimile of the wicker basket they carried him in underneath the table. This is what she needed to see, what her husband needs to see. She leans into his shoulder, walks with him from picture to picture like any couple at a gallery. Dillinger's public execution, the expression on the bystanders' faces one common face of horror and of fascination.

These are the real blood-stained trousers, this is his face frozen in anguish. This is the room you can be angry in, the one where Dillinger is murdered over and over in photograph after photograph. His is the face you want to smash, and here is the scream that waits in your throat for the moment it can rise up clear and clean to the edges of the universe, the defiant *no*, the *why*, your fist finding its home, finally, in Dillinger's white and perfect teeth.

And still, somehow, it's not enough. There's one more room to see, across the hall. They walk toward it. She looks at her husband's face to see if here in the John Dillinger Museum he can see what she's afraid of, how treacherous the road they're on.

Room Four regrets the passion. Calmly, the room says that it isn't right, revenge that hot and sudden. It won't do. It leaves you cold. The room shifts suddenly to the Lindbergh baby thief.

This is his room. Here's the real revenge, the room says, Hauptmann with his weasel face sitting in the electric chair, the slow
rational burn the only satisfaction. Dillinger should have died this
way but didn't. By comparison, Dillinger in his satin coffin, fresh
from a comedy, is peaceful, about to wake from sleep. Hauptmann has the look of a man who's seen the wrong, a man who
knows he's going to die.

She stares at Hauptmann's face. She stares and stares at it. The
room is windowless and cold. They've been in here too long.
There's nothing for them here, no explanations.

Her husband turns away from her and heads back down the
stairs and out the door. She runs behind him.

Outside, a man is playing a kazoo. Outside, the day is clear
and filled with sun. Someone's hanging wind chimes on a clothesline. Her husband's eyes are lonely as a child's. Whatever is behind those eyes is dark and hidden.

They're pulled into the rush of people on the sidewalk. She
holds onto his hand like the string of a kite. Please, she says as he
begins to fly away from her, don't leave me here alone in the
John Dillinger Museum.

Nominated by Michael Martone and Sycamore Review

CHOOSING YOUR NAMES

by KOTHAR WA-KHASIS

from RARITAN: A QUARTERLY REVIEW

Personal names survive, absurdly, as fixed signifiers. The aspiring scholar or intellectual wants to "make a name" for herself, even after the death of the author and the discovery of "text." If everything is text, then names are, too, and it is time to abandon the pretense that they refer to definite persons. They refer to other names or to other texts, beginning with the title of the article next to which they appear. For this reason, the custom of the unchanging name should be abandoned, along with its implicit metaphysics of self and immortality, and the writer should use a new name each time. She should make names for herself. An immediate practical benefit would be a modest increase in the size of the c.v., in which, for the first few years of a career, the list of the publications always seems too short. The length of each citation will be increased by the pseudonym. And interviewers will no longer say, "So you are . . . ," but, "So you were . . . and . . . and. . ." You will be judged by your names as well as by your publications. In fact, your names may have won you the interview.

In 1987, at age twenty-nine, James A. Hogue decided to apply to Ivy League colleges. He had already been enrolled at the University of Washington, the University of Texas, and Palo Alto High School, in that order. His name in Palo Alto was Jay Huntsman. Posing as a Stanford Ph.D., he then worked as a coach at a sports cross-training camp in Vail, Colorado. When his credentials came under scrutiny, he departed for Aspen and then Utah, apparently taking with him $20,000 worth of bicycle frames and tools. In this period, as the police were closing in on him, he invented the new identity that he would present to the Ivy League. He became Alexi Indris-Santana, ranch hand and autodidact. In his admissions essay, he wrote about his horse Good Enough. Both Brown and Princeton admitted him. He deferred his matriculation at Princeton for a year while he served time in a Utah prison.

Hogue had grasped the semiotic power of the personal name. His multicultural Russian-Indian-Hispanic name by itself filled in the large, blank space of his application—the lack of a high school transcript, the missing facts, the fuzzy details, the absence of letters of recommendation, except for a note from the (nonexistent) Lazy T Ranch. Here was the ideal candidate, the son of an Indian mother and a Hispanic father (or vice versa) with perhaps also a few drops of Russian blood. This man was thus worth, on the chart of diversity, three other students. He was in himself what academic administrators want their student bodies as a composite to be. If there was any doubt about him, his horse's name provided the answer.

Principle 1: Hogue's success points to the first principle in the choosing of names: be multicultural. As "cultural studies" take institutional root, the competition for jobs and perks, not to mention access to scholarly journals, will depend upon the correct choice of names. Consider the table of contents of a recent number of the *Yale Journal of Criticism,* as it appeared in an advertisement (*NYRB* 16 May 1991, p. 43). The authors' names were printed in bold type, no doubt to enhance their semiotic impact, the titles in regular:

Jeff Nunokawa AIDS and the Age of Mourning
Gauri Viswanathan Raymond Williams and British Colonialism
Joan DeJean Marriage and the Novel in Crisis in France (1690–1715)
Christopher Norris Heidegger, de Man, and Lacoue-Labarthe
Toril Moi Beauvoir and the Intellectual Woman
Wai-chee Dimock Rightful Subjectivity
Dudley Andrew Renoir's *La Marseillaise*

David Bromwich Edmund Burke, Revolutionist
Ngugi wa Thiong'o English: A Language for the World?
Akeel Bilgrami Rushdie and Postcolonial Defensiveness

The construction of this list illustrates the only possible use of Anglo- or WASP-sounding names. They must be sandwiched between multicultural names. If this list had been alphabetical, "Dudley Andrew" would have come first and "David Bromwich" third—a sure disaster, since no one would have read further. **Corollary 1:** In general, however, the Anglo- or WASP-sonic name should be avoided, both as an obvious corollary of the first principle and also because intellectual acumen is not usually associated with WASPS. Clearly Brit-sounding, as distinguished from vaguely Anglosonic, names are discussed below. **Strategy 1:** "Jeff Nunokawa" and "Wai-chee Dimock" are multicultural unto themselves. These names represent a straightforward strategy for the fulfillment of the first principle. "Jeff" is also an example of the endearing nickname (see below). **Strategy 2:** "Ngugi wa Thiong'o" is an excellent choice, since it suggests that the author is so "other" that his (or her?) name can hardly be transliterated into the Roman alphabet. Under what better name to write about the English language?

The relationship between name and title of article, as in "Ngugi's" ("wa Thiong'o's"?) case, should always determine the choice of the name, since this is the juxtaposition that the potential reader will first encounter, either on the cover or on the title page of the journal. Journals that use only last names on their covers, in the form

$$X \text{ on } Y,$$

where X = writer and Y = another writer, present grave difficulties. If you had to write on someone calling himself "Fish," you would not call yourself "Rivers," because

Rivers on Fish

would sound like an Aesopean pronouncement by rivers on their longtime parasites.

477

Faced with the "X on Y" form, you should follow, insofar as possible,

Principle 2: Be confrontational, "Ngugi wa Thiong'o," like other names in the table of contents, illustrates the principle. In case there was any doubt, the table was preceded by this paragraph:

> Published in association with the Whitney Humanities Center, Yale University, *The Yale Journal of Criticism* provides a new forum for acts of confrontation and discovery in all fields of the humanities.

The author's name itself performs the first act of confrontation. It is a Brechtian Gestus. Thus

Rotterdam on Fish

would be a solution to the "X on Y" problem, not only because the polysyllabic "Rotterdam" overpowers the wimpish "Fish" but still more because of its **Strategy 3:** semantic ghosts. A "dam" is potentially inimical to "fish," and "Rotter" suggests "rotting fish," the putative effect of "Rotterdam's" assessment of "Fish."

It would be difficult to overestimate the confrontational value of semantic ghosts. While some subjects, such as AIDS, cancer, refugees, and the homeless, should be paired only with friendly names (see Principle 4), nearly any article on sex or gender is more likely to be read if the author's name sounds hostile. Therefore, writing on feminism, you should use "Dwight Mailer" (ghost: "white male"), "Dick Draper" (ghost: "dick rape"), "Eberhard Coxmann" (ghost: "hard cock man"), or the like. "Dwight Mailer" of course also suggests Norman Mailer, who was one of the butts of Kate Millett in *Sexual Politics*. Still worse, "Coxmann" sounds like a Mannheim School sociologist. The potential reader practices onomancy willy/will she-nilly/nill she, and the effect is proleptic outrage.

Women should, however, feel outrage at the very existence of proper names. Hélène Cixous stood Jacques Lacan on his head, cleverly seeing that the "Nom du père" (= the Law) was really the name of the son and that women existed only to create sons (= names = the Law): "Oedipe peut faire l'amour avec sa "mère" tant qu'elle n'est pas nommée tandis que Jocaste, celle qui sait

au-delà de tout savoir, et qui vit par delà les mots, tente de dé-
livrer l'amour des noms qui font la Loi. Le sort tient à un fil(s),
un nom. . ." (blurb from Cixous on the back of André
Boucourechliev, *Le nom d'Oedipe: Chant du corps interdit,* an
opera to which Cixous contributed the libretto).

What if you are reviewing

Domestic Chores and the Corporal Punishment of Children in the Midi 1100–1230 AD

by a famous exponent of the daily-life school of French historiog-
raphy, translated into English sixteen days after its appearance in
French, and published by Harvard University Press (826 + lviii
pages)? Here respect must be shown. French culture is, after all,
the only one of any interest to most American intellectuals (despite Principle 1). Your first name is best a gambit chosen from
the nongender-specific repertory:

Alex	Lee	Rolly
Ashley	Marion	Schuyler
Hadley	Morgan	Shirley
Hilary	Parker	Sprague
Holt	Pat	Stevie
Jackie	Robin	Vivian

The most enabling surname will be French (cf. above, "Joan De-
Jean" in the *Yale Journal of Criticism*), showing sympathy and
correct orientation. A good source of French surnames is the
Plan de Paris par Arrondisement (*Nomenclature des rues avec la
station du métro la plus proche*), provided they are chosen from
arrondisements that Americans do not usually visit and the street
names of which they will therefore not recognize.

The slight deformation of a famous name in "Dwight Mailer"
illustrates

Principle 3: onomastic piggy-backing. Sometimes you can entice
readers by using a name that sounds like the name of a known
expert on your subject. Writing in the field of anthropology, you
are "Cliff Rupestrine" or "James Geer" or "Margherita Clifford"
and, in this way, not only do you make a potential reader think
that you might somehow *be* one of the famous anthropologist
Cliffords, Jameses, or Geertzes, you also begin to destabilize and

fragment their names. You oppose the intellectual colonialism by which persons, conceiving themselves as autonomous, authoritative subjects, carve out "fields" to dominate. Dominating and authorial mono-self-denominating go hand in glove. With the spread of onomastic pluralism, this now obsolete subject will be replaced by a true, i.e., fictive, individual. "Then perhaps the subject returns, not as illusion, but as *fiction*. A certain pleasure is derived from a way of imagining oneself as *individual*, of inventing a final, rarest fiction: the fictive identity. This fiction is no longer the illusion of a unity; on the contrary, it is the theater of society in which we stage our plural: our pleasure is *individual*—but not personal" (Roland Barthes, *The Pleasure of the Text*, p. 62).

Principle 4: Contrary to Principle 2, it may be desirable to appear not as confrontational but as the friendly native informant. Let us imagine that, in an ethnological experiment, camcorders are distributed to a tribe of Bushmen. Then a journal devotes a thematic issue to the experiment, and on its cover appear such names and titles as:

N!ai, "The First Tribal Cinema"
Bayly Spawforth-Jones, "Can Tribal Cinema Stabilize San Culture?"
Marie Desséchée, "The Male Gaze in Tribal Cinema"

N!ai is the native informant. The exclamation point is one of the ways of representing the clicks in the Bushman tongues. In future articles on the same subject, "N!ai" could call him- or herself "Chum!Kwe" or "!Khu" or "XKo" or "Hie//om." The sandwiching of the Anglosonic name is a device already observed in the table of contents quoted above. The name has, however, its own integrity here. It is, in a word, confrontational, since it suggests an unsympathetic Brit anthropologist. Similarly, if you are publishing

"12% Unemployment: A 'Rational Expectation'?"

a Brit name will suggest that you are a die-hard British socialist attacking the New Classical Macroeconomics.

But, to repeat, **Corollary 1:** Americans should, if possible, avoid Brit-sounding names. They rarely sound good in the United States, except to classicists, and, in the United Kingdom, the chances of error are great. Americans, who do not understand the semiotics of British names, should not experiment with formations like "Hugo Williams" and "Eric Korn." Americans do not know how to pronounce British names, either, so that the apparent triumph of something like "Mappledurham" falls flat in England, where it is pronounced "Mum." In situations in which it is absolutely necessary to use a Brit-sounding name, one should be chosen that (1) simply sounds British to Americans and (2) will do nothing more than perplex Englishpersons. Names may be chosen from the following lists:

Brit-sounding first names	Brit-sounding last names
Angela	Bayly
Bossy	Crabbe
Bushey	Bossy
Caroline	Hawtree
Cyril	Hebblethwaite
Galen	Hogwood
Grevel	-Jones, preceded by any
Hugh (better: Hew)	other name in this list
Ian	except Rees-Mogg
Lord	Nokes
Martyn	Nye
Merlin	Peacocke
Muriel	Pumfrey
Nye	Rees-Mogg (cf. Strategy 5)
Toby	Shrimpton
Warwick	Spawforth
Wintle	Warwick
	Wormald
	Yapp (cf. Strategy 5)

(It is in the nature of Brit first names that there are fewer feminine than masculine.) In general, surnames ending in -spoon, -berry, -shend, and -shire will also serve.

Multiculturalism has its own pitfalls, and **Caveat:** authors must be attentive to changing fashions. A name like "Little Running Bull," which would have drawn the pious attention of potential readers in the 1960s, will now meet with derision. While outrage at colonial and expansionist treatment of native Americans is still

481

welcome, American Indian names are not. A shrewd choice of names depends upon recognition that Messrs. Hierarchy, Colonialism, and Hegemony, barred at the front door, always slip in through the postern gate. Indian names have now been sent back to the reservation or left in an Indian gambling casino. With glasnost, yet another large repertory of names goes into desuetude. For three decades, the Slavic names of dissident poets and intellectuals melted Western hearts, no matter how dreadful the poems, no matter how pretentious the accounts of the Russian, Polish, Slakan, etc. soul. Now that dissidence is losing its meaning, Slavic names will lose their panache (and one will be able to express one's honest opinion of the writings of a Bohumil Hrabal). The only Slavic names that will be useful any longer will be those that, ornamented with hačeks and accents in unexpected places, have pure orthographical glamour (see Principle 7 below), e.g.,

Pál Ševčenko.

It is questionable, however, whether such a name achieves the goal of absolute onomastic otherness. "Pál" might be just another dissident poet trying to dine out on the charm of yester-decades. In fact, despite the curiosity of the accent, "Pál" is readable as English "pal," and, in this way, represents a completely different strategy (see on semantic ghosts above). A much more successful creation is "Slavoj Zižek," which opened a column-bottom blurb in *TLS* concerning a collection of papers on Lacan. None of the other contributors was mentioned until the fifth line of the blurb, properly, since they had names like "Judith Miller" and "Henry W. Sullivan" (*TLS* 28 June 1991, p. 7). These names arouse the suspicion that the authors are using their "real" names. But if "it would be frivolous to think that 'Descartes,' 'Leibniz,' 'Rousseau,' 'Hegel,' etc., are names of authors" (Jacques Derrida, *Of Grammatology*, p. 99), why think that your surname, which, if not Miller or Sullivan, is probably something like Oshinsky or O'Neill, could be the name of an author?

If a Slavic name is unavoidable, then **Strategy 4:** it should be one that is unpronounceable. Serbo-Croatian tends to have this characteristic and, if perceived as Serbo-Croatian, may also suggest that you were a Croatian freedom-fighter or that you are now an up-to-date dissident, a Serbian one (though, at the date of this writing [9/18/91], the prospects are unclear).

Serbo-Croatian First Names	Serbo-Croatian Last Names
Biljana (f.)	Biljić
Ciga (m.)	Džukić
Ljiljana (f.)	Krstić
Ljubica (f.)	Prstić
Ljubomir (m.)	Rockić
Miodrag (m.)	Smiljanić
Siniša (m.)	Tadić
Smiljan (m.)	Tašić
Srboljub (m.)	Trtić
Srdjan (m.)	
Zdravko (m.)	
Zika (m.)	

If you do not use any of these and are also somewhat unsure of whatever name you have chosen, then dedicate your book or article to a hyper-Slavic name, which will also suggest that you have exotic friends. (It is too late for "Zajačik-Ušičik," preempted by Patrice Pavis for the dedicand of *Languages of the Stage: Essays in the Semiology of the Theatre*.)

But as fashions change, it will be necessary to find new sources of multicultural names and literally to go farther afield. Two places at the greatest remove from the United States are Australia and the Philippines. The Australian Aboriginal languages and the Philippine language Tagalog are both rich in names for American intellectuals. Examples (any of the following can be either a first or a last name and either masculine or feminine; pronounce as if English or Spanish):

Australian Aboriginal	Tagalog
Alkuntjipirna	Ang Kaputian Nang Itlog
Apiyalpintjipirna	Bumubouís
Gugu-Yalanji	Gaso
Iiyimp	Getumup
Kintjangam	Hámak Na Táuo
Lesbin	Hingkod
Murrumurru	Kimosabe
Ngay	Mabubulaanan

Nhimpitimarnti	Magandá
Nintang	Magbabalibalitang
Nquir	Naaararo
Pitjanjatara	Patayin
Tiwi	Páñgit
Tjanaymungaku	Tiniklop
Yumpunga	

In order to avoid the difficulty of detecting subtle changes in onomastic fashions (cf. Caveat), apply **Principle 5:** indeterminacy within multiculturalism. In one reality, Toril Moi is a Duke-based Norwegian; in the only reality with which readers of this article need be concerned, that of the text, "Toril Moi" is a fine example of indeterminacy. Is the first name masculine or feminine? Is "Moi" Chinese "Moy?" Or French *moi,* so that "Moi" is really in apposition to the other name, and "Moi, Toril," implies "Quant à Moi, Toril, je pense. . ."? In this case, the name "Moi" is a free-floating *instance de discours,* outside of but always ready on the margin of any discourse, an enunciative self-reference that, content less, still in its very liminality beckons Siren-like to an interlocutor.

Whenever possible, any of the above principles should be combined with one or two others. The first of these **Principle 6:** is euphony, brilliantly displayed in James Hogue's handling of the vocalic palette. "Alexi" deploys the first three vowels in the alphabet, creating the expectation of a progression. The final *i* of "Alexi" is, however, a bridge to the next name (-*i I*-), which tarries on a twice-repeated *i* vocalism, a suspenseful retard broken by the forward-pointing hyphen. Then the repeated *a* vocalism of "Santana" balances out the initial vowel of "Alexi" and the name attains closure. Note also the bridge between the final -*s* of "Indris" and the initial *S*- of "Santana." Simultaneously, however, within this tightly contained vocalic system, Hogue achieved a rhythmic contrast between (1) the clausular cadence of Ĭndrĭs-Săntānă (˘˘˘˘˘) alluding precisely to the pattern of the last two feet of the dactyllic hexameter, after the tribrach Ălĕxĭ (˘˘˘) and (2) the complementarity of the trisyllabic and like-accented names "Aléxi" and "Santána." A less sophisticated application of these techniques can be observed in "Joan DeJean."

The second of the supplementary principles is **Principle 7:** orthographic glamour. A name can have this quality even if it is completely lacking in euphony, like "Clyde de L. Ryals." Who knows what "L." stands for? Who cares? It is a glyph composed of a vertical and a horizontal line having a common terminus. It organizes the space between the two symmetrical y's like a gazebo in a garden. Someone who could combine the sensitive ear of a James Hogue with the architectural eye of a "Clyde de L. Ryals" would be the consummate auto-onomast. Measured against this standard, such efforts as "Jeff Nunokawa" and "Wai-chee Dimock" seem leaden. A daring technique **Strategy 5:** for achieving a beautiful look is the orthographic supplement. Even a name like "Sue" becomes possible with the addition of a nonalphabetic ornament, for example, "Sue/" (cf. the Bushman names above) or "Sue°." This strategy should not be employed, however, until conventional means have been exhausted. Underused letters are useful as embellishments: ø, ÿ, β, and several others. Orthographic stuttering, i.e., the reduplication of initial or final consonants, can also be tried, as in "Ffinch" or "Grampp" (cf. "Rees-Mogg" and "Yapp" above).

In spite of everything here proposed, authors will face **Dilemmas:** There will be times when any name is too committal or confrontational or when the right name eludes the imagination. Several strategies are available. One is simple **Strategy 6:** avoidance. Persons at the Center for Poetic Studies at the University of Liège publish jointly under the name "Group μ." You could be "Group α," or β, γ, σ, etc., or β1, etc. To feel compunction about pretending to be a group is simply to endorse the whole set of prejudices that Michel Foucault exploded in "What Is an Author?" (in *The Foucault Reader*, pp. 101–20). Indeed, it could be wondered, as in the cases of "Centers" within one's own experience, whether the Liège Center exists and if the group is not really one person with a lot of funding. If to be a group seems too much, then **Strategy 7:** be two persons, using the old trick of the dissident poet, who would present himself thus:

The Blood of Slaka
by Bábl Šlok
[text of dissident poem]
Translated by Bábl Šlok and Kenneth Bly

Here the American-sounding name also sounds like the name of a poet. In fact, "Bly" did not exist and the translation was done by a fellow Slakan, a graduate student at CCNY. Bábl implied that, while he was bilingual, only the soul of "Bly" could filter the beauties of the poem into English. If, on the other hand, the poem failed, it was because its beauties were simply ineffable in any tongue but Slakan. (For a description of Bábl's native land, see Malcolm Bradbury, *Why Come to Slaka?* [Penguin Books: New York, 1986]). The pairing of names is such a clever device precisely because it accepts credit but refuses blame. If, writing on the overpopulation of Mexico City, you are "Clifford Shame and Angel José-Maria Gutiérrez," and your article succeeds, you get whatever you get; if it is offensive, no one's to blame, because the best of both worlds wrote it.

To avoid, in the case of difficult subjects, any appearance of confrontation, use **Strategy 8:** the endearing nickname. Here the trick is to be sufficiently disarming without sounding unintellectual. Thus you would not call yourself "Tookie" or "Gunny." An alternative to the nickname would be one of the feminine names taken from flowers:

Dahlia	Iris	Posey
Daisy	Lily	Veronica
Heather	Pansey	Violet
Impatience	Poppy	

but not Daphne, Fern, Ivy, Juniper, Laurel, Myrtle or Rose. These examples also illustrate **Strategy 9:** the conversion of common adjectives and nouns into proper names. Just as cigarettes are advertised in terms of qualities that they do not possess, your article on disease in third-world countries can have an author who is "Cool," "Mild," "Fresh," or "Low," e.g., "Lowell Mild Edmunds." Many common nouns can be elevated to proper surnames, e.g., "Child," "Care," "Help," "Hope," "Strength," and the like.

This article has eschewed theory since nothing but a pragmatics of the proper name was at stake. If, however, it were necessary to subtend a theoretical line, one could perhaps allude to the Jean-François Lyotard. If one positions oneself in his argument, the proper name is an embarrassment no matter which way one looks. On the one hand, it implies a personal history that one would like to forget: "The addresser who will sign the name

486

'Kant' was first the addressee of an 'I baptize you Kant' and the referent of a 'Kant has grown a lot this week' " ("The *Différend*, the Referent, and the Proper Name," *diacritics* 14.3 [1984] 10). On the other, the name is vacuous: "The proper name is a designator of reality, like a deictic; it does not, anymore than a deictic, have a signification; it is not, anymore than a deictic, the abridged equivalent of a definitive description or of a bundle of descriptions. It is a pure mark of the designative function" (ibid.). A photograph on a dustjacket is not, then, the occasion for a desperate grab at a signification for your name. On the contrary, as "Pico Iyer" has pointed out: "Perhaps the best idea, in these Milli Vanilli days, when so many celebrities hire ghost-writers, is for writers to hire ghost-celebrities. Could any first novelist with Rob Lowe's face, or Greta Scacchi's, on his cover, fail?" (*TLS*, 28 June 1991, p. 12).

To conclude, the naming of authors is a difficult matter. It is not just a holiday pastime. At first, you might think it madness that an author must have several different names. But armed with the principles and strategies offered here, you will be able to find a new name to stand before any article you may write: "The Japanese Buyout of England," "The Kikuyu Clitoridectomy Controversy Again," "Specificity, Classicity and Canonicity," "The Metaphoricity of Urban Space," "The Rhetoricity of Urban Planning," "The Cityicity of Las Vegas," "The Opening of the SS Sturm-Abteilung Archive," "A *Lebenswelt* Approach to the Homeless," "Interculturalness as Diffusion of the Local," "Wit and Self-Irony in Susan Sontag," "The Failure of U.S. Policy Toward [name of country]," "Meta-Everything," "Godzilla and the Hulk: Deconstruction Takes On Virtual Reality," "The Supposed Theft of All French Ideas from German Philosophy," or "Communication As Fetish."

Nominated by Raritan: A Quarterly Review

SYCAMORE CANYON NOCTURNE

by CHRISTOPHER BUCKLEY

from POETRY

> *But home is the form of the dream, & not the dream.*
>
> Larry Levis

Home again in dreams, I'm walking the middle of the foothill
   road
just after a last morning star slips away over canyon walls—
red and gold riprap of creek rock, ferns splayed in the fervent
shade of oaks, the high yellow sycamores, oat straw catching sun
at my feet.
      Some wind-switch, and the stone-blue stillness
saying *angels*, who come down here to dip their wings
and give the water its color.
           Yet even when I'm allowed back
along the weedy path of sleep to this first green and singing
   space,
I know someday air will be set between my shoulder blades
and arms and all my bones, and little more than clouds,
the clouds will be my final lesson until I'm taken off
into some clearer imagining. . . .
          In exile, it is hard to love God.
What, then, must I never ask for again? The Psalter of shade
ringing from evergreens along Sheffield Drive? The loquat
and acacia overcome with salt-spray riding the ocean fog?
Can I speak of love almost a life ago, those unguent syllables
repeating the skin's fire and salt like lemon blossoms
riding the August heat?

I love the life slowly taken from me,
so obviously spun out flower-like, and for my own use, it seems,
against some future sky—the world, just a small glory of dust
    above
a field one autumn afternoon—the resinous pines and a back
    road
full of birds inside you.
            What more could wishes be,
who would live there again, sent back among the blue
acanthus to lift unconsciously with morning and with mist?
I would.
        And where this canyon levels out, I'd eat the wild sun—
            red plums, the sweet light of the juice carrying through me
my only hymn. Moonlight or dreamlight, I thought I'd lost
that frame of days I have in me always—that is the way of this
    world,
giving and taking away with one unseen hand—the way we were
    told
to unravel desires around the soul like rings of flesh on a tree.

I know God, old flame wearing through the damp sponge
of the heart, that candle I cannot put out, coming back
each time it seems extinguished. And so I must bless
    everything,
take anything given me—these words, their polish and pity,
the almost bearable absence they hold like the trees ascending
foothills each winter and resembling starving angels
in the early dusk, and then the dark, and the broken order
of prayer. . . .
        I know you are listening. Like the sky.
But aren't the birds going over always full of light? To shine
like these trees again, that air hovering on the canyon walls—
sometimes, all I want to be is the dreaming world.

Nominated by Timothy Geiger

TOMORROW, WE'LL DANCE IN AMERICA

by JAMES HARMS

from THE DENVER QUARTERLY

In America, there is an answer for everything,
though little has been asked.
We stand around the water cooler comparing notes.
If it is Friday, we discuss hope.

In America, in a bar, I sit beside . . .
well, her, for instance.
I feel like the subject of protest.
The sight of love will draw grease from a driveway—
I expect the shadow boys in satin jackets
to emerge from their rented corners
and distribute the bruised carnations.
Flowers are only a dollar, sometimes more.
It hurts to sit this close to someone
I will never know.

In America, I am thirty. I am not married.
I am alone but I am happy.
Until I am sad. This won't last forever.

In America, I would be the first to say
someone has lied to us. Oh well.
I will propose marriage to a pool of guppies.

Now *that* is fear.
Last year my lung turned black with empathy.
Please believe me when I say
all of this is a ruse for honesty.

In America I stand around wondering how to say
I love you, until she asks, Coffee?
I think I could live my whole life
waiting for someone to say the word
Love, knowing a cup of coffee was on its way.

Nominated by The Denver Quarterly

WOMAN KILLS SWEETHEART WITH BOWLING BALL

by LAURA KASISCHKE

from WILD BRIDES (New York University Press)

The moon is loose in the gutter tonight
and it rolls without kisses
or handprints between us   its mouth
is an O of surprise

O Tonight the phantasma of love
climbs the stairs while we sleep   She
sags with exhaustion and booze
and pills   while her skin hangs heavy
and empty as hate
She floats so slow she floats
as if she is swimming through blood

   Shhh   Shhh   the lights are out
   and the little suspicion
   sleeps and dreams
   and whimpers in its crib
   Its tongue is ugly and blue

She climbs   She climbs
in silence and fury   spinning groggy

in darkness and wind   Look
her left hand bears for you sweetly
a gift of lightning
and lilies to please you   Though
O   tonight
in her right hand she   she
has invented gravity

Nominated by Ehud Havazelet, William Matthews, Sharon Olds

SAME OLD BIG MAGIC

fiction by PATRICIA HENLEY

from THE SECRET OF CARTWHEELS (Graywolf Press)

HE KEPT the maps. They'd had a cardboard Kahlúa box of maps, forest service maps, topo maps, road maps, some of them from the early sixties when his parents had taken him and his brothers on road trips in the summers. She had to admit they were mostly his maps, though she'd grown to love them, their gift of anticipation, their memory of blind stabs at settling down, of wilderness euphoria. After thirteen years the Kahlúa box was soft as dish towels along the corners.

"That's my favorite boulder in the Cascades," she told her sister. They were both on the wagon, drinking cranberry tea and talking early marriages. "We camped under it in February one year and walked up into the mountains and hugged trees." Her sister said, "You were stoned, right?" "Yeah," she said, smiling and shaking her head yes and flipping the photo album page. "And we lived to tell the tale."

Hitchhiking can make you hate one another—or forge a link between you that can't be broken. They had taken two major trips by thumb: one from Oregon to Arizona in the middle of winter and one from Lumby, British Columbia, to Seattle, also in the winter. During these trips, life went on. They made love in the A-frame North Face mountain tent; she complained about how cramped she was on top. She sometimes cried at night, missing her sisters. They fed fragile, hopeful camp fires, drinking brandy and talking, weaving the toughest cloth of their fears and desires, finding out what they believed in. They fought over whether to eat in a restaurant or cook over a camp fire. They never had any money to speak of, but there was a stamina to their love. They prided themselves on having endured. Seventeen below; Nevada; camping in an arroyo among cages of snowy sagebrush. That's love of a different color, her girlfriends said. Hardcore. They did it to see Monument Valley in the winter, rime like crystal sugar everywhere. They did it because they thought they were both born to the road.

Once they had a cabin with a big black Monarch cookstove. This was in the beginning. Lightning pinwheeled into their bedroom and he leaped from the bed and found a book of poems and read her a poem in the storm. They carried water from the creek and shared a zinc tub of steaming bathwater. She scrubbed his back with a loofah. They made love in the parsnip patch in broad daylight. At night there were always the stars and he knew them by name. At a garage sale, they bought a cast-iron skillet and an Oriental rug. From secondhand hardbacks, they read short stories aloud to one another. There were always pileated woodpeckers, red whips of willows, evening sunlight only a gold band above the mountain; there were always animal tracks, lichened stones, creeks, applewood, fir, wild plums; there were always, always, the stars, and his arm around her as he named them: *Orion, Cygnus, Sirius.* He smelled like Balkan Sobranie tobacco and wool Woolrich shirts, and his arms were archetypal arms, arms of the woodsman who'd saved her from the wolf within.

The day they moved away from the cabin they stood on the porch and cried in one another's arms. That was the first loss they'd ever shared, shocked at its sweetness.

In town, the first town, the elementary school blazed white as sand in the winter sun. He was a student at the college and she taught at the elementary school. Kites tattered from the cottonwoods beside the playground. Their wantonness required practice. "Talk to me," she said. "You have to have a bit of the ham, the rake, in you to do this. Coax me. Be sly. You know how easy I am." Beyond the shutters an evening snowstorm muffled streets; all the cars had forgotten how to travel; they moved as though forced awry by enchantment, into berms and woodpiles. "The words," she said, "can be about how much you know I'll like it." "How does it feel for you to come?" he said. "It's like stealing something." "Stealing home," he said. She was a ma-

495

rauder, slip of a woman in the flying night, stealing whatever she could, fingers tender and blind, grafting bliss to truancy, crazed absence of self. It was something like an old blues song: that bad, winsome, visceral. She knew how it worked. They found them— the very words—and they became his charm and code, his mojo, sweetbone totem, the rib and thorn in their fenny winter bed.

They each had private dreams and these were difficult to realize together. The first time she talked about moving away, she cried into a brakeman's bandana until her eyes were puffy. Finally he said, "Maybe it's a good idea. Maybe I need to be on my own too." She said no. She said she'd figure out some other way to make her dreams come true. That was in the second year and they had eleven more years to go.

For a long time they took turns moving for one another; the one who followed always felt cheated.

Even now, when she peruses certain maps, she imagines all the places they slept outdoors together. Beside rivers, with that rushing, that glassy green blooming of the waves: Clark Fork, Gallatin, Yellowstone, Lochsa, Columbia, Methow, Okanogan, Entiat, Wenatchee, Skagit, Rogue, Klamath, Williamson, Santiam, Umpqua, Bella Coola, Fraser, Thompson, Quesnel, Chilcotin. Too numerous to mention were the creeks and lakes. And the mountains they ranged: the Cascades, the Rainbows, the Monashees, the Purcells, the Selkirks, the Tobacco Roots, the Big Belts. Field mice; blackened pots; woodsmoked sleeping bags zipping together; their breath visible in the mornings; aspens shimmering; cutthroat winds. They were caught in the bite of the mother's moon tooth.

At shi-shi beach near Neah Bay, they slept together outdoors for the last time. To the Indians, *shi-shi* meant "big magic." The unrestrained Pacific dumped rain on them four days running. Deer cavorted in the surf. They visited a man in a nearby cabin and drank mescal and traded life stories and waited out the weather. He was drunk enough to eat the worm. She has a crescent-shaped scar—petite petroglyph—on the back of her right hand, from falling into a rocky swollen creek on the walk out. She thinks it's a scar that won't fade and that pleases her, to have the mark of *shi-shi*.

Before that particular July, for several years, they practiced moving away from each other. They were getting used to the

496

idea. First there were separate pleasure trips. Then they began going away to work, a month here, two months there, a summer. Finally she took a job in another state, seventeen hundred miles away. They thought they could manage; they were good at reunions.

They broke the rules like pottery, with that little regret. Their letters of breakup crossed in the mail, one of many blessings that befell them over the years. When next they met—after the divorce was final—they were rife with happy grief, a blessing in itself they realized. He lived in a small wooden house beside a gang of McIntosh trees. The apples were nearly ripe. The whole tiny house smelled of fresh pocket bread; he baked bread so often that the muslin curtains gave off the odor of yeast and sugar. They cried, made love, slept. They had left an open bottle of Polish vodka on the kitchen table. Once, in the middle of the night, she went out to the screened-in porch. An inverted yellow kayak glowed under the clothesline. She couldn't deny feeling free, a kind of joy in the soles of her feet. The night had grown frost on the dull grass; smudge pots tilted under the trees. Stars stirred above them like fading fires, trying to focus through mottled clouds. This is how she thought of the stars: blurry, a little drunk, still there.

Nominated by Graywolf Press

THE DIG

by LYNN EMANUEL

from PLOUGHSHARES and THE DIG (University of
Illinois Press)

Beyond the dark souks of the old city, beyond the Dome of the
    Rock
gray and humped and haunted, beyond the eyes of the men at
    the café
where they drink their thimblefuls of hot tea, beyond the valley
with its scar of naked pipe, the perfect geometrical arcs of
    irrigation,
and someone incising a dark furrow in a field, some plowman's
    black
gutter opening through the green, she is waist deep in this open
    grave,
staring at the delicate puzzle of my feet. Beyond her, in the
    shadow
of Tel Hesi, daubing and dampening the earth, another woman
    finds
the faint brickwork of floor spidering the dust, on the hearth's
wedge-shaped arc of shadow a scattering of charred millet.
Nothing else for miles. Nothing but this bluff of ruin,
one decapitated tower, one "window" staved into the brick,
the bougainvillea crawling across a wall dragging its little bloody
    rags.
She is standing here thinking she cannot bear the way this foot—
my foot—wants to step out of the earth. I don't care. I am using
    her
to leave the grave. And so we go on. We go on until we cannot
    go on

deepening my grave, and the trowel hits stone and I lie staring
while she makes the earth recede, reaches in and pulls me out,
my jaw wired shut by roots, my skull so full of dirt that suddenly
the intricate sutures come loose and, in her hands, the whole
   head opens.
In the shallow setting where I lay is the small triangular sail
of a scapula, the ribs like the grill of a car. She bones me like a
   fish.
She lays the little pieces, the puzzling odds and ends, into the
   dishes
of shellac and formalin. One carpal still wears the faint blue
stain of a ring. Wearily, I lean my reassembled head,
sutures rich with glue, against the wall of the filled beaker.
A fine sweat of bubbles on my chin. All night, through the
   window
of my jar, I watch her mend with glue and wire the shallow
saucer of my pelvis. We are nothing. Earth staring at earth.

Nominated by William Matthews

THE OLD TESTAMENT

by PHILIP LEVINE

from HUDSON REVIEW

My twin brother swears that at age thirteen
I'd take on anyone who called me kike
no matter how old or how big he was.
I only wish I'd been that tiny kid
who fought back through his tears, swearing
he would not go quietly. I go quietly
packing bark chips and loam into the rose beds,
while in his memory I remain the constant child
daring him to wrest Detroit from lean gentiles
in LaSalle convertibles and golf clothes
who step slowly into the world we have tainted,
and have their revenge. I remember none of this.
He insists, he names the drug store where I poured
a milkshake over the head of an Episcopalian
with quick fists as tight as croquet balls.
He remembers his license plate, his thin lips,
the exact angle at which this 17 year old dropped
his shoulder to throw the last punch. He's making
it up. Wasn't I always terrified?
"Of course," he tells me, "that's the miracle,
you were even more scared than me, so scared
you went insane, you became a whirlwind,
an avenging angel."
                         I remember planting
my first Victory Garden behind the house, hauling
dark loam in a borrowed wagon, and putting in

carrots, corn that never grew, radishes that did.
I remember saving for weeks to buy a tea rose,
a little stick packed in dirt and burlap,
my mother's favorite. I remember the white bud
of my first peony that one morning burst
beside the mock orange that cost me 69¢.
(Fifty years later the orange is still there,
the only thing left beside a cage for watch dogs,
empty now, in what had become a tiny yard.)
I remember putting myself to sleep dreaming
of the tomatoes coming into fullness, the pansies
laughing in the spring winds, the magical wisteria
climbing along the garage, and dreaming of Hitler,
of firing a single shot from a foot away, one
that would tear his face into a caricature of mine,
tear stained, bloodied, begging for a moment's peace.

Nominated by Christopher Buckley, Henry Carlile, David Jauss,
Dorianne Laux, Len Roberts, Laurie Sheck.

WOULDN'T A TITLE JUST MAKE IT WORSE?

a story by GORDON LISH

from WITNESS

I DON'T GET IT. I just don't get it. I mean, how come is it that I am always telling people stories of my life and people are always construing my stories to be stories as in *stories*? Why would I want to tell people made-up stories? I can't stand made-up stories. It makes me sick to hear a made-up story. Look, if your story is a made-up story, then do me a favor and keep it to yourself. Me, I would never tell a made-up story about anything, let alone about myself. I respect myself much too much for me ever to stoop to just making something up about myself. I don't get it why anybody would want to tell a made-up story about himself. But the even bigger mystery to me is why, when you tell them the truth, people go ahead and look at you and say, "Oh, come on, quit it—nooooooooooooooo." Take this one, for instance. I mean, suppose we just get a squint at how this one works with someone like you instead of with anyone like them, okay? It was when I was lecturing in Austin once. I was there for the week, had to be there for the week, was signed up to teach fiction-writing there for the week—and was, for the week, being put up at the home of some very fancy folks, dignitaries in the English department or in the literature department or in one of those departments like that, both husband and wife. Anyhow, they were very grand and very nice and very kind, and I accordingly start to begin to feel so tremendously and irredeemably in debt to these folks even before I'd even slept under their roof for even one night. Well, I wasn't actually under their roof, as it were, but was in a sort of apartment affair attached to the main house by a sort of connective passageway, you might say, since passageways, I suppose, connect. I only mean to say that my place, my borrowed place, the place lent to me, that is, had its own window and its own door and when you went out of it, the door, you stepped into a little connective consideration that put you right up against the kitchen door of the grown-up house, as it also were—which is to say, the house of one's hosts. Anyhow, to get right to it if you don't mind all the hurry—you just have to appreciate the fact that I am the most fastidious little thing in all the wide and untidy world. In other words, let's say I happened to have been your house-guest for a period of ten years. Look, to give you an idea of how fastidious a little thing I am—at my usual base rate of one squillion tidinesses per year, it works out to the fact that you would find not just your house but your next-door neighbors' houses about ten squillion times tidier than they were when I had first put in an appearance in your neighborhood ten years ago. So I guess it goes without saying that this little tiny sort of garage apartment I was in was the last word in presentability the morning I was—the week's work now a job safely behind me—making ready to leave. Okay, I had to catch a plane, you see. So here's the deal—had positioned a box of candy on the table by the door, had leaned up against the box of candy a square of writing paper on which had been entered the written expression of my gratitude, had situated the key on the table so as for the key to act as a discouragement against the thank-you note's drifting to the floor, had taken one last look about to make certain nothing would offer the slightest invitation to reproach. Ahhhh. Good Gordon. I tell you, I felt as if, praise God, I was getting away with murder and was fooling them here and there and everywhere . . . *one . . . more . . . time*. And at this he shoulders his carry-all and goes for the knob with his other hand. But lets go of it, the doorknob, in the instant, it having just been disclosed to him that he is going to have to race to the latrine, and this with all possible speed. Now, then, we are hastening ahead in order that we might consider the forthcoming event from the dainty standpoint of hindsight, eh? Are you following me? Try to follow me. I have wiped. I have, as is my custom, wiped—wiping with soap, wiping with water—and wiped and wiped and wiped, flushing all the while. Good. I have not tarried for too long a time. I can make it to the airport in more than enough time. Wonderful, wonderful. I get to my feet, draw up my trousers, fasten them, yank a handful of toilet tissue free from the roll for to give a last finishing touch to the porcelain, to the seat, to the whole fucking glistening commode. When I see—in the bowl—*in the bowl*—a single, rock-hard, well-formed, fair-sized, freshly minted stool. So I activate the flushing mechanism. The water goes into its routine commotion, the excretum gets itself sucked out of sight, but in due course—just as I had guessed, just as I had guessed—hell, *guessed*—KNEW, KNEW, KNEW—from the instant I was *born* I knew!—are you kidding, are you kidding?—it, this thing, this twist of Lishness lifts itself back into blatant view, grinning, I do believe—even, it seemed to me, winking. Fine, fine—I hit the plunger again, already knowing what there is to be known, what there is *always* to be known—namely, that I and that all my descendants might stand here at our frantic labors flushing toilets until the cows came home, that when they did come home, this malicious, hainted, evil turd would still be here for them to see, and see it—it idly, gaily, gigantically turning in the otherwise perfect waters below—they, the bovine police, would. What to do, what to do, what to do? I mean, I could *see, foresee,* feel myself beaten by *forecast* galore. This blightedness, this fouledness, it would never be gone. If I snatched it up and hid it away in my carry-all, the contents thereof would smash into it and mash it into a paste that would then smear itself irremeably onto my favorite stuff, the best of which I had toted with me to Austin to show myself off in in front of whosoever might show up in my class. If instead I went to the window with it and dumped it overboard, would my hosts not come and discover it (it!) beneath the very porthole the very minute fate had seen me gone? What of taking it in hand, going to the door with it, and then going with it (oh, God, *it* again!) with me thither, thereafter to dispose of same in a suitable municipal receptacle as soon as I was well clear of the neighborhood? Yes, yes, yes, this seemed the plan! Until foresight (*stories, stories, stories*) made me to read in my mind—*in my mind*— the sentence predicating the presence of my hosts there in the passageway on the other side of the door, they foregathered in beam-

504

ing bonhomie for the very purpose of embracing me the one last time, thereupon to send me all the more cheerily off. So are you seeing what I in my mind—*in my mind*—saw? I would fling open the door and *he* would be there to reach for my hand to clasp it quickly to his own. Whereas were I to have taken the precaution of having shifted the turd into my *other* hand, then would that not be the hand that *she* would then shoot out her hand to seize, *no es verdad?* I mean, I do not know what this means, *no es verdad?*—but can you think of what else there is for me to say? Except, to be sure, to report to you—yes, yes, yes—that, yes, yes, yes, I ate it. Well, of course, I ate it. After all, had it not been written that I would? Come on, quit it—has not every outcome by the teller—by me, by you, by Willie, by your aunt Tillie—already been foretold?

So now which is it, do you say—story or *story*, truth or *truth*, or words just working out as words?

Nominated by Diane Williams

505

IN THE CLOUD CHAMBER

by ROGER WEINGARTEN

from AMERICAN POETRY REVIEW

Weightless in the shower,
I was gliding on my own
adolescent current of song, my voice
breaking into suds and spray
when the stall door cracked
open to a slice
of my father sliding the knot
in his tie toward his throat
asking was it all right with me
if he remarried. Can't hear,
I shouted, soap in my eyes.
His new shoe's perfect
shine took a giant step
backward into the billowing
steam. Years later, I told
my four-year-old in the tub
I'm leaving your mother, then
asked if he understood I wasn't
leaving him. He left
his wind-up scuba diver sputtering,
stepped into a towel and without a word
closed the mirror-backed door
in my dripping face. My reflection

distorted in the chrome
doorknob turned counter-clockwise.
My red-eyed boy returned
an angel of vengeance in pajamas,
threw a punch then another
I caught in flight. We tumbled
to the bath mat. He cried,
kneed and scratched, his entire
being flailing at mine. Seven years
of weekends and holidays into the future,
dreaming I'm on my knees at the foot
of the porcelain throne clipping my dead
father's toenails, the white
crescents growing back
as I go, the sound of bathwater
lapping turns me around to the skinny
frame of my son afloat, raging
at someone he can't see, calling out
the garbled words of a child in sleep,
the steam rising.

Nominated by Genie Chipps

"NEARER GOD, NEARER REALITE"

—Gwen John

by JOELLEN KWIATEK

from THE INDIANA REVIEW

I'm safe—safe in a mood.
The quiet of trees after snowfall
is in my room. The same
sterling expectancy. I
could read now or sew.
Occasionally look up.
To read is to lower
oneself into time as if it were
a bath. I believe
in slowness, in the loss that
precedes harmony.

Listen! If I paint a thing
over and over, it's
not for security or to show
faith; the only way
in for me is to repeat my subject
endlessly, like a chant. (Once

against the pressure of aloneness
I thought the friezework
on the church had the momentum of a herd—
the saints like young bulls with their heads down.)

Each weekday I travel from
my room to my studio and
back. On Saturdays I ride
the trams, sketching.
Sundays I go to mass.
To tame my happiness I sleep.

Nominated by Karen Fish

THREE PROTRUSIONS

fiction by DAVID FOSTER WALLACE

from GRAND STREET

WHERE WAS THE woman who said she'd come. She said she
would come. He thought she'd have come by now. He sat and
thought. He was in the living room. When he started waiting one
window was full of yellow light across the floor and he was still
waiting as that shadow began to fade and was intersected by a
brightening shadow from a different wall's window. There was an
insect on one of the steel shelves that held his audio equipment.
The insect kept going in and out of one of the holes on the gird-
ers that the shelves fit into. The insect was dark and had a shiny
case. He kept looking over at it. Once or twice he started to get
up to go over closer to look at it, but he was afraid that if he came
closer and saw it closer he would kill it, and he was afraid to kill
it. He did not use the phone to call the woman who'd promised
to come because if he tied up the line and if it happened to be
the time when maybe she was trying to call him he was afraid she
would hear the busy signal and think him disinterested and get
angry and maybe take what she'd promised him somewhere else.

She had promised to get him a quarter of a pound of marijuana, four ounces of unusually good marijuana, for $550. He had
tried to stop smoking marijuana maybe seventy or eighty times
before. Before this woman knew him. She did not know he had
tried to stop. He always lasted a week, or two weeks, or maybe
two days, and then he'd think and decide to have some in his
home one more last time. One last final time he'd search out
someone new, someone he hadn't already told that he had to stop

510

smoking dope and please under no circumstances should they procure him any dope. It had to be a third party, because he'd told every dealer he knew to cut him off. And the third party had to be someone new, because each time he got some he knew this time had to be the last time, and so told them, asked them, as a favor, never to get him any more, ever. And he never asked a person again once he'd told them this, because he was proud, and also kind, and wouldn't put anyone in that kind of contradictory position. Also he considered himself creepy when it came to dope, and he was afraid that others would see that he was creepy about it as well. He sat and thought and waited in an uneven X of light through two different windows. Once or twice he looked at the phone. The insect had disappeared back into the hole in the steel girder a shelf fit into.

She'd promised to come at one certain time, and it was past that time. Finally he called and it rang and he was afraid of how much time he was taking tying up the line and he got her answering machine, the message had a snatch of radio music and her voice and a male voice saying we'll call you back, and the "we" made them sound like a couple, the man was a handsome black man who was in law school, she designed sets, and he didn't leave a message because he didn't want her to know how much now he felt like he needed it. He had been very casual about the whole thing. She said she knew a guy over in Enfield who sold high-resin dope in moderate bulk, and he'd yawned and said well, maybe, well, hey, why not, sure, special occasion, I haven't bought any in I don't know how long. He said he guessed he'd have her get a decent amount, he said he'd had some friends call him in the recent past and ask if he could get them some. He had this thing where he'd frequently say he was getting dope for friends. Then if the woman didn't have it when she said she'd have it for him and he became anxious about it he could tell the woman that it was his friends who were becoming anxious, and he was sorry to bother the woman about something so casual but his friends were anxious and bothering him about it and he just wanted to know what he could tell them. He was caught in the middle, is how he would represent it. He could say his friends had given him their money and were now anxious and exerting pressure. This tactic was not possible with this woman who'd said she'd come because he hadn't yet given her the $550. She would not let him. She was well off. Her family was well off, she'd said to explain how her condominium was how it was when she worked designing sets for a Cambridge theater company that seemed to do only German plays, dark smeary sets. She didn't care much about money, she said she'd cover the cost when she got out to Enfield to see whether the guy was at home as she was certain he would be this particular afternoon, and he could pay her back when she got it. This arrangement, very casual, made him anxious, so he'd been even more casual and said sure, fine, whatever. Thinking back, he was sure he'd said "whatever," which in retrospect worried him because it might have sounded like he didn't care at all, not at all, so little that it wouldn't matter if she forgot to get it or call, and once he'd made the decision to have marijuana in his home one more time it mattered a lot. It mattered a lot. He'd been too casual, he should have made her take $550 from him up front, claiming politeness, claiming he didn't want to inconvenience her financially over something so trivial and casual. He didn't care much about money either, money was not where his greed lay. He had his share of the emotion of greed, but somehow it wasn't for money. But money did create a sense of obligation, and he did want the woman to feel obliged to do what she'd said once what she'd said she'd do had set him off inside. It mattered so much somehow he was afraid to show how much it mattered. Once he had asked her to get it, he was committed to several courses of action. The insect on the shelf was back. It didn't seem to do anything. It just came out of the hole in the girder onto the edge of the steel shelf and sat there. After a while it would disappear back into the hole in the girder, and he was pretty sure it didn't do anything in there either. He felt similar to the insect inside the girder his shelf was connected to but was not sure just how he was similar. Once he'd decided to own marijuana one more last time, he was committed to several courses of action. He had to call in to the agency and say there was an emergency and ask them to put a note in a colleague's box asking her to cover his calls for the rest of the week because he'd be out of town for several days due to this emergency. He had to put a message on his answering machine saying that starting that afternoon he was going to be unreachable for several days. He had to clean his bedroom, because once he had dope he would not leave his bedroom except to go to the refrigerator and the

512

bathroom, and even then the trips would be very quick. He had to throw out all his beer and liquor, because if he drank alcohol and smoked dope at the same time he would get dizzy and ill, and if he had alcohol in the house he could not be relied on not to drink it once he started smoking dope. He had to do some shopping. He had to lay in supplies. Now just one of the insect's antennae was protruding from the hole in the girder. It protruded but did not move. Somehow he formed the analogy that when he had committed himself to one last vacation with marijuana, but the marijuana had not yet arrived, something in him protruded but did not move. He spent several hundred clicks of the portable clock next to the telephone on this analogy, not extending the analogy or trying to analyze it, but simply letting it sit there. He had had to buy soda, Oreos, bread, sandwich meat, mayonnaise, tomatoes, M&M's, Almost Home cookies, ice cream, a Pepperidge Farm frozen chocolate cake, and four cans of canned chocolate frosting to be eaten with a large spoon. He'd had to rent film cartridges from the entertainment service. He'd had to buy antacids for the discomfort that eating all he would eat would cause late at night. He'd had to buy a bong, because each time he finished what had to be his last bulk-quantity of marijuana he decided that that was it, he was through, he didn't even like it anymore, that was it, no more hiding, no more putting different messages on his answering machine and moving his car away from his condominium and closing his windows and curtains and blinds and living in vectors between his television and VCR and his refrigerator and his toilet, and he would throw the bong away wrapped in numerous paper bags. His refrigerator made its own ice in little cloudy crescent blocks and he loved it, when he had dope in his home he always drank a great deal of cold soda and ice water. His tongue almost swelled at the thought. He looked at the phone and the clock. He looked at the windows but not at the foliage and driveway beyond the windows. He had already vacuumed his venetian blinds and curtains, everything was ready to be shut down. Once the woman who'd said she'd come had come, he would shut the system down. It occurred to him that he would disappear into a hole in a girder inside him that supported something else inside him. He was unsure what the thing inside him was and was unprepared to commit himself to the course of action that would be required to explore the question. It was now almost three hours past the time when the woman had said she would come. A counselor, Randi, with an *i*, with a mustache like a Mountie, had said in the outpatient treatment program he'd gone through two years ago that he seemed insufficiently committed to the course of action that would be required to remove substances from his life. He'd had to buy a new bong at Bogarts in Cambridge because whenever he finished the last of the substances on hand he always threw out his bong and pipes, screens and tubes and rolling papers and roach clips, lighters and Visine and Pepto-Bismol and cookies and cakes, to eliminate all temptation. He wrapped everything in Star Market shopping bags and drove it out to some dumpster in some disreputable location, and discarded it. He removed all dope-related materials from his life each time. He always felt a great relief and optimism after he'd discarded the materials. He'd bought the new bong and laid in supplies this morning, getting back home with everything well before the woman had said she'd come. He thought of the new bong and new little packet of brass screens in the Bogarts bag on his kitchen table in the sunlit kitchen and could not remember what color this new bong was. The last one had been orange, the one before that a dusky rose color that had turned muddy at the bottom from resin in just four days. He could not remember the color of this new last bong. He considered getting up to check the color of the bong he'd be using but decided that obsessive checking and convulsive movements could compromise the atmosphere of casual calm he needed to maintain while he waited, protruding but not moving, for the woman he'd met at a design session for his agency's small campaign for her small theater company's new Brecht festival, while he waited for this woman, with whom he'd had intercourse twice, to honor her casual promise. He tried to decide whether she was pretty. Another thing he laid in when he'd committed himself to one last marijuana vacation was petroleum jelly. When he smoked marijuana he tended to masturbate a great deal, and the petroleum jelly kept him from returning to normal function all sore. He was also hesitant to get up and check the color of his bong because he would have to pass right by the phone to get to the kitchen, and he didn't want to be tempted to call the woman who'd said she would come again because he felt creepy about bothering her about something so casual, and was afraid that several hang-ups

514

on her answering machine would look even creepier, and also he felt anxious about tying up the line when she called, as she certainly would. He decided to get Call Waiting added to his phone service for a nominal extra charge, then remembered that since this was positively the last time he would or even could indulge what Randi, with an *i*, had called an addiction every bit as destructive as pure alcoholism, there would be no real need for Call Waiting, since a situation like the present one could never arise again. This line of thinking almost caused him to become angry. To ensure the composure with which he sat waiting in light in his chair he focused his senses on his surroundings. No part of the insect he'd seen was now visible. The clicks of his portable clock were really composed of three smaller clicks, signifying he supposed preparation, movement, and readjustment. His left thumbnail was noticeably longer than his right thumbnail, which was puzzling, since he clipped all his nails at the same time and never bit his nails. His necktie had bunched into a small arc between the top of his vest and the collar of his shirt. He began to grow disgusted with himself for waiting so anxiously for something that had stopped being fun anyway. He didn't even know why he liked it anymore. It made his mouth dry and his eyes dry and red and his face sag, and he hated it when his face sagged, it was as if all the integrity of all the muscles in his face was destroyed by marijuana, and he got terribly self-conscious about the fact that his face was sagging, and had long ago forbidden himself to smoke dope around anyone else. And the dope gave him a painful case of pleurisy if he smoked it for more than two straight days of heavy continuous smoking in his bedroom. It made his thoughts jut out crazily in jagged directions and made him stare like a rapt child at anything convulsive or bright—he favored video cartridges in which a lot of things blew up and there was little dialogue when he laid in video cartridges for a vacation with marijuana. He gathered his intellect, will, self-knowledge, and conviction and determined that when this woman came as she surely would this would simply be his last marijuana debauch. He'd simply smoke so much so fast that it would be so unpleasant and the memory of it so repulsive that once he'd gotten it out of his home and his life as quickly as possible he'd never even want to do it again. He would create a really bad association with the stuff. The dope scared him. It made him afraid. It wasn't that he

515

was afraid of it, it was that it made him afraid of everything else. He would smoke the whole quarter-pound in four days, an ounce a day, all in tight heavy economical one-hitters off a bong, an incredible, insane amount per day, he'd treat it like a penance, he'd smoke one ounce per day, starting right when he woke up and detached his tongue from the roof of his mouth and took an antacid, two or three hundred bong hits per day, an insane, unpleasant, brain-damaging amount, even though if it was good after the first ten hits he wouldn't want any more until he wanted more. He would smoke it even if he did not want it. He would use discipline and persistence and make the whole experience so unpleasant, so debased and degrading and painful, that his behavior would be henceforth modified, he'd never even want to do it again, the memory of the debauched four days to come would be so firmly, terribly emblazoned in his memory. He'd cure himself by excess. He predicted that the woman, when she came, might want to smoke some of the four ounces with him, hang out, hole up, listen to some of his impressive collection of Tito Puente recordings, and probably have intercourse. He had never once had intercourse on marijuana. The idea frankly repelled him. Two dry mouths bumping at each other, trying to kiss. His thoughts jutting and twisting around on themselves like a snake on a stick while he snorted and grimaced above her, his face sagging so that its loose folds maybe touched, limply, the folds of her loose face as it went back and forth spread out over his pillowcase. He decided he'd have her toss him what she'd promised and then would toss the $550 in large bills back at her from a distance and tell her not to let the door hit her on the bottom on the way out. He'd say "ass" instead of "bottom." He'd be so rude to her that the memory of his lack of courtesy and of her tight offended face would be a further disincentive ever, in the future, to risk calling her and repeating the course of action he had committed himself to.

He had never been so anxious for the arrival of a woman he did not want to see. He remembered clearly the last woman he'd involved in his trying just one more vacation with dope and drawn blinds. The last woman had been something called an appropriation artist, which meant she copied and embellished other art, then sold it. She had an artistic manifesto that involved radical feminist themes. He'd let her give him one of her smaller

516

paintings, which covered half the wall over his bed and was of a famous film actress whose name he had a hard time recalling and a less famous film actor, the two of them in a scene from a well-known film, a romantic scene, an embrace, copied from a film magazine and much enlarged and made stilted, with obscenities scrawled all over it in bright brave red letters. The last woman had been sexy but not pretty, as the woman he now didn't want to see but was waiting for was pretty in a tight tanned withered Cambridge way that made her seem pretty but not sexy. The appropriation artist had been led to believe that he was a recovering speed addict, intravenous addiction to methamphetamine hydrochloride is what he remembered telling that one, he had even described the terrible taste of hydrochloride in the addict's mouth immediately after injection, he had researched the subject carefully. She had been further led to believe that marijuana kept him from using the drug with which he really had a problem, and so that if he seemed anxious to get some once she'd offered to get him some it was only because he was heroically holding out against much darker deeper more addictive urges, and he needed her to help him. He couldn't quite remember when or how she'd been given all these impressions. He had not sat down and outright bold-faced lied to her, it had been more of an impression he'd nurtured and allowed to gather its own life and force. The insect was now entirely visible. It was on the shelf that held his amplifier and equalizer. The insect might never actually have gone back into the hole in the shelf's girder. The girder protruded from the wall and was a triangle of dull silver metal with holes for shelves to fit into. The shelves that held his audio equipment were metal painted a dark industrial green and were originally made for holding canned goods. They were designed to be extra kitchen shelves. The insect sat with an immobility that seemed like the gathering of a force, it sat like the hull of a vehicle from which the engine had been for the moment removed. It was dark and had a shiny case and antennae that did not move. He had to use the bathroom. His last piece of contact from the appropriation artist, with whom he had had intercourse, and who during intercourse had sprayed perfume into the air from a mister she held in her left hand as she lay beneath him making a wide variety of sounds and spraying perfume into the air, so that he felt the cold mist of it settling on his back and shoulders and was terribly chilled, his last piece of contact after he'd disappeared with the marijuana she had gotten for him had been a card that was a pastiche photo of a doormat of rough false plastic green with WELCOME on it and next to it a flattering publicity photo of her from her Back Bay gallery, and between them an unequal sign, an equal sign with a diagonal slash through it, and an obscenity he had assumed was directed at him scrawled in red grease pencil at the top and bottom. She had been offended because he had seen her every day for ten days, then when she'd obtained two ounces of marijuana for him he had said that she had saved his life and he was grateful and the friends to whom he'd promised to give some were grateful and she had to go right now because he had an appointment and had to leave, but that he would doubtless call her that day, and they had shared a moist kiss, and she had said she could feel his heart pounding right through his suit coat, and she had driven away in her unmuffled car, and he had gone and moved his own car to a garage several blocks away, and had walked back and drawn the blinds and curtains, and changed the message on his answering machine to one that described an emergency departure from town, and had drawn and locked his vacuumed bedroom blinds, and had taken the new rose-colored bong out of its Bogarts bag, and was not seen for three days, and ignored over a dozen messages from the appropriation artist on his answering machine expressing concern over the emergency, and had never contacted her again. He had assumed she would assume he had succumbed again to methamphetamine hydrochloride and was sparing her the agony of his descent into the hell of addiction. What it really was was that he had again decided those two ounces of reasonably good marijuana represented his final debauch with dope and that he had to cut himself off from all possible future sources of temptation and supply, and that surely included the appropriation artist. His shame at what she might perceive as his slimy conduct toward her made it easier for him to avoid her, too. Though not shame, really. More like being very uncomfortable. He had had to launder his bedding twice to get the smell of the perfume out. He went into the bathroom to use the bathroom, making it a point to look at neither the insect that sat still on the shelf to his left nor the telephone and answering machine on the small stand to his right. He was committed to touching neither. Where was the woman who had said she'd come. The new bong in the bag was a rich green that paled when the device was held up to the late-afternoon light of the window over the kitchen sink. The metal of his new stem and bowl was rough silver, with a grain, unpretty and all business. The bong was two feet tall and had a weighted base and its plastic was thick and its carb had been raggedly cut so that some rough shards of plastic protruded from the little hole and might hurt his thumb, which he decided to consider just part of the penance he would undertake after the woman had come. He left the door to the bathroom open so that he would be sure to hear the phone when it rang or the buzzer to the front door of his condominium when it sounded. In the bathroom he wept hard for only two or three seconds before the weeping stopped abruptly and he could not get it to start again. It was now over four hours since the time the woman had casually committed to come. Was he in the bathroom or in his chair near the window and near his telephone and answering machine and the insect and the window that had admitted a straight spilled bar of light when he began to wait. The light through this window was coming at an angle more and more oblique, its shadow had become a parallelogram. The light through the west window was straight and reddening. He had thought he needed to use the bathroom but was unable to. He tried putting a whole stack of video cartridges into the VCR and turning on the large television in his bedroom. He could see the bold-colored piece of appropriation art in the mirror above the television. He lowered the volume all the way and pointed the remote control device at the television like some sort of weapon. He sat on the edge of his box spring and mattress with his elbows on his knees and scanned the stack of cartridges. Each dropped and began to spin in the machine with an insectlike click and whir, and he scanned it. He was unable to distract himself with the VCR because he was unable to stay with any one entertainment cartridge for more than a few seconds. The moment he recognized what was on one cartridge he had a strong unpleasant feeling that there was something better on another cartridge and that he was missing it. He scanned for some time. The bedroom was dim because the curtains over the big window that overlooked the street had been vacuumed and pulled shut tight, so it was difficult to gauge how long he scanned. The phone rang during this interval of scanning. He was moving back out toward it before the first ring was completed, flooded with excitement, or relief, the remote control device still in his hand, but it was only a friend, calling, and when he heard that it was not the woman who had promised to bring what he'd committed the next several days to banishing from his life forever, he was shocked with disappointment, with a great deal of mistaken adrenaline shining and ringing in his system, and he got off the line with the friend to clear the line and keep it available so fast that he was sure his friend perceived him as either angry with him or just plain rude. He was further upset because his answering the phone this late in the afternoon did not jibe with the emergency message that would be on his answering machine if the friend called back after the woman had come and he'd shut the system down, and he was standing by the phone machine trying to decide whether the risk of the friend calling back was sufficient to justify changing the message on the answering machine to describe an emergency departure starting this evening instead of this afternoon, but he decided he felt that since the woman had committed to coming some time ago, his leaving the message intact would be a gesture of fidelity to her commitment, and might somehow in some oblique way strengthen that commitment. He returned to his chair. The television and VCR were still on in his bedroom and he could see through the angle of the doorway the lights from the television screen blink and shift from one primary color to another in the dim room, and for a while he killed time casually by trying to imagine what scenes on the unwatched screen the changing colors and intensities might be depicting. Reading while waiting for marijuana was out of the question. He considered masturbating but did not. He didn't reject the idea so much as not react to it and watch as it floated away. He thought very broadly of desires and ideas being watched but not acted upon, he thought of impulses being starved of expression and drying out and floating drily away, and felt on some level that this had something to do with him and his circumstances and what, if the last debauch he'd committed himself to didn't perhaps resolve the problem, would surely have to be called his problem, but he could not even begin to try to see how the image of desiccated impulses floating related to either him or the insect that was back in its hole in the girder, because at this precise time the telephone and the buzzer to the door downstairs both sounded at once, both loud and tortured and so abrupt they sounded yanked through a very small hole into the great balloon of silence he sat in, waiting, and he moved first toward the telephone, and then toward his intercom module, and then tried to move back to the phone, and then tried to move toward both at once, so that he stood splay-legged, arms wildly out as if something had been flung, splayed, entombed between the two signals, without a thought in his head.

Nominated by Mary Karr

SPECIAL MENTION

(The editors also wish to mention the following important works published by small presses last year. Listing is in no particular order.)

POETRY

Thirty One Flavors of Houses—Rodney Jones (New England Review)

Union Camp Bag Plant—Kathleen Berotti (Sou'wester)

The Raptors—William Olsen (Poetry Northwest)

Poppy Field Near Giverny—Stephen Corey (Yellow Silk)

To Dream A Tongue Loose—Judy Chalmer (Spoon River Anthology)

The Boy Who Had No Shadow—Michael Burkhard (The American Voice)

The Gladiolas—Deborah DiNicola (Embers)

Scar—C.K. Williams (Kenyon Review)

Growing Up With A Sears Catalogue—Khaled Mattawa (Michigan Quarterly Review)

Musica Reservata—John Ashbery (Paris Review)

Broadway—Mark Doty (The American Voice)

Circe—Dian Shoaf (*Hurricane Walk*, BOA Editions)

River Bridge—Lynda Hull (Denver Quarterly)

One Story Conversation—Sally Ball (Threepenny Review)

Removes—Michael Klein (Kenyon Review)

Halloween—Frankie Paino (Kenyon Review)

Net of Jewels—Barbara Siegel Carlson (Passages North)

Flights to Another Kingdom—Juan Felipe Herrera (High Plains Review)

Gloves—Claire Bateman (Passages North)

Praising Dark Places—Yusef Komunyakaa (Southern Review)

Shame—Tom Sleigh (TriQuarterly)
A Necessary Story—Dionisio D. Martinez (Kenyon Review)
Donuts, the Color of—Jim Daniels (Tampa Review)
The Secret Life—Chana Bloch (Poetry)
In A Motel Room In Nebraska—Jim Shugrue (Poetry East)
The Dyke with No Name Thinks About A Landscape—Judith Barrington (The American Voice)
Dawn—Campbell McGrath (Ohio Review)
Lawn Mower—Michael Heffernan (Iowa Review)
The Friend—Rachel Hadas (The Formalist)
Aunt Mary Jean—Andrew Hudgins (Paris Review)
The Sad Art of Making Paper—Ramon C. Sunico (Manoa)
Restlessness—Barbara Guest (New American Writing)
Letter to My Mother in Spanish—Judith Ortiz Cofer (Prairie Schooner)
Trakl & Grete—Michael J. Bugeja (Prairie Schooner)
The Business of Love Is Cruelty—Dean Young (Poetry East)

ESSAYS

Wistman's Wood—Stanley Plumly (Ohio Review)
The Messenger of the Lost Battalion—Gregory Orfalea (*Visions of America: Personal Narratives*, Persea Books)
Lost Cowboys (But Not Forgotten)—William Kittredge (Antaeus)
South of the Ultima Thule—Emily Hiestand (Georgia Review)
A Liberal Education: Mentors, Fomenters, and Tormentors—W.D. Snodgrass (Southern Review)
The Rat Historian—David Morse (Boulevard)
Via Negativa: From Croatia to Yale Divinity—Josip Novakovich (Hungry Mind Review)
My Mother Will Never Forgive Them—Mary-Claire King (Grand Street)
The Dark American Bar—Robert Pinsky (Southwest Review)
The Gulf of Unknowing—Will Baker (Georgia Review)
Karachi—Sara Suleri (Raritan: A Quarterly Review)
Symbols In The Rock—Frank Stewart (Southwest Review)
Swiss Wilderness—Reg Saner (Gettysburg Review)

FICTION

Schlafstunde—Yehudit Katzir (Grand Street)

Those Hands, That Hair—Daniel Barden (Western Humanities Review)

My Summer of Love—Alyce Miller (New England Review)

Citadel—T.L. Toma (Black Warrior Review)

Ed and Dave Visit The City—Ann Beattie (Southern Review)

Babies—Abraham Rodriguez (*The Boy Without A Flag*, Milkweed Editions)

Moonwalk—Susan Power (Ploughshares)

Witness—D.J. Waldie (Massachusetts Review)

So Long—Lucia Berlin (ZYZZYVA)

Beverly Home—Denis Johnson (Paris Review)

Rupert Killamarsh's Other Life—Paul West (Conjunctions)

Heaven Is No Use If You're Dead When You Get There—Nanci Kincaid (Shenandoah)

Widow—Joyce Carol Oates (The Southern Review)

Spinach—Dan Leone (Paris Review)

Pawnbroker to the Stars—Ellen Herman (Other Voices)

The Taking of Charlotte—Joan Marcus (Georgia Review)

The Cracker Man—Helen Norris (Gettysburg Review)

My Mother, Jolene and Me—Gregory Spatz (New England Review)

Glissando—Robert Boswell (Iowa Review)

This Is It—Sigrid Nunez (Fiction)

Selma's Weddings—Deborah Najor (Michigan Quarterly Review)

Love and Work—Alice Adams (Southwest Review)

Light of This World—Ehud Havazelet (Tikkun)

Talking Dog—Francine Prose (Yale Review)

The Ghost of Magnetism—William T. Vollmann (Paris Review)

Safe At Home—Robert Spencer Wilson (American Short Fiction)

In The South—Jack Lopez (Quarterly West)

Potato Women—Teresa Jordan (Yellow Silk)

Angela's Story—Domenic Stansberry (*Exit Paradise*, Lynx House)

A Bad Outfit—Donald Mangum (Mississippi Review)

Wernher Von Braun's Last Picnic—Robin Hemley (Another Chicago Magazine)

Gulf War—Joyce Carol Oates (Boulevard)

Jalousie—Anthony Bukoski (Quarterly West)

Or Live So Long—Sharon Solwitz (Boulevard)

The Iron Road—Cary Holladay (Shenandoah)

The Fay Wray Day Memorial Party—Robert Phillips (Boulevard)
The Personals—Leslee Becker (Prism International)
Landing Zone X-Ray—Thomas E. Kennedy (New Letters)
The Poorest Boy In Chicago—Mitch Berman (Southwest Review)
The Arrival of the Queen of Sheba (in Galway)—Philip Brady (Massachusetts Review)
Wisconsin—James McManus (Other Voices)
A Night in Newark—Michael Lee (Temper)
Two After Four—Mark Wisniewski (Painted Hills Review)
Rubato—Sussy Chako (Hawaii Review)
Where It Belongs—Louisa Ermelino (Italian Americana)
from Elongated Figures—Tom Whalen (Red Dust)
Condolences—Ed Weyhing (Calliope)
from The Crow Eaters—Bapsi Sidhwa (Milkweed Editions)
The Donor—Victoria Bilski (Black Warrior Review)
Shooting The Dog—Bobbie Ann Mason (The Southern Review)
Flying Lessons—Thomas E. Kennedy (Gettysburg Review)
Send Me Meat—Jacoba Hood (Crazyhorse)
The Lufbery Circle—James Spencer (Ontario Review)
The Logic of Angels—Karen S. McElmurray (Alaska Quarterly)
My Father's Heart—Tony Earley (TriQuarterly)
Buddy's Best Work—Abigail Thomas (Missouri Review)
Marine Mammal Guy—Gerald Shapiro (Gettysburg Review)
Bread—Frederick Busch (Gettysburg Review)
The Greek Head—Peter Weltner (American Short Fiction)
How It Is—Kyle Anne Bates (Glimmer Train)
Radon—Edward Falco (Virginia Quarterly)
I Am The Other—K.C. Frederick (Fiction International)
Sister—Richard Bailey (Oxford Magazine)
Angel—Philip Graham (Missouri Review)
My Body To You—Elizabeth Searle (Kenyon Review)
Cutter—C.E. Poverman (Ontario Review)
The Monster—Melanie Sumner (Boulevard)
The Chief's Bridge—Elizabeth Inness-Brown (Boulevard)
Risk—Cornelia Nixon (Boulevard)
The Surgeon—Elizabeth Inness-Brown (Glimmer Train)
Book of Songs—John Dalton (Story)
Hawk of the Night—Ewing Campbell (Cimarron Review)
The Weight of the Soul—Robin Green (Sou'wester)
Spirit Voices—Dan Chaon (American Short Fiction)

The War That Never Ends—Michael Martone (High Plains Literary Review)
The Address—Josip Novakovich (Chelsea)
Home Base—Courtney Henry (Folio)
The Heaven of Animals—Alison Baker (Alaska Quarterly Review)
Rumanian Legends—Barbara Scheiber (Whetstone)
Merit-Making—Leslie Bienen (The Journal)
Revenge—Christine Benvenuto (William and Mary Review)
Preparation—Robert Olen Butler (Sewanee Review)
Evening—Richard Bausch (The Southern Review)
The Happy Day—Antonya Nelson (Kenyon Review)
The Tyranny of the Visual—Barry Hannah (Southern Review)
The Visitors—Josephine Jacobsen (Ontario Review)
Blazo—Ron Carlson (Ploughshares)
from The Queen of Diamonds—Stephen Wright (Ontario Review)
The Gulf—J.D. Dolan (Shenandoah)
Terrific Mother—Lorrie Morre (Paris Review)
Queen Wintergreen—Alice Fulton (TriQuarterly)
June Afternoon—Christa Wolf (Grand Street)
The Channah Tales—Bradford Morrow (Conjunctions)
Lakeview—Gerald Shapiro (Greensboro Review)
Eros Manque—Randall Reid (Antioch Review)
They, The Living—Lane von Herzen (Greensboro Review)
Absent Without Leave—Jessica Treadway (Agni)
My Own Vanity—Daniel Wallace (Glimmer Train)
from The Cleveland Indian—Luke Salisbury (The Smith)
Buffalo Medicine—Diane Glancy (Michigan Quarterly Review)

PRESSES FEATURED IN THE PUSHCART PRIZE EDITIONS (1976–1993)

Acts
Agni Review
Ahsahta Press
Ailanthus Press
Alaska Quarterly Review
Alcheringa/Ethnopoetics
Alice James Books
Ambergris
Amelia
American Literature
American PEN
American Poetry Review
American Scholar
The American Voice
Amicus Journal
Amnesty International
Anaesthesia Review
Another Chicago Magazine
Antaeus
Antietam Review
Antioch Review
Apalachee Quarterly
Aphra
Aralia Press
The Ark
Ascensius Press
Ascent

Aspen Leaves
Aspen Poetry Anthology
Assembling
Bamboo Ridge
Barlenmir House
Barnwood Press
The Bellingham Review
Bellowing Ark
Beloit Poetry Journal
Bennington Review
Bilingual Review
Black American Literature Forum
Black Rooster
Black Scholar
Black Sparrow
Black Warrior Review
Blackwells Press
Bloomsbury Review
Blue Cloud Quarterly
Blue Unicorn
Blue Wind Press
Bluefish
BOA Editions
Bookslinger Editions
Boulevard
Boxspring
Bridges

Brown Journal of the Arts
Burning Deck Press
Caliban
California Quarterly
Callaloo
Calliope
Calliopea Press
Canto
Capra Press
Carolina Quarterly
Cedar Rock
Center
Chariton Review
Charnel House
Chelsea
Chicago Review
Chouteau Review
Chowder Review
Cimarron Review
Cincinnati Poetry Review
City Lights Books
Clown War
CoEvolution Quarterly
Cold Mountain Press
Colorado Review
Columbia: A Magazine of Poetry
    and Prose
Confluence Press
Confrontation
Conjunctions
Copper Canyon Press
Cosmic Information Agency
Crawl Out Your Window
Crazyhorse
Crescent Review
Cross Cultural Communications
Cross Currents
Cumberland Poetry Review
Curbstone Press
Cutbank
Dacotah Territory
Daedalus
Dalkey Archive Press

Decatur House
December
Denver Quarterly
Domestic Crude
Dragon Gate Inc.
Dreamworks
Dryad Press
Duck Down Press
Durak
East River Anthology
Ellis Press
Empty Bowl
Epoch
Exquisite Corpse
Fiction
Fiction Collective
Fiction International
Field
Firebrand Books
Firelands Art Review
Five Fingers Review
Five Trees Press
The Formalist
Frontiers: A Journal of Women
    Studies
Gallimaufry
Genre
The Georgia Review
Gettysburg Review
Ghost Dance
Goddard Journal
David Godine, Publisher
Graham House Press
Grand Street
Granta
Graywolf Press
Green Mountains Review
Greenfield Review
Greensboro Review
Guardian Press
Hard Pressed
Hayden's Ferry Review
Hermitage Press

Hills
Holmgangers Press
Holy Cow!
Home Planet News
Hudson Review
Icarus
Iguana Press
Indiana Review
Indiana Writes
Intermedia
Intro
Invisible City
Inwood Press
Iowa Review
Ironwood
Jam To-day
The Kanchenjuga Press
Kansas Quarterly
Kayak
Kelsey Street Press
Kenyon Review
Latitudes Press
Laughing Waters Press
Laurel Review
L'Epervier Press
Liberation
Linquis
The Literary Review
The Little Magazine
Living Hand Press
Living Poets Press
Logbridge-Rhodes
Lowlands Review
Lucille
Lynx House Press
Magic Circle Press
Malahat Review
Mānoa
Manroot
Massachusetts Review
Mho & Mho Works
Micah Publications
Michigan Quarterly

Milkweed Editions
Milkweed Quarterly
The Minnesota Review
Mississippi Review
Mississippi Valley Review
Missouri Review
Montana Gothic
Montana Review
Montemora
Moon Pony Press
Mr. Cogito Press
MSS
Mulch Press
Nada Press
New America
New American Review
The New Criterion
New Delta Review
New Directions
New England Review
New England Review and Bread
    Loaf Quarterly
New Letters
New Virginia Review
New York Quarterly
New York University Press
Nimrod
North American Review
North Atlantic Books
North Dakota Quarterly
North Point Press
Northern Lights
Northwest Review
O. ARS
Obsidian
Oconee Review
October
Ohio Review
Ontario Review
Open Places
Orca Press
Orchises Press
Oxford Press

Oyez Press
Painted Bride Quarterly
Painted Hills Review
Paris Review
Parnassus: Poetry in Review
Partisan Review
Passages North
Penca Books
Pentagram
Penumbra Press
Pequod
Persea: An International Review
Pipedream Press
Pitcairn Press
Ploughshares
Poet and Critic
Poetry
Poetry East
Poetry Northwest
Poetry Now
Prairie Schooner
Prescott Street Press
Promise of Learnings
Provincetown Arts
Puerto Del Sol
Quarry West
The Quarterly
Quarterly West
Raccoon
Rainbow Press
Raritan: A Quarterly Review
Red Cedar Review
Red Clay Books
Red Dust Press
Red Earth Press
Release Press
Review of Contemporary Fiction
Revista Chicano-Riquena
River Styx
Rowan Tree Press
Russian *Samizdat*
Salmagundi
San Marcos Press

Sea Pen Press and Paper Mill
Seal Press
Seamark Press
Seattle Review
Second Coming Press
Semiotext(e)
The Seventies Press
Sewanee Review
Shankpainter
Shantih
Sheep Meadow Press
Shenandoah
A Shout In the Street
Sibyl-Child Press
Side Show
Small Moon
The Smith
Some
The Sonora Review
South Florida Poetry Review
Southern Poetry Review
Southern Review
Southwest Review
Spectrum
The Spirit That Moves Us
St. Andrews Press
Story
Story Quarterly
Streetfare Journal
Stuart Wright, Publisher
Sulfur
The Sun
Sun & Moon Press
Sun Press
Sunstone
Sycamore Review
Tar River Poetry
Teal Press
Telephone Books
Telescope
Temblor
Tendril
Texas Slough

13th Moon
THIS
Thorp Springs Press
Three Rivers Press
Threepenny Review
Thunder City Press
Thunder's Mouth Press
Tikkun
Tombouctou Books
Toothpaste Press
Transatlantic Review
TriQuarterly
Truck Press
Undine
Unicorn Press
University of Illinois Press
University of Massachusetts Press
University of Pittsburgh Press
Unmuzzled Ox
Unspeakable Visions of the
    Individual

Vagabond
Virginia Quarterly
Wampeter Press
Washington Writers Workshop
Water Table
Western Humanities Review
Westigan Review
Wickwire Press
Willow Springs
Wilmore City
Witness
Word Beat Press
Word-Smith
Wormwood Review
Writers Forum
Xanadu
Yale Review
Yardbird Reader
Yarrow
Y'Bird
ZYZZYVA

CONTRIBUTORS' NOTES

ANTLER makes a living reading poetry around America in Walt Whitman's tradition of poets as "itinerant gladness scatterers." He is the recipient of the 1987 Witter Bynner Prize and the 1985 Walt Whitman Award. His work is included in several recent anthologies.

TONY ARDIZZONE is the author of two novels and two story collections including Milkweed's *Larabi's Ox* and *The Evening News,* winner of the Flannery O'Connor Award. He teaches at Indiana University.

RICK BASS first appeared in the *Pushcart Prize XIII* with his story "Where the Sea Used to Be." (*Paris Review.*) His story "Wejumpka" (*Chariton Review*) was reprinted in PPXV. His collected stories, *The Watch,* was published by Norton in 1989. His most recent book is *The Ninemile Wolves.*

ROBIN BEHN's books of poems are *Paper Bird* (Texas Tech) and *The Red Hour* (HarperCollins). She teaches in the MFA program at Alabama.

MARVIN BELL's latest poetry collection is *Iris of Creation* (Copper Canyon). He is a former co-poetry editor of this series and he resides part on Long Island, New York, and teaches at The University of Iowa.

KAREN BENDER is a 1991 graduate of the Iowa Writer's Workshop. Her work has appeared in various journals and she is completing a novel.

MICHAEL BENDZELA lives and writes in Maine and is a former student of the Stonecoast Writers Conference. This is his first story in a national publication.

SUSAN BERGMAN lives near Chicago with her husband and four children. "Estivation" is excerpted from *Anonymity*, due to be published by Farrar, Straus & Giroux.

SCOTT BRADFIELD is the author of *Dream of the Wolf* and *The History of Luminous Motion*, both from Vintage.

CHRISTOPHER BUCKLEY's fifth book of poems, *Blue Autumn*, was published by Copper Beech Press in 1990. He is a former poetry co-editor of this series.

MARK COX's first book, *Smoulder*, was published in 1989 by Godine. His second book, *Slam-Dancing At The Paradise Club*, is due from Godine in 1994.

PETER COYOTE writes: "Like his father, and his father before him, Peter Coyote came from nowhere and is working his way back." He is currently in Spain filming a movie.

ALISON DEMING is director of the Poetry Center at the University of Arizona. Her book, *Science and Other Poems* (L.S.U. Press) has been selected to receive the 1993 Walt Whitman Award. Her poems have also appeared in *Crazyhorse, Denver Quarterly, Nimrod* and elsewhere.

DEBORAH DIGGES is the author of two books of poems, *Vesper Sparrows* and *Late In the Millennium*. Her memoir, *Fugitive Spring*, was recently published by Knopf.

LYNN EMANUEL's new collection, *The Dig*, was a National Poetry Series winner and was published by The University of Missouri Press in 1992. She teaches at the University of Pittsburgh.

ALICE FULTON's books of poems include *Palladium* (University of Illinois, 1986) and *Powers of Congress* (Godine, 1990). Recent works have appeared in *Atlantic, Grand Street* and elsewhere.

TESS GALLAGHER's *Portable Kisses* is just out from Capra Press. She lives in Port Angeles, Washington and has written the introduction to *No Heroics, Please*, the first volume of *The Uncollected Works of Raymond Carver*.

SUZANNE GARDINIER is the author of *Usahn: Ten Poems and A Story* (Grand Street Press, 1990) and *Above the New Word* (University of Pittsburgh Press, 1993). She lives in Sag Harbor, New York.

MOLLY GILES teaches creative writing at San Francisco State University. Her collection of stories, *Rough Translations*, won the Flannery O'Connor Award.

DIANE GLANCY lives in St. Paul, Minnesota. Her books include *Lone Dog's Winter Count* (West End Press, 1991) and *Iron Woman* (New Rivers Press, 1990).

ALBERT GOLDBARTH's recent books include *A Sympathy of Souls* (Coffee House Press) and *Heaven and Earth* (University of Georgia Press), which won the 1991 National Book Critics Circle poetry award. *Across the Layers, Poems Old and New* is just out from the University of Georgia Press.

MARK HALLIDAY's *Tasker Street* is the winner of the Juniper Prize for Poetry. His first book of poems, *Little Star*, was a National Poetry Series selection in 1987. He teaches at Wilmington Friends School and lives in Philadelphia.

JAMES HARMS lives in Stroudsburg, Pennsylvania and teaches at East Stroudsburg University. His book *Modern Ocean* (1992) is available from Carnegie Mellon Press.

ROBERT HASS is a poet and essayist who teaches at the University of California, Berkeley. He is the author of *Human Wishes* and *Twentieth Century Pleasures*, and other books.

PATRICIA HENLEY's first collection of stories, *Friday Night At The Silver Star* (Graywolf, 1986) won the Montana First Book Award and was selected by the American Library Association as one of the thirty most notable books of 1986. She divides her time between Indiana and the American West.

EDWARD HIRSCH has published three books of poems: *Sleepwalkers*, *Wild Gratitude*, and *The Night Parade*. A new collection is due next year from Knopf.

TONY HOAGLAND won the 1992 Brittingham Prize in poetry for his first collection, *Sweet Ruin*. His work appears in *New American Poets of the 90's*, an anthology recently issued by Godine. He lives in Waterville, Maine.

MARK JARMAN's book-length poem, *Iris*, was published by Story Line Press recently. He is also the author of *The Black Riviera* (Wesleyan, 1990).

DIANE JOHNSON is the author of *Persian Nights*, *The Shadow Knows* and other novels. "White Hunter" appears in her recent book of travel essays, *Natural Opium*, out from Knopf.

DENNIS LOY JOHNSON's stories have appeared in *Columbia*, *Black Warrior Review* and *The New Generation* (Anchor). He lives in Saratoga Springs, New York.

EDWARD P. JONES grew up in Washington D.C. and now lives in Virginia. "Marie" is his first fiction in a magazine and appears in his short story collection, *Lost In The City*, (Morrow) winner of the 1993 PEN/Hemingway Award for a first book of fiction, and a finalist in the 1992 National Book Awards.

LAURA KASISCHKE lives in Ann Arbor, Michigan. She received her B.A. and M.F.A. from the University of Michigan.

JOELLEN KWIATEK's *Eleven Days Before Spring* will be out soon from HarperCollins. She lives in Syracuse, New York.

DAVID LEHMAN is the author of two books of poems, most recently *Operation Memory* (Princeton, 1990). He is the author of *Signs of the Times: Deconstruction and the Fall of Paul de Man* (paperback edition just out from Poseidon) and the forthcoming *The Line Forms Here*, a gathering of his essays and reviews (University of Michigan Press).

PHILIP LEVINE is a former poetry co-editor of this series. He is the author of numerous books of poems. His essay "Mine Own John Berryman" from *The Gettysburg Review* appeared in last year's *Pushcart Prize*.

GORDON LISH's next novel is *Zimzum* (Pantheon). He is the editor of *The Quarterly*, now published by New York University Press, and an editor at Knopf.

BARRY LOPEZ is the author of *The Rediscovery of North America* and *Arctic Dreams*, which won a National Book Award.

D. R. MACDONALD's short story collection is *Eyestone* (Pushcart Press, 1987; Penguin, 1989). He lives in Palo Alto, California. His "The Flowers of Bermuda" appeared in *Pushcart Prize XI*.

JOSEPH MAIOLO's stories have appeared in *Ploughshares*, *Sewanee Review* and *Shenandoah*. He has received three PEN Syndicated Fiction awards and two NEA Fellowships.

WILLIAM MATTHEWS's *Selected Poems and Translations 1969–1991* was published by Houghton Mifflin in 1992. He lives in New York City.

REBECCA MCCLANAHAN is the author of two poetry collections and a recent gathering of essays and stories, *One Word Deep* (Ashland Poetry Press). She is at work on a collection of stories, including "Somebody" and is seeking a publisher. She lives in Charlotte, North Carolina.

LEONARD MICHAELS is the author of *Going Places, Sylvia, The Men's Club* and other works of fiction and non-fiction. He lives in Kensington, California.

SUSAN NEVILLE won the Flannery O'Connor Award for her collection of stories, *The Invention of Flight*, published by The University of Georgia Press. Her collection of essays and stories, *Indiana Winter*, is due soon from Indiana University Press.

ROBERT PINSKY's most recent books are an essay collection, *Poetry and the World* (Ecco, 1988), and a volume of poems, *The Want Bone* (Ecco, 1990).

STANLEY PLUMLY teaches at the University of Maryland. His most recent collection of poems, *The Boy on the Step*, was recently published by Ecco.

DAVID RATTRAY died earlier this year. He was an outlaw scholar, prose writer, poet and translator whose work appeared everywhere from scholarly journals to fanzines. His books have been published by City Lights, North Point Press, Station Hill, Diwan Press and Vincent Fitzgerald, and his short works have appeared in *Bomb, Conjunctions, Sulfur* and elsewhere.

DAVID RIVARD's first book of poems, *Torque* (Pittsburgh, 1988) won the Starrett Poetry Prize. He is a 1991 National Endowment for the Arts Fellow.

TOMAŽ ŠALAMUN's *Selected Poems* is available from Ecco Press and recent poems appear in *American Poetry Review* and *Antaeus*. He lives in Slovenia. His translator, Sonya Kravanja, lives in Santa Fe, New Mexico.

DENNIS SCHMITZ has just published *About Night: New & Selected Poems* with Oberlin College Press as part of their new Field Editions series. He lives in Sacramento, California.

JOANNA SCOTT's latest novel, *Arrogance*—a finalist for the PEN/Faulkner Award—is available from W.W. Norton. She is working on a collection of stories.

BÁRBARA SELFRIDGE has received fellowships from the NEA, the Fine Arts Work center in Provincetown, and Poets & Writers. Her stories appeared in *The Caribbean Writer, Other Voices, Soujourner, Five Fingers Review,* and two fiction anthologies from Cleis Press. A story collection is looking for a home.

DANIEL STERN is the author of numerous books. His *Twice Told Tales* (Paris Review Editions, 1989) won the Fiction Award of The American Academy of Arts and Letters. A second collection, *Twice Upon A Time,* is just out from Norton. He teaches at the University of Houston Creative Writing Department.

GERALD STERN's latest book is *Bread Without Sugar* (Norton). He teaches at the Writers' Workshop at the University of Iowa.

KOTHAR WA-KHASIS (Lowell Edmonds) is Professor of Classics at Rutgers University. He has recently published books with the University of North Carolina Press and Mill Brook Press.

DAVID FOSTER WALLACE is the author of *The Broom of the System,* a novel, *Girl With Curious Hair,* a short story collection, and *Signifying Rappers,* a book about music. His stories have appeared in the *O'Henry* collection and *Best American Short Stories.* "Three Protrusions" is part of a larger work in progress.

BRUCE WEIGL's most recent collection is *What Saves Us* (Tri-Quarterly Books, 1992). He directs the writing program at Penn State University.

ROGER WEINGARTEN is the author of seven books of poetry including *Infant Bonds of Joy* and *Shadow Shadow* (both from Godine). With Jack Myers he co-edited Godine's *New American Poets of the '90's.*

MARIE SHEPPARD WILLIAMS is an artist, journalist and social worker. She has published stories in *The Yale Review, Alaska Quarterly, Hurricane Alice* and elsewhere.

DAVID WOJAHN teaches at Indiana University. The University of Pittsburgh will publish his *Late Empire* next year.

TOBIAS WOLFF's most recent book is the memoir, *This Boy's Life* (Atlantic Monthly Press 1989; Harper Perennial 1990). "The Life of the Body" is part of a collection of stories in progress.

LOIS-ANN YAMANAKA is a native of Hawaii who writes in the pidgin passed down through the third and fourth generation descendants of Hawaiian plantation workers of the 1800's. She lives in Kaneohe, Hawaii.

CONTRIBUTING
SMALL PRESSES

(These presses made or received nominations for this edition of *The Pushcart Prize*. See the *International Directory of Little Magazines and Small Presses*, Dustbooks, P.O. Box 100, Paradise, CA 95967, for subscription rates, manuscript requirements and a complete international listing of small presses.)

A

Agni, Boston Univ., 236 Bay State Rd., Boston, MA 02215
Ahsahta Press, Boise St. Univ., 1910 Univ. Dr., Boise, ID 83725
Alaska Quarterly Review, Univ. of Alaska, Anchorage, AK 99508
Albatross, see Anabiosis Press
Alice James Books, 33 Richdale Ave., Cambridge, MA 02140
Ally Press, 524 Orleans St., St. Paul, MN 55107
Alpha Beat Press, 31 Waterloo St., New Hope, PA 18938
Amelia, 329 "E" St., Bakersfield, CA 93304
American Poetry Review, 1721 Walnut St., Philadelphia, PA 19103
American Short Fiction, English Dept., Univ. of Texas, Austin, TX 78712
The American Voice, 332 W. Broadway, Ste. 1215, Louisville, KY 40202
Americas Review, see Arte Publico Press
Amherst Writers & Artists Press, P.O. Box 1076, Amherst, MA 01004
Ampersand Press, Roger Williams College, Bristol, RI 02809
Anabiosis Press, Inc., 125 Horton Ave., Englewood, FL 34223
Anamnesis Press, P.O. Box 14304, Tallahassee, FL 32317
Another Chicago Magazine, 3709 N. Kenmore, Chicago, IL 60613
Antaeus, 100 W. Broad St., Hopewell, NJ 08525
Antietam Review, 82 W. Washington St., Hagerstown, MD 21740
The Antioch Review, P.O. Box 148, Yellow Springs, OH 45387
Applezaba Press, P.O. Box 4134, Long Beach, CA 90804
Archae, 10 Troilus, Old Bridge, NJ 08857
Arte Publico Press, Univ. of Houston, Houston, TX 77204
Artful Dodge, English Dept., College of Wooster, Wooster, OH 44691
Ascent, P.O. Box 967, Urbana, IL 61801
Aslan Publishing, P.O. Box 108, Lower Lake, CA 95457
Aspects, 5507 Regent St., Philadelphia, PA 19143
Asylum, P.O. Box 6203, Santa Maria, CA 93456
Axelrod Publishing, P.O. Box 14248, Tampa, FL 33690

B

Bagman Press, P.O. Box 81166, Chicago, IL 60681
Bakunin, P.O. Box 1853, Simi Valley, CA 93062
Bamberger Books, P.O. Box 1126, Flint, MI 48501
Barnwood Press, P.O. Box 146, Selma, IN 47383
The Barrelhouse, 1600 Oak Creek Dr., Edmond, OK 73034
Bastard Review, P.O. Box 422820, San Francisco, CA 94142
bear creek haiku, 1177B Bear Mt. Dr., Boulder, CO 80303
Being, P.O. Box 417, Oceanside, CA 92049
Bellingham Review, 1007 Queen St., Bellingham, WA 98226
Bellowing Ark, P.O. Box 45637, Seattle, WA 98145
Beloit Fiction Journal, P.O. Box 11, Beloit College, Beloit, WI 53511
Beloit Poetry Journal, RFD 2, Box 154, Ellsworth, ME 04605
Big Head Press, Box 137, 1212 Bellflower Blvd., Ste. 256, Long Beach, CA 90815
Bilingual Review/Press, Hispanic Research Center, Arizona St. Univ., Tempe, AZ 85287
Black Heron Press, P.O. Box 95676, Seattle, WA 98145
Black Oak Press, Box 4663, Univ. Place Sta., Lincoln, NE 68504
Black Thistle Press, 491 Broadway, New York, NY 10012
Black Warrior Review, P.O. Box 2936, Tuscaloosa, AL 35486
Blue Gables Publ. Co., 17320 97th Pl, SW, #601, Vashon, WA 98070
Blue Heron Publ'g, Inc., 24450 NW Hansen Rd., Hillsboro, OR 97124
Blue Unicorn, 22 Avon Rd., Kensington, CA 94707
Bluff City, P.O. Box 7697, Elgin, IL 60121
Bone & Flesh, P.O. Box 349, Concord, NH 03302
Borderline, 425 W. Meyer Blvd., Kansas City, MO 67113
Bottom Dog Press, Firelands College, Huron, OH 44839
Boulevard, P.O. Box 30386, Philadelphia, PA 19103
Breakthrough!, 204 Millbank Dr., SW, Calgary, Alberta, CANADA T2Y 2H9
Brick Books, Box 38, Sta. B, London, Ontario, N6A 4V3, CANADA
Broken Moon Press, P.O. Box 24585, Seattle, WA 98124
Brownbag Press, see Hyacinth House Publications

C

Cafe Solo, Box 2814, Atascadero, CA 93424
Calapooya Collage, P.O. Box 309, Monmouth, OR 97361
Calliope, see Ampersand Press
The Camel Press, Big Cove Tannery, PA 17212
Caravan Press, 15445 Ventura Blvd., Ste. 279, Sherman Oaks, CA 91403
Carolina Quarterly, Univ. of North Carolina, Chapel Hill, NC 27599
Carpenter Press, P.O. Box 14387, Columbus, OH 43214
Catbird Press, 44 N. Sixth Ave., Highland Park, NJ 08904
The Chattahoochee Review, 2102 Womack Rd., Atlanta, GA 30338
Chelsea, Box 5880, Grand Central Sta., New York, NY 10163
Chestnut Hills Press, see New Poets Series, Inc.
Chicago Review, 5801 S. Kenwood, Chicago, IL 60637
Chiron Rising, P.O. Box 2589, Victorville, CA 92393
Chrysalis, Rte. 1, Box 184, Dillwyn, VA 23936
Cimarron Review, Oklahoma St. Univ., Stillwater, OK 74078
Cleveland State Univ. Poetry Center, English Dept., CSU, Cleveland, OH 44115
Clockwatch Review, English Dept., Illinois Wesleyan Univ., Bloomington, IL 61702

Coffee House Press, 27 N. 4th St., Minneapolis, MN 554
Coldwater Press, Inc., 9806 Coldwater Circle, Dallas, TX 75228
Concho River Review, English Dept., Angelo St. Univ., San Angelo, TX 76909
Confluence Press, Lewis-Clark St. College, Lewiston, ID 83501
Confrontation, English Dept., C. W. Post of L.I.U., Brookville, NY 11548
Conjunctions, Bard College, Annandale-on-Hudson, NY 12504
The Connecticut Poetry Review, P.O. Box 3783, New Haven, CT 06525
Cooper House Publ'g, Inc., P.O. Box 54947, Oklahoma City, OK 73154
Cornerstone Publ'g, Inc., 306 Barnstable Quay, Virginia Beach, VA 23452
Crazyhorse, English Dept., Univ. of Arkansas, Little Rock, AR 72204
CrazyQuilt, P.O. Box 632729, San Diego, CA 92163
Cream City Review, Univ. of Milwaukee, P.O. Box 413, Milwaukee, WI 53201
Creative With Words, P.O. Box 223226, Carmel, CA 93922
The Creative Woman, Governors St. Univ., University Park, IL 60466
The Crescent Review, 1445 Old Town Rd., Winston-Salem, NC 27106
Crooked Roads, see Wheel of Fire Press
The Crossing Press, P.O. Box 1048, Freedom, CA 95019
Crucible, Barton College, College Sta., Wilson, NC 27893
CutBank, English Dept., Univ. of Montana, Missoula, MT 59812

D

Daedalus Press, P.O. Box 1374, Las Cruces, NM 88004
Dalkey Archive Press, Illinois St. Univ., Normal, IL 61761
Damascus Works, One East Univ. Pkwy, #1101, Baltimore, MD 21218
John Daniel & Co., Publrs., P.O. Box 21922, Santa Barbara, CA 93121
Daughters of Sarah, 3801 N. Keeler, Chicago, IL 60641
Denver Quarterly, English Dept., Univ. of Denver, Denver, CO 80208
Devil's Millhopper, College of Humanities, USC, 171 Univ. Pkwy, Aiken, SC
  29801
A Different Drummer, 84 Bay 28th St., Brooklyn, NY 11214
Dimitri Publications, 2425 First Ave., San Diego, CA 92101
Distinctive Publ. Corp., P.O. Box 17868, Plantation, FL 33318
Dog River Review, see Trout Creek Press
Downstate Story, 1825 Maple Ridge, Peoria, IL 61614

E

Eagle Publ'g, P.O. Box 403, Red Bluff, CA 96080
Earth Books, P.O. Box 740, Redwood Valley, CA 95470
EduCare Press, P.O. Box 31511, Seattle, WA 98103
Egg In Hand Press, 4927 N. Bernard St., Chicago, IL 60627
Epicenter Press, Inc., 18821 64th Ave NE, Seattle, WA 98155
Epiphany, P.O. Box 2699, Univ. of Arkansas, Fayetteville, AR 72701
Epoch, 251 Goldwin Smith Hall, Cornell Univ., Ithaca, NY 14853
Evanston Publ'g, Inc., 1216 Hinman Ave., Evanston, IL 60202
Exit 13 Magazine, 22 Oakwood Ct., Fanwood, NJ 07023
Experiment in Words, P.O. Box 470186, Fort Worth, TX 76147
Exquisite Corpse, English Dept., Louisiana St. Univ., Baton Rouge, LA 70803

F

Farmer's Market, P.O. Box 1272, Galesburg, IL 61402
Fiction, English Dept., City College of N.Y., 138th St. & Convent Ave.,
  New York, NY 10031

Fiction International, English Dept., San Diego Univ., San Diego, CA 92182
Fine Madness, P.O. Box 31138, Seattle, WA 98103
Folio, Lit. Dept., Gray Hall, The American Univ., Washington, DC 20016
For Poets Only, P.O. Box 4855, Schenectady, NY 12384
Forbidden Lines, P.O. Box 23, Chapel Hill, NC 27514
Ford-Brown & Co., Publ'rs, P.O. Box 2764, Boston, MA 02208
The Formalist, 320 Hunter Dr., Evansville, IN 47711
Frontiers, Mesa Vista Hall 2142, Univ. of New Mex., Albuquerque, NM 87131

G

Gaslight, P.O. Box 21, Cleveland, MN 56017
The Georgia Review, Univ. of Georgia, Athens, GA 30602
Gettysburg Review, Gettysburg College, Gettysburg, PA 17325
Glimmer Train, 812 SW Washington St., Ste. 1205, Portland, OR 97205
Grand Street, 131 Varick St., Rm. 906, New York, NY 10013
Grasslands Review, English Dept., N.T., Box 13706, Univ. of No. Texas, Denton, TX 76203
Graywolf Press, 2402 Univ. Ave., Ste. 203, St. Paul, MN 55114
Green Meadow Press, 105 Betty Rd., East Meadow, NY 11554
Green Mountains Review, Johnson St. College, Johnson, VT 05656
Green Zero, 3401 N. Columbus Blvd., #23G, Tucson, AZ 85712
Greensboro Review, English Dept., Univ. of No. Carolina, Greensboro, NC 27412
Gypsy, 10708 Gay Brewer Dr., El Paso, TX 79935

H

Haight-Ashbury Literary Jour., 558 Joost Ave., San Francisco, CA 94127
Hammers, 1718 Sherman Ave., Ste. 205, Evanston, IL 60201
Hawaii Review, English Dept., Univ. of Hawaii, Honolulu, HI 96822
Hayden's Ferry Review, Matthews Ctr., Arizona St. Univ., Tempe, AZ 85287
Haypenny Press, 211 New St., W. Paterson, NJ 07424
Headwaters Press, Inc., 331 Fairway Dr., New Orleans, LA 70124
The Higginsville Reader, P.O. Box 141, Three Bridges, NJ 08887
High Plains Literary Review, 180 Adams St., Ste. 250, Denver, CO 80206
Hob-Nob, 994 Nissley Rd., Lancaster, PA 17601
Hold the Pickle, 7942 Convoy Ct., San Diego, CA 92111
Home Planet News, P.O. Box 415, Stuyvesant Sta., New York, NY 10009
Honeybrook Press, P.O. Box 883, Rexburg, ID 83440
Hope Publ'g House, 696 So. Madison Ave., Pasadena, CA 91106
Horror's Head Press, 140 Dickie Ave., Staten Island, NY 10314
Hot Pepper Press, P.O. Box 39, Somerset, CA 95684
Hubbub, 5344 S.E. 38th, Portland, OR 97202
The Hudson Review, 684 Park Ave., New York, NY 10021
Hyacinth House Publications, P.O. Box 120, Fayetteville, AR 72702
Hyphen Magazine, 3458 W. Devon Ave., Ste. 6, Lincolnwood, IL 60659

I

Icarus, 29 E. 21st. St., New York, NY 10010
Illinois Writers Review, English Dept., Illinois St. Univ., Normal, IL 61761
Indiana Review, 316 N. Jordan Ave., Indiana Univ., Bloomington, IN 47405
InQ. Publ'g Co., P.O. Box 10, No. Aurora, IL 60542

Interim, English Dept., Univ. of Nevada, Las Vegas, NV 89154
International Poetry Review, Dept. of Romance Lang., Univ. of N.C., Greensboro, NC 27412
International Publ'rs Co., Inc., 239 W. 23rd St., New York, NY 10011
Iota Press, see The Poet Tree
The Iowa Review, 308 EPB, Univ. of Iowa, Iowa City, IA 52242
Iowa Woman, P.O. Box 2938, Waterloo, IA 50704
ipsissima verba, see Haypenny Press
Italian Americana, Univ. of Rhode Island, 199 Promenade St., Providence, RI 02908

J

Jabberwocky, 2461 Lanrell Dr., Tallahassee, FL 32303
James Dickey Newsletter, Dekalb College, Dunwoody, GA 30338
Jeopardy, 132 College Hall, Bellingham, WA 98225
Jewish Lights Publ'g, P.O. Box 237, Rte. 4, Woodstock, VT 05091
The Journal, English Dept., Ohio St. Univ., Columbus, OH 43210
Journal of New Jersey Poets, County College of Morris, 214 Center Grove Rd., Randolph, NJ 07869

K

Kaleidoscope, 326 Locust St., Akron, OH 44302
Kalliope, Florida Comm. College, 3939 Roosevelt Blvd., Jacksonville, FL 32205
Kelsey Review, Mercer Co. Comm. College, P.O. Box B, Trenton, NJ 08690
Kelsey Street Press, P.O. Box 9235, Berkeley, CA 94709
The Kenyon Review, Kenyon College, Gambier, OH 43022

L

Lactuca, P.O. Box 521, Suffern, NY 10901
Laurel Review, NW Missouri St. Univ., Maryville, MO 64468
The Ledge, 64-65 Cooper Ave., Glendale, NY 11385
Left Bank, see Blue Heron Publ'g
Letter Press, 6606 Soundview Dr., Gig Harbor, WA 98335
Lilliput Review, 207 S. Millvale Ave., #3, Pittsburgh, PA 15224
LILT, Liberal Arts Dept., Kansas City Art Inst., 4415 Warwick Blvd., Kansas City, MO 64111
The Literary Review, Fairleigh Dickinson Univ., Madison, NJ 07940
Literary Sketches, P.O. Box 810571, Dallas, TX 75381
Longshanks Book, 30 Church St., Mystic, CT 06355
Loonfeather Press, Bemidji Arts Ctr, 426 Bemidji Ave., Bemidji, MN 55601
Los Hombres Press, P.O. Box 632729, San Diego, CA 92163
Lost & Found Times, c/o Luna Bisonte Prods, 137 Leland Ave., Columbus, OH 43214
Lotus Press, Inc., P.O. Box 21607, Detroit, MI 48221
The Louisville Review, Univ. of Louisville, Louisville, KY 40292
Lucidity, Rte. 2, Box 94, Eureka Springs, AR 72632
Lynx House Press, 1326 West St., Emporia, KS 66801

M

The MacGuffin, Schoolcraft College, 18600 Haggerty Rd., Livonia, MI 48152
MacKinations, see Southwest Writers Inst.

Mad Poets Review, c/o E. M. D'Angelo, 1074 Hopkins Ave., Glenolden, PA 19036
Mad River, Philosophy Dept., Wright St. Univ., Dayton, OH 45435
Magic Realism, see Pyx Press
Maisonneuve Press, P.O. Box 2980, Washington, DC 20013
Maize Press, see Bilingual Review/Press
Manhattan Review, 440 Riverside Dr, #45, New York, NY 10027
Manic D Press, P.O. Box 410804, San Francisco, CA 94141
Manoa, Univ. of Hawaii, 1733 Donaghho Rd., Honolulu, HI 96822
March Street Press, 3413 Wilshire Dr., Greensboro, NC 27408
The Massachusetts Review, Univ. of Mass., Amherst, MA 01003
Mastication Publications, 1700 Constitution, #D-24, Pueblo, CO 81001
Maverick in the Chaparral, see Maverick Press
Maverick Press, Rt. 2, Box 4915, Eagle Pass, TX 78852
Mayapple Press, P.O. Box 5743, Saginaw, MI 48603
Metropolitan, 6307 N. 31st St., Arlington, VA 22207
Mho & Mho Works, Box 33135, San Diego, CA 92163
Michigan Quarterly Review, Univ. of Mich., 3032 Rackham Bldg., Ann Arbor, MI 48109
Mid-American Review, English Dept., Bowling Green St. Univ., Bowling Green, OH 43403
Midmarch Arts Press, 300 Riverside Dr., New York, NY 10025
Milkweed Editions, 528 Hennepin Ave., Ste. 505, Minneapolis, MN 55403
Mindscapes, c/o Juno Press, 2252 Beverly Glen Pl., Los Angeles, CA 90077
Minnesota Review, English Dept., E. Carolina Univ., Greenville, NC 27858
Mississippi Review, Box 5144, Southern Sta., Hattiesburg, MS 39406
Mississippi Valley Review, English Dept., W. Illinois Univ., Macomb, IL 61455
The Missouri Review, 1507 Hillcrest Hall, Univ. of MO, Columbia, MO 65211
Monesson, Harry (Publ'r), 35 Magnolia Rd., Pemberton, NJ 08068
Moving Parts Press, 220 Baldwin St., Santa Cruz, CA 95060
Mudfish, c/o Turtle Press, Inc., 184 Franklin St, New York, NY 10013
Mulberry Press, 105 Betty Rd., East Meadow, NY 11554

N

The Naiad Press, P.O. Box 10543, Tallahassee, FL 32302
Nalta Publ'g, P.O. Box 3578, Boulder, CO 80307
Nebraska Review, Writer's Workshop, Univ. of Nebraska, Omaha, NE 68182
New American Writing, 2920 W. Pratt, Chicago, IL 60645
New Chapter Press, Inc., Old Pound Rd, Pound Ridge, NY 10586
New Delta Review, English Dept., Louisiana St. Univ., Baton Rouge, LA 70803
New England Review, Middlebury College, Middlebury, VT 05753
New Hampshire College Journal, N.H. College, Manchester, NH 03106
New Letters, UMKC, 5100 Rockhill Rd, Kansas City, MO 64110
New Native Press, Rt. 67, Box 128, Cullowhee, NC 28723
New Poets Series, Inc., 541 Picadilly Rd, Baltimore, MD 21204
The New Press, 53-35 Hollis Court Blvd, Flushing, NY 11365
New Sins Press, P.O. Box 7157, Pittsburgh, PA 15213
New Spirit Press, see The Poet Tree
New York University Press, Washington Square, New York, NY 10012
A New World Rising, Box 33, 71 Hope St, Providence, RI 02906
Next Phase, 33 Court St, New Haven, CT 06511
Night Roses, P.O. Box 393, Prospect Heights, IL 60070
Nightshade Press, P.O. Box 76, Troy, ME 04987
Nimrod:Int'l Jour. of Prose & Poetry, 2210 S. Main, Ste. B, Tulsa, OK 74114
Ninety-Six Press, P.O. Box 30882, Furman Univ., Greenville, SC 29613

North Carolina Literary Review, Eng. Dept., ECU, Greenville, NC 27858
North Dakota Quarterly, Univ. of No. Dak., P.O. Box 8237, Grand Forks, ND 58202
Northwest Review, Univ. of Ore., Eugene, OR 97403
Now and Then, Box 19180A, ETSU, Johnson City, TN 37614

O

The Ohio Review, Ellis Hall, Ohio Univ., Athens, OH 45701
Old Mole Press, P.O. Box 313, Rosendale, NY 12477
Old Red Kimono, Box 1864, Floyd College, Rome, GA 30162
Omnation Press, 5548 N. Sawyer, Chicago, IL 60625
Onionhead, 115 N. Kentucky Ave, Lakeland, FL 33801
Ontario Review, 9 Honey Brook Dr., Princeton, NJ 08540
Orchises Press, P.O. Box 20602, Alexandria, VA 22320
Oregon Wordworks, P.O. Box 514, Manzanita, OR 97130
Organica Press, 4419 N. Manhattan Ave, Tampa, FL 33614
Osiris, Box 297, Deerfield, MA 01342
Other Voices, Eng. Dept., Box 4348, Univ. of Ill., Chicago, IL 60680
Oxalis, P.O. Box 3993, Kingston, NY 12401
Oxford Magazine, Bachelor Hall, Miami Univ., Oxford, OH 45056
Oxygen, 535 Geary St, #1010, San Francisco, CA 94102

P

Painted Hills Review, P.O. Box 494, Davis, CA 95617
Paisano, see Maverick Press
Pancake Press, 163 Galewood Circle, San Francisco, CA 94131
Papier-Mache Press, 795 Via Manzana, Watsonville, CA 95076
The Paris Review, 541 E. 72nd St, New York, NY 10021
Parnassus Literary Journal, P.O. Box 1384, Forest Park, GA 30051
PBW, 130 West Limestone, Yellow Springs, OH 45387
Pendragon, VSC Box 7110, Valdosta St. College, Valdosta, GA 31698
Peregrine, see Amherst Writers & Artists Press
Perivale Press, 13830 Erwin St., Van Nuys, CA 91401
Permeable Press, 900 Tennessee, Studio 15, San Francisco, CA 94107
Phrygian Press, 58-09 205th St, Bayside, NY 11364
Pig Iron Press, P.O. Box 237, Youngstown, OH 44501
The Pikeville Review, Pikeville College, Pikeville, KY 41501
The Pinehurst Journal, P.O. Box 360747, Milpitas, CA 95036
The Pittsburgh Quarterly, 36 Haberman Ave, Pittsburgh, PA 15211
Pivot, 250 Riverside Dr, #23, New York, NY 10025
Plain View Press, P.O. Box 33311, Austin, TX 78764
Ploughshares, 100 Beacon St, Boston, MA 02116
The Plum Review, P.O. Box 3557, Washington, DC 20007
Poesflesh, P.O. Box 7157, Pittsburgh, PA 15213
Poet, see Cooper House Publ'g
Poet Lore, 4508 Walsh St, Bethesda, MD 20815
The Poet Tree, 82-34 138 St, 6F, Kew Gardens, NY 11435
Poetic Page, P.O. Box 71192, Madison Heights, NJ 48071
Poetry, 60 West Walton St., Chicago, IL 60610
Poetry Break Journal, P.O. Box 417, Oceanside, CA 92049
Poetry New York, P.O. Box 3184, Church St. Sta., New York, NY 10008
Poetry USA, 2569 Maxwell Ave, Oakland, CA 94601
Political Diction, see Texture Press

Potato Eyes, see Nightshade Press
Potpourri, P.O. Box 8278, Prairie Village, KS 66208
Prairie Schooner, 201 Andrews, Univ. of Neb., Lincoln, NE 68588
Primal Publ'g, 107 Brighton Ave, Allston, MA 02134
The Prose Poem, Eng. Dept., Providence College, Providence, RI 02918
Provincetown Arts, 650 Commercial St, Provincetown, MA 02657
Prudhomme Press, P.O. Box 11, Tavares, FL 32778
Pschotrain, see Hyacinth House Publctns
Puck, see Permeable Press
Puckerbrush Review, 76 Main St, Orono, ME 04473
Puerto del Sol, Eng. Dept., Box 3E, N.M. St. Univ., Las Cruces, NM 88003
Pynchon House, Publ'rs, 6 Univ. Dr., Ste. 105, Amherst, MA 01002
Pyx Press, P.O. Box 620, Orem, UT 84059

Q

The Quarterly, 201 E. 50th St., New York, NY 10022
Quarterly West, 317 Alpin Union, Univ. of Utah, Salt Lake City, UT 84112

R

Rag Mag, Box 12, Goodhue, MN 55027
Raritan, Rutgers Univ., 31 Mine St, New Brunswick, NJ 08903
Raw Dog Press, 128 Harvey Ave, Doylestown, PA 18901
The Raystown Review, RD 1, Box 205, Schellsburg, PA 15559
Red Brick Review, 315 Canal St, Manchester, NH 03101
Red Cedar Review, English Dept., Mich. St. Univ., E. Lansing, MI 48823
Red Crane Books, 826 Camino de Monte Rey, Santa Fe, NM 87501
Red Dancefloor Press, P.O. Box 7392, Van Nuys, CA 91409
Red Dust, Inc., P.O. Box 630, New York, NY 10028
Redneck Review of Lit., 2919 N. Downer Ave, Milwaukee, WI 53211
Review of Contemporary Fiction, see Dalkey Archive Press
Rhiannon Press, 1105 Bradley Ave, Eau Claire, WI 54701
The Ridgeway Press, P.O. Box 120, Roseville, MI 48066
Riverside Quarterly, P.O. Box 958, Big Sandy, TX 75755
Ruddy Duck Press, P.O. Box 424906, San Francisco, CA 94142

S

Sabotage Press, 71 Richmond St, Providence, RI 02903
Sachem Press, P.O. Box 9, Old Chatham, NY 12136
Salmagundi, Skidmore College, Saratoga Springs, NY 12866
San Jose Studies, Eng. Dept., San Jose St. Univ., San Jose, CA 95192
San Miguel Writer, Tenerias 9, San Miguel de Allende, GTO 37700, MEXICO
Santa Fe Lit. Review, P.O. Box 8018, Santa Fe, NM 87504
Santa Monica Review, Santa Monica College, Santa Monica, CA 90405
Scots Plaid/Persephone Press, 22B Pine Lake Dr, Whispering Pines, NC 28327
Scuipsit?, Wallace 217, EKU, Richmond, KY 40475
The Seal Press, 3131 Western Ave, #410, Seattle, WA 98121
Seneca Review, Hobart & William Smith Colleges, Geneva, NY 14456
Shenandoah, Box 722, Lexington, VA 24450
Shockbox Press, P.O. Box 7226, Nashua, NH 03060
Short Fiction by Women, Box 1276, Stuyvesant Sta., New York, NY 10009
Side Show (see Somersault Press)

Sifrut, 88 First St, Ste. 300, San Francisco, CA 94105
Signal Books, P.O. Box 940, Carrboro, NC 27510
Sing Heavenly Muse!, P.O. Box 13320, Minneapolis, MN 55414
Singular Speech Press, Ten Hilltop Dr, Canton, CT 06019
6IX Magazine, 44 W. Washington Lane, Philadelphia, PA 19144
Skylark, Purdue Univ. Calumet, 2200 169th St, Hammond, IN 46323
Slipstream, Box 2071, New Mkt Sta., Niagara Falls, NY 14301
A Slow Tempo Press, 2746 Everett, Lincoln, NE 68502
The Small Pond Magazine, P.O. Box 664, Stratford, CT 06497
The Smith, 69 Joralemon St, Brooklyn, NY 11201
The Snail's Pace Review, RR2, Box 363, Brownell Rd, Cambridge, NY 12816
So To Speak, George Mason Univ., Fairfax, VA 22030
Somersault Press, P.O. Box 1428, El Cerrito, CA 94530
Sonora Review, Eng. Dept., Univ. of Ariz., Tucson, AZ 85721
Southern Exposure, P.O. Box 531, Durham, NC 27702
Southern Review, 43 Allen Hall, Louisiana St. Univ., Baton Rouge, LA 70803
Southwest Review, 6410 Airline Rd, So. Methodist Univ., Dallas, TX 75275
Southwest Writers Inst., P.O. Box 1660, Dickinson, TX 77539
Sou'wester Magazine, Eng. Dept, So. Illinois Univ., Edwardsville, IL 62026
Sow's Ear Press, 245 McDowell St, Bristol, TN 37620
Sparrow Press, 103 Waldron St, W. Lafayette, IN 47906
Spoon River Quarterly, Eng. Dept., Ill. St. Univ., Normal, IL 61761
St. Andrews Press, St. Andrews College, Laurinburg, SC 28352
The Stake, see III Publ'g
Starlight Poets, c/o Starlight Press, Box 3102, Long Island City, NY 11103
Steam Press, 5455 Meridian Mark Rd, Ste. 100, Atlanta, GA 30342
Steamshovel Press, 5927 Kingsbury, St. Louis, MO 63112
Sticks Press, P.O. Box 399, Maplesville, AL 36750
Stone Bridge Press, P.O. Box 8208, Berkeley, CA 94707
Stone Soup Poetry Gazette, 70 Joy St, Boston, MA 02114
Story, 1507 Dana Ave, Cincinnati, OH 45207
Sucarnochee Review, Station 22, Livingston Univ., Livingston, AL 35470
Sulpher River Review, P.O. Box 402087, Austin, TX 78704
The Sun, 107 N. Roberson St, Chapel Hill, NC 27516
Sun Dog, 406 Williams, Fla. St. Univ., Tallahassee, FL 32306
Suntop Press, P.O. Box 98, Kodak, TN 37764
Sycamore Review, Eng. Dept., Purdue Univ., W. Lafayette, IN 47907

T

Talisman, Box 321, Beech Grove, IN 46107
Tampa Review. 401 W. Kennedy Blvd., Univ. of Tampa. P.O. Box 19F, Tampa, FL 33606
Tar River Poetry, Eng. Dept., E. Carolina Univ., Greenville, NC 27834
Temporary Culture, P.O. Box 43072, Upper Montclair, NJ 07043
Texas Tech. Univ. Press, Lubbock, TX 79409
Texture Press, 3760 Cedar Ridge Dr, Norman, OK 73072
Thema Literary Society, Box 74109, Metairie, LA 70002
Thinker Review, see White Fields Press
Third Side Press, 2250 W. Farragut, Chicago, IL 60625
III Publ'g, P.O. Box 170363, San Francisco, CA 94117
Threepenny Review, P.O. Box 9131, Berkeley, CA 94709
Tilbury House, Pub'rs, 132 Water St, Gardiner, ME 04345
Tornado Alley Quarterly, P.O. Box 9390, St. Louis, MO 63117
Touchstone, P.O. Box 8308, Spring, TX 77387
TriQuarterly, Northwestern Univ., 2020 Ridge Ave, Evanston, IL 60208

Trout Creek Press, 5976 Billings Rd, Parkdale, OR 97041
Tucumcari Literary Review, 3108 W. Bellevue Ave, Los Angeles, CA 90026
Turnstile, 175 Fifth Ave, Ste. 2348, New York, NY 10010
Tyger Press, 88 Parkway South, Apt. A, New London, CT 06320

U

United Artists Books, Box 2616, Stuyvesant Sta., New York, NY 10009
Univ. of Massachusetts Press, P.O. Box 429, Amherst, MA 01004

V

Verse, 213 N. Narberth Ave, Narberth, PA 19072
Verve, P.O. Box 3205, Simi Valley, CA 93093
The Vincent Brothers Review, 4566 Northern Circle, Mad River Twnshp, Dayton, OH 45424

W

We Press, P.O. Box 1503, Santa Cruz, CA 95061
Webster Review, Webster College, Webster Groves, MO 63119
West Branch, Eng. Dept., Bucknell Univ., Lewisburg, PA 17837
Western Humanities Review, Univ. of Utah, Salt Lake City, UT 84112
Wheel of Fire Press, P.O. Box 32631, Kansas City, MO 64111
Whetstone, P.O. Box 1266, Barrington, IL 60011
White Eagle Coffee Store Press, P.O. 383, Fox River Grove, IL 60021
White Fields Press, Univ. of Louisville, Louisville, KY 40292
The William & Mary Review, P.O. Box 8795, Williamsburg, VA 23187
Willow Springs, Eng. Dept., MS-1, EWU, Cheney, WA 99004
Wisconsin Review, Univ. of Wis., Oshkosh, WI 54901
Without Halos, P.O. Box 1342, Pt. Pleasant Beach, NJ 08742
Witness, Oakland Comm. College, Farmington Hills, MI 48334
Wordcraft of Oregon, P.O. Box 3235, La Grande, OR 97850
Words of Wisdom, 612 Front St, East, Glendora, NJ 08029
The Wormwood Review, P.O. Box 4698, Stockton, CA 95204
Writers' Craft Guild, 4009 Weed-Sparksville Rd, Columbia, KY 42728
Writers' Forum, P.O. Box 7150. Univ. of Colo, Colorado Springs, CO 80933
Writing on the Wall, P.O. Box 8, Orono, ME 04473 Y

Y

Yellow Silk, P.O. Box 6374, Albany, CA 94706
Yucca Tree Press, 2130 Hixon Dr, Las Cruces, NM 88005

Z

Zuzu's Petals Quarterly, P.O. Box 4476, Allentown, PA 18105
ZYZZYVA, 41 Sutter St, Ste. 1400, San Francisco, CA 94104

INDEX

The following is a listing in alphabetical order by author's last name of works reprinted in the first eighteen *Pushcart Prize* editions.

553

555

558

560